A rugby compendium

A Rugby Compendium

An Authoritative Guide to the Literature of Rugby Union

Compiled by

John M Jenkins

With a Review of the Literature by Huw Richards
Introduction by Michael Green

Edited by Cynthia McKinley

THE BRITISH LIBRARY
1998

First published 1998 by

The British Library
Boston Spa, Wetherby
West Yorkshire LS23 7BQ

ISBN: 0 7123 1096 7

Series Editor: A E Cunningham

Printed by Redwood Books, Trowbridge

Acknowledgements

The compiler would like to pay special thanks to Rhidian Griffiths for the use of facilities at the National Library of Wales, Aberystwyth. And to staff of the National Library of Wales, especially Brian Lile, Ceris Gruffudd, Gareth Lloyd Hughes, Richard Huws and Vernon Jones. My appreciation to the following for drawing my attention to material for inclusion in this bibliography: Dónall Ó Luanaigh and the staff of The National Library of Ireland, Dublin; Veronica Morrow and the staff of the Library, Trinity College Dublin; the staff of the South African Library, Cape Town; English Sports Council; Rex King and Jed Smith of the Library, Rugby Football Union, Twickenham; Tom Graham and Sylvia Ross of the South African Rugby Football Union, Newlands; the late Keith Clayton, Rodney Constantine, Paul Dobson, and David McLennan (all Cape Town); Jean-Pierre Bodis (University of Pau, France); Ian Buchanan; Richard W. Cox; Peter Crittle; Alan Evans; Stuart Farmer; Dave Fox; Robert Gate; Michael J. Kelly (Northern Territory, Australia); Tony Lewis; Cathy McKenna (City University New York, USA); Andy Mitchell; Piers Morgan; Willow Murray (Dun Laoghaire, Dublin); Duncan Pierce; Harry Smith; Malcolm Spark, Fiona White and Gareth W. Williams.

Assistance in the compilation of this bibliography was also kindly offered by the National Library of Australia, the National Library of New Zealand, the State Library, Pretoria, and The Old College Library, University of Wales, Aberystwyth.

Chapter H would have looked decidedly bare without the assistance of Lowri Wyn Bevan and John Gardener (Cape Town, South Africa). Gareth Williams I mention again for being magnanimous with advice, perspective and wisdom.

I owe a substantial debt to Michael Green and Huw Richards for their contribution to this work, and I never could have ventured forth without the patient and scrupulous guidance of Cynthia McKinley and Arthur Cunningham who, as editors, had the intuitive sense to gently coax me through the occasional crisis by offering the thought or word that inspires new thinking. It is they who piloted this work to its destination.

Finally, to the following: Timothy Auty, Andrew Baster, John McI. Davidson, Brian Edwards, John Gaustad, John Griffiths, Chris Harte, Steve Lewis, Allan J. Martin, Dave McLaren, and Dai Richards, thank you for your interest and encouragement.

The publisher has been unable to trace the copyright holders of 'The last of the Mohicans' reproduced on page 213. Any information enabling the publisher to do this would be gratefully received.

Contents

Introduction

ONE DOES NOT IMMEDIATELY ASSOCIATE rugby and literature. The robust world of sweat, liniment, gumshields and scrum-caps seems a far cry from the sentimental poem or delicately turned simile. Shaven-headed front-row forwards with no necks are unlikely topics for a gifted pen. However, as John Jenkins shows, a surprising amount has been written about the game even though no one writer has managed to achieve the literary reputation Neville Cardus gained in cricket. But then, the two games are totally different, one lasting up to five days, the other concentrated into eighty furious minutes. There's hardly time for a spectator to read the programme, let alone anything else. Perhaps that's why rugby players are not really avid readers during their playing days. When I played for the local Extra B this applied even to important communications from Twickenham such as changes in the laws. I well recall forty-odd years ago, following some drastic amendments, a despairing referee asking our hooker, 'Don't you know the new Laws?' and getting the reply, 'What new Laws?'. After the referee had patiently explained them he commented, 'Well, I think the old ones were better'.

Browsing through *A rugby compendium* I came across a publication which was issued by Twickenham just to deal with players like that, the famous *Why the whistle went*, by H. F. Ellis. This was quite a landmark in rugby literature, as the first attempt to explain the Laws in a less serious manner and it was a runaway best-seller.

Alas, it was wasted on our hooker, who was a squat little man with no teeth nicknamed Gnasher. His father had been a miner and had lost a leg in a colliery accident, and one of Gnasher's earliest memories was of his mother rubbing his father's stump with turpentine to harden it. The lesson sank in and although he had no stump he did have false teeth and a pair of gums, which he massaged daily in order to harden them. He would then take his teeth out before a match and use his gums freely upon opponents. People who suffered said it was rather like being gripped by a dying octopus. One rather posh young opponent objected he had been bitten on the forearm and showed the referee a strange mark like a plague token. But Gnasher confronted the ref with open mouth and said, 'Look, I can't have bitten him – got no teeth, ref.'

The young man thought for a moment and then replied, 'Well if he didn't bite me, he gave me a very unpleasant suck'.

One rather surprising literary association for rugby, is that of Sherlock Holmes. Conan Doyle based a complete Sherlock Holmes story ('The missing threequarter') on a game of rugby, the Varsity match to be precise. Holmes' fans will recall that the Great Detective was consulted by the desperate captain of Cambridge, whose finest threequarter had vanished the day before the match ('When it comes to passing, tackling or dribbling there's no one to beat him, Mr Holmes'). Holmes set off for Cambridge immediately, accompanied by Watson of course, and met with a wall of silence from the Principal of the medical school (whom they rightly suspected of being involved, somehow).

After much investigation and sending of telegrams, Holmes finally discovered the awful truth by hiring a bloodhound and squirting aniseed on the Principal's pony and trap so the dog would follow. It transpired that the missing threequarter had secretly married a girl of whom his guardian disapproved. She had contracted a fatal disease, and he missed the match to attend her dying moments. To make a sad story sadder, Cambridge lost heavily.

Furthermore, Holmes' companion, the bluff Dr Watson, is revealed in another story as a former rugby player. 'The adventure of the Sussex Vampire' begins with a client writing to Holmes for his help and adding the postscript, 'I believe your Watson played rugby for Blackheath'. To which Watson comments, 'Of course I remember Big Bob Ferguson, the finest threequarter Richmond ever had'.

When he calls at Baker Street, however, Ferguson, is not so complimentary about Watson, whom he greets by saying, 'You don't look quite the same man you did when I threw you over the ropes into the crowd at Old Deer Park'. Which suggests Watson was not a particularly good player. What sort of man lets himself be thrown over the ropes? Was the good doctor a terrible weed, promoted at the last minute from Richmond Extra C? And what position did he play? There's a book there, somewhere.

And if there should be such a book it would undoubtedly finish up in this astonishing bibliography of rugby literature. The enormous breadth of writing about the game is quite surprising. Everyone knows there are books on coaching and the history of the game, but how many people know there are several volumes of rugby poetry? The offerings are perhaps not quite up to the standard of Francis Thompson's famous poem on Lord's which includes the immortal lines:

> For the field is full of shades as I near the shadowy coast,
> And a ghostly bowler bowls to the batting of a ghost.

But although rather more earthy, the rugby collections do include one by Roger McGough, the well-known Liverpool poet, which starts:

> Big Arth from Penarth
> was a forward and a half.

Another collection of poems dates back to 1893 under the pseudonym Alfred Jingle and includes this gem:

> The forwards blamed the quarters, while in turn the halves they blamed,
> In self-defence the halves declared the back should be ashamed –

To which one can only comment, 'plus ça change...'.

And of course, all the works of rugby's great Welsh musician Max Boyce are here. Indeed Max Boyce occupies a unique niche as perhaps the only true bard of any sport. No other game can boast its own musical chronicler and one to reach the top of the Hit Parade at that.

I certainly did not realise that Rugby Union had inspired several plays. I always believed Rugby League had a monopoly of the stage with *The changing room* and *Up 'n under*. It was equally surprising to find the game had inspired several novels, often involving crime, kidnap and murder (off the field, fortunately). Indeed, the climax of one murder mystery is set during an international at Twickenham.

Most surprising of all, though, was to find a list of children's books devoted to rugby. One, *Freddy's football*, was printed in 1890 and shaped like an oval ball. One of the latest is *Sir Gawain and the rugby sevens*, published in 1995, which describes how King Arthur held a seven-a-side tournament among his knights to stop their constant squabbling, and the surprising events which followed.

Rugby's literature reflects the way the game has changed. In the earlier part of the century Rugby spawned a whole genre of books which treated it not as a sport but as a branch of moral improvement. Growing up at Grammar School in the thirties I read some of them. I always remember a book by a famous international who captained a London club, which stressed the importance of monk-like asceticism. The writer told how he saw one of his players actually entering a tea-dance in his plus-fours on the evening before a big game. Unhesitatingly the captain strode into the dance, went up to the offending player as he sat at a table, and said sternly, 'You may consider yourself dropped from tomorrow's team'.

Glancing down the list of titles I spotted another book with a strong moral tone: E. H. D. Sewell's *Rugger: the man's game*. I can't resist quoting one passage: 'It is something more than a mere game, is this man-maker. It possesses character-building virtues to an extent no other game can claim. It inculcates self-control and discipline to a degree unknown in any other sport. To play rugger well you must play it fiercely, and at the same time, and all the time, remember while doing so that you are a Sahib.' There was unfortunately, a gap between the noble sentiments preached and real life, a gap which I described in my own book *The art of coarse rugby*, first published in 1960. Rugby players in those days were supposed to be fit young men with thighs like oak trees, impervious to pain, playing fair at all times and living lives of purity and chastity. While that might (or might not) have been so in the first team of a good club, most players weren't in that category.

In reality a typical player in the lower sides might be an unfit sales rep, approaching middle-age and praying for the match to end as he panted round some sodden suburban meadow. And I write as one who was invariably sick at half-time (probably because I used to light up a cigarette the moment the whistle went). However, I wasn't as depraved as some of the side, who used to keep a packet of fags hidden behind the posts and light up for a quick drag when there was a conversion. The posts were covered in scorch marks where they had stubbed them out.

It was altogether a rather different game from the one envisaged in some of the literature.

I shall not easily forget the matches I played in for various teams ranging from Ealing Extra B to Leicester Thursday. For one thing neither side ever had fifteen men (having that number I had always assumed was the basis of Rugby Union as distinct from Rugby League). Trouble would begin before the match. Mysterious messages would be left from the team secretary in the pub where we met beforehand, such as

'Bert won't be coming because he's got to take the cat to the vet, so tell Mike he is to play for the Second XV and to go to Hanger Lane and pick up Charlie and give him a lift to Finchley. The replacement for Mike will be Fred and Jack will have to go to Gunnersbury Park and get him away from the fourth team, and I myself will play for the fifth team.'

Invariably these complicated arrangements ended with people speeding madly all over the Home Counties and teams kicking off with either twelve men or sixteen (it was not unknown for teams deliberately to start with sixteen until the referee or their opponents noticed). Sometimes a gap would be filled at the last minute by borrowing a spectator or even, as I recall, a goalkeeper on the soccer pitch next door who didn't have much to do as his side were winning ten-nil. Occasionally men the club were trying to get rid of had to be called in, such as the team psychopath. I always remember one chap who was 'on tablets' and we had to warn the opposition he might behave peculiarly. He had a strange stare and sometimes his limbs would jerk uncontrollably and he would flail about in a line-out. Worse, he had an eerie laugh and boomed 'Hur-Hur-Hur' all over the field whenever something unpleasant happened, such as a serious injury.

Another of our men was over sixty and used to foam at the mouth as he ran round the field. Perhaps 'run' is not the word. He moved slowly from scrum to scrum, wheezing terribly and with a bubble coming out of his lips. Opponents were afraid to tackle in case he dropped dead.

Usually the discrepancy between sides was lessened by lending a player, so twelve men to ten became eleven each. We had a special player for lending, a weedy, short-sighted youth of eighteen who could see nothing without his glasses and who was liable to burst into tears if roughly treated. The damage such a player did to the opposition can be imagined. Although selected for every game, he usually went through the entire season playing for the opposition. We reckoned he was worth ten points a fixture to us.

Playing short of a full side meant some desperate switching of positions. Frequently one might find a threequarter line composed entirely of hookers. I remember having to play scrum-half at the age of thirty-five after originally being selected at full-back. I knew it was going to be a difficult afternoon when at the first scrum I bent down to pick up the ball and the opposing scrum-half didn't bother to tackle me, he just trod on my hand. But he was Welsh, and valley rugby had its own laws and customs.

A commendable number of books for referees are listed in this volume but I often wonder if they would have been much use to our referees who had to deal with crises that don't normally occur in the better class of rugby. For instance, if a man was sent off he didn't just meekly leave the field, he would keep turning round to shout abuse at the referee or the opposition. That is assuming he condescended to go off at all; there were several instances where players just refused to go. One did go off but then stood on the touchline jeering and hooting and making rude signs at the referee and making such a nuisance of himself the ref asked him back on condition he behaved. I don't think any books give advice on what to do if that happens, nor on how to cope with a player who has got drunk in the pub before the match (or even at half-time, when some players were inclined to use a bottle of rum kept on the touchline.)

I have seen several conversions foiled because the defending team started to make the post sway and the ball passed outside, which was easy enough on the local park, where the posts were inserted into slots before the game. Once, a side picked up the posts bodily and carried them sideways as the kicker struck the ball.

And I don't think any of the books listed tell what to do if a touch-judge stops a certain try by thrusting a flag between a winger's legs to bring him down. The culprit in this case was actually a woman, the mother of a young lad in the team. Another touch-judge set his dog on to a winger, shouting, 'Good dog, seize him boy, seize him, kill kill' to such effect the player dropped the ball.

One of the most extraordinary referees I knew was a priest, hauled off the touchline by an Irishman in our side when the usual ref failed to turn up. Everybody was unusually careful in their language in front of him, until the Irishman himself went down groaning in pain.

'What is the matter my son?' asked the priest kneeling by him. 'Father,' he said, 'some bloody swine has kicked me in the balls'.

'Hush, my son,' said the priest. 'Tell me who it was and I will send the bastard off.'

Priests, of course, used to be an integral part of Irish rugby, which is not surprising when you consider one captain of the international side always sprinkled holy water over the forwards in the dressing-room. A year or two back, an Irish side turned up for a seven-a-side competition in Amsterdam with no fewer than seventy-two players but the following Saturday couldn't even field a full side for a second XV match twenty miles away at Shannon. When the local priest asked why, the secretary told him, 'Well Father, to the best of my knowledge there is no red light district in Shannon'.

Mercifully, within an hour of the final whistle our game was usually consigned to oblivion over beer. By seven o'clock we were singing 'The muffin man' and balancing pints on our heads and vowing the opposition splendid fellows really. All that clouded the horizon was the game we had to play before the beer next Saturday.

Rugby teams don't seem to sing so much these days, which is a pity because it was a long tradition. I was surprised at the great number of volumes listed devoted entirely to rugby songs and they evoked many happy memories. Although the rugby song is often criticised as being a mere bellow, the best ones did have a crude folk-culture of their own. Keir Hardie himself would have approved of the socialist appeal of 'They're digging up father's grave to build a sewer', the story of an honest British workman who was exhumed for the building of a drain 'up to some dirty posh's residence' and who retaliated by haunting the aristocrat's lavatory seat. Some songs told a narrative story of heroic proportions such as 'Eskimo Nell' or 'The wild west show' while others, like 'Oh you Zulu warriors', depended for their appeal on violent physical action, usually involving pouring beer over everybody.

And what better description of the classic Welsh rugby braggart than the sardonic verse:

> Oh I have a brother Rupert
> And he used to play for Newport
> And they thought so much about him
> That they always played without him.

In the second half of the century society began to change. People began to question the old gods; the sixties saw the growth of the anti-establishment movement and *A rugby compendium* shows how rugby literature reflected (perhaps not always consciously) this trend. Rugby, with its insistence on public-school values was always going to be vulnerable. My own little spoof *The art of coarse rugby*, devoted to life in the lower sides, surprised everybody by its success in 1960 (the publishers warned me solemnly to expect a sale of 2,000 copies and it finished up selling nearly a quarter of a million and staying in print for nigh on forty years). This was certainly not due to the literary quality, so it must have caught the mood of the moment. Perhaps people were tired of being preached at in rugby books, in the manner I've described earlier.

The literary mood quite definitely moved in the seventies. Whereas previously books confined themselves to playing matters and were usually deferential to the authorities, the new genre put the boot in. Nothing was sacred any more and rugby literature became as investigative and controversial as any. As the game has become more professional, harder and more competitive, so has the literature. Rugby books are no longer books about what a clean healthy sport it is and good for the soul, too. They are more likely to expose, probe, criticise and shock. Naturally, they make more money that way although sometimes one yearns for an age when a game could exist without permanent controversy.

I am bitterly aware that my own *The art of coarse rugby* is now as out-of-date as Mr Sewell's comment about playing the Sahib. Even the third team trains today, and trains hard. A player who strolled on the pitch with a fag in his mouth or left the field for a rest after a long run (as one of my friends always did) would be banned by the coach. Few teams change in cowsheds, pubs or even old buses like we used to do. The old bus, incidentally, was from Nottingham Corporation, and situated in a field near Ratcliffe-on-the-Wreake, on the Leicestershire-Notts. borders. It was the home of a side called Notts. Tigers (they don't exist any longer) and I played against them in 1951 for Stoneygate Second XV.

We were actually given a map reference to guide the coach driver and this turned out to be where a path diverted from the road. Here we were met by a bald-headed, elderly individual who appeared to be in the last stages of some hideous disease and who introduced himself as the vice-captain. He led us up the path and through a wood into a field.

'Before we start,' he said, 'I wonder if you'd mind helping us move the pavilion four feet to the left?'

This unusual request was explained by the fact that the pavilion was the aforesaid bus, which stood proudly beside the pitch and was at present occupied by a sheep. After we'd solemnly pushed the bus the required four feet, we asked him why this had to be done.

'We have to move it every week,' he explained, 'because of the planning regulations. It'd never pass as a permanent fixture but if we move it four feet every week it counts as a mobile dwelling.'

So we changed in the bus – home team downstairs, visitors upstairs. And afterwards we bathed in oil drums cut in half and heated over fires. I think that was the time the posts fell down and we had to take all the kicks at goal at one end. I also seem to remember play stopping while players watched the copulation of a sheep and a ram on the touchline and when it was over we all applauded.

We may sneer at the old books with their insistence on stern moral values and sportsmanship but looking at the modern game with its millionaire bosses, highly-paid players, agents, cheer leaders, scandals and domination by money, I sometimes feel nostalgic for the time when the game was played for fun. But then, fun is a dirty word today. Perhaps it will be rediscovered sometime.

However, rugby, like life, goes on. Who could have foreseen that women would take to the game so enthusiastically and in such large numbers? Today, they too, have their own ever-growing body of literature. Indeed, of the making of rugby books there is no end.

Michael Green
London, 1997

How To Use This Book

✳ *Scope*

A rugby compendium is a bibliography of books on rugby union published in the United Kingdom or Republic of Ireland in any language, and of books on rugby union published in the English language anywhere in the rest of the world. The cut-off date for inclusion is December 1997. It does not include newspapers, boys' annuals, programmes, club yearbooks, testimonial brochures, unpublished research, promotional items, or public records, although occasional instances of these categories may be included to make or illustrate a specific point. Reprints are not included, but new editions *are* listed. In the case of serial publications such as *Yearbooks*, *Guides*, and *Annuals* the entry gives the year in which the title started publication and, if known, the year in which publication ceased.

Periodicals are included at title level; individual articles are not. Journal literature is invaluable in providing news and up-to-date information on current topics of interest, on research and work-in-progress. It is also often the means by which new topics for study and research are introduced, trends reported and general communication within a discipline or subject area facilitated. Such information dates quickly and is readily and best accessed through secondary sources of information – specialist indexing and abstracting services, such as *Sport bibliography*, a database with international coverage produced by the Sport Information Resource Centre (SIRC) in Toronto. Many such services have long been available as online databases, and many are now available as CD-ROMs or through the World Wide Web, where specialist sites and discussion groups are rapidly taking the place of the traditional learned journal. In the case of rugby, such sites abound and a number of these services have now come together on the *SportQuest* site which acts as a referral centre to a vast range of organisations and sports sites and also acts as a gateway for (priced) online literature searches of the *Sport bibliography* database, now retitled *SPORTS discus* (http://www.silverplatter.com/catalog/spts.htm). *SportQuest* epitomises the completely new type of resource which the development of the Internet has made possible – where information which it would never have been economic to disseminate in printed form, can be made available in a structured way to users, often free or at low cost. The last year has seen an explosion in the number of web sites offering information on practically every subject in which there is an academic or hobbyist interest.

The resources made available by this burgeoning technology are beyond the scope of this compilation, but the reader's attention is drawn to Richard Cox's *The Internet as a resource for sports historians* (Frodsham: Sports History Publishing, 1995).

It is such Web resources, readily accessed through the desktop PC, which have made it possible to include so many overseas publications in this compilation. Increasingly, national and other major reference libraries are making their catalogues freely available on the Internet. This has led, and will lead, to tremendous benefits for researchers who are now able to determine what publications exist and where they are held. A subsidiary benefit is that it allows authoritative bibliographic records to be garnered from a range and number of sources which it would have been impractical to attempt only a year or two ago.

The result is that in this bibliography it has been possible to list and record the bulk of overseas English-language titles likely to be of interest to the researcher or general rugby reader. Many of the catalogues accessed in the course of this work have not yet extended their coverage back beyond the introduction of automated cataloguing systems. Thus there is still significant lack of coverage of many early titles. As more catalogues are converted to the new format, so the editors hope it will be possible to rectify this omission in subsequent editions.

In the main, the entries in this bibliography are derived from the holdings of the British Library (the national library of the United Kingdom), and the National Library of Wales. In some instances, however, full bibliographic information has not been available to the compiler. Such entries have been included only where the compiler is confident that the item actually exists, even though it has not been possible to obtain full details. Further information on these items, and indeed on any omissions or mistakes in this bibliography, will be gratefully received by the editor and incorporated in any future edition.

As a specialist subject bibliography, *A rugby compendium* does not include those general reference sources which are to be found in any major reference library. These are no substitute for a subject's own specialist literature but can sometimes supply hard to find or otherwise unavailable information, for example most titles in the *Victoria history of the counties of England* series have a chapter on sport which, depending on its standing in the county, will include references to rugby. Another example is professional or other directories which may include elusive biographical information not readily found elsewhere. Equally, general indexing and abstracting services should not be overlooked for the material they might throw up from journals in other disciplines.

For a similar reason, books on sport in general, or which contain only a section or chapter on rugby, are only included if the compiler has judged their rugby content to be of particular significance (these books are listed in the Additional References sections). There is a vast and ever-growing literature on sport and sports history, subjects which are increasingly the focus of academic study and research. Such research is illuminating whole areas of British social history, and what has already appeared has more than proved the worth of such study. Unless the compiler of this bibliography has felt such items to be particularly relevant to the literature of rugby union they have been omitted. The researcher is referred to those bibliographic tools specific to the literature of sports history, such as Cox's *History of sport: a guide to the literature and sources of information* (Frodsham: Sports History Publishing, 1994).

✳ *Arrangement & Layout*

The chapter headings used reflect the categories to be found in the literature and it has thus been possible to list most items just once. Where the scope of a work cuts across the boundaries of the chapter headings, the book has been listed in the most relevant chapter and index entries created under all other appropriate headings. In a few cases where it has been judged more helpful to the user, books have been listed in more than one section. There are four indexes at the end of the bibliography: name, club, title, subject.

Each chapter has its own contents page, showing the span of numbers for each topic covered in that chapter. The order in which books have been listed is in most cases immediately apparent, and is always the order considered most useful for the reader. For example, biographies are arranged in alphabetical order by the name of the biographee; club histories are arranged alphabetically by club name; tours and competitions are arranged chronologically by event. Elsewhere the usual arrangement is by date of publication. When more than one book has been published in the same year, they are further arranged alphabetically by title.

Within each lettered chapter books are numbered sequentially, e.g. A1, A2. A new sequence of numbers starts with each chapter. In this way every book listed has a unique reference made up of the chapter letter and the number of the book within the chapter.

The bibliographic information within each record and its format are in accordance with current bibliographic standards. Not all records will contain the same level of information. Some books, for example, do not give their place of publication. In such instances the entry may therefore omit this information.

All records, whether derived from the catalogue of the British Library or elsewhere, have been arranged in a uniform way. Every effort has been made to include all the information necessary to uniquely identify the item in order to facilitate its purchase, or enable users to obtain it on loan from a public or other library.

The location numbers for books held in the British Library refer to books which are not available for loan. They are only available for consultation in the British Library, when it is not possible for a reader to consult them elsewhere. Various restrictions may also apply to particular items. Enquiries concerning use of the Library's Reading Rooms should be made in writing to:

British Library
Reader Admissions Office
96 Euston Road
London NW1 2DB

A typical entry is set out below:

ENTRY NUMBER   TITLE   AUTHOR/EDITOR   PLACE OF PUBLICATION

27 Land of sport and glory: sport and British society,
1887-1910 / Derek Birley. Manchester: Manchester
University Press, 1995.

PUBLISHER

YEAR OF
PUBLICATION

PAGINATION +
ENHANCEMENTS

x, 287p; index
(International studies in the history of sport)

SERIES

ISBN: 0719044944 (cased) • 0719044952 (pbk)
BL: YC.1995.b.3402

ISBNs

BRITISH LIBRARY
LOCATION

A study of sport in the late Victorian and
Edwardian period. Describes the background
leading to the division in rugby and the birth of
rugby league.

COMPILER'S ANNOTATION

✳ *Abbreviations used in the Entries*

BL	British Library
D	BL copy destroyed during WW2
ed.	edition
illus	illustrated
ISBN	International Standard Book Number
ISSN	International Standard Serial Number
p	pages
pbk	paperback
pseud.	pseudonym
rev.	revised
SBN	Standard Book Number
t.p.	title page
vol.	volume

Review of the Literature

by *Huw Richards*

WHEN C. L. R. JAMES COINED one of the most famous sporting aphorisms, asking 'What do they know of cricket, that only cricket know?' in 1963, it is unlikely he knew that a rugby player had anticipated his warning against tunnel vision, if not his elegant Kiplingesque formulation, three decades earlier.

Thus Welsh international winger Rowe Harding, marking the end of his playing career with his *Rugby reminiscences and opinions* [H184], one of the first rugby memoirs, warned his readers against obsession with the game: 'I have known men whose whole life was sacrificed to rugby, who played it until they were middle-aged, who refused to give it up until their health gave way. Their only literature was rugby literature, their only interest in life was rugby.' Such lives, he argued, might not be regretted by those who lived them, but they were 'lives thrown away'.

Not the least striking element of this is the suggestion that as early as 1929 a man, albeit one suffering from chronic cultural malnutrition, might have found all his reading matter in books and articles devoted to the game. It all depends, of course, on what one means by literature. There is an arguable case that the most significant literary form associated with the various codes of football has been the newspaper match report, with which Harding's rugby obsessives would have been as fully supplied as their counterparts seventy years later.

Welsh novelist Gwyn Thomas considered the game's success in Wales actively inimical to literature and the arts: 'This game, with its magnets of remembrance, has drained off much of the ardour which might have gone into a more sedulous cultivation of the arts.' Rugby has been accused of being 'twin sister of the drinking system', the peculiar preserve of unreflective masculinity, a breeding ground for unthinking conservatism and one of the key underpinnings of South African apartheid.

There is sufficient truth in each of these accusations to give pause to the most dedicated enthusiast.

Some might consider 'rugby literature' the classic oxymoron. Doubts about the game's ability to inspire the literate and analytical are even to be found in one of the last places where such scepticism might be expected, an early rugby anthology. The passage in question, buried deep within Kenneth Pelmear's *Rugby football* [H137] was penned by his co-compiler, J. E. Morpurgo: 'It is not surprising that rugby football has produced no Borrow or Walton, no Francis Thompson, Meredith or Hazlitt, to turn its movement into literary art. Angling is an accompaniment to contemplation. Prize-fighting has that spirit of violent personal conflict which makes it particularly susceptible to symbolic interpretation. Cricket, with its complexity of skills and the perfect simplicity of its setting, is justly the most tempting of all games to the literary observer. But rugby football is too rapid for the contemplative, too co-operative for those who seek symbolism and too vigorous for aesthetic delight.'

The philistine 'muddied oaf' image of the game and its culture has been underlined by humorists. P. G. Wodehouse knew his rugby and followed the fortunes of his old school Dulwich with an enthusiasm which even he acknowledged might be disproportionate – writing in 1936 to his lifelong friend Bill Townend: 'Isn't it amazing that you and I, old buffers of about fifty-five with civilisation about to crash, can worry about school football? It is really about the only thing I do worry about.'

Michael Green, in his trio of 'coarse rugby' books, [J3-4, J12], brilliantly managed simultaneously to celebrate and debunk rugby culture. In *The art of coarse rugby*, he addresses the issue of rugby's relationship with literature: 'I am frequently asked for advice on what a Coarse Rugby player should read. Very little suitable is published, and most of it has been banned, but I would certainly recommend *An actor's approach to his part* by Constantin Stanislavski. The annual report of Watney, Combe and Read is also interesting reading. For a good laugh I would suggest the Rugby Union handbook, quite the funniest book ever written on the game. Why not read pieces to each other at half time?'

While the humour of Green and Wodehouse may be England's great contribution to rugby literature, it should also be noted that Reginald Hill, one of the most readable and intellectually satisfying of modern crime novelists, uses a convincing picture of a rugby club and its social tensions as the setting for his *A clubbable woman* [H12], the first of his extremely popular Pascoe and Dalziel series.

The reflectiveness of the bat and ball games – baseball possibly even more than cricket – and the elemental nature of boxing have certainly appealed more to writers with a capital 'W' than have the football codes. Yet, within the last fifteen years, each oval-ball code has inspired writing which passes the test set by John Gaustad, founder of the specialist Sportspages bookshop: 'The best sports books are as much about life as about sport.' Rugby League inspired Geoffrey Moorhouse's book of essays, *At the George* (1989), and Gaelic football and hurling Brendan OhEithir's *Over the bar* (1984). American football has H. G. Bissinger's painfully penetrating analysis of the over-importance of high school football in small-town Texas *Friday night lights* (1990) and

Australian Rules Brian Matthews' *Oval dreams* (1991), essays on cricket, literature and why 'following the St Kilda Football Club for so long taught one a great deal about the meaning of life – which was struggle, defeat and hope springing eternal'.

In spite of Morpurgo's doubts, there is little reason why rugby union should not also encourage good writing. There is sufficient variety and complexity, a mix of the elemental and intellectual, to appeal to the most sophisticated observer. New Zealander Spiros Zavos, writing in Auckland's *Metro* magazine (1987), has produced one of the best delineations of its appeal:

'At its most basic rugby is a simple game. And that is one of its joys. A group of players, of any age, build and degree of skill, can enjoy themselves scrambling around a big paddock, occasionally belting into each other, trying to place a piece of inflated leather over a line or kick it through some posts. Nothing could be more elemental, and therefore so easy to enjoy than this.

'But another of the game's joy is that its art and artifice, within these seemingly simple parameters, can take a lifetime to learn and appreciate. How and when to wheel a scrum; the right time to throw a dummy and scuttle through a gap; the angles that come into play when the ball goes through the backline to the centres; the lovely arch of the leg as someone like Allan Hewson kicks a goal; the bruising choreography of the scrum; and the terrible beauty of a well-drilled pack of forwards driving into a ruck.'

Wavell Wakefield, the dominant personality and tactical innovator of England's brilliant spell in the 1920s, made the case for intelligence in his *Rugger* (with Howard Marshall) [F147]: 'It is above all the game for the tactician and for the man who is mentally alert, for so quickly does it move and so unexpected are its phases, that only a keenly intelligent player can seize openings which come and are gone in a flash, or can check his opponents when prompt decisions and actions are essential.' Carwyn James, coach of the 1971 British Lions side which won in New Zealand, and leading contender – with South Africa's Danie Craven – for the title of sharpest intellect ever applied to the game, put it more directly: 'Rugby union is a thinking game'.

That game has, for better or worse, become the favoured sport of the male populations of New Zealand, white South Africa, South Wales, South-West France, the business classes of England, Scotland and Ireland (not to mention most classes in Gloucester, the Scottish borders and Limerick), of Fijians, West Samoans and Tongans. Any activity inspiring such widespread enthusiasm deserves serious attention.

It has had an impact in unexpected quarters. Mexican historian Jorge Castanada, in *Compañero*, (1997), his biography of revolutionary icon Ernesto 'Che' Guevara, notes the formative role of the game in the asthmatic Guevara's youth in Argentina: 'The position of scrum-half held for Ernesto the great advantage of being more static and strategic, less mobile and tactical. It benefited him in two ways, offering him an opportunity to develop his skills as a leader and strategist and allowed him to play without running from one end of the field to another throughout a match; thus preventing him from tiring too early.' The French journalist Jacques Verdier has pointed out that Guevara also contributed to rugby literature, writing a column on the game for an Argentinian paper for several years.

This contribution to the eventual success of the Cuban Revolution offers some absolution against accusations that rugby automatically incubates conservatism, although not against a parallel charge that it propagates authoritarians – others who played the game before they were famous include Benito Mussolini, Idi Amin and Ian Smith (the Rhodesian Premier, not to be confused with the Scottish winger of the 1920s).

If to know nothing but rugby is still to court cultural deprivation, today's enthusiast has a much wider choice of reading. To read everything would leave little time for any other form of literature – where Rowe Harding's enthusiast might have a choice of ten new books, mostly technical in nature, in a good year, the World Cup year of 1995 brought over a hundred new entries for this *Compendium*.

John Jenkins' painstaking research, three years specifically on this project, but based on the accumulation of many previous years' expertise in the parallel fields of rugby and librarianship, has located in excess of 3,000 items. Much inevitably is ephemeral, parochial and of interest only to the specialist. The reader with a more general interest in the game will nevertheless find much that offers both pleasure and enlightenment and whose quality of writing, analysis and evocative power matches anything in the canon of other sports.

Four elements account for around two-thirds of the entries. The earliest form to emerge was technical – rule books and advice on how to play the game. Next came history, the largest single category, with the stories of clubs forming the bulk of entries. Then biography and autobiography. None of these categories is mutually exclusive, particularly in the earlier days – the massive, multi-authored *Football: the rugby union game*, edited by the Rev. Frank Marshall [A9] is, for instance, both technical and historical. Nor are they peculiar to rugby. The final major category, the tour account, is rugby and cricket's distinctive contribution to sportswriting – part sports book, part travelogue, detailing the experiences of teams on the long overseas tours made necessary by the giant distances between the two games' major centres.

Rugby writing is predominantly the output of rugby people – administrators, players and journalists. Marshall's clerical garb, for instance, concealed a second identity as one of the most important figures in the late nineteenth century Rugby Union, the hammer of the clubs eventually driven into secession in the 1893-5 split which led to the creation of Rugby League. Only recently have academics started to make a serious study of the game, although one would be intrigued to know the precise circumstances under which Francis Peabody Magoun, the Professor of Comparative Literature at Harvard University not only chose in the 1930s to research a *History of football from the beginnings to 1871* [A19] but had it published not in Boston, New York or London, but Cologne.

It is not necessary to be an academic to write good history, but serious historians do provide basic guarantees, particularly in terms of quality of evidence. Much rugby history is written with the narrowness of vision against which Harding counselled. It concentrates on matches won and lost, shows only a limited sense that the game exists in any sort of social context and unquestioningly recycles myth and anecdote.

This sort of 'history' is exemplified by the game's founding legend, famously summarised in the plaque at Rugby School proclaiming the 'Exploit of William Webb

Ellis, who, with a fine disregard for the rules of football, as played in his time, first took the ball in his arms and ran with it, thus originating the distinctive feature of the Rugby game. AD 1823.' It is an attractively subversive founding legend, with the cardinal defect that the finest disregard displayed is for the rules of evidence at any time. Its perfection as an 'invented tradition' is shown by the almost exact parallel with baseball's founding legend, similarly fixed in place by a committee of those with a vested interest in the traditional version, working about sixty years after the alleged event and not above browbeating octogenarian 'witnesses' into acceptable testimony. There is no evidence that Ellis ever did anything of the sort.

The myth has been further sanctified by naming the World Cup the Webb Ellis Trophy. It is in any case missing the point. To kick, or pick up and run with, a ball is to respond to basic human instinct. Nobody invents so elemental a game as rugby. The key point is codification – the point at which rules are agreed which make it possible to take the game further afield. This – and not invention – was the genius of eighteenth and nineteenth century Britons. Webb Ellis's alleged action may be a myth, but the claim of his school, well chronicled in Jennifer Macrory's *Running with the Ball* [A22] is hard to contest.

Rugby literature is however a reliable barometer of two factors – the centrality of the game in local and national cultures and the success of national teams. It is no fluke that Wales and New Zealand should account for so high a proportion of the best writing on rugby, that relatively unbookish South Africa should have generated so many books, that the English game should have inspired surges of publication in the 1920s and 1990s, or that Australia's limited literature should be almost entirely the product of the last fifteen years.

This can particularly be seen in the game's histories. There is no single authoritative English-language volume on its development – although good judges have spoken very highly of the French historian Jean-Pierre Bodis's *Histoire mondiale du rugby: dimensions économiques et sociales* (1987), based on his doctoral thesis. For those who do not read French the best introduction – in spite of a somewhat episodic style, reflecting its origins as the companion volume for a television series – remains Carwyn James and John Reason's *The world of rugby* [A57]. Its credentials as a piece of history rather than retelling of old legends is established on the very first page, where the Webb Ellis story is cheerfully discounted, while the combination of the outstanding British coach (James) and one of its most sharply analytical journalists (Reason) ensures that the account of the game's on-field evolution is particularly strong.

Those who combine an interest in the game's social history with fearlessness in the face of sociological terminology will find much of interest, particularly on early developments, in Eric Dunning and Kenneth Sheard's *Barbarians, gentlemen and players* [A55], although a more approachable work is John Morgan and Geoffrey Nicholson's *Report on rugby* [A42], a pioneering volume by two Welsh journalists combining social history with perceptive analysis of the state of the game in the late 1950s which is particularly interesting on the social dynamics underpinning the emergence of distinctive national playing styles in the four home countries. Nicholson was later responsible for *The great bike race* (1977), a study of the Tour de France which is one of the best books on any sport in any language.

That there are as many books under the heading of 'Wales' as for the other three British nations combined in the History & Development chapter is a reflection of the immense cultural importance of the game in Wales; in historian Gareth Williams's words, 'a pre-eminent expression of Welsh consciousness, a signifier of Welsh nationhood'. The list includes undoubtedly the outstanding work on the game's history – Gareth Williams and David Smith's *Fields of praise* [A132].

Recognising that the story consisted of much more than matches won and lost, the Welsh Rugby Union's Publications Committee, chaired by former college principal Hermas Evans, bypassed the more obvious resort offered by a journalist or administrator, to commission two young academic historians – both as it happens former pupils of Gwyn Thomas at Barry Grammar School – to write their centenary history. They were rewarded by the last world-class performance by any team selected by the WRU, a book which as Williams has written, is 'as much an orthodox institutional history as *Moby Dick* is a book about a whale'. While not stinting on the detail of who played, who won and lost and why, it is a social history of modern Wales seen through the filter of one of its defining activities. It is at its strongest, and most entertaining, in its evocation of great players. The portrait of Cliff Morgan encapsulates his brilliance as a player and his place in the context of his society and times: 'The succession of William Benjamin Cleaver by Clifford Isaac Morgan as Triple Crown fly-half confirmed a long-held suspicion that, years ago, one of the lost tribes of Israel had somehow wandered into South Wales. Cliff always played with the passionate urgency of a man trying to get out again. With the ball held at arm's length in front of him, his tongue out almost as far, his bow legs pumping like pistons, eyes rolling, nostrils flaring in a range of facial expressions seldom seen north of Milan… he was an amalgam of the currents that were defining Welshness anew in the second half of the twentieth century. Cliff came from Trebanog, a precipitous offshoot of the Rhondda, on whose windy ridge people clung together for warmth and safety lest the storms of the world blew away; he would never lose a sense of this induced Welsh, almost cosy togetherness. His was the Welshness of the nonconformist home where Mam ruled and Sunday was for chapel.' The portrait perhaps has extra passion for being of a giant of the authors' youth (Morgan played for Wales from 1951 to 1958, both writers were born in 1945) but equal justice is done many others. Williams has further explored themes of rugby and identity in *1905 and all that* [A146], essays whose distinction doubtless failed to halt a posthumous snort from Gwyn Thomas, old pupil or not, at an acknowledgement of assistance from the Welsh Arts Council.

Contemporary with *Fields of praise* came *A touch of glory* [A135] by Alun Richards – less a history than a brilliantly evocative essay, which peaks in its treatment of Arthur Gould, the first of the Welsh game's authentic giants. His subsequent rugby book *Carwyn* [C133], a tribute to Carwyn James, comes closer to catching the essence of one of the most remarkable figures of the century commemorated in *A touch of glory* than anyone before or since.

Yet Richards' most distinctive contribution to the game's literature comes in a trio of short stories, 'Hon Sec RFC', 'Fly half' and 'The drop-out', written in the 1970s (all three can be found in *The former Miss Merthyr Tydfil and other stories* [H79]). 'Hon Sec RFC' in particular, with its cast of committee men and roaring prop forwards, evokes both rugby culture and its place within wider Welsh society with humorous, humane precision. That a serious writer like Richards, one of Wales' leading literary figures, should devote such attention to rugby is further evidence of the game's cultural centrality.

This Welsh example finds a close parallel in New Zealand where a significant novelist, Maurice Gee, gave a rugby theme to the title story of his early book of short stories *The big season* [H10]. Just as Americans are prepared to use baseball as a metaphor for life and their society – Thomas Boswell is only half-joking in his titles *Why life imitates the World Series* and *Why time begins on opening day* – so rugby acts as a metaphor for New Zealand society and its fault-lines in *Foreskin's lament* [H149], a play written in 1976 by former All Black trialist Greg McGee and described by one critic as 'a quantum leap forward in New Zealand drama'.

It should be noted that British rugby league can claim, via the pen of ex-professional David Storey, a significant, filmed novel in *This sporting life* (1960) and a play whose implication extends beyond the immediately sporting in *The changing room* (1972), not to mention a modern reworking of Chaucer via Alan Plater's *Trinity tales* and an immense popular theatrical success in John Godber's *Up 'n under* (1985). Union also has yet to develop anything comparable to the group of, mostly self-publishing, historians who have emerged over the last fifteen years in rugby league. The work of Trevor Delaney, Robert Gate, Michael Latham, Graham Williams and most recently Tony Collins has shed important light not only on their own game, but on the split between the codes in the 1890s and their subsequent relationship.

Collins' *Rugby's great split* (1998), which should become the standard text on the schism, is still a relative rugby history rarity in being based on a British doctoral thesis. By contrast the number of Canadian and US theses on a game which enjoys only minority status in those countries testifies to the much greater strength and standing of sports history in North American universities.

The largest single history category is the club history, more often than not a labour of love by a fan or member timed to coincide with a significant anniversary – note the twenty-five year sequence of books on Bristol (founded 1888). Among Welsh accounts Gareth Hughes' books on Llanelli [B558-560] stand out for their use of period press coverage, not just to explain who scored and what happened in matches, but to provide a real sense of the town and its community through the last century and more. The most imaginative junior club histories explicitly place a club in the context of its community – Denver Evans' *Bont: the story of a village and its rugby club* [B593] and Howard Jones' *Yr Hendy* [B551] are good examples dealing with near-neighbours Pontardulais and Hendy. Notable works on clubs in England include Paul Beken and Stephen Jones' painstaking examination of the peculiar duality of London Welsh *Dragon in exile* [B566], David Hands' histories of Leicester [B155, B157] and Chris Ducker's *Rugby Bristol fashion* [B60], whose evocation of the club's traditional brilliance makes poignant reading in the year when Bristol lost top-flight status. Those who doubt that the level of publishing is a barometer of the cultural significance of rugby should note that there are seven books on Cornish county rugby – most reflecting its spectacular renaissance in the 1990s.

This importance of success is further underlined when Welsh and English autobiographies are compared. As columnist Alan Watkins has noted, the biography is a relative rarity: 'Great rugby players are rarely the subject of full biographies as great cricketers are.' It is a measure of Will Carling's fame that he should have inspired two substantial biographies, one of which (much the more critical) was by Peter Bills [C28], who has also written a distinguished study of Jean-Pierre Rives [C191]. Biographies are almost entirely contemporaneous; the historical biography, such as Michael Latham's *Buff Berry and the Mighty Bongers* [C11], remains a rarity, although the Welsh journalist David Parry-Jones plans to publish a biography of Gwyn Nicholls, captain of Wales in the early years of this century.

Until the 1970s the player autobiography was a rarity. There was a trickle of volumes by journalists and broadcasters. Notable among these are the BBC pioneers H. B. T. Wakelam [C219] and G. V. Wynne-Jones [H190] while *Rugby recollections* (1948) by W. J. T. Collins, 'Dromio' of the Newport *South Wales Argus*, is a lucidly perceptive recounting of more than sixty years watching the game. Players who went into print generally did so on the strength of other achievements. This makes Stephen Gwynn [C93], Dai Lewis [C129], Sir Robert Bruce-Lockhart [C140-142], Robert Collis [C40-41], and Peter Howard [109] much more interesting men, but inevitably leaves the rugby element marginal. Rowe Harding's 1929 effort [H184] is the first straightforward player memoir, and the second had to wait until 1956 and Bleddyn Williams' *Rugger my life* [C228], noted for his view (p37) that actor Richard Burton might have been an international forward. Burton was to write (1970) that '…one of the curious phenomena of my library is that when you take out Bleddyn's autobiography from the shelves it automatically opens at the very page mentioned above'.

Williams was followed in 1958 by two Welsh converts to league, Gus Risman and Lewis Jones. But it was not until the 1970s that British commercial publishers became convinced that autobiographies of famous players, normally ghosted, were a commercial proposition. Timing was dictated by the rule that anyone taking money for a book was deemed professional and excluded from any involvement in the game. The rule was rigidly enforced – asking a senior Rugby Union official in the mid 1980s about the absence of Bill Beaumont, England's most popular recent player, from a flagging national set-up, I received the snorted response 'Beaumont? Man's a professional' – a status based solely on the fee received for his post-retirement (1982) autobiography [C8].

The 1970s surge in interest in the game rested on a number of linked phenomena. Rule changes in the late 1960s produced, for a time at least, a fluid and attractive game in which a brilliantly gifted Welsh generation flourished and, as well as providing magnificent entertainment in televised home internationals, made up the bulk of the British Lions sides who enjoyed unprecedented success in New Zealand in 1971 and South Africa in 1974.

The 1970s player autobiography was even more a Welsh monopoly than the Five Nations Championship. Starting with *The Barry John story* [C114] the retirements of most of the great Welsh players of the era were followed rapidly by a book. Of these *Gerald Davies: an autobiography* [C52] stands out for sheer (unghosted) literacy and a magnificent description of his childhood and the role of rugby in the Carmarthenshire village of Llansaint, while another fine account of the society that produced this brief explosion of genius is contained in *Rugby: body and soul* [C196] – the memoirs of Bill Samuel, early mentor to Gareth Edwards. But the flow of Welsh memoirs halts abruptly in the mid 1980s, and the unprecedentedly unsuccessful years since have seen only Ieuan Evans [C66], Paul Thorburn [C211], Jonathan Davies [C53-54], and Jonathan Humphreys [C110] appear between hard covers. Another charismatic league convert David Watkins also managed two books [C221-222].

The Welsh hegemony of the 1970s was even acknowledged in the title of the first of the recent English autobiographies. Coventry winger David Duckham, who could walk unrecognised near his office in Birmingham but could not go five yards without being spotted in Cardiff or Swansea, called his book *Dai for England* [C61]. It took the Grand Slam won in 1980 by Bill Beaumont's side to make the English memoir a selling proposition. Seven of the team made it into print. Where the bulk of Welsh memoirs were, and are, written by backs, the strength of Beaumont's side was faithfully reflected by four of the front five-front-rowers; Phil Blakeway [C12], Peter Wheeler [C225] and Fran Cotton [C42] plus Beaumont himself [C8] producing autobiographies. A lull followed as England lapsed back into the doldrums, but since Will Carling's teams became the dominant force in European rugby – and the loosening then abolition of amateur regulations has allowed players to write books while still playing – it has begun to look as though England players are issued with publishing contracts along with their caps or Lions blazers. Amid this surge of literary activity, much the most interesting efforts have come inevitably from those whose efforts are driven as much by having something to say as the attractions of a publisher's advance. Carling's England teams won more games than friends with their ultra-controlled approach. The abrasively intelligent hooker Brian Moore displays both qualities in expounding the case for them in his *Brian Moore: an autobiography* [C165] – much more interesting than its title promises – while the highly literate outside-half-turned-journalist Stuart Barnes, English rugby's most articulate dissident, puts the case against with considerable power in *Smelling of roses* [C5].

Scottish and Irish autobiographies are conspicuous by absence. Tony O'Reilly is a special case, with his business career, more than his rugby, inspiring two biographies. Players of the stature of Tom Kiernan, Fergus Slattery and Mike Gibson would have had to beat off aspirant ghost-writers and importunate publishers had they been Welsh or English, and Gibson's much-anthologised humorous essay on the Irish outside-half tradition [A146] points to genuine literary talent. In Ireland they went undisturbed. Three players and a coach – Willie John McBride [C147], Nick Popplewell [C183], Tony Ward [C220] and Mick Doyle [C60] – are the extent of Ireland's modern autobiographers while ultra-charismatic 1970s full-back Andy Irvine [C111] and lock

Gordon Brown [C19] were the only modern Scots to write memoirs before a surge from members of the 1984 or 1990 Grand Slam teams.

All of which is in striking contrast to New Zealand, and sales figures explain why. *Colin Meads, All Black* [C157] sold 57,000 copies, Andy Haden's *Boots 'n all* [C94] 44,000 and the first volume of Bob Howitt's *New Zealand rugby greats* [C259] 33,000. New Zealand is admittedly, and against stereotype, a bookish society where the most impressive public building in a town is not infrequently the public library. These books had some international sales. But in the context of a population of just over three million these figures would not displease John Grisham, Nick Hornby or Catherine Cookson.

Rugby in New Zealand has had, for the male population at least, a near-universality unrivalled elsewhere. It has been estimated that forty per cent of New Zealand males were involved in the game in the early 1950s. John Mulgan, in his autobiographical *Report on experience* (1947), wrote: 'Rugby football was the best of all our pleasures, it was religion and desire and fulfilment all in one. Most New Zealanders can look back on some game in which they played to win and whose issues seemed to them then a good deal more important than a lot that has happened since. This phenomenon is greatly deprecated by a lot of thinkers who feel that an exaggerated attention to games gives the young a wrong sense of values. That may well be true, and if it is true, the majority of New Zealanders have a wrong sense of values for the whole of their lives.'

New Zealand's rugby followers have supported a comprehensive *Rugby almanac* since 1935 [H131]. Compare this with Rothmans début as late as 1972 [H83] and the erratic career of the Playfair [H75, H90, H116] in Britain. It has also provided a market for consecutive reissues of A. C. Swan's voluminously comprehensive *History of the New Zealand Rugby Union* [H181-182], and for the coffee table volumes (assuming an extremely sturdy table) produced by R. H. Chester and N. A. C. MacMillan [H207].

Howitt's three volumes of *New Zealand rugby greats*, now compressed in a single 1,000-page volume [C310] whose seventy-five interviews extend from hooker Has Catley's memories of pre-war play with Otago to Jonah Lomu's reflections on his meteoric rise in the 1990s, are an oral history of post-war All Black experience and lore unmatched in the records of any other rugby nation.

Most significant players since the 1970s have gone into print themselves or, more frequently than those of other nations, been the subject of biographies. There were also earlier books – George Nepia's 1963 memoirs [C170], a quarter of a century after his retirement, reflect a career that left such indelible memories that the grandstand at St Helens, Swansea rose to him before the Swansea-Maoris game of 1982, no less than fifty-eight years after he had played there for New Zealand against Wales. T. P. McLean, Nepia's co-author, had also assisted with the first post-war All Black memoir, by another full-back, Bob Scott in 1956 [C197]. Other early works recorded the memories of Peter Jones [C121] and Don Clarke [C38] while among more recent books Chris Laidlaw's *Mud in your eye* [C126] and the best-selling Haden are notable for polemics against rugby's *status quo* – Haden, who gave 'rugby player' as his occupation in his passport deriding the conventions of amateurism while Laidlaw lacerates, *inter alia*, conservative administrators, mindlessly macho coaches and the game's relationship with South African apartheid.

New Zealand, by force of location, looks outwards. The first New Zealand touring team to Britain, the 1888 Maoris, have been efficiently rescued from relative obscurity by Greg Ryan's *Forerunners of the All Blacks* [E210]. The key formative moment, however, came with the first All Black tour to Britain in 1905. Historian Jock Phillips has suggested that this was a crucial moment in the merging of sport and national identity, which 'created idols of the All Blacks and turned them into formal representatives of the nation's manhood endorsed by the highest political leaders'. Gareth Williams sees the Welsh victory by 3-0 over the tourists as one of the decisive moments in the cultural history of modern Wales, and the tour as a whole was a vital step in the internationalisation of the game, a process culminating in the creation of the World Cup in 1987.

There is a strong case, implied in the title of Williams' *1905 and all that* [A146] for regarding that year rather than 1823 as the most memorable date in rugby history, to use *1066 and all that's* distinctive typology. That case is strengthened by the tour's contribution to one of the seminal works on the game, *The complete rugby footballer on the New Zealand system* [F117] by Dave Gallaher and W. J. Stead, captain and vice-captain respectively of the 1905 team. The second part of the title is significant and instructive. By the first years of this century, New Zealand rugby was sufficiently advanced that it could generate a 322 page coaching textbook, of which Gareth Williams has written: '[Their] penetrating discussion of the game – lines of running, angles of packing, miss moves, compiling statistics on different phases of play – brought a startlingly new technical discussion to rugby literature, raising it to a level of sophistication previously unheard of and rarely exceeded since.'

Little wonder that New Zealand's subsequent history has been one of rarely broken success particularly since, as Williams also notes, Gallaher and Stead's lessons took a long time to be accepted in Britain. Subsequent outbreaks of deep thinking on the game include, conspicuously, the South African Danie Craven's *Rugby handbook* [F244] and Carwyn James' posthumously-published *Focus on rugby* [F305]. New Zealand's capacity for tactical innovation in the game's early days is further chronicled in Graeme Barrow's *Up front* [A199] in which an informed technical analysis of the idiosyncrasies and successes of All Black forward play before the 1930s is ingeniously topped and tailed by chapters containing just about every known humorous rugby anecdote.

While the 1905 tour of Britain was New Zealand's formative moment, its great rivalry, conducted with unmatched intensity since 1921, has been with South Africa. The game there has been fortunate in a succession of devoted historians, in particular Paul Dobson whose *Thirty super Springboks* [C303] is, as John Jenkins notes, a history of the game told via the experiences and memories of its greatest figures.

Any discussion of the South African game is inevitably overlain by apartheid. It is sadly in the nature of underprivileged communities that they are less likely to leave the sort of records on which historians rely, but examination of the consequences of apartheid for rugby in South Africa's non-white communities received an excellent start in Albert Grundlingh, Andre Odendaal and Burridge Spies' *Beyond the tryline* [A170].

The consequences of apartheid for New Zealand, culminating in the civil strife associated with the 1981 Springboks tour, are testified to by no fewer than fifteen titles in this *Compendium* [E189-193, G12-24]. The divisiveness of 1981 was a consequence of the immense importance both societies accorded rugby, and in particular their own rivalry – expressed in no fewer than six histories of All Black-Springboks games; the invocation in *Foreskin's lament* [H149] of 'the Bokkies in '73 – the ones that never came, that never more will come'; and former Springbok Boy Louw's instruction to the 1949 Bokke: 'When South Africa plays New Zealand at rugby, consider your country at war', which, if showing a certain lack of proportion, was at least not said lightly or unknowingly – Louw had served in the western desert.

The post-war peak of this rivalry is brilliantly described in Warwick Roger's *Old heroes* [C178], whose evocation of the 1956 Springbok tour of New Zealand, its impact on the host nation and the subsequent lives of those who watched and took part is, considered as literature, the best book ever written on the game. Roger was ten years old in 1956 and the mix of his and others' memories, of contemporary reportage and his tracing of every surviving player – culminating in a tragi-comic pursuit of Springbok captain Basie Viviers – recaptures the extraordinarily charged atmosphere of the tour. He quotes one observer: 'New Zealand was committed to rugby for three months. I'm sure it was like the feeling people would have had on VE Day in London. Or maybe the Carnival in Rio, where the Latin Americans take off most of their clothes to enjoy themselves. Here we did it in our gumboots and our sou'westers and gabardine raincoats and hats, with bottles of beer.' John Nauright has accused Roger of a nostalgic celebration of New Zealand as a patriarchal rugby-obsessed society. But Roger's affectionate, non-judgmental portrait of 1950s New Zealand acknowledges 'a rather flat mental and social landscape'. If there is nostalgia, it is for the people and landscape of his childhood. His evocation of 'another time, another country' is the nearest thing rugby has to Roger Kahn's *Boys of summer* (1972), one of the classics of baseball's much larger literature.

It is also a remarkable variation, being both historical rather than contemporary and as much concerned with the social context as the rugby, on that most distinctive of rugby books – the tour account. The appeal of these books was understandable in times when each country undertook a tour only every three or four years at the most; foreign travel was an exotic adventure in itself and fans at home were unlikely to see even newsreel film of the matches. All of New Zealand and South Africa's test matches were involved either making or hosting tours.

In *Mud in your eye* [C126], Chris Laidlaw proffered a typically crisp if jaundiced summation of the type: 'The tour book is and probably forever will be characterised by an introduction detailing the history of earlier confrontations between the two countries concerned, a middle which gives a match-by-match analysis interspersed by precise diaries of schools visited, cocktail parties attended at every town and an end containing a set of tables which are designed for and can usually only be understood by a qualified statistician.'

The bulk were written by journalists, with J. B. G. Thomas of the (Cardiff) *Western Mail* standing out as a particularly assiduous chronicler of British Lions fortunes amid a formidable *oeuvre* that eventually comfortably exceeded twenty-five books. The writing is somewhat pedestrian and attitudes more reverential than analytical – rugby is always capitalised as 'The Game' and administrators and players are invariably good fellows – but Thomas' great service to the modern reader with an interest in the game's history is that when rugby books were a rarity in the 1950s and 1960s he managed to get published regularly, ensuring the survival of a contemporary record other than newspaper reports. In New Zealand his contemporary and equivalent was T. P. (Terry) McLean, a much more astringent commentator with a wider frame of reference, while South African tours were habitually followed by a book from A. C. Parker.

Accounts of British Lions tours burgeoned in the 1970s on the back of the expansion in rugby books in general and, in particular, successful tours to New Zealand in 1971 and South Africa in 1974 – the latter tour producing one of the most interesting accounts. Some British followers felt the Lions should not have gone to South Africa. John Reason, the *Daily Telegraph* correspondent had no problem with the tour, but as a writer who combined a keen analytical view of the game with robust unconcern about who his views offended, showed that journalists are not invariably uncritical backers of successful national teams by offering a sharply critical view, *The unbeaten lions* [E58], of the forward-oriented tactics of Willie John McBride's team.

The tour book expires suddenly after the early 1980s – there is no account of the Lions 1990 tour of Australia, in spite of its success on the field, and only one of the 1993 visit to New Zealand. Foreign travel had become much more of a commonplace, both for rugby players and for the population as a whole. Television and press coverage had become much more comprehensive, while videos provided an alternative for those seeking a more permanent record.

One of my strongest early personal rugby memories is of going to hear Lions coach Carwyn James lecture, in a school hall in Shropshire, on the successful 1971 Lions tour of New Zealand. James, sufficient attraction in himself, was accompanied by a film of action from the tour. Television had shown only newsreel clips while the tour was on. This article is being completed following a weekend on which satellite television offered live coverage of Ireland playing a South African province, followed by full as-live coverage of the Auckland v Canterbury Super 12 final from Eden Park. Under such circumstances, there is little new that a journalists' account published some months after the end of a tour can say.

Where the tour book has resurrected itself is in the first-person diary account by a player, coach or manager. Several, most in company with a journalist 'ghost' were published following the 1997 Lions tour of South Africa – and while good sales reflected the unexpected success of Martin Johnson's team, the bulk of contracts were signed before the tour, suggesting that publishers see a renewed future for the tour book, win or lose. This pattern of the decline of the traditional journalist's tour account and its replacement, after a hiatus, by the first-person player diary almost exactly reflects the pattern in cricket, where the 1997 England v Australia series inspired several such accounts.

The 1997 Lions tour was the first to be fully professional. The events of the last decade, incorporating the first World Cup in 1987, inexorable pressure leading to the acceptance of professionalism in 1995, the subsequent proliferation of international games and (in Britain at least) domestic chaos, will provide a terrific story for some future writer. They will be able to lean on some impressive contemporary accounts. Stephen Jones' *Endless winter* [H191-192] is the definitive account of the immediate pre-professional era, quite possibly the best state-of-the-game analysis of any period. Peter FitzSimons, an intriguing combination of Australian test lock, lawyer and French-speaking journalist, calls on all three areas of expertise to give the manoeuvrings accompanying the attempt to create a professional international rugby circus after the 1995 World Cup the flavour of a good thriller in *The rugby war* [G69].

There are two good accounts of the British game in the early stages of open professionalism. Stuart Barnes's *Rugby's new age travellers* [G72] concentrates on the highest levels and includes an outstanding essay on England's Lawrence Dallaglio as an emblematic figure for the new dispensation. Ian Malin's *Mud, blood and money* [G71] ranges more widely and looks with particular sympathy at those, like Orrell and the Cornish clubs, in danger of marginalisation.

If that brings the current survey of rugby literature up to date, the question remains of what changes we might expect to see if a second edition of this book is published in the early years of the next millennium.

There is no doubt that academics will be more fully represented. They, and their institutions, are finally accepting that sport is a legitimate subject of study. *The International Journal of Sports History* has run a number of significant scholarly articles on rugby since its foundation in 1984, and dedicated centres like The International Centre for Sports History and Culture at De Montfort University should, through the efforts of both academic staff and research students, add considerably to our knowledge of the game. Issues such as the relationship between rugby and both national identity and masculinity will bear considerable further examination. Though *Making men: rugby and masculinity* [G58], edited by John Nauright and Timothy Chandler is uneven in quality and often over-judgmental, it points towards important and still relatively unexplored aspects of the game. The same editors will publish another book of essays, *The rugby world: race, gender, commerce and rugby union* in 1999.

One of the game's healthiest recent developments has been the loss of its exclusive identification as a male sport through the rapid growth of women's rugby both in Britain and abroad. In some countries, such as the United States, Spain, and Kazakhstan, the women's national XVs have enjoyed considerably greater success than their male counterparts, although the crushing victories of New Zealand in the 1998 World Cup were a reminder that there are points in common. The growth of women's rugby has been rooted in colleges and universities, which should help ensure that the women's game generates a literature to match its rapid on-field development by the time the *Compendium* reaches a second edition.

The shift to professionalism and the flounderings of both clubs and unions should undoubtedly provoke greater interest in the economics of the game. Too little is known, both historically and sociologically, about the people who pay to watch the game.

Commercial publishers are likely to continue looking for the big-name autobiography – or at least the interim version – and for the coach or player's diary of a season or tour. But it must be hoped that there is also still space, and writers brave enough to attempt the job in the face of the reckless rate of change promoted by market forces and the game's rulers, for intelligent, historically-informed state-of-the-game analyses in the tradition of *Report on rugby* and *Endless winter*.

There are numerous opportunities too for historians. Nobody has yet examined a major British club as institution against the context of its local society as the American urban historian Chuck Korr's *West Ham United* (1986) illuminates the experience of London's East End or Bruce Kucklik's *To everything a season* (1991) mixed business, sporting and urban history in a vivid chronicle of Shibe Park, Philadelphia.

More too needs to be known about the players of the past – and at greater length than the thumbnail sketches, however brilliant, in *Fields of praise* [A132] or essays commissioned for the new *Dictionary of national biography*. Commercial publishers may take some persuading of the market possibilities of a biography of, say, Wavell Wakefield or Albert Jenkins, but there are other possible models. The self-publishers of rugby league, enterprising exploiters of the opportunities offered in recent years by desktop publishing, show one example. Another is offered by Frank Keating's *The great number tens* [C294], a series of portraits linked by a common theme, expounded with all the flamboyance of the great outside-halves; while one of those greats, Cliff Morgan, showed the potential of the multi-author collection of essays as editor of *Rugby: the great ones* [C255]. The British game also awaits its equivalent of *Old heroes* [C178] or David Kynaston's *W. G.'s birthday party* (1990), which illuminated a cricket era through the prism of the 1898 Gentlemen v Players match, while the tour genre is still to generate anything comparable to Mike Marqusee's *War minus the shooting* (1996), an account of the 1996 Cricket World Cup which puts the action into the context of modern Indian society, its relations with Pakistan and the changing game as a whole.

We need also to know more about the game outside the former empire. In particular it must be hoped that at least some of the burgeoning French literature on rugby finds its way into an English translation to follow one of the acknowledged classic tour books, Denis Lalanne's account of the 1958 France tour to South Africa *The great fight of the French XV* [E138]. Alongside Bodis's *Histoire mondiale*, suitable candidates might include *Le rugby c'est un monde* (1990) and *Voyous et gentlemen* (1993) by Jean Lacouture, whose other subjects have included Ho-Chi Minh and Charles de Gaulle, Pierre Sansot's *Le rugby est une fête* (1990), Sebastian Darbot's ethnographic study of the St Vincent-de-Tyrosse club *Rugby: mode de la vie* (1995) and André Herrero's *Passion ovale* (1989).

The French have also made something of a speciality of coffee-table books like the *Livres d'or* and Richard Escot and Jacques Rivière's *Un siècle de rugby*. Like Norman Barrett's informative and useful *Daily Telegraph chronicle of rugby* (1996), but with more lavish presentation and a different perspective, these volumes offer a synoptic view of the game's history.

Other European nations too need their chroniclers – why for instance has Germany, which had rugby before France, failed to develop in the same way ? How has Italy moved so far ahead of Spain, which once regarded it as an equal?

Then there is the rugby of the Pacific Islands, and its at times equivocal relationship with New Zealand; the hidden history of the non-white game in South Africa and the full story of how rugby did, and much less frequently did not, buttress apartheid; and the stories of those fiercely dedicated groups who have sustained the game in Argentina, Japan and British Columbia.

All of these deserve serious study. Some will get it before the next edition of this *Compendium*, as will other topics undreamed of here. The one absolute certainty about the second edition is that it will require either much smaller print or a lot more pages.

Chapter A

History &
Development

Contents

The Victorian Era

1   Beeton's football / Frederick Wood. London: Frederick Warne, 1867.

96p; illus   BL: D

    Wood writes that football 'has risen considerably in public estimation, and has spread over much new ground'. But its rising popularity has been hindered by 'the great diversity, nay, absolute incongruity of the codes of rules in force in the various seats of the game; and the indisputably dangerous nature of the modes of play generally in vogue in our great schools – too rough, indeed, for the more brittle bones and less reckless temperaments of adult players'. In any attempt to reconstruct the game of football 'it is worth while to make some endeavour in this direction outside the great schools'. The author describes the 'theory of the game; the rules for play; ground, stock dress, treatment of ball; practical instructions for beginners; special qualifications of the players in their respective positions'.

2   Routledge's handbook of football. London: George Routledge, 1867.

60p   BL: Mic.A.12484(1) (microfilm copy)

    Includes: the history of the game; how the game is played; rules of the game of football as observed at schools where no 'carrying' or 'handling' the ball is allowed; Westminster rules; rugby game – plan of the field; explanation of rugby football; rules of rugby football; definition of terms used in rugby football; a simplification of the rugby game as played at Marlborough; Football Association rules; costume.

3   Football: our winter game / Charles W. Alcock. London: 'Field', 1874.

ix, 139p   BL: D

    Written by the then secretary of the Football Association, this work covers football at the various schools; 'soule' in Brittany; and, the Shrovetide Festival at Derby,

4   Foot-ball: its history for five centuries / Montague Shearman and James E. Vincent. London: Field and Tuer, 1885.

vi, 72p

(Historical sporting series)   BL: 7908.c.43

5   Athletics and football / Montague Shearman, with a contribution on paper-chasing by W. Rye and an introduction by Sir Richard Webster. London: Longmans, Green, 1887.

xxvi, 446p; illus; index

(The Badminton library of sports and pastimes)

BL: K.T.C.103.a.1/5

    The rugby union game is covered in chapter III, pages 294-333, in the second section of the book, under the generic term 'Football'. Avoiding the complexities of the laws, the author concentrates on the theoretical side of the game, and though mention is made of the personalities who fashioned the game, the name of William Webb Ellis is not among them.

    ☞ Subsequent ed. A17

6   Camsell's game of football. 1889.

BL: Mic.A.9961(13) (microfilm copy)

    ☞ Subsequent ed. A8

7   Football: the rugby union game / Harry Vassall, with a chapter on professionalism by Arthur Budd. London: George Bell, 1889.

vi, 73p

(The All England series)   BL: 7908.df.23/31

    ☞ Subsequent ed. A16

8   Camsell's game of football: description and rules. New ed. 1890.   BL: Mic.A.9961(14) (microfilm copy)

    ☞ Previous ed. A6

9   Football: the rugby union game / edited by F. Marshall, with special chapters by A. G. Guillemard, G. Rowland Hill, H. Vassall, Arthur Budd, H. H. Almond, C. J. B. Marriott, and W. Cail; with numerous illustrations. London: Cassell, 1892.

xvi, 515p; illus   BL: 7908.c.41

    ☞ Subsequent ed. A10

10   Football: the rugby union game / edited by Rev. F. Marshall, with special chapters by A. G. Guillemard, G. Rowland Hill, H. Vassall, Arthur Budd, H. H. Almond, C. J. B. Marriott, and W. Cail. Rev. and enlarged ed. London: Cassell, 1893.

xvi, 560p; illus   BL: 07905.i.6

    An appendix containing a review of the seasons 1892-93 and 1893-94, illustrated by portraits and groups of players together with statistics relating to international, county, and other matches, is added to this edition.

    ☞ Previous ed. A9; subsequent ed. A11

11   Football: the rugby union game / edited by Rev. F. Marshall. Rev. and enlarged (2nd) ed. London: Cassell, 1894.

xvi, 564p; illus   BL: 7922.b.18

    ☞ Previous ed. A10; subsequent ed. A35

12   The rugby union game / C. J. B. Marriott; The association game / C. W. Alcock. London: Routledge, 1894.

120p; illus

(The 'Oval' series of games)   BL: D

    History and instructional text.

    ☞ Also listed at: F109; subsequent ed. A28

13   Football / Arthur Budd, C. B. Fry, T. A. Cook and B. F.
     Robinson. London: Lawrence and Bullen, 1897.
     95p; index
     (Suffolk sporting series)   BL: 7912.df.13

     *Reprinted, with additions and alterations, from part
     7 of the 'Encyclopædia of sport' (London: Lawrence &
     Bullen, 1897-1898). The content is a mix of the
     historical and instructional.*

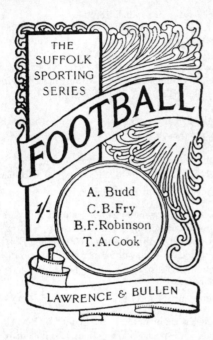

14   Football: association and rugby / J. Jeffery, known as
     'Straw Hat'. London: Dean, 1897.
     2 parts
     (Dean's champion handbooks)   BL: D

15   The origin of rugby football: report (with appendices) of
     the sub-committee of the Old Rugbeian Society,
     appointed in July 1895 / Harry F. Wilson, Herbert H.
     Child, Arthur G. Guillemard and Harry L. Stephen.
     Rugby: Rugby School, 1897.
     49p; pbk

16   Football: the rugby game / Harry Vassall with chapters
     on professionalism, refereeing, and the Northern Union
     by Arthur Budd. Rev. ed. London: George Bell, 1898.
     78p
     ☞   Previous ed. A7; subsequent ed. A31

17   Football history / Sir Montague Shearman. New ed.
     London: Longmans Green, 1899.
     xii, 379p; illus
     (The Badminton library of sports and pastimes)

     *Contains: 'The association game' by W. J. Oakley and G. O.
     Smith; 'The rugby union game' by F. Mitchell.*
                                                   BL: 7913.pp.1/20

     ☞   Previous ed. A5; subsequent ed. A29

18   Minutes of the International Board for the years 1886 to
     1921 inclusive / R. G. Warren. Dublin: The Board, 1922.
     93p; pbk
     ☞   See also: A36

19   History of football from the beginnings to 1871 /
     Francis Peabody Magoun. Köln: Bochum-Langendreer,
     1938.
     ix, 151p; index
     (Kölner Anglistische Arbeiten; Bd. 31)   BL: W.P.4979/31

     *Written by the professor of comparative literature at
     Harvard University, this book traces the development
     of football from the earliest times to the
     establishment of the Football Association and the
     Rugby Football Union.*

20   Early stages in the development of football as an
     organised game / Eric Dunning. University of Leicester,
     1961. *Doctoral thesis.*

21   The origins and early days of rugby football: how the
     game began / Eddy Rawlings. Rugby: The author, 1989.
     12p; illus; pbk

     *Replete with bibliography, the booklet sketches the
     game of football as played in Roman times; the type
     of football played at Rugby School before 1823; the
     birth of rugby following William Webb Ellis' alleged
     misdemeanour on the school playing field in 1823;
     extracts from the 'Laws of football played at Rugby
     School' and anecdotes on the game.*

22   Running with the ball: the birth of rugby football /
     Jenny Macrory; foreword by M. R. Steele-Bodger.
     London: CollinsWillow, 1991.
     viii, 216p; illus, maps; index

     Bibliography: p213-4   ISBN: 0002184028
                                           BL: YK.1991.b.4089

     *A well researched and well presented look at the
     game's development. Includes extracts from seminal
     articles which illustrate and entertain.*

23   Rugby football 1839-1900: a glance back at the first
     referees' societies / Derek Homfray-Davies. The author,
     1993.
     17p; pbk

✳   *Additional References*

24   Every boys' book: a complete encyclopædia of sports and amusements with more than six hundred illustrations from original designs / edited by Edmund Routledge. London: Routledge, 1856.

BL: Mic.A.7129(9) (microfilm copy)

The brief section on 'foot-ball' is concerned with the conflicting sets of rules in use at the time. The editor then goes on to present his preferred version of rules.

25   Modern English sports: their use and their abuse / Frederick Gale ('The Old Buffer'). London: Sampson Low, Marston, Searle & Rivington, 1885.

xx, 201p; illus   BL: 7906.ccc.15

In a brief review of the history of rugby the author views the sport as a 'very great mystery ... [where] the ball appears to be very much like a mutton-chop which A is about to devour with a keen appetite, which B snatches from him, where A collars B, and B throws it to C, who is collared by D, and so on by E, till every one is collaring each other. Whatever the points of the game may be, which are too complicated for any but experts to master, be they what they may, the game itself is a fine manly sport, and very funny to look at, and very exciting.'

26   The 'House' on sport / by Members of the London Stock Exchange; compiled and edited by W. A. Morgan. London: Gale & Polden, 1898.

xv, 470p; illus   BL: 7908.h.10

Written by members of the Stock Exchange. There are two chapters on rugby: W. Maclagan and G. L. Jeffery's 'The different epochs of the rugby game: a comparison of Scotch and English styles in each'; and, Aub. Sperling's, 'Rugby', which is instructional.

27   Land of sport and glory: sport and British society, 1887-1910 / Derek Birley. Manchester: Manchester University Press, 1995.

x, 287p; index

(International studies in the history of sport)

ISBN: 0719044944 (cased) • 0719044952 (pbk)

BL: YC.1995.b.3402

A study of sport in the late Victorian and Edwardian period. Describes the background leading to the division in rugby and the birth of rugby league.

The Early Twentieth Century

28   Football: the rugby union game / Charles J. B. Marriott; The association game / C. W. Alcock. 2nd ed. London: Routledge, 1903.

127p; illus

(The 'Oval' series of games)

Pages 1-54: Rugby union football; pages 91-117: Rugby union and the laws of rugby union football.

☞   Also listed at: F114; previous ed. A12

29   Football history / Sir Montague Shearman. New ed. London: Longmans, Green, 1904.

xii, 387p; illus; index

(The Badminton Library of sports and pastimes)

Contents: The association game / W. J. Oakley & G. O. Smith; The rugby union game / Frank Mitchell; other contributions by R. E. MacNaghten, M. C. Kemp, J. E. Vincent, Walter Camp, and A. Sutherland

BL: 2270.c.1

☞   Previous ed. A17

30   The book of football: a complete history and record of the association and rugby games with numerous illustrations and photographs. London: Amalgamated Press, 1906.

xii, 292p; illus   BL: 7912.k.14

A series of some 60 articles on association and rugby football.

☞   See also: A34

31   Football: the rugby game / Harry Vassall and Arthur Budd. New ed. revised by Charles J. B. Marriott. 1909.

vi, 87p; illus

(The All England series)   BL: 7908.df.23/32

☞   Previous ed. A16

32   The book of football / E. H. D. Sewell. London: Dent, 1911.

xiv, 304p; illus; index   BL: 7911.c.14

33 British sports and sportsmen: cricket and football /
compiled and edited by 'The Sportsman'. London:
British Sports & Sportsmen, 1917.
xiii, 579p; illus
(British sports and sportsmen past & present; vol. 5)
BL: L.R.255.b.1

*Rugby is represented by: 'The rise of rugby football' by
Henry V. L. Stanton, 'Rugby football at the universities'
by C. J. B. Marriott, and 'Strategy and tactics in the
Welsh rugby game' by T. J. Pryce Jenkins. There then
follows a single alphabetic list of prominent players
and their performances (cricket, rugby and
association football).*

34 The book of football / edited by Clive Leatherdale.
Westcliff-on-Sea: Desert Island Books, 1997.
298p; illus; index
ISBN: 1874287139
BL: YK.1997.b.6729

*The original, 'The book of football: a complete history
and record of the association and rugby games
1905-1906', was published in twelve fortnightly
instalments from 20 October 1905 to 23 March
1906.*
☞ See also: A30

The Inter-War Years

35 Football: the rugby union game / edited by the late Rev.
F. Marshall. New ed. edited and revised by Leonard R.
Tosswill. London: Cassell, 1925.
xi, 408p; illus; index
BL: 7904.f.25
☞ Previous ed. A11

36 Minutes of the International Board for the years 1922 to
1925 inclusive / R. G. Warren. Dublin: The Board, 1925.
31p; pbk
☞ See also: A18

✻ *Additional References*

37 They're off!: a journalistic record of British sports by
leading writers of the press / edited by C. W. Miles with
a foreword by the Earl of Derby. London: Denis Archer,
1934.
278p; illus
BL: 2271.d.22

*Leo Munro contributes a chapter on rugby. He
describes the international matches in the years
immediately prior to publication, and his impression
of the players who featured in those matches.*

38 Playing the game: sport and British society, 1914-1945 /
Derek Birley. Manchester: Manchester University Press,
1995.
x, 342p; index
(International studies in the history of sport)
ISBN: 0719044960 (cased) • 0719044979 (pbk)
BL: YC.1996.b.2112

*Examines amateurism, professionalism and social
values in rugby in the aftermath of the Great War
and before the Second World War.*

They're Off!

A Journalistic Record of British Sports
by
LEADING WRITERS OF THE PRESS

Edited by
C. W. MILES
with
A Foreword by
THE RIGHT HON.
THE EARL OF DERBY, K.G.

Denis Archer
London

The Post War Years & General Histories

39 A history of football / Morris Marples. London: Secker & Warburg, 1954.
xi, 276p; illus; index

Bibliography: p263-5 BL: 7922.bb.3

Examines the history of football through the ages. Among the chapters which consider the game of rugby are: school football in the early nineteenth century; the public school games cult; rugby and association; the twentieth century; and, football as a world game.

40 Football through the ages / Percy Marshall Young, with illustrations by Reginald G. Haggar. London: Methuen, 1957.
68p; index; pbk
(Methuen's outlines) BL: W.P.A.543/31

Written for young readers. The development of rugby is introduced in headings such as: Tom Brown's schooldays; William Webb Ellis; rugby football union; developments in rugby football; spread of rugby union.

41 Rugby football: the Gilbert story / James Gilbert. Rugby: James Gilbert, 1957.
51p; illus; pbk

Nine chapters: the makers of the rugby ball; the evolution of the rugby ball; the centenary of rugby caps; the historic ground (Rugby School); ancient history; the origin and development of the rugby game; the laws of football as played at Rugby School before hacking was abolished; ici est né le rugby; some rugby milestones.

42 Report on rugby / William John Morgan and Geoffrey Nicholson. London: Heinemann, 1959.
231p BL: 7925.b.36

43 Football / B. J. W. Hill. Oxford: Basil Blackwell, 1961.
vii, 94p; illus; index BL: X.449/555

'This is an outline of the history of football … to the development of the nineteenth century and modern times. All types of football are mentioned and most aspects of the game are discussed.'

44 An analysis of schoolboy rugby / McInnes and Hill. Loughborough College, 1964. *Master's thesis*.

45 The world of rugby / Wallace Reyburn with Ross Reyburn; additional statistics by Leslie J. Parsons. London: Elek, 1967.
154p; illus BL: X.441/1000

46 The rugby union football book / edited by Jack Cox. London: Purnell, 1968.
157p; illus

47 Rugby: men, matches and moments: impressions of the game in post-war years / J. B. G. Thomas. London: Pelham, 1970.
224p; illus SBN: 720700515
  BL: X.629/2930

The book is 'intended as a mirror, reflecting a cross-section of the matches, players, administrators and occasions of the post-war years in the game'. Brief biographies of 12 administrators, 13 players and 9 members of the press are also included.

48 Football history map of England and Wales / John Carvasso. Edinburgh: Bartholomew, 1971.
1 sheet (101 x 70 cm)

Scale ca. 1:1,050,000
Includes text and colour illustrations

49 A history of rugby / Wallace MacDonald Reyburn. London: Arthur Barker, 1971.
ix, 147p; illus SBN: 213004860
  BL: X.629/3876

50 The world of rugby, 1971-1972 / edited by Jack Cox. London: Purnell, 1971.
92p; illus
(World of sport) SBN: 361017650
  BL: X.62/1004

51 Football!: the story of all the world's football games / Nicholas Mason. London: Temple Smith, 1974.
xvi, 256p; illus ISBN: 0851170633
  BL: X.620/7717

Rugby is covered in two sections: 'The missionary spirit: rugby football 1863 to 1896', and 'The long divorce – rugby union and rugby league football 1896 to 1940'.

52 The report of the Mallaby Committee, constituted by the RFU in November 1972. Twickenham: Rugby Football Union, 1974.
71 leaves; pbk

Chaired by Sir George Mallaby, the Committee, which had been appointed on 10 November 1972, examined 'the necessity of restructuring the organisation of the Rugby Football Union in the light of geographical changes in local government areas and other relevant factors and of altering the basis of representation on the Rugby Union Committee accordingly'. The report was submitted to the President of the Rugby Football Union on 15 February 1974.

53 Rugby in the Royal Navy. 1974.
7p; pbk

54   Rugby: a history of rugby union football / Chris Rea.
London: Hamlyn, 1977.
216p; illus; index   ISBN: 0600375919
                                      BL: X.622/2565

55   Barbarians, gentlemen and players: a sociological study
of the development of rugby football / Eric Dunning,
Kenneth Sheard. Oxford: Martin Robertson, 1979.
xiii, 321p; illus; index   ISBN: 0855201681
                                      BL: X.629/12433

      The study includes five sections: the development of
      rugby football as a sociological problem; folk
      antecedents and traditional forms of football in the
      public school; the modernisation of rugby football; the
      development of rugby football as a modern sport;
      towards a sociological theory of modern sport.

56   Rugby in focus: a review of rugby union football, 1978 /
J. B. G. Thomas. London: Pelham, 1979.
216p; illus; index   ISBN: 0720711371
                                      BL: X.629/12450

57   The world of rugby: a history of rugby union football /
John Reason and Carwyn James. London: BBC, 1979.
288p; illus   ISBN: 0563162805
                                      BL: BS.129/174

      In the 1960s and 1970s a virtual explosion in world
      rugby came about following tours from and to the
      British Isles, South Africa, the Antipodes and other
      countries. Tracing the development of the game from
      the nineteenth century to the present, topics such
      as coaching, violence, professionalism and
      sponsorship are discussed.

58   Rugby. London: Hamlyn, 1982.
95p; illus; pbk   ISBN: 0600346471
                                      BL: X.622/14986

      Includes: The evolution of rugby; famous rugby union
      clubs; great union players; the Five Nations
      Championship; the overseas sides; rugby now; and,
      three chapters on rugby league.

59   Run with the ball!: a brisk dash through 150 years of
rugby / Derek Robinson. London: Collins Willow, 1984.
144p; illus   ISBN: 0002180774

60   Side-steps: a rugby diary, 1984/85 / Gerald Davies and
John Morgan. London: Hodder and Stoughton, 1985.
156p; illus   ISBN: 0340381132
                                      BL: X.950/47683

61   The history of army rugby / John McLaren. Aldershot:
The Army RFU, 1986.
xiv, 295p; illus

62   Rugby: a way of life: an illustrated history of rugby /
edited by Nigel Starmer-Smith; foreword by Bill
Beaumont. London: Stanley Paul, 1986.
192p; illus; index   ISBN: 0091657105
                                      BL: LB.31.b.2039

63   Rugby in focus: twenty years of rugby action /
photographed by Colin Elsey; written by John Taylor.
Newton Abbot: David & Charles, 1986.
187p; chiefly illus   ISBN: 0715388827
                                      BL: YK.1987.b.3554

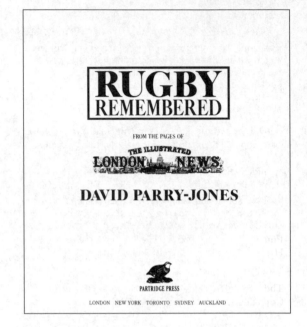

64   Rugby remembered: from the pages of The Illustrated
London News / David Parry-Jones. London: Partridge,
1988.
188p; illus   ISBN: 1852250453
                                      BL: YK.1989.b.2779

65   Rugby: a history of the game / text by Harry Langton.
London: Sports Design, 1991.
50p; illus; pbk

      'An illustrated catalogue for the 1991 London
      Exhibition of the Langton Collection of pictures,
      antiques and souvenirs illustrating the development
      of one branch of football games over a period of at
      least 1,000 years.' It includes chapters on: ancient
      European football; a school that gave its name; 1871
      and all that; and, a description of the items in the
      collection.

      ☞   Also listed at: G100

66   Rugby the international game: a photographic
celebration / Colin Whelan; text by Pat Booth; foreword
by Ian McGeechan. London: Queen Anne Press, 1994.
112p; pbk   ISBN: 1852915544
                                      BL: LB.31.c.7110

67   William Cail, amateurism and the Rugby Football Union
/ P. Blackledge. University of Northumbria, 1994.
Master's thesis

68 The Daily Telegraph chronicle of rugby / compiled and edited by Norman Barrett. Enfield: Guinness, 1996.
192p; illus   ISBN: 085112626X
BL: YK.1997.b.346

Following a brief introduction to the game and decade-by-decade coverage, the period from 1990 to the final of the 1995 Rugby World Cup in South Africa, is given year by year from the pages of The Daily Telegraph.

✱   *Additional References*

69 Association football / edited by A. H. Fabian and Geoffrey Green. London: Caxton, 1960.
4 vols.   BL: 7925.c.19

J. R. Witty examines the different football codes in 'Early codes'.

70 Sport in Britain: a social history / edited by Tony Mason. Cambridge: Cambridge University Press, 1989.
363p; illus; index   ISBN: 0521351197
BL: YK.1990.b.5610

Gareth Williams's chapter on the birth of rugby union appears on pages 308-43.

Folk Football

71 Survivals of folk football, Great Britain / Frank N. Punchard. King's Norton: The Editor of 'School Hygiene and Physical Education', 1928.
12p   BL: D

72 The Ashbourne custom of Shrovetide football / G. J. Corbishley. Yeldersley: P. J. Wood, 1953.
20p; illus   BL: 7921.e.63

73 The ancient game of cnapan and the beginnings of rugby football / Brian John. Newport: Greencroft, 1985?
20p; illus; pbk   ISBN: 0905559568
BL: YK.1988.a.4726

The game of cnapan is native to north Pembrokeshire and was at its peak of popularity during Tudor times. This little booklet reprints George Owen's 1603 account of the game originally contained in 'Description of Penbrokeshire'.

74 Ashbourne Royal Shrovetide football: the official history / Lindsey Porter. Ashbourne: Ashbourne Editions, 1992.
206p; illus

75 Ashbourne Shrovetide football: 100 years in photographs / Lindsey Porter. Ashbourne: Ashbourne Editions, 1995.
112p; illus; pbk   ISBN: 1873775148

Photographs from 1892 (the earliest known photograph of the game peculiar to Ashbourne) through to 1995.

76 The working-class origins of modern football: an examination of the influence of folk football on the development of the association and rugby codes / John Goulstone. Bexleyheath: The author?, 1997.
8 leaves   BL: YK.1997.b.7188

England

77 The history of the Rugby Football Union / O. L. Owen. London: Playfair Books, 1955.
368p; illus   BL: 7920.l.57

78 English football in the nineteenth century: a social history / Richard Kitto. Princeton University, US, 1969. *Thesis.*

79 Centenary history of the Rugby Football Union / Uel Addison Titley and Alan Ross MacWhirter. London: Rugby Football Union, 1970.
216p; illus, maps   BL: X.625/50
☞ Also listed at: C254

80 The men in white: the story of English rugby / Wallace Reyburn. London: Pelham, 1975.
150p; illus; index   ISBN: 0720708311
BL: X.629/10143

81 England rugby: a history of the national side, 1871-1976 / Barry Bowker; with a foreword by M. R. Steele-Bodger. London: Cassell, 1976.
xiv, 199p; illus; index   ISBN: 0304295469
BL: X.629/11081

☞ Subsequent ed. A82

82 England rugby: a history of the national side, 1871-1978
    / Barry Bowker; with a foreword by M. R.
    Steele-Bodger. Rev. ed. London: Cassell, 1978.
    xiv, 207p; illus; index   ISBN: 0304302147
                                               BL: X.629/12190

    ☞ Previous ed. A81

83 The book of English international rugby 1871-1982 /
    compiled and edited by John Griffiths. London: Willow,
    1982.
    496p; illus   ISBN: 0002180065
                                               BL: X.622/14842

84 Rugby union football and English society 1871-1914 /
    James W. Martens. University of Manitoba, Can., 1988.
    Doctoral thesis.   ISBN: 0315441046

    In order to accurately assess the development of
    amateur rugby up to the eve of the First World War, it is
    necessary to understand England's broader social
    history. As the southern middle-class administrators
    and players were more committed to the amateur code
    it was their northern counterparts who led the
    secession from the Rugby Football Union in the 1890s.

85 English rugby: a celebration / edited by Ted Barrett;
    introduction by Bob Hiller. Edinburgh: Mainstream,
    1991.
    192p; illus
              ISBN: 1851584307 (cased) • 1851584358 (pbk)
                                               BL: YK.1992.b.4335

86 Double grand slam / Peter Cullimore. Taunton: T.
    Williams Publications, 1992.
    144p; illus   ISBN: 1869833058

    Charts the progress of the England team from the
    beginning of 1990 to 1992 when they won the Grand
    Slam for the second time running. Also contains
    match reports of England's progress in the 1991
    World Cup and profiles the players off the field.

87 The history of the Northern Rugby Football Union,
    1895-1915 / P. A. Greenhalgh. Lancaster University,
    1992. *Doctoral thesis.*
    433p   BL: DSCDX180240

    Covers the history of rugby union before the birth of
    rugby league.

88 The code war / Graham Williams. Harefield: Yore, 1994.
    192p; illus

       Bibliography: p190-1   ISBN: 1874427658
                                               BL: YK.1995.a.5421

    Analyses the history, development and organisation
    of association and rugby football in England. Also
    includes the history of individual clubs and the
    development of the two codes of rugby.

89 Re-defining amateurism in English rugby union / B. S.
    Ryan. University of Leicester, 1994. *Master's thesis.*

90 England rugby roadshows in the eastern counties and
    the growth of youth rugby in the region during the
    period 1990-1994 / P. J. Kennedy. Cambridge: Eastern
    Counties Rugby Union, 1995.

91 A five year development plan for rugby union football in
    the West Midlands / edited by K. H. Bonser. London?:
    Sports Council, 1995?
    pbk

92 Rugby union development plan for London and south
    east regions 1995-1999. Colchester?: Sports Council
    London and South East Region, 1995.
    44p; pbk

    A development plan providing a co-ordinated
    approach to the spread of rugby in London and the
    south east.

93 Band of brothers: a celebration of the England rugby
    squad / written by Frank Keating with the England
    players; photographs by Jon Nicholson. London:
    Michael Joseph, 1996.
    224p; illus; index   ISBN: 0718141733

94 The Carling years: England rugby 1988-96 / Mick
    Cleary; photographs by Colorsport. London: Gollancz,
    1996.
    157p; illus   ISBN: 0575064021
                                               BL: YK.1996.b.16090

95 Class, commercialism and community in the origins and
    development of the Northern Rugby Football Union,
    1857-1910 / Tony Collins. Sheffield Hallam University,
    1996. *Doctoral thesis.*

96 Will Carling's England dream team. London: Sunburst
    Books, 1996.
    80p; illus; index; pbk

       With additional text by Nigel Blundell

                                               ISBN: 1857782461

    Carling, the 1996 England captain, chooses his
    England dream team.

97 Rugby's blazered buffoons: a critical analysis of English
    rugby / Jeff Gage; foreword by John Gallagher;
    consultant editor: Mark Reason. Leicester: Kairos, 1997.
    160p; illus; index; pbk   ISBN: 1871344166
                                               BL: YK.1998.a.2546

❋ *Public Schools & Universities*

98 Cradle of rugby: a history of rugby in prep schools /
    Nick Eynon. Great Glemham: Catt Educational, 1995.
    158p; illus; pbk   ISBN: 1869863755
                                               BL: YK.1995.b.11635

    Looks at the schools which have traditionally
    produced some of the finest players. Also examines
    the state of the game in prep schools.

RUGBY'S BLAZERED BUFFOONS by JEFF GAGE

Foreword by JOHN GALLAGHER former Rugby Union All Black and Rugby League professional

consultant editor:
Mark Reason
of the Sunday Telegraph

✳ *Additional References*

99 Fifty years of sport at Oxford, Cambridge, and the great public schools / arranged by the Right Hon. Lord Desborough; edited by A. C. M. Croome. London: Walter Southwood, 1913-1922.
3 vols; illus

Vol. 1, 2: Oxford and Cambridge; vol. 3: Eton, Harrow and Winchester / edited by Hon. R. H. Lyttleton, Arthur Page and Evan B. Noel   BL: L.R.37.a

100 Arnold and organised games in the English public schools of the nineteenth century / Brian T. P. Mutimer. University of Alberta, Can., 1972. *Doctoral thesis.*

101 The Victorian public school: studies in the development of an educational institution: a symposium / edited by Brian Simon and Ian Bradley. Dublin: Gill and Macmillan, 1975.
vii, 215p; illus; index

Bibliography: p207-9   ISBN: 071710740X
BL: X.529/30301

This book is based on papers delivered at a conference held at Digby Hall, Leicester, in September 1973 and organised by the University of Leicester Adult Education Department in conjunction with the Victorian Studies Centre and the Victorian Society. In his paper, 'The origins of modern football and the public school ethos', Eric Dunning traces the development of the versions of football played by the different public schools during the latter part of the nineteenth century. Rugby is covered on pages 173-6.

102 Origins of athleticism, games in the English public schools, 1800-1880 / Timothy J. L. Chandler. University of Stanford, US, 1984. *Doctoral thesis.*

The study discovers how and why organised games emerged and developed in four groups of public schools in the nineteenth century. Cricket, rowing, and rugby and association football in the public schools were organised initially through the ingenuity and enthusiasm of the older boys. These young men took their love of games to the universities and after graduation many of them returned to teach in the growing caucus of schools. Their interest in and enthusiasm for games was embraced by the school staff and parents. Explanations are sought as to why a belief in the educational value of games and sports became such a widely held and lasting belief.

Scotland

103 The story of Scottish rugby / R. J. Phillips. Edinburgh & London: Foulis, 1925.
239p; illus   BL: 7904.ee.28

Covers the establishment and early progress of the game in Scotland; school (rugby) football; Edinburgh and Glasgow inter-city rivalry; international football; and, antipodean visitors.

104 Scottish rugby fifty years ago / Norman Lang Stevenson. 1950s.

105 The history of Scottish rugby / Sandy Thorburn. London: Johnston & Bacon, 1980.
vi, 346p; illus   ISBN: 0717942759

106 Ian McLauchlan's Scottish rugby scrapbook. London: Pictorial Presentations, 1982.
128p; illus

ISBN: 028562542X (cased) • 0285625438 (pbk)

107   A portrait of Scottish rugby / Allan Massie. Edinburgh:
      Polygon, 1984.
      ix, 198p; illus   ISBN: 0904919846
                                                         BL: X.622/24093

108   The Scottish Rugby Union official history / A. M. C.
      Thorburn. Edinburgh: The Union in association with
      Collins, 1985.
      xviii, 210p; illus, 1 coat of arms   ISBN: 0004356977
                                                         BL: X.622/25819

      ☞ See also: A111

109   Feet, Scotland, feet!: the book of Scottish rugby / Bill
      McLaren, Bill McMurtrie, Brian Meek and David Steele;
      edited by Derek Douglas. Edinburgh: Mainstream, 1991.
      208p; illus
      (The Glasgow Herald full 1991 World Cup reports)
                                                         ISBN: 1851584250
                                                         BL: YK.1992.b.4265

      Examines the game in Scotland from its inception to
      the present.

110   Young Scotland rugby squad. Edinburgh: Scottish Sports
      Council, 1993.
      2p; pbk

111   International rugby union: a compendium of Scotland's
      matches / John McI. Davidson based on an original
      volume by A. M. C. Thorburn. Edinburgh: Polygon, 1994.
      xii, 295p; illus; pbk   ISBN: 0748661867
                                                         BL: YK.1995.b.6375

      ☞ See also: A108

112   The changing social composition in Scottish rugby /
      Fiona White. University of Edinburgh, 1996. *Master's
      thesis.*

      Questions whether or not Scottish rugby, which
      originated as a pastime of the upper classes, is still
      predominantly confined to this strata of society, or
      whether it has since become a 'game for all classes'.

113   Strategy for Scottish success in the open future: a report
      from the Rugby Division. Edinburgh: Scottish Rugby
      Union, 1996.
      23 leaves; pbk

114   Strategic report 1997-2002 / Scottish Rugby Union.
      Edinburgh: The Union, 1997?
      36p; illus

115   Structure and governance of the Scottish Rugby Union:
      a report from the SRU General Committee. Edinburgh:
      Scottish Rugby Union, 1997.
      8p; illus; pbk

116   The thistle: a chronicle of Scottish rugby / Derek
      Douglas. Edinburgh: Mainstream, 1997.
      207p; illus   ISBN: 1851587373

117   Unity for shared success in Scottish rugby: a report from
      the Rugby Division. Edinburgh: Scottish Rugby Union,
      1997?

Ireland

118   Twenty years of Irish rugby: a rugby review, Ireland's
      international matches / F. J. Murphy. Dublin: The
      author, 1946.
      52p; pbk

119   Ireland's golden rugby years / edited by Barry S. Nolan.
      Dublin: Independent Newspapers, 1953?
      136p; pbk

      A number of contributors record Ireland's triumphs in
      the seasons 1947 to 1952 – the winning of the Triple
      Crown in successive seasons, 1948 and 1949, and
      championship winners in 1951. Also included are
      results at international and provincial level, and lists
      of International players from Ireland, England,
      Scotland and Wales.

120   The men in green: the story of Irish rugby / Sean
      Diffley. London: Pelham, 1973.
      156p; illus; index   ISBN: 0720707277
                                                         BL: X.629/5895

121   One hundred years of Irish rugby: the official history of
      the Irish Rugby Football Union / Edmund Van Esbeck.
      Dublin: Gill and Macmillan (for the Irish Rugby Football
      Union), 1974.
      246p; illus   SBN: 717107159
                                                         BL: X.629/6259

122   Irish rugby scrapbook / Edmund Van Esbeck. London:
      Pictorial Presentations, 1982.
      128p; illus
                                         ISBN: 0285625454 (cased) • 0285625462 (pbk)
                                                         BL: X.622/14574

The Men in Green

THE STORY OF IRISH RUGBY

Sean Diffley

PELHAM BOOKS

123 The Carlsberg book of Irish rugby / David Guiney.
Blackrock: Desmond Barry, 1983.
138p; illus; pbk

124 Schoolboy rugby in Ireland / Muriel Butler. Blackrock:
Desmond Barry Associates, 1985.
50p; illus; pbk

> Fifteen short chapters extend to the reader a 'feel'
> for the game, with comments on: competitions in
> Leinster, Ulster, Munster and Connacht; mini rugby;
> laws and aspects of play; and, the role of the coach,
> referee, touch judges and groundsmen.

125 The story of Irish rugby / Edmund Van Esbeck.
London: Stanley Paul, 1986.
256p; illus   ISBN: 0091662702

Wales

126 History of Welsh international rugby / John Billot.
Ferndale: Ron Jones Publications, 1970.
x, 285p; illus   SBN: 950162302X
                            BL: X.629/3160

☞ Subsequent ed. A128

127 Rugby in Wales / edited by John B. G. Thomas & Rowe
Harding. Llandybïe: C. Davies, 1970.
156p; illus   SBN: 85339024X
                            BL: X.629/2689

128 History of Welsh international rugby / John Billot. Rev.
ed. Ferndale: Ron Jones Publications, 1971.
ix, 292p; illus   BL: X.629/4203
☞ Previous ed. A126

129 The men in scarlet: the story of Welsh rugby football /
John B. G. Thomas. London: Pelham, 1972.
176p; illus; index   ISBN: 0720704510
                            BL: X.629/4129

The Men in Scarlet

THE STORY OF WELSH RUGBY FOOTBALL

J. B. G. Thomas

PELHAM BOOKS

130   Rugby '76 / edited by Barry John. Swansea: Christopher
       Davies, 1976.
       107p; illus; pbk
                                                    ISBN: 071540346X
                                                    BL: YK.1989.b.670

131   Decade of the dragon: a celebration of Welsh rugby
       1969-1979 / John Taylor. London: Hodder and
       Stoughton, 1980.
       248p; illus; index
                                                    ISBN: 0340252731
                                                    BL: X.622/10823

132   Fields of praise: the official history of the Welsh Rugby
       Union 1881-1981 / David Smith and Gareth Williams.
       Cardiff: University of Wales Press on behalf of the
       Welsh Rugby Union, 1980.
       xii, 505p; illus, coats of arms; index

          Bibliography: p489-95   ISBN: 0708307663
                                                    BL: X.629/14555

133   100 years of Welsh rugby / Western Mail in association
       with the Welsh Rugby Union. Cardiff: Western Mail,
       1980.
       46p; illus; pbk

          Contents: In the beginning / J. B. G. Thomas; The first
          golden era of Welsh rugby / John Billot; The dark ages /
          Rowe Harding; Rugby in the thirties / Wilfred Wooller; The
          game in the 1940/50s / J. A. Gwilliam; The sixties / John
          Dawes; The last decade, or, The second golden era / J. B. G.
          Thomas

          Newspaper supplement celebrating the centenary of
          the WRU.

134   The illustrated history of Welsh rugby / J. B. G.
       Thomas. London: Pelham, 1980.
       256p; illus; index
                                                    ISBN: 0720712688
                                                    BL: X.622/8373

135   A touch of glory: 100 years of Welsh rugby / Alun
       Richards. London: Joseph, 1980.
       176p; illus; index
                                                    ISBN: 071811938X
                                                    BL: X.622/8304

136   Welsh rugby: the crowning years, 1968-80 / Clem
       Thomas and Geoffrey Nicholson. London: Collins, 1980.
       263p; illus; index
                                                    ISBN: 0002116413
                                                    BL: X.629/14202

137   Can llwyddiant!: cyfrol i ddathlu canmlwyddiant Undeb
       Rygbi Cymru / golygwyd gan Royston James. Abertawe:
       Gwasg Christopher Davies, 1981.
       333p; illus   ISBN: 0715405829
          'One hundred successes!: a volume to celebrate the
          centenary of the Welsh Rugby Union'.

138   A historical study of the formative years of the Welsh
       Rugby Union, 1870-1900 / Kenneth Evans. University
       of Liverpool, 1981. *Master's thesis.*

139   The golden years of Welsh rugby / Gareth Edwards;
       edited by David Parry-Jones; additional commentary by
       J. P. R. Williams and others. London: Harrap, 1982.
       144p; illus
                                                    ISBN: 0245538364
                                                    BL: X.622/14729

140   Welsh rugby scrapbook / Gerald Davies. London:
       Souvenir, 1983.
       112p; illus
       (Pictorial presentations)
              ISBN: 028562590X (cased) • 0285625950 (pbk)
                                                    BL: X.622/18534

141   Report on the state of Welsh rugby / Welsh Rugby
       Union Investigative Committee. Cardiff: Welsh Rugby
       Union, 1985.

142   Rugby / Gareth Edwards. Haywards Heath: Partridge,
       1986.
       168p; illus   ISBN: 1852250178
          A study of post-war Welsh rugby union.

143   Rugby Wales '87 / edited by Barry John and Clem
       Thomas. Swansea: Christopher Davies, 1986.
       102p; illus; pbk   ISBN: 0715406817
                                                    BL: YK.1988.b.2705

       A well illustrated book which considers the future of
       Welsh rugby. In addition to the editors, there are
       contributions by John Taylor, Gerald Davies, J. B. G.
       Thomas and referee Clive Norling.

144   Medi'r corwynt / Thomas Davies. Capel Garmon:
       Gwasg Carreg Gwalch, 1989.
       146p; illus; pbk   ISBN: 0863811450
                                                    BL: YK.1990.a.7174

       Records the 1988-89 Welsh season: the Five Nations
       championship; the Schweppes Cup; the Western Mail
       championship; youth and schools rugby; tours from
       Wales and other countries; and, the New Zealand tour
       of Wales.

145   The quest for excellence: a strategy for Welsh rugby in
       the 1990s. Cardiff: Welsh Rugby Union, 1990.
       16p; pbk

       Four main headings: Excellence – the aim; the plan to
       excel; the means to excel; the attainment of
       excellence, each with sub-headings.

146   1905 and all that: essays on rugby football, sport and
       Welsh society / Gareth Williams. Llandysul: Gomer,
       1991.
       xiv, 250p; illus; index; pbk   ISBN: 0863837581
                                                    BL: YK.1992.a.3747

       The social history of Welsh rugby is given in a series of
       reprinted articles. One of the two chapters written in
       Welsh covers the rugby careers of George Nepia (New
       Zealand), Lucien Mias (France), Michael Gibson
       (Ireland), and Gerald Davies, Gareth Edwards, Barry
       John, Lewis Jones and Bleddyn Williams (Wales).

147   The history of the Welsh Schools Rugby Union
      1903-1939 / Carl French. University of Wales, Cardiff,
      1991. *Master's thesis.*

148   The socio-cultural development of Welsh rugby union
      1890-1914 / David L. Andrews. University of Illinois at
      Urbana-Champaign, US, 1991. *Master's thesis.*

149   Adroddiad ar arolwg rygbi yn yr ysgolion, or, Report on
      rugby in schools survey / G. E. Jones, S. Addicott, S.
      Davies. Aberystwyth: Faculty of Education, University of
      Wales Aberystwyth, 1992.
      20p, 20p; illus; spiral

      *Cover title: Rugby in schools survey; English/Welsh text
      bound tête-bêche*

      Published bilingually, nine pages are taken up with the
      'Rugby in Schools' questionnaire. The questionnaire
      survey is used as the basis for the report in which the
      authors try to deduce whether changes in the
      education systems have affected the development of
      rugby in schools. Two LEAs — Dyfed and West
      Glamorgan — were approached to air their views.

✳   *Additional References*

150   Pleasure, profit, proselytism: British culture and sport at
      home and abroad, 1700-1914 / edited by J. A. Mangan.
      London: Frank Cass, 1988.
      296p; illus
                    ISBN: 0714632899 (cased) • 0714640506 (pbk)

      Gareth Williams has contributed 'From popular
      culture to public cliché: image and identity in Wales
      1890-1914'. Despite financial inducements, rugby as
      an amateur game remained the national sport of the
      Welsh up to 1914. Opposing open professionalism in
      order to keep their place and preserve their identity,
      where elsewhere the accession of the working man
      inevitably led to professionalism in sport, the Welsh
      game played a unifying role in Welsh society.

151   The global sports arena: athletic talent migration in an
      interdependent world / edited by John Bale and Joseph
      Maguire. London: Frank Cass, 1994.
      xii, 289p; illus, maps
                    ISBN: 0714634891 (cased) • 0714641162 (pbk)
                                        BL: YC.1995.b.5689

      Originally presented during a colloquium at Keele
      University in April 1991, the papers include one by
      Gareth Williams, 'The road to Wigan Pier revisited: the
      migration of Welsh rugby talent since 1918'
      (pp25-38). Unemployment in South Wales, and the
      chance to earn a good wage in the north of England,
      meant that many rugby players at club and
      international level took the road out of Wales.

France

152   The rise of French rugby / Alex Potter and Georges
      Duthen. London: Bailey & Swinfen, 1961.
      218p; illus   BL: X.449/644

      A Franco-British partnership tells the story of
      French rugby in English for the first time.

✳   *Additional References*

153   Sport and society in modern France / Richard Holt.
      London: Macmillan in association with St Antony's
      College, Oxford, 1981.
      xiii, 256p; illus; index

            Bibliography: p237-50   ISBN: 0333259513
                                              BL: X.529/42829

      An important work with good rugby content.

South Africa

154   Impressions of South African rugby / W. H. Davy.
      Tauranga, NZ: Bay of Plenty Times Office, 1921.
      iv, 38p

> *Cover title: The Springboks: impressions of South African rugby by a New Zealander*

155   The history of South African rugby football, 1875-1932
      / Ivor D. Difford; with an introduction by A. J. Pienaar.
      Wynberg, SA: Specialty Press, 1933.
      xv, 736p; illus   BL: 07912.i.60

> Difford was in fact the editor.

> ☞ See also: A156

156   Supplement to the first edition of, The history of South
      African rugby football: laws of the game as framed by
      the Rugby Football Union; plan of the field: rules as to
      professionalism articles of association and regulations
      and bye-laws of the South African Rugby Football
      Board; how to play rugby / A. F. W. Marsberg, P. S.
      Twentyman-Jones, H. W. Carolin and B. H. Heatlie;
      some notes on rugby football / Revd. H. Ewbank. Cape
      Town, SA: Specialty Press of South Africa, 1933.
      96p; illus

> ☞ See also: A155

157   Springbok rugby trials souvenir. 1949.
      124p; illus

158   Springboks down the years / Danie Craven. London:
      Bailey & Swinfen, 1956.
      vii, 203p; illus   BL: 7923.ff.3

> Matches starring the Springboks.

159   Rugby in South Africa: 1889-1964 / edited by Herman
      Steytler and A. C. Parker. Cape Town, SA: Johnston &
      Neville on behalf of the South African Rugby Board,
      1964.
      216p; illus

> Divided into three parts: historical; articles by
> prominent rugby men; details of the jubilee plans.

160   The Springboks, 1891-1970 / Arthur C. Parker. London:
      Cassell, 1970.
      x, 364p; illus   SBN: 304935913
                                                   BL: X.629/2567

161   Toyota Springbok saga: a pictorial history from 1891 /
      Chris Greyvenstein. Cape Town, SA: Don Nelson, 1977.
      271p; illus

> *Bibliography: p5*   ISBN: 0909238278

> ☞ Subsequent ed. A167

162   Focus on rugby / photographs by Wessel Oosthuizen.
      Johannesburg, SA: The author, 1980.
      chiefly illus

> Captions by Gerhard Burger.

163   A history of the South African Referees' Society,
      1914-1981 / Johannes A. M. Hoefnagels. University of
      Stellenbosch, SA, 1983. *Master's thesis.*

164   Great Springbok rugby tests: 100 years of headlines: a
      rugby centenary scrapbook / Chris Greyvenstein. Cape
      Town, SA: Don Nelson, 1989.
      87p; illus; pbk   ISBN: 1868060616

> Reproduction of newspaper reports of famous South
> African tests.

165   Green & gold: 100 years of rugby in South Africa, or,
      100 jaar se rugby in Suid-Afrika / Paul Dobson. Cape
      Town, SA: Cameron Design CC, 1989.
      52p; illus; pbk

> A brief account of momentous occasions in South
> African rugby. Text in English and Afrikaans.

166   Rugby in South Africa: a history 1861-1988 / Paul
      Dobson. Newlands, SA: South African Rugby Board,
      1989.
      272p; illus; index

> *Bibliography: p256-8*   ISBN: 062014100X

167   Springbok saga: 100 years of Springbok rugby / Chris
      Greyvenstein. 3rd ed. Cape Town, SA: Don Nelson,
      1989.
      334p; illus; index

> *Bibliography: p334;*
> *Cover title: Toyota Springbok saga centenary edition*
>   ISBN: 1868060578

> First published in 1977, the 1981 (2nd) edition has
> not been listed as the evidence suggests that it was
> only published in Afrikaans.

> ☞ Previous ed. A161; subsequent ed. A169

168   A century of tests: one hundred years of Springbok test
      rugby 1891-1991 / Richard Whittingdale and Paul
      Dobson. Newlands, SA: On the Ball Publications, 1991.
      64p; illus; pbk

169   Springbok saga: from 1891 to the new beginning / Chris
      Greyvenstein. 4th ed. Cape Town, SA: Don Nelson,
      1992.
      344p; illus; index

> *Bibliography: p344*   ISBN: 1868060950

> ☞ Previous ed. A167

170   Beyond the tryline: rugby and South African society /
Albert Grundlingh, André Odendaal and Burridge Spies.
Johannesburg, SA: Ravan, 1995.
viii, 135p; illus; pbk   ISBN: 0869754572
                                         BL: YA.1996.a.8955

A sociological survey. Among the issues assessed
are: South Africa's rugby past; the make-up of South
African teams and the contribution of the Jewish
player; black rugby; international relations —
apartheid, anti-apartheid protests, Afrikaner
nationalism and English imperialism; nabobs such as
Luis Luyt and Danie Craven, administrators and
players.

171   Springbok rugby: an illustrated history: the proud story
of South African rugby from 1891 to the 1995 World
Cup / Chris Greyvenstein. London: New Holland, 1995.
288p; illus; index

   Bibliography: p288   ISBN: 1853687499
                                         BL: YK.1996.b.11753

Includes a complete list of Springboks from 1891 to
World Cup 1995.

172   One team, one country: the greatest years of Springbok
rugby / Edward Griffiths. Parktown, SA: Viking, 1996.
xi, 228p; illus; index   ISBN: 0670873578

Griffiths, who served as Chief Executive of the South
African Rugby Football Union in 1995, chronicles
events in South African rugby, culminating in the
winning of the Rugby World Cup.

173   Forgotten heroes: a history of black rugby 1882-1992 /
Abdurahmam (Manie) Booley. Cape Town, SA: The
author?, 1997.
328p; illus   ISBN 0620224819

✳   *Additional References*

174   South African sports: cricket, football, athletics, cycling,
tennis, racing, polo, golf, gymnastics, boxing, shooting,
&c.: an official handbook with portraits of leading
athletes and officials / G. A. Parker. London: Sampson
Low, Marston, 1897.
liii, 234p; illus

Contains some early coverage of the rugby game on
pages 61-72. The author was honorary secretary of
the South African Football and Cricket Association.

175   Football and the men who made it / Alfred Gibson and
William Pickford. South African ed. Cape Town, SA: D.
E. McConnell, 1906.
ix, 265p; index

The rugby game is included in the chapter 'Football in
South Africa'.

176   Sports and sportsmen: South Africa / compiled and
edited by the 'Cape Times'. Cape Town, SA: Atkinson,
1929.
2 vols: 526p; illus   BL: L.R.259.c.1
Rugby appears on pages 145-218.

177   Green and gold: a sporting miscellany / R. K. Stent.
London: Longmans, Green, 1954.
188p; illus   BL: 7922.bb.14

Chronicles the Springboks from their earliest days,
with a look at some of the personalities, the tours
and the inevitable politics. The second half of the
volume covers cricket, boxing and tennis.

178   The Springbok story from the inside / Eric Litchfield.
Cape Town, SA: Howard Timmins, 1960.
231p; illus   BL: 7925.b.96
The 'inside' story of cricket, rugby, boxing, golf and
soccer.

New Zealand

179   Rugby football in New Zealand: its development from
small beginnings / W. W. Robinson; with an
introduction by Hamish Stuart. London: Pall Mall Press,
1906.
16p; pbk   BL: Mic.A.12577(7) (microfilm copy)
Reprinted from the *Pall Mall Gazette*, the contents
include: 'Secret of the All Blacks success' by Hamish
Stuart; 'Rugby football in New Zealand: a ludicrous
beginning'; 'The introduction of wing forwards'; 'Origin
of the "five-eights"'; and, 'Scrum formation'.

180   Players and slayers / Leo Fanning (with some remarks
and reminiscences of Bernard Fanning). Wellington, NZ:
Gordon & Gotch, 1910.
149p; pbk
General rugby history. Of the thirty-five chapters, six
are revised versions of newspaper articles from the
Wellington *Post*.

181 History of New Zealand rugby football 1870-1945: a
complete and authentic history compiled under official
sanction / Arthur C. Swan. Wellington, NZ: Reed for
the New Zealand Rugby Football Union, 1948.
xiii, 736p; illus

☞ See also: A182; A207

182 History of New Zealand rugby football. Volume 2:
1946-1957 / Arthur C. Swan. Christchurch, NZ: New
Zealand Rugby Football Union, 1958.
ix, 527p   BL: 7923.bbb.8

☞ See also: A181; A207

183 Rugby in my time, including, A gallery of rugby greats /
Winston McCarthy. Wellington, NZ: Reed, 1958.
200p; illus

'Rugby in my time' was first published in the New
Zealand Listener, April-September 1958.

184 Great days in New Zealand rugby / Terry McLean.
London: Bailey & Swinfen, 1959.
198p; illus   BL: 7925.bb.13

☞ Subsequent ed. A192

185 Champagne rugby: the story of secondary school rugby
in New Zealand / Peter B. Minogue. Wellington, NZ:
Reed, 1961.
204p; illus

Records the birth and growth of secondary school
rugby in New Zealand.

186 The New Zealand Rugby Football Union (Inc.),
1892-1967 / A. C. Swan. Wellington, NZ: Rugby
Football Union in association with Reed, 1967.
277p; illus

187 Evolution of rugby football with an emphasis on New
Zealand / R. N. Hair. Otago University, 1968. *Dissertation.*

188 Haka!: the All Blacks story / Winston J. McCarthy.
London: Pelham, 1968.
348p; illus; index

A record of the game in New Zealand.

189 Black, black, black! / J. M. MacKenzie. Auckland, NZ:
Minerva, 1969.
176p; illus

As well as surveying great matches and famous
players, the author questions standards within the
game, such as the lack of recognition for the Maori
players in New Zealand rugby, and calls for the
abolition of the International Board.

190 On the ball: the centennial book of New Zealand rugby
/ Gordon Cyril Slatter; foreword by Billy Wallace.
Christchurch, NZ: Whitcombe & Tombs, 1970.
274p; illus   BL: X.620/1565

191 All Blacks come back: Terry McLean looks at New
Zealand and world rugby / T. P. McLean. London:
Pelham, 1975.
165p; illus   ISBN: 0720708443
                                                BL: X.629/10019

☞ Also listed at: E267

192 Great days in New Zealand rugby / Terry McLean. Rev.
ed. Auckland, NZ: Collins; Fontana Silver Fern, 1976.
216p; illus

The new edition contains two additional chapters.

☞ Previous ed. A184

193 New Zealand international rugby 1884-1975: the
international matches / Arthur H. Carman. Tawa
Sporting Publications, 1976.
viii, 206p; illus

194 The history of rugby union football in New Zealand /
Stuart Carter. California State University, US, 1977.
Master's thesis.
107p

195 Maori rugby, 1884-1979 / Arthur H. Carman. Linden,
NZ: Sporting Publications, 1980.
xii, 256p; illus; index

196 Haka, the Maori rugby story / Winston McCarthy and
Bob Howitt. Auckland, NZ: Rugby Press, 1983.
158p; illus   ISBN: 0908630077

197 Centenary: 100 years of All Black rugby / R. H. Chester
& N. A. C. McMillan. Poole: Blandford, 1984.
592p; illus, 1 map   ISBN: 0713715561
                                                BL: X.622/24011

198 All Blacks almost: 15 hard-luck stories from 25 years of
rugby / Mark Taylor. Havelock North, NZ: TC
Publications, 1985.
ix, 215p; illus: index   ISBN: 0473003287

199 Up front: the story of the All Black scrum / Graeme
Barrow. London: Kingswood, 1985.
106p; illus   ISBN: 0434980773
                                                BL: X.629/28050

200 Black magic / Graham Hutchins. Auckland, NZ: Moa,
1988.
232p; illus   ISBN: 1869470303

201 The game for all New Zealand: through the lens of Peter
Bush. Auckland, N.Z: Moa in Association with
Television New Zealand, 1989.
198p; chiefly illus

Commentary by Ron Palenski

                                                ISBN: 1869470451

Photographs of the 1988 New Zealand rugby season.

202 21 years of Rugby news. Auckland, NZ: Rugby Press, 1991.
240p; illus ISBN: 0908630352
☞ See also: I253

203 The All Blacks / T. P. McLean. London: Sidgwick & Jackson, 1991.
vii, 168p; illus; index ISBN: 0283060786
BL: YK.1993.b.3723

204 Magic matches: great days of New Zealand rugby / Graham Hutchins. Auckland, NZ: Moa in association with TVNZ Enterprises, 1991.
256p; illus ISBN: 1869470877

205 The beginning / Kevin Boon; edited by Allan R. Kirk. Wellington, NZ: Kotuku, 1992.
24p; illus, 1 map; pbk
(The story of the All Blacks; 1)
For children.

206 Cradle of rugby: the history of New Zealand college rugby / Arthur W. V. Reeve; edited by Lynn McConnell. Lower Hutt, NZ: Imprint, 1992.
x, 220p; illus; pbk ISBN: 0864641753

207 History of New Zealand rugby football / A. C. Swan. Auckland, NZ: Moa, 1992.
4 vols.; illus
Vols. 1 and 2 are reprints; Vols. 3 and 4 written by R. H. Chester and N. A. C. McMillan
☞ See also: A181; A182

208 Our national game: a celebration of 100 years of NZ rugby / Ron Palenski. Auckland, NZ: Moa, 1992.
192p; illus; index
Bibliography: p187-8 ISBN: 1869471008

209 Pride power & pain: an era of All Black excellence, 1987-1991 through the lens of Peter Bush; text by Geoff Blackwell. Auckland, NZ: Moa, 1992.
160p; chiefly illus ISBN: 186947094X

210 The invincibles / Kevin Boon; edited by Allan R. Kirk. Wellington, NZ: Kotuku, 1993.
24p; illus, 1 map; pbk
(The story of the All Blacks; 3)
The story of the 1924 All Blacks, for children.

211 A new beginning / Kevin Boon; edited by Allan R. Kirk. Wellington, NZ: Kotuku, 1993.
24p; illus, 1 map; pbk
(The story of the All Blacks; 7) ISBN: 0908947038
For children.

212 The originals / Kevin Boon; edited by Allan R. Kirk. Wellington, NZ: Kotuku, 1993.
24p; illus, 1 map; pbk
(The story of the All Blacks; 2)
The story of the 1905 All Blacks, for children.

213 The super sixties / Kevin Boon; edited by Allan R. Kirk. Wellington, NZ: Kotuku, 1993.
24p; illus, pbk
(The story of the All Blacks; 9) ISBN: 0908947054
For children.

214 From All Blacks to All Golds: New Zealand rugby league pioneers / John Haynes. Limited ed. Christchurch, NZ: Ryan and Haynes, 1996.
165p; illus; index ISBN: 0473038641
An account of the New Zealand All Black team who were cast out of the union in 1907.

215 The game of our lives: the story of rugby and New Zealand, and how they've shaped each other / text, Finlay Macdonald; photographs, Bruce Connew; picture research, Ann Andrews. Auckland, NZ: Viking, 1996.
vi, 138p; illus; index
Bibliography: p135-6 ISBN: 0670869074
'The television series upon which the book is based set out to look at New Zealand's social history through rugby.... Like the series, the book is peppered with the anecdotes of several generations of rugby players, fans and even detractors. This is neither definitive social history, nor exhaustive rugby history. Rather, this is one story of how a game and its country shaped each other.'

Up Front

The Story of the All Black Scrum

Graeme Barrow

The Kingswood Press

216   Season of glory: the historic 1996 All Blacks season /
      text by Bob Howitt; foreword by Brian Lochore.
      Auckland, NZ: Hodder Moa Beckett in association with
      TVNZ, 1996.
      48p; illus; pbk
                                              ISBN: 1869584546

217   They gave us rugby: the beginning of New Zealand
      rugby and New Zealand secondary school rugby from its
      origins at Nelson College / Alan Turley. Nelson, NZ:
      Nelson College, 1996.
      60p; illus; index; pbk
         Bibliography: p60   ISBN: 047303753X

218   Rugby: developments in the field of play / J. J. Stewart.
      Palmerston North, NZ: Dunmore Press for Massey
      University, 1997.
      115p; illus; pbk
                                              ISBN: 047305034X

✱   *Additional References*

219   The nature and meaning of sport in New Zealand: a
      selection of papers presented at a seminar on sport
      arranged by the Centre for Continuing Education,
      University of Auckland, in association with the New
      Zealand Council for Recreation and Sport, April 1978 /
      edited by John Hinchcliff. Auckland, NZ: University of
      Auckland, Centre for Continuing Education, 1978.
      90p; illus
         Includes 'The place of rugby in New Zealand' by Warren
         L. Butterworth (pp 52-62) which poses the question
         of whether rugby is a sport or a religion and proposes
         that it is a healthy fanaticism that is neither
         political nor religious. Offers a brief history of the
         game, considers rugby's place in politics, both
         nationally and internationally, and discusses the
         effects of participation on the individual and on the
         populace.

Australia

220   Australian rugby union: the game and the players / Jack
      Pollard; foreword by Sir Nicholas Shehadie. North Ryde,
      Aust.: Angus & Robertson in association with the
      Australian Broadcasting Corporation, 1984.
      xiii, 945p; illus
         Bibliography: p943-5   ISBN: 0207150060
      ☞   Also listed at: C268; subsequent ed. A225

221   The first twenty-one years: Australian Services Rugby
      Union 1963-83 / Jeff S. Partington. Drummoyne, Aust.:
      The author, 1984?
      120p; illus; index
                                              ISBN: 0959098100

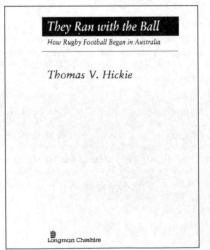

They Ran with the Ball
How Rugby Football Began in Australia

Thomas V. Hickie

Longman Cheshire

222   Path to victory: Wallaby power in the 1980s / Mark Ella,
      Terry Smith; foreword by Alan Jones, Wallaby coach;
      introduction by Andrew Slack, Wallaby captain. Sydney:
      ABC Enterprises for the Australian Broadcasting
      Corporation, 1987.
      182p; illus; pbk   ISBN: 0642527660
         Looks at the years 1984-86 in Australian rugby,
         when the national side defeated England, Scotland,
         Ireland and Wales, and recaptured the Bledisloe Cup
         in 1986.

223   Australian rugby panorama, 1990. Pymble, Aust.:
      Playbill, 1990.
      70p; illus; pbk

224   They ran with the ball: how rugby football began in
      Australia / Thomas V. Hickie. Melbourne, Aust.:
      Longman Cheshire, 1993.
      xviii, 243p; illus, maps; index; pbk
         Bibliography: p196-7   ISBN: 0582910625
                                              BL: YK.1994.b.2202

225   Australian rugby: the game and the players / Jack
      Pollard; edited by David O'Neil. Rev., enlarged updated
      ed. Chippendale, Aust.: Ironbark, 1994.
      712p; illus
         Bibliography: p711-2   ISBN: 0330356194
         Like the previous 1984 edition this work details the
         history of rugby in Australia, biographies of players,
         tours from and to Australia.
      ☞   Also listed at: C295; previous ed.: A220

226 Gordon Bray presents the spirit of rugby: a tribute to Australian rugby union. Pymble, Aust.: Harper Sports, 1995.
198p; illus

> *Bibliography: p198;*
> *Subsequently published: London: HarperCollins, 1996*
> ISBN: 0732251583

❋ *Additional References*

227 Sport in Australia: a social history / edited by Wray Vamplew and Brian Stoddart. Cambridge: Cambridge University Press, 1994.
xiv, 346p; illus; index
ISBN: 0521435137
BL: YC.1995.b.2676

> Murray G. Phillips' paper on 'Rugby' (pp 193-212) looks at the birth of the game (both codes) in Australia, its success in the international arena, the social background, sponsorship and television coverage.

Canada

228 A history of Canadian football, 1909-1958 / Frank Cosentino. University of Alberta, Can., 1969. *Master's thesis.*
375p

> Traces the growth of Canadian football. The game of football evolved from a game akin to rugby to one closely resembling American football.

229 A history of rugby football in Canada / Douglas Norman Sturrock. University of Alberta, Can., 1971. *Master's thesis.*
387p

> Describes the development of rugby in the different provinces from the game's origins to 1967.

❋ *Additional References*

230 Canada learns to play: the emergence of organized sport, 1807-1914 / Alan Metcalfe. Toronto, Can.: McClelland and Stewart, 1987.
243p; illus
(The Canadian social history series) ISBN: 0771058705

> Under the sub-heading 'British sport', mention is made of English rugby which 'gained root in only two areas of the country, the Maritimes and British Columbia. This was to remain the case until after the First World War, although some interest was expressed in Toronto in the mid 1870s and in Winnipeg after 1908. Rugby developed in the 1880s in settings with a strong British presence – in this case, naval garrisons...'.

Rest of the World

❋ East Africa

231 Rugby football in East Africa 1909-59 / edited by M. Campbell and E. J. Cohen. Nairobi: Rugby Football Union, 1960.
131p; illus

❋ Fiji

232 Rakavi 60 / D. Robinson. Fiji: Rugby Football Union, 1973.
80p; illus

❋ Japan

233 The development of rugby football in Japan, 1874-1996 / Alison Nish. University of Sheffield, 1996. *Master's thesis.*
52p

❋ Kenya

234 Rugby 1909-1982: a magazine of Kenya's rugby history. Nairobi: Gulf (K), 1982.
92p; illus; pbk

✳ *Namibia*

235 Namibian rugby: a story of courage and dedication /
Gert J. Kruger. Windhoek: The author, 1991.
152p; illus; pbk   ISBN: 9991630090

✳ *Rhodesia*

236 Rhodesia rugby: a history of the national side, 1898-1979
/ Jonty Winch. Salisbury, Zimbabwe Rhodesia:
Zimbabwe Rhodesia Rugby Union, 1979?
151p; illus   ISBN: 079740421X

The first game of football in Rhodesia was a rugby
match which took place in the bed of the Shashi river
on 5 July 1890.

✳ *Additional References*

237 A history of sport in Southern Rhodesia, 1889-1935 / J.
de L. Thompson. 1935.

This is the first volume of a three volume history of
Rhodesian sport encompassing the years 1889 to
1976. Rugby is covered on pages 133-88. A reprint in
reduced format with a new foreword and author's
preface was published in 1976 (Bulawayo: Books of
Rhodesia).

✳ *Sri Lanka*

238 1879-1978 history of a hundred years of rugby football
in Sri Lanka / S. S. Perera. Sri Lanka: Sri Lanka Rugby
Football Union, 1978.
xii, 208p; illus

Cover title: 100 years of rugby football in Sri Lanka
1879-1978   BL: DSC83/27972

✳ *Trinidad*

239 A history of rugby union football in Trinidad. Port of
Spain, Trinidad: Trinidad RFC, 1960.
illus; pbk

Contains a series of short articles by a number of
authors on: rugby in the West Indies; rugby football in
Trinidad; Caribs RFC; the MacGregor Cup (awarded
since 1929 to the winners of the annual
Trinidad-British Guiana match); and, intercolonial
rugby before the war. Includes photographs of
individual players and teams.

✳ *United States*

240 Football: the American intercollegiate game / Parke Hill
Davis. New York, US: Scribner's, 1911.
xii, 504p; illus   BL: X.629/5872

Looks at the evolution of the football game in
American colleges.

241 Football: the story of a sport which developed from
basic rugby to the collegiate and powerhouse pro games
played today: inspiring tales of its all-time greats / Paul
Staments and J. S. Chilton. New York, US: Grosset and
Dunlap, 1967.
154p; illus; index

242 A survey of rugby union football in American
universities / Paul Gerard Anderson. California State
University, 1977. *Master's thesis.*
80p

✳ *Additional References*

243 Individualism reconsidered, and other essays / David
Riesman. Glencoe, US: Free Press, 1954.
529p   BL: 8476.d.8

'Football in America: a study in culture diffusion', a
chapter written jointly by David Riesman and Reuel
Denney, traces the birth of American football via the
game of rugby. Rugby was introduced to Yale
University by D. S. Schaft who entered the university
in 1873 having previously been at Kornthal School in
Germany (and not at Rugby School as a number of
histories believe). The Americans found some aspects
of the rugby game not to their liking and they
therefore 'tampered' with the existing rules (which
were in the process of development themselves). The
scrum was abandoned and a crude line of scrimmage
was constructed across the field. The combined
running and kicking possible under rugby rules was
shifted almost entirely in the direction of an
emphasis on ball-carrying. It is significant how often
Riesman and Denney's essay is cited.

244 Play and culture: 1978 proceedings of the Association
for the Anthropological Study of Play / edited by Helen
B. Schwartzman. West Point, US: Leisure Press, 1980.
328p; pbk   ISBN: 0918438527
                                                     BL: DSC80/24222

A paper by James H. Duthie, 'Athletics: the ritual of a
technological society?', shows how a sport form which
arose in one country needed to be modified before
acceptance in another. Demonstrates how rugby was
transformed into American football in the United
States.

☞ Also listed at: G49

Chapter B

Club Histories

Contents

British & Irish Grounds

1 One hundred years at Raeburn Place, 1854-1954: a short history of the Edinburgh Academy's playing field. Edinburgh: Edinburgh Academical Club, 1954.
48p; illus; pbk BL: 7919.ff.47

2 Guide to safety at sports grounds (football) / Home Office and Scottish Home and Health Department. London: HMSO, 1976.
iv, 30p; pbk ISBN: 0113407610
BL: BS.18/1086

A guide to measures for improving spectator safety at rugby union, rugby league and soccer grounds.

3 Twickenham: the story of a rugby ground / Wallace Reyburn. London: Allen and Unwin, 1976.
176p; illus ISBN: 0047960442
BL: X.622/5417

Covers games played at Twickenham during the New Zealand tours of 1925, 1936, 1967 and 1974.

4 Undeb Rygbi Cymru Welsh Rugby Union centenary year 1980-1981: gala opening at the National Ground, Cardiff Arms Park, Saturday 26th July 1980 official souvenir programme. Cardiff: Welsh Rugby Union, 1980.
40p; illus; pbk

Contributions by former players, broadcasters, and writers.

5 Taffs acre: history & celebration of Cardiff Arms Park / edited by D. Parry-Jones. London: Collins Willow, 1984.
198p; illus

6 Cardiff Arms Park tribute spectacular: Saturday 14 September 1996, or, Teyrnged mawreddog i Barc yr Arfau: Dydd Sadwrn 14 Medi 1996 / presented by the Welsh Rugby Union and the Rod Gunner Organisation. Cardiff: Welsh Rugby Union, 1996.
39p; illus; pbk

Includes sections in Welsh.

7 Arwerthiant hanesyddol: mewn cyfrannau yn y maes cenedlaethol cynnwys Parc yr Arfau Caerdydd cartref i rygbi Cymru am dros 100 mlynedd, dydd Sul 27 Ebrill, or, Historic sale by auction: in lots at the national ground the contents of Cardiff Arms Park home of Welsh rugby for over 100 years, Sunday 27th April 1997. Cardiff: Welsh Rugby Union, 1997.
46p; illus; pbk

A unique event in the history of the game when everything from the spoons and the bandages to the turf off the pitch went under the hammer. Only the goalposts were spared.

8 A farewell to arms. Cardiff: Western Mail in association with the Welsh Rugby Union, 1997.
63p; illus; pbk ISBN: 1900477025
BL: YK.1998.b.45

A celebration of Cardiff Arms Park in words and pictures. Following the Cup Final in April 1997, the stadium was dismantled to make way for the Millennium Stadium which is being assembled on the site.

✳ *Additional References*

9 Lawns for sports: their construction and upkeep / Reginald Beale. London: Simpkin, Marshall, Hamilton, Kent, 1924.
xvi, 276p; illus; index BL: 7077.h.33

Rugby football fields are covered in chapter 11.

Overseas Grounds

10 Great days at Lancaster Park / Gordon Cyril Slatter. Christchurch, NZ: Whitcombe & Tombs, 1974.
234p; illus ISBN: 0722303894
BL: X.629/6422

Lancaster Park has played host to a number of sports and teams including 'New South Wales rugby team' (chapter 4), 'England rugby team' (chapter 7), and 'British rugby team' (chapter 12).

11 Newlands 100: one hundred years at Newlands 1890-1990. Claremont, SA: On the Ball Publications, 1990.
88p; illus

12 Newlands, the story of the stadium: an illustrated history of South Africa's most famous rugby ground. Newlands, SA: Western Province Rugby Football Union, 1995.
25p; illus; pbk

England

Altrincham (Kersal)

13 Altrincham (Kersal) RFC 1897-1997 / Don Williams and others. Altrincham: The Club, 1996.
27p; illus; pbk

Ashbourne

14 50 years of rugby: Ashbourne Rugby Union Football Club golden jubilee, 1933-1983 / P. A. Harries. Derby: Breedon Books for The Club, 1983.
29p; illus; pbk

Ashford

15 100 years of Ashford Rugby Football Club: a sort of history! / edited by Derek Wyatt. Ashford: Robquest, 1986.
72p; illus, 1 map; pbk   ISBN: 0561003335
                                BL: YK.1987.b.1033

Ashton-under-Lyne

16 Ashton-under-Lyne Rugby Club 1884-1984: 100 years of rugby / edited by Mike Crebbin. Ashton-under-Lyne: The Club, 1984.
48p; illus; pbk

Askeans

17 Askean RFC golden jubilee, 1929-79. London: The Club, 1979.
48p; illus; pbk   BL: X.622/8755

A club history, confessions of a team secretary, team tactics, pen pictures, cartoons and a tour quiz all find a place in this jubilee magazine.

Aspatria

18 Aspatria Rugby Union Club centenary 1875-1975. Aspatria: The Club, 1975.
16p; illus; pbk

19 Aspatria: the history of a rugby union football club / Terry Carrick. Worksop: The author, 1991?
95p; illus; pbk

Aston Old Edwardians

20 Aston Old Edwardians Rugby Football Club 75th anniversary 1889-1964. Aston: The Club, 1965.
53p; illus; pbk

21 Aston Old Edwardians Rugby Football Club 1889-1989 / Brian Roberts. Aston: The Club, 1989.
86p; illus; pbk

Avonvale

22 Avonvale RFC centenary 1883-1983: 100 years of village rugby / George Atchison. Bath: The Club, 1983.
141p; illus

Baildon

23 Baildon RUFC golden jubilee 1912-1962 / John Bell. Baildon: The Club, 1962.
32p; illus; pbk

Bank of England

24 The House: a history of the Bank of England Sports Club (1908-1983) / A. J. N. Bond and M. O. H. Doughty. Roehampton: The Club, 1984.
403p; illus   ISBN: 0950977705

Covers rugby, soccer, hockey and cricket.

Barclays Bank

25 Barclays Bank Football Club rugby union: a dinner to celebrate the 50th season at Barclays Bank Sports Club, Park View Road, Ealing 21 October 1970 / edited by John Robinson. London: The Club, 1970.
24p; illus; pbk

Contains a short history of the club on pages 3-9.

Barnstaple

26   Barnstaple Rugby Football Club 1877-1977. Barnstaple: The Club, 1977.
45p; illus; pbk

Bath

27   Bath Football Club centenary 1865-1965. Bath: The Club, 1965.
63p; illus; pbk

28   Gladiators of a Roman city: a history of Bath Football Club / Harry W. Barstow. Bath: The Club, 1986.
180p; illus; pbk
      ISBN: 0948914009
      BL: YK.1987.a.1378

29   Bath Football Club (RFU) 125: a celebration of 125 years of rugby history / Harry Barstow and others. Bath: The Club, 1990.
48p; illus; pbk

30   Bath: ace of clubs / Brian Jones. Derby: Breedon, 1993.
252p; illus; index
      ISBN: 1873626452
      BL: YK.1994.b.14674

31   Triple triumph / edited by K. Johnstone. Bath: Bath Rugby Football Club, 1994.
48p; illus
    A review of Bath's 1993-4 season.

Bath Public Schools

32   Bath Public Schools RFC & CC 1939-1941 / compiled by Malcolm Spark. Ripley: The author, 1996.
24p; illus; pbk
    Pages 1-18 are devoted to rugby.

Bedford

33   Bedford Rugby Union Football Club: winners of the RFU club competition 1974/75 Twickenham 26th April 1975: souvenir booklet / Don Riddy. Bedford: The Club, 1975.
33p; illus; pbk
    Contains a brief history of the club.

34   100 years of the Blues: the Bedfordshire Times centenary history of Bedford RUFC 1886-1986 / edited by Neil Roy. Bedford: Bedford County Press, 1986.
x, 270p; illus

35   Bedford Rugby Union Football Club 1886-1986: souvenir centenary brochure. Bedford: The Club, 1986.
55p; illus; pbk
    A brief history of the club compiled by Jack Pope.

Bedford Athletic

36   A history of Bedford Athletic RUFC / Alan Cox. Bedford: The Club, 1970.
43p; pbk

Berry Hill, Gloucester

37   'Breathe on 'um Berry!': a history of 100 years of playing the game at Berry Hill / John Belcher. Berry Hill: The Club, 1993.
174p; illus; pbk

Biggleswade

38   1949-1974, Biggleswade Rugby Union Football Club: 25th anniversary souvenir. Biggleswade: The Club, 1974.
20p; illus; pbk

Bingley

39   Bingley Rugby Union Football Club centenary brochure 1876-1976 / Gary Firth. Bingley: The Club, 1976.
24p; illus; pbk

Birkenhead Park

40   Birkenhead Park: the first hundred years: a rugby union centenary / Philip J. Beacall. Birkenhead: The Club, 1971.
viii, 70p; illus; pbk

Birmingham Welsh

41   'Half a ton of Welsh': the story of fifty years of Birmingham Welsh rugby / Richard Williams. Birmingham: The Club, 1986.
38p; illus; pbk
    Cover title: Birmingham Welsh RUFC golden jubilee season 1986-1987: 'half a ton of Welsh': the story of fifty years of Birmingham Welsh rugby

Bishop's Stortford

42   1920-1971, Bishop's Stortford Rugby Football Club. Bishop's Stortford: The Club, 1971.
32p; illus; pbk

Bishopston, Bristol

43   The first hundred: a review of the history of Bishopston Rugby Football Club 1894-1994 / Ivor Woodman. Bishopston: The Club, 1993.
76p; illus; pbk
    The compilation of the history was based on notes compiled by Vic Ball in 1969.

Blackburn

44   1877-1977 centenary season: Blackburn RUFC / edited
     by J. Michael Green and Kenneth J. Ainsworth.
     Blackburn: The Club, 1977.
     55p; illus; pbk

Blackheath

45   The Blackheath Rugby Football Club: records
     1862-1898. Southwark: The Boys' Home, 1898.
     76p; illus

          Cover title: The Blackheath Rugby Football Club: records
          1875-1898   BL: X.449/737

46   100 years: story of Blackheath Football Club / A. C.
     Shanahan. Lewisham: Lewisham Borough News, 1958.
     xviii, 28p; illus; pbk   BL: X.449/1951

47   Blackheath since the war: the continued story of
     Blackheath Football Club / Owen Dixson. Blackheath:
     The author, 1971.
     iv, 71p; illus; index; pbk   ISBN: 095019980X

48   Blackheath Football Club: some highlights from the
     history of the oldest independent rugby club in the world
     / Hugh Brodie. Blackheath: The Club, 1997.
     14p; illus; pbk

Blackpool

49   Blackpool RUFC silver jubilee 1959-1984. Blackpool:
     The Club, 1984.
     32p; illus; pbk

Blaydon

50   Blaydon RFC: the first 75 years. Blaydon: The Club?,
     1963.
     7p; pbk

51   Blaydon Rugby Football Club centenary brochure.
     Blaydon: The Club, 1988.
     106p

Bowdon

52   Bowdon RUFC 1877-1977: the first hundred years /
     Brian Fallon. Cheshire: The Club, 1978.
     31p; illus; pbk

Bradford

53   Bradford Rugby Union Football Club centenary
     brochure 1866-1966. Leeds: The Club, 1966.
     26p; illus; pbk

Bradford Northern

54   Bradford Northern: the history 1863-1989 / compiled
     by Nigel Williams. Bradford: M. Q. Printing, 1989.
     395p; illus; pbk   BL: YK.1991.a.12074

Bramley

55   Bramley Rugby Union Football Club 1921-1971.
     Bramley: The Club, 1972.
     5p; pbk

Bridgwater and Albion

56   Bridgwater and Albion centenary season 1975-1976:
     1875-1975 / edited by Bob Collard, Mike Squibbs and
     David Watkins. Bridgwater: The Club, 1975.
     123p; illus; pbk

Brighouse Rangers

57   The rise and fall of rugby league Brighouse Rangers
     Football Club 1879-1906 / David Adams. Halifax: The
     author, 1995.
     64p; illus

     Before becoming a founder member of the Northern
     Union in 1895, Brighouse Rangers had enjoyed
     success on the playing field against local teams able
     to call on a greater population. Formed in 1879,
     Rangers produced teams of distinction, winning the
     Yorkshire Challenge Cup and the Yorkshire Senior
     Competition, and finally a few months before the
     Great Split, the club dashed the hopes of such
     teams as Bradford, Hunslet, and Manningham by
     winning the Yorkshire Cup against Morley at
     Headingley in front of a crowd of approximately
     20,000. Limited to 250 copies and written by a
     one-time director of Hunslet RLFC.

Bristol

58   Bristol Football Club jubilee book 1888-1938 / W. T.
     Pearce and others. Bristol: The Club, 1938.
     102p; illus

59   Bristol Football Club (rugby union) 1888-1963: a review
     of the history of the club to celebrate the 75th
     anniversary of its foundation / Horace Hutt. Bristol:
     The Club, 1963.
     56p; illus; pbk

60   The Bristol Rugby Football Club centenary book
     1888-1988: rugby – Bristol fashion / Chris Ducker.
     Bristol: The Club, 1988.
     vi, 160p; illus; pbk

Brixham

61   Brixham Rugby Football Club 1875-1975. Brixham: The
     Club, 1975.
     9p; pbk

Bromsgrove

62 Bromsgrove RFC 1872-1972.
6p; pbk

Broughton Park

63 Broughton Park FC centenary 1882-1982. The Club,
1982.
25p; illus; pbk

Burton-on-Trent

64 Burton-on-Trent FC: 70th season 1870-1940 / compiled
by J. R. Pennington. Burton-on-Trent: The Club, 1939.
14p; illus; pbk

65 Burton (Rugby Union) Football Club centenary.
Burton-on-Trent: The Club, 1970.
8p; pbk

Cainscross, Gloucestershire

66 The ragged and dangerous: the story of 100 years of
Cainscross Rugby Club 1894-1994 / Norman Hall and
Bill Tocknell. Cainscross: The Club, 1993.
92p; illus; pbk

Calder Vale

67 Calder Vale RUFC 1926-76. Lancashire: The Club, 1976.
48p; illus; pbk

Camborne

68 Camborne Rugby Football Club, 1878-1978: the story of
a proud club / compiled by Phillip Rule and Alan
Thomas. Camborne: The Club, 1977.
92p; illus; pbk

> *Cover title: Camborne RFC centenary programme,
> 1878-1978*

BL: X.611/7915

Camborne School of Mines

69 The first hundred years of the Camborne School of
Mines Football Club (1896 to 1995-96) / C. V. Phillips.
Redruth: The Club, 1996.
130p; illus; pbk

> *Bound tête-bêche; includes bibliography: p130*

Cambridge University

70 Oxford v. Cambridge: the story of the university rugby
match / Howard Marshall in collaboration with J. P.
Jordan. London: Clerke & Cockeran, 1951.
256p
BL: 7920.l.36
☞ Also listed at: B225

71 The Bowring story of the varsity match / David Frost.
London: Macdonald, 1987.
256p; illus
ISBN: 0356120066
BL: YK.1989.b.2035

☞ Also listed at: B227

Camp Hill Old Edwardians

72 Sixty years of Old Boys' rugger: a history of Camp Hill
Old Edwardians Rugby Football Club, 1893-1953 / B.
M. Bowker. Birmingham: Camp Hill Grammar School,
Camp Hill Old Edwardians Rugby Football Club, 1954.
34p; illus; pbk
BL: 7921.b.45

73 Camp Hill Rugby Football Club centenary 1893-1993: a
history, incorporating 'Sixty years of Old Boys' rugger
1893-1953' by B. M. Bowker, forty years on, 1953-1993
/ K. P. Birrell. Birmingham: The Club, 1993.
196p; illus; pbk

> Reprints and updates the previous item.

Cantabrigian

74 Choicer Cantabrigian tales: a history of the first fifty
years of the Cantabrigian Rugby Union Football Club /
R. C. Griggs and P. B. Harvey. Cambridge: The authors,
1996.
xi, 171p; illus; pbk

Carlisle

75 Carlisle RFC centenary 1873-1973 / Harry Watson.
Carlisle: The Club, 1973?
28p; illus

Castle Cary

76 Castle Cary Rugby Club 1888-1988 centenary booklet.
Castle Cary: The Club, 1988.
50p; illus; pbk

Centaurs

77 Centaurs Rugby Football Club golden jubilee 1923-1973.
Middlesex: The Club, 1973.
42p; illus; pbk

Charlton Park

78 A centenary history of Charlton Park Rugby Football
Club 1893-1993 / Andy Potts. London: The author,
1993.
64p; illus; pbk

Cheltenham

79 Cheltenham Rugby Football Club: 75th anniversary
1889-1964. Cheltenham: The Club, 1964.
24p; illus; pbk

80 Cheltenham Rugby Football Club 1889-1989 / J.
Woodward. Cheltenham: The Club, 1989.
102p; illus; pbk

Cheltenham Civil Service

81 Cheltenham Civil Service RFC from the kick off
1947-1997: the club history spanning 50 years /
compiled by Geoffrey Hardy and Brian Didlick.
Cheltenham: The Club, 1997.
28p; illus; pbk

Cheltenham Colts

82 Cheltenham Colts silver jubilee 1960-1985. Cheltenham:
The Club, 1985.
65p; illus; pbk

Chesterfield

83 Chesterfield Rugby Union Football Club: the first 50
years / Les Collins and Graham Bell. Chesterfield: The
Club, 1978.
24p; illus; pbk

Chingford

84 1928-1978: fifty years of Chingford Rugby Club / Ken
Ball. Chingford: The Club, 1978.
32p; illus; pbk

> *Limited edition of 500 copies*

Cinderford

85 1886-1986: one hundred years of Cinderford rugby /
Robert Williams. Cinderford: The Club, 1986.
207p; illus; pbk

Civil Service

86 A history of the Civil Service RFC 1863-1929 / J. R.
Patterson. London: The Club, 1929.
12p; illus; pbk

87 Civil Service Football Club: its first 100 years of playing
rugby football 1863-1963 / D. Emlyn Davies. London:
The Club, 1963.
20p; illus; pbk

Cleckheaton

88 Cleckheaton RUFC: 50 jubilee season 1924/25-1974/75.
Cleckheaton: The Club, 1975.
24p; illus; pbk

> HISTORY
>
> OF THE
>
> ## Clifton Rugby Football Club
>
> 1872 - 1909
>
> WITH
>
> LIST of MEMBERS—PAST and PRESENT
>
> ————
>
> BY
>
> FRANK C. HAWKINS
>
> (THE "CHIEL").

Clifton

89 History of the Clifton Rugby Football Club 1872-1909:
with list of members past and present / Frank C.
Hawkins (The 'Chiel'). Bristol: Bristol Times and Mirror,
1909.
200p; illus

> *Limited ed. of 200 numbered copies*   BL: 7904.bbb.12

90 Fifty years with the Clifton Rugby Football Club,
1872-1922 / Frank C. Hawkins and E. Seymour Bell.
Bristol: J. W. Arrowsmith, 1922.
xv, 172p; illus   BL: 07911.g.28

91 Clifton Rugby Football Club 1872-1972 / edited by
Horace Hutt. Bristol: The Club, 1972.
ix, 116p; illus

> *Cover title: One hundred years with the Clifton Rugby
> Football Club 1872-1972*

Coventry

92 Souvenir and brief history with photographs of the
Coventry Football Club past and present / edited by
Herbert Coulson. Coventry: Coventry FC Supporters'
Association, 1921.
56p; illus; pbk

93 Coventry Football Club (RU), 1874-1974: one hundred
years of Coventry Blue / edited by J. R. Barker-Davis.
Coventry: The Club?, 1974.

Crediton

94　1878-1978. Crediton RFC centenary. Crediton: The
　　Club, 1978.
　　52p; illus; pbk

Cullompton, Devon

95　Cullompton RFC founded 1892: one hundred years of
　　rugby football. Cullompton: The Club, 1992.
　　32p; illus

Darlington

96　Darlington Rugby Football Club: the first half-century
　　1863-1914 / Bob Jackson. Darlington: The Club, 1994.
　　62p; illus; pbk

De Havilland

97　De Havilland Rugby Football Club golden jubilee
　　1986/87 / Phil Missing and others. Hertfordshire: The
　　Club, 1986.
　　114p; illus; pbk

　　　*Cover title: Evolution of a rugby football club, the first fifty
　　　years: de Havilland RFC jubilee 1986/7*

Devonport Services

98　A history of Devonport Services Rugby Football Club
　　1912-1981 / T. F. Dunbar. Devonport: The Club, 1981.
　　212p; pbk

Dorchester

99　A history of Dorchester Rugby Football Club / H. W.
　　M. Brewer. Dorchester: The Club, 1984.
　　109p; illus; pbk

Drybrook

100　One hundred years of Drybrook rugby / Paul Mason.
　　Drybrook, Glos.: Drybrook RFC, 1992.
　　89p; illus; pbk

Durham City

101　Durham City Rugby Football Club 1872-1950 / edited
　　by Walter Douglas. Durham: The Club, 1950.
　　104p; illus; pbk

102　DCRFU 1872-1972: Durham City Rugby Football Club:
　　a centenary review / G. S. Shaw.
　　19p; illus; pbk

Durham University

103　1875-1975 centenary magazine: Durham University.
　　Durham: The University RFC, 1975.
　　28p; illus; pbk

Eastleigh

104　Eastleigh Rugby Football Club golden jubilee 1931-81.
　　Eastleigh: The Club, 1981.

Eccles

105　A hundred years 1897-1997: a history of Eccles Rugby
　　Union Football Club / Arthur Gilbody. Eccles: The
　　Club, 1996.
　　58p; illus; pbk

Exeter

106　100 years of rugby at the County Ground: Exeter Rugby
　　Football Club County Ground, Exeter: special
　　commemorative match, Exeter v. Barbarians, Tuesday
　　28 September 1993. Exeter: The Club, 1993.
　　34p; illus; pbk

Five Ways Old Edwardians

107　Five Ways Old Edwardians Football Club (rugby union):
　　a centenary collection including a short history,
　　memories, photographs and records. Birmingham: The
　　Club, 1995?
　　35p; illus

Frome

108　Frome Rugby Football Club 1883-1983: centenary
　　booklet. Frome: The Club, 1983.
　　31p; illus; pbk

　　　Author is B. J. Convery

Fylde

109　History of the Fylde Rugby Club: jubilee 1919 to 1969 /
　　F. F. Pastore. Fylde?: The author?, 1969?
　　22p; illus

Gloucester

110　Double Gloucester: the city and county of Gloucester
　　are part of the world of rugby football / Nico Craven.
　　Seascale: The author, 1972.
　　44p; pbk　　　　　　　　　　　ISBN: 0905467035
　　　　　　　　　　　　　　　　　　BL: X.619/16759

111　One hundred cherry & white years, 1873-1973 / edited
　　by Arthur Russell. Gloucester: The Club, 1973.
　　128p; illus

112　Kingsholm 1891-1991 Gloucester Rugby Football Club:
　　the first 100 years / Peter Arnold. Northampton: Byline
　　Publishing, 1992.
　　32p; illus; pbk

Gloucester Old Boys

113   Gloucester Old Boys Rugby Club: 75 years on (1904-79)
      / compiled by Norman Partridge. 1979.
      84p; illus; pbk

Gosforth

114   Gosforth FC: 1877-1977. Gosforth: The Club, 1977.
      17p; illus; pbk

Guildford & Godalming

115   Guildford & Godalming Rugby Football Club
      1922-1972. Guildford: The Club, 1972.
      20p; illus; pbk

Handsworth

116   Handsworth RUFC centenary year brochure: 100 years
      of rugby. Birmingham: The Club, 1986.
      72p; pbk

Harlequins

117   A record of the matches played by the Harlequin
      Football Club during the season 1888-9. London: The
      Club?, 1888.
      31p; pbk

118   A record of the matches played by the Harlequin
      Football Club during the season 1889-90. London: The
      Club?, 1889.
      35p; pbk

119   Harlequin story: the history of the Harlequin Football
      Club / H. B. T. Wakelam. London: Phoenix House,
      1954.
      172p; illus   BL: 7922.b.20

120   Harlequin Football Club centenary season
      1866/67-1966/67. London: Harlequin FC, 1966.
      17p; illus; pbk

121   The Harlequins: 125 years of rugby football / Philip
      Warner. Derby: Breedon, 1991.
      253p; illus   ISBN: 1873626002
                                      BL: YA.1993.b.10100

Harrogate

122   Harrogate Rugby Union Football Club 1871-1971 /
      Brian Forshaw. Harrogate: The Club, 1971.
      20p; illus; pbk

123   Harrogate Rugby Union Football Club 1871-1996 /
      compiled by Brian Forshaw. Harrogate: The Club, 1996.
      24p; illus; pbk

Harrogate Old Boys

124   Harrogate Old Boys RUFC: coming of age souvenir
      1926. Leeds: Bramley, 1926.
      16p; illus; pbk

Harrow

125   100 years 1891-1991: Harrow Rugby Football Club
      centenary souvenir magazine. Harrow: The Club, 1991.
      96p; illus

Hartlepool

126   Hartlepool Rugby Football Club: one hundred years of a
      rugby club (and a bit of monkey business to boot) /
      edited by John Bradley. Hartlepool: The Club, 1993.
      159p; illus

Hartlepool Rovers

127   History of the Hartlepool Rovers Rugby Football Club /
      Fred J. Theaker; with supplementary article on the
      original Hartlepools club and introduction by F. H. R.
      Alderson. Hartlepool: The Club, 1901.
      90p; illus; pbk

128   Five-star year / edited by D. Hornby. Hartlepool:
      William Barlow, 1969.
      106p; illus; pbk   BL: X.619/10637

      The article 'Hartlepool Rovers FC' by F. Lister traces
      the history of Hartlepool Rovers since 1879; their
      participation in the Durham Senior Cup and county
      rugby; players' appearances for the county and brief
      pen pictures of 19 players who were in the 1968
      teams.

Hayle

129   Hayle Rugby Football Club centenary magazine,
      1877-1977.
      68p; illus; pbk

Headingley

130   Headingley Rugby Union Football Club 1878-1948: 70th
      anniversary. Headingley: The Club, 1948.
      56p; illus; pbk

131   Headingley Football Club: centenary souvenir brochure,
      1878-1978 / edited by Paul A. W. Stephens. Leeds: The
      Club, 1979.
      111p; illus; pbk   BL: X.611/8703

Heath

132   1928/9-1978/9: Heath Rugby Union Football Club
      (formerly Heath Old Boys) golden jubilee brochure / M.
      Hiller, N. Wheelwright. Halifax?: The Club, 1978.
      64p; illus; pbk

Heaton Moor

133   75 anniversary: Heaton Moor Rugby Club 1899-1974.
Lancaster?: The Club, 1974.
34p; illus; pbk

Henley

134   Henley RFC golden jubilee, 1930-1980 / compiled by C.
Bowsher. Henley: The author, 1980.
49p; pbk

Hereford

135   Hereford Rugby Football Club founded 1870: a short
history / J. F. Escott; with additional contributions from
M. T. McCarthy, Nicki Pryor, J. Leeuwaugh, G.
Griffiths. Hereford: The Club, 1996.
60p; illus; pbk

   Cover title: 125 years of Hereford Football Club
   1870/71-1995/96

Hertford

136   OHRFC 1932-1982 HRFC golden jubilee: Hertford
Rugby Football Club / edited by Jim Goodman.
Hertford: The Club, 1981.
52p; illus; pbk

Hinckley

137   Hinckley Rugby Football Club: 1893-1993 centenary /
compiled by A. Gildroy. Hinckley: The Club, 1993.
208p

Honiton

138   Centenary booklet & history of club 1883-1983: Honiton
Rugby Football Club season 1983-84. Honiton: The
Club, 1983.
32p; illus; pbk

Hornets

139   Hornets RFC silver jubilee 1987-1988 season: 'the first
25 years' / Brian Collard and Mike Thomas.
Weston-Super-Mare: The Club, 1988.
32p; illus; pbk

Huddersfield

140   Huddersfield Rugby Union Football Club: the first 75
years (1909-1985) / K. T. Shaw.
202p; illus; pbk

Hull

141   Old faithful: a history of Hull Football Club, 1865-1987
/ Michael E. Ulyatt with rugby league statistical records
by Bill Dalton and foreword by Lord Derby. Beverley:
Hutton, 1988.
125p; illus; pbk   ISBN: 0907033636
                                                    BL: YK.1990.b.1426

142   A tale of two roads: an early history of Hull FC and Hull
KR / Michael E. Ulyatt. Beverley: Hutton, 1996.
136p; illus; pbk   ISBN: 1872167780

   A history of Hull FC and KR compiled through the
   reproduction of newspaper reports, minutes from
   annual general meetings and letters.

Isle of Wight

143   50 years of island rugby. Isle of Wight: Isle of Wight
RFC, 1975.
22p; illus; pbk

Kendal

144   History of football in Kendal from 1871 to 1908 / Jim
Clarke. 1908.
408p; illus

   Includes both rugby and association football with a
   complete list of results and short accounts of most
   of the matches played.

Kesteven

145   Kesteven Rugby Football Club 1947-1997: fiftieth
anniversary, 26th-28th September 1997. Grantham: The
Club, 1997.
16p; illus; pbk

Keswick

146   Keswick RUFC centenary year, 1879-1979 / edited by
W. R. Taylor. Keswick: McKane for Keswick RUFC,
1979.
44p; 1 illus; pbk   BL: X.619/22424

Kettering

147   Kettering Rugby Football Club 1875-1975 / edited by
Tony Hewitt. Kettering: The Club, 1975.
72p; illus; pbk

Keynsham

148   Keynsham Rugby Football Club: the first 50 years
1923-1973 / compiled by David Whittington.
Keynsham: The Club, 1973.
24p; pbk

King's College Hospital

149 King's College Hospital Rugby Football Club. London?:
Lara-Rae Partnership, 1995?
32p; illus; pbk   BL: YK.1996.b.494

King's College School Old Boys

150 A history of KCS Old Boys Rugby Football Club / D.
G. Dalziel. Esher: The Club, 1979?
100p

Kingsbridge

151 Kingsbridge and the handling code 1889-1989: a history
of Kingsbridge Rugby Football Club / Steve Ball.
Kingsbridge: The Club, 1989.
57p

Kodak

152 Jumping for joy: 50 years of Kodak rugby / N. A. Davis.
Harrow: The Club, 1986.
204p; illus; pbk

Leamington

153 A history of the Leamington Rugby Union Football
Club: the first 50 years / B. C. Harrison. Leamington:
The Club, 1976.
84p; illus; pbk

     *Cover title: Leamington Rugby Union Football Club
1926-1976*

Leicester

154 Leicester Tigers: a history of the Leicester Football Club
/ Brian Thompson. Leicester: Edgar Backus, 1947.
51p; illus; pbk   BL: 7918.aaa.17

155 Leicester Football Club 1880-1980: one hundred years of
rugby from the 'Death or Glory' boys to the present-day
'Tigers' / David Hands. Leicester: The Club, 1981.
xvi, 246p; illus

     Limited ed. of 150 copies

156 Tigers review / Martin Johnson. Leicester: 1983?
23p; illus; pbk

    Documents the progress of Leicester RFC during
seasons 1980/81 and 1981/82.

157 The Tigers tale: the official history of Leicester Football
Club, 1880-1993 / Stuart Farmer & David Hands.
Leicester: ACL & Polar, 1993.
416p; illus   ISBN: 095148625X
             BL: YK.1994.b.3992

    Includes 'A who's who of celebrated Tigers', pages
126-94.

Liverpool

158 Red, black & blue: the first 125 years of Liverpool
Football Club (rugby union) / J. R. A. Daglish.
Manchester: N. Richardson, 1983.
41p; illus; pbk   ISBN: 0907511295
            BL: X.622/18885

Lloyds Bank

159 Lloyds Bank RFC 1913/14-1963/64. London?: The
Club, 1963.
16p; pbk

Luctonians

160 The first 40 years: 1948-1958, 1958-1968, 1968-1978,
1978-1988 / W. A. (Bill) Thomas and others. Kingsland:
Luctonians RFC, 1988.
56p

Lydney

161 Black & white 'oops: the story of 100 years of Lydney
Rugby Club 1887-1987 / John Powell. Lydney: The
Club, 1987?
54p; illus; pbk

Lymm

162 Out on a Lymm / Dave Berry. Lymm, Cheshire: Lymm
RUFC, 1990.
232p; illus; pbk   BL: YK.1993.a.10124

Maidstone

163 Maidstone Football Club centenary season: one hundred years of rugby football (1880-81) to (1979-80) / compiled by Roger Craske. Maidstone: The Club, 1980.
82p; illus; pbk

Manchester

164 Centenary of the Manchester Football Club: 26th September 1959 souvenir brochure. Manchester: The Club?, 1959.
14p; illus; pbk

165 125: 1860-1985 MFC / Len Balaam. Manchester: Manchester Football Club, 1985.
96p; illus; pbk

Manningham

166 Putting Valley Parade on the map: a short history of the development of Valley Parade as the home of Bradford City and an impression of that period / written and compiled by Richard Halfpenny. Wetherby: City Gent, 1995.
66p; illus, maps; pbk   ISBN: 0952079909
This booklet also chronicles the growth of Manningham Rugby Club from 1886-1908.

Market Rasen & Louth

167 1950-1975: twenty five years of Market Rasen and Louth Rugby Union Football Club / George Geeson and others.
18p; illus

Middlesbrough

168 Middlesbrough Rugby Union Football Club: eightieth anniversary 1872-1952 souvenir. Middlesbrough: The Club, 1952.
34p; illus; pbk

169 Middlesbrough RUFC 1872-1972: centenary brochure / John Taylor. Middlesbrough: The Club, 1972.
52p; illus; pbk

Midsomer Norton

170 Golden jubilee 36-86: MNRFC.
42p; illus; pbk

Mill Hill

171 Mill Hill Rugby Football Club 1937-1987: souvenir golden jubilee brochure. 1987.
32p; illus; pbk

Morley

172 1878 Morley RFC / edited by Paul Robinson. 1978.
40p; illus; pbk

Moseley

173 Moseley Football Club 1873-1973. Moseley: The Club, 1973.
80p; illus; pbk
Cover title: The centenary of Moseley Football Club 1873-1973

National Westminster Bank

174 100 years of rugby 1886-1986: National Westminster Bank RFC. London: The Club, 1985.
118p; illus; pbk

New Brighton

175 New Brighton Rugby Football Club souvenir booklet for opening new clubrooms 20th September 1969.
56p; illus

176 New Brighton Rugby Union Football Club 1875-1975 / Maurice Eggleshaw. New Brighton: The author, 1975.
82p; illus; pbk

Newark

177 Newark Rugby Football Club 1919-1969. Newark: The Club, 1970.
17p; pbk   ISBN: 0950187607

Newbold-on-Avon

178 Newbold-on-Avon RFC: 'in the red and the black' / Michael R. Scott. Newbold-on-Avon: The Club, 1994.
224p; illus; pbk

Newport (Salop)

179 The story of Newport (Salop) Rugby Union Football Club and of rugby in the district from 1871 / Gavin Goulson. Newport, Shropshire?: The author, 1993?
86p; pbk   BL: YK.1994.b.8990

North Bristol

180 North Bristol Rugby Football Club jubilee 1933-1983. Bristol: The Club, 1983.
56p; illus; pbk

North Petherton

181 North Petherton RFC centenary season: founded 1893. Bridgwater: The Club, 1993.
40p; illus

Northampton

182 Northampton Football Club, the Saints 1880-1948: the story of a great club, the record of a great season / edited by D. A. Reid. Northampton: The Saints' Supporters Club, 1948.
51p; illus; pbk

183 Northampton Football Club centenary 1880-1980 / R. B. Taylor. Northampton: The Club, 1980.
52p; illus; pbk

184 The 'Saints' history by the 'Scouts': the first 100 years 1880-1980. Northampton: The Club, 1980.
20p; illus; pbk

185 Oh when the Saints: the official history of Northampton Football Club / Brian Barron. Northampton: Byline, 1990.
250p; illus

186 The Saints: Northampton Football Club (rugby union): official souvenir brochure of the 1989/90 Courage Division Two champions / edited by Mark Harris. Northampton: Byline, 1990.
66p; illus

Norwich

187 100 years of rugby football: history of Norwich FC 1885-1985. Norwich: The Club?, 1985.

Nottingham

188 Nottingham Rugby Football Club: history, information, player profiles, statistics to season 1992/93 / edited by John L. Drapkin. Nottingham: The Club, 1993.
157p; illus; pbk

Oadby Wyggestonians

189 One hundred years of rugby in Oadby 1888-1988 / Martin Bromley. Leicester: Oadby Wyggestonian RFC, 1988.
133p; illus; pbk

Old Aldwinians

190 Old Aldwinians RUFC golden jubilee, 1936-1986. Manchester?: The Club, 1988.

Old Alleynians

191 Old Alleynian Rugby Football Club, 1898-1948 / Dulwich College, Old Alleynian Rugby Football Club. London: Clowes, 1950.
x, 182p; illus

The introduction is signed: N. H. Blundell   BL: 7920.d.15

Old Brodleians

192 1930-1980 brochure to commemorate the golden jubilee of the Old Brodleians Rugby Football Union Football Club. Halifax: The Club, 1980.
72p; illus; pbk

Old Caterhamians

193 A history of the Old Caterhamians RFC 1928-1978. Caterham: The Club, 1978.
33p; pbk

Old Cranleighans

194 A history of the Old Cranleigh Rugby Football Club / M. J. P. Fawcett. Thames Ditton: The Old Cranleighan Society, 1994.
181p; illus   ISBN: 0952431408

Old Dunstonians

195 History of the Old Dunstonian Rugby Football Club 1903-1953. Beckenham: The Club, 1952.
91p; illus; pbk

Old Edwardians

196 Old Edwardians RFC, founded 1967: silver jubilee. Romford: The Club, 1992.
24p; illus; pbk

Old Elthamians

197 The history of the Old Elthamians' Rugby Football Club 1911-1961 / edited by Geoffrey W. Lovelock. Chislehurst: The Club, 1961.
46p; illus; index; pbk

Old Gaytonians

198 Old Gaytonians Rugby Football Club 1934-1984. Harrow: The Club, 1984.
52p; illus; pbk

Old Haberdashers

199 Making a mark: a history of Old Haberdashers Rugby Football Club from 1923 to 1957 / compiled by George Jamieson. Hertfordshire: The Club, 1957.
54p; pbk

Old Haileyburians & Imperial Service College

200 Old Haileyburian & Imperial Service College Rugby Football Club 1902-1952. 1952.
11p; pbk

Old Halesonians

201 Old Halesonians RFC 1930-1980 / edited by Martin Baker and Philip Worsley. Halesowen: The Club, 1980.
32p; illus; pbk

Old Isleworthians

202 50 years of football with the Old Isleworthians, 1902/3-1952/3. London: Old Isleworthians Football Club, 1953.
46p

Old Leysians

203 Old Leysian Football Club: jubilee 1877-1927 / compiled and edited by J. H. S. McArthur. Cambridge?: The Club, 1928.
39p; illus; pbk

204 The Old Leysian Rugby Football Club centenary issue 1877-1977. Cambridge?: The Club, 1976.
32p; illus; pbk

Old Merchant Taylors

205 Old Merchant Taylors Rugby Football Club: records of twenty seasons 1882-1902 / L. H. Gunnery, N. Parham. London: The Club, 1902.
264p

206 A short history of the Old Merchant Taylors' Rugby Football Club 1882-1949 / B. H. St. J. O'Neil. Rickmansworth: The Club, 1949.
12p; pbk

207 Old Merchant Taylors' Rugby Football Club centenary season 1882-1982: souvenir programme / compiled by Jeremy Birch. London: The Club, 1982.
35p; illus; pbk

208 OMTRFC centenary 1882-1982: a history of the Old Merchant Taylors' Rugby Football Club / edited by C. L. Bywater. London: Foremost Colour for the Club, 1983.
108p; illus; pbk

Old Millhillians

209 Nobis: the story of a club: the Old Millhillians Club 1878-1978 / Gowen Bewsher. London: The Club, 1979.
203p; illus; index
    Limited edition

210 Old Millhillians Rugby Football Club: the first hundred seasons 1879-1979 / edited by J. D. M. King. Middlesex: The Club, 1979.
73p; illus; pbk

Old Patesians

211 Old Patesians RFC 75 years 1913-1988: a celebration of the Old Patesians Club's illustrious past: seventy-five years of sporting endeavour.
20p; pbk

Old Paulines

212 Old Pauline Football Club 1871-1971. Surrey?: The Club, 1971.
13p; illus; pbk

Old Rishworthians

213 Old Rishworthian RUFC: golden jubilee booklet 1930-1980. Halifax: The Club, 1980.
44p; illus; pbk

Old Uppinghamians

214 Records of the Old Uppinghamian Football Club. Uppingham: John Hawthorn, 1913.
xii, 120p

Old Westcliffians

215 Souvenir of the first twenty-five years of the Old Westcliffians Rugby Football Club 1922-1947. Southend: The Club, 1947.
14p; illus; pbk

Old Whitgiftians

216 Old Whitgiftian Rugby Football Club 1901-1951 / edited by Ian S. Hubbard. London: Wightman, 1952.
69p; illus; pbk

217 Old Whitgiftian Rugby Football Club: part II, 1951-1960 / edited by Ian S. Hubbard. London: Wightman, 1961.
36p; illus; pbk

218 Old Whitgiftian Rugby Football Club: part III, 1960-1976 / edited by Ian S. Hubbard. London: Wightman, 1977.
68p; illus; pbk

Old Windsorians

219 Old Windsorians RFC 1925-1975. Windsor: The Club, 1975.
27p; illus; pbk

Old Yardleians

220 Old Yardleians Rugby Football Club golden jubilee 1927-1977. West Midlands: The Club, 1977.
16p; illus; pbk

Oldham

221 Photographs, history record and blotter yearbook, 1925-26: (incorporating over half a century of rugby in Oldham 1873-1925) / Oldham Rugby League Football Club. Leeds: Bramley, 1925.

Coverage has been extended to cover 22 years of rugby union.

Orrell

222 Orrell RUFC golden jubilee 1927-1977. Orrell: The Club, 1978.
78p; illus; pbk

Orrell Colts, Wigan

223 Orrell Colts 1956-1990: an anniversary brochure. Orrell: Orrell Rugby Union Football Club, 1989.
38p; illus; pbk

Osterley

224 Osterley RFC founded 1922 / Tennent Eastman. Osterley: The Club, 1978.
145p; pbk

Oxford University

225 Oxford v. Cambridge: the story of the university rugby match / Howard Marshall in collaboration with J. P. Jordan. London: Clerke & Cockeran, 1951.
256p   BL: 7920.l.36
☞   Also listed at: B70

226 Centenary history of Oxford University Rugby Football Club / Ross McWhirter, Sir Andrew Noble. Oxford: The Club, 1969.
211p; illus   BL: YA.1993.c.60

A biographies section follows the history of Oxford RFC and the annual encounter with Cambridge University. The latter section is divided into: 'honorary treasurers; those who have represented Oxford versus Cambridge 1872-1968; war time Blues 1939-1945; international players who did not gain their Cap or Blue while in residence at Oxford'.

227 The Bowring story of the Varsity Match / David Frost. London: Macdonald, 1987.
256p; illus   ISBN: 0356120066
                                       BL: YK.1989.b.2035
☞   Also listed at: B71

Paignton

228 Cherry and white: a century of rugby at Paignton 1873-1973 / C. H. Patterson. Paignton: The Club, 1973.
72p; pbk

Painswick

229 Proud Painswick: the Cotswold rugby queen 1872-1972 / Nico Craven. Seascale: The author, 1973?
20p; pbk

Park House

230 Park House Football Club: rugby union centenary 1883-1983 / B. J. Harding and others.
60p; illus; pbk

Penzance & Newlyn

231 Newlyn, Penzance and the Pirates: an illustrated rugby history / Ben G. Batten. Penzance?: The Club, 1978.
107p; illus; pbk   ISBN: 0950630101

232 50 golden years: an illustrated history of the Penzance & Newlyn Rugby Football Club 1945-1995 / compiled and written by Phil Westren, Johnny Thomas and Harry Matthews. Penzance?: The Club, 1995.
160p; illus; pbk

Percy Park

233 Percy Park Rugby Football Club: a history 1872-1972. North Shields: The Club, 1972.
132p; illus; pbk   BL: YA.1988.a.17836

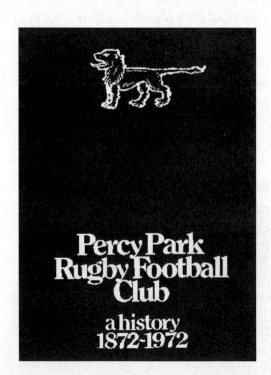

Plymouth Albion

234 Plymouth Albion RFC: centenary season 1876-1976.
     Plymouth: The Club, 1976.
     60p; illus; pbk

Plymouth Argaum

235 Plymouth Argaum: a history 1887-1987 / D. I. Dobell.
     Plymouth: The Club, 1987.
     77p; pbk

Pocklington

236 A century of Pocklington rugby 1885-1985 / P. G.
     Gilbank. Pocklington: Pocklington RFC, 1985.
     32p; illus; pbk

Portsmouth

237 Portsmouth Rugby Football Club 1899-1900 / Kevin
     Ricketts. Portsmouth?: Wessex Sports Agency, 1996.

Preston Grasshoppers

238 A short history of the Preston Grasshoppers Rugby
     Football Club / A. Marsden. Preston: The Club, 1969.
     36p; illus; pbk

Redruth

239 The centenary of Redruth Rugby Football Club
     1875-1975. Redruth: The Club, 1975.
     85p; illus; pbk

Richmond

240 Richmond Football Club: from 1861 to 1925 / E. J.
     Ereaut. London: Howett, 1925.
     250p; illus; index

241 Richmond Football Club: 1925 to 1961 / T. S. Rider and
     W. C. O. Munks. Richmond: The Club, 1961.
     172p   BL: YA.1994.a.1050

Rochdalians

242 Rochdalians RUFC golden jubilee 1930-80: souvenir
     brochure.

Rockliff

243 Rockliff Rugby Football Club: a hundred years of rugby
     football. Newcastle?: The Club, 1987.
     ix, 79p; illus; pbk

Rosslyn Park

244 Fifty years of Rosslyn Park / written and compiled by C.
     C. Hoyer Millar; with a foreword by W. J. A. Davies, a
     description of the club's services' fifteens during the war
     period by A. Podmore and some impressions of the
     club's annual dinners by Mark Waters, with 20
     illustrations. London: Wyman, 1929.
     284p; illus   BL: 07911.f.41

245 One hundred years of rugby football: a history of
     Rosslyn Park Football Club, 1879-1979 / edited by Rex
     Alston. London: The Club, 1979.
     60p; illus; pbk

Rugby Lions

246 The Rugby Lions: a history of the Rugby Football Club
     1873-1991 / Dennis Keen. Rugby?: The author, 1991.
     ix, 166p; illus; pbk   ISBN: 0951820400
                                       BL: YK.1993.a.14835

St. Day

247 St. Day Rugby Football Club: the first 100 years
     1894-1994 / Paul Newcombe. Redruth: The Club, 1995.
     60p; illus; pbk

St. Edward's College Old Boys

248 St. Edward's College OBRUFC: a brief history / Mark
     Seddon. Liverpool: The Club, 1991.
     12p; illus; pbk

     *Cover title: The blue and the gold (a brief history of St.
     Edward's Old Boys RUFC)*

St. Ives

249 Alright in the end!: the St. Ives Rugby Football Club
     1887-1987 / Peter Murrish. St. Ives: St. Ives Printing, 1987.
     88p; illus
           ISBN: 094838509X (cased) • 0948385065 (pbk)
                                       BL: YK.1988.b.3097

St. Just, Cornwall

250 St. Just Rugby Football Club silver jubilee 1967-92:
     souvenir programme. St. Just: The Club, 1992.
     29p; pbk

Salcombe

251 Salcombe RFC centenary year 1888-1988: centenary
     celebration magazine. Salcombe: The Club, 1987.
     32p; pbk

Sale

252   A century of rugby at Sale / editor, Monty Barak. 1962.
104p; illus

253   Sale Football Club: 125 years 1861-1986 commemorative brochure.
46p; illus; pbk

Saracens

254   Saracens Football Club (rugby football union): a brief outline of its first fifty years / O. R. G. Williams. London: The Club, 1926.
84p; illus; pbk

255   Saracens Football Club 1876-1976 / compiled by Haydn Perry. London: The Club, 1976.
64p; illus; pbk

Scunthorpe

256   Scunthorpe Rugby Union Football Club, 1929-1979 / Barry Holmes. Scunthorpe: The Club, 1979?
56p; illus; pbk

Selby

257   Selby Rugby Union Football Club jubilee brochure / edited by Kevin Pitchford and Bill Wharram. Selby: The Club, 1983.
52p; illus; pbk

Sheffield

258   Sheffield Rugby Union Football Club: the history / Andrew Reichwald. 1993.
155p; illus; pbk

Sheffield Tigers

259   Tigers: the first fifty years / Mike Joel. 1981.
32p; illus; pbk

Sheppey

260   Sheppey Rugby Football Club: centenary (1892-1992) / Neil Golding. Sheppey: The Club, 1992.
60p; illus; pbk

Sidcup

261   The history of Sidcup Football Club, 1883-1983 / Walter Bennet. Bromley: Media Bureau, 1983.
106p; illus; pbk

Sidmouth

262   Sidmouth Rugby Football Club centenary season 1983-84: a souvenir handbook including a history of the club. Sidmouth: The Club, 1983.
36p; illus; pbk

Skipton

263   Skipton Rugby Union Football Club: centenary brochure 1874-1974. Skipton: The Club, 1974.
17p; illus; pbk

Staines

264   1926-1976 Staines Rugby Football Club: 50th season / A. R. Partner and others. 1976.
23p; illus; pbk

Stoneygate

265   Stoneygate Football Club 1888-1988: a centenary history, recollections and reminiscences / compiled by Robert M. L. Kemp. Leicester: The Club, 1988.
220p; illus

Streatham-Croydon

266   Streatham-Croydon Rugby Football Club 1871-1971. Croydon: The Club, 1971.
36p; illus; pbk

Stroud

267   Stroud Rugby Football Club centenary 1873-1973 handbook. Stroud: The Club, 1973.
48p; illus; pbk

Sunderland

268   To Ashbrooke and beyond / prepared by E. Watts Moses in collaboration with D. G. Greig and others. Sunderland: 1963.
204p; illus, maps   BL: 7926.k.7
The history of the Sunderland Cricket and Rugby Football Club, 1802-1962.

Sutton

269   The Sutton Football Club (RFU): the first fifty years 1881-1931. London: Whittington Press, 1931.
65p

Taunton

270   Taunton RFC centenary 1875-1975. Taunton: The Club, 1975.
67p; illus; pbk
Cover title: 100 years of Taunton rugby

Thanet Wanderers

271   Thanet Wanderers Rugby Union Football Club: one hundred years old, a club history 1886-1986 / compiled by John Treharne. Kent: The Club, 1986.
35p; illus; pbk

Thornbury

272 ...The nite were dark & stormy: Thornbury Rugby Football Club 1963-1983 / Tom Gracey.
54p; illus; pbk

Tiverton

273 Tiverton Rugby Football Club: 125 years of rugby. Tiverton: The Club, 1993.
52p; illus; pbk

Totnes

274 Totnes Rugby Football Club 1889-1989 centenary. Totnes: The Club, 1989.
60p; illus; pbk

Trinity Guild

275 Blood, sweat & beers: Trinity Guild RFC from 1898 / John Collings. Kineton: Roundwood, 1972.
xvii, 172p; illus   ISBN: 0900093382
                                     BL: X.629/5118

   The author was the President of Trinity Guild Rugby Football Club. The foreword is by T. A. Kemp.

University College School Old Boys

276 UCS Old Boys Rugby Football Club centenary season 1992-3 / edited by Quentin Bozeat. Hampstead: The Club, 1992.
32p; illus; pbk

   The University College School OB RFC is in the London & South East – Middlesex Division.

Upper Clapton

277 A retrospect. Upper Clapton FC, 1929.
37p; pbk

Wakefield

278 Wakefield Rugby Football Club: golden jubilee 1901/02-1950/51. Wakefield: The Club, 1951?
24p; illus; pbk

Walcot Old Boys

279 Walcot Old Boys RFC centenary 1882-1982 / Mike Greensides. Walcot: The Club, 1983.
172p; illus; pbk   ISBN: 0950859206
                                     BL: X.622/22939

Warlingham

280 Warlingham Rugby Football Club 1922-1954. Warlingham, Surrey: Committee of the Warlingham RFC, 1954.
24p; index; pbk

Wasps

281 The centenary of Wasps Football Club 1867-1967 / edited by Jack Cox. Sudbury: The Club, 1967?
70p; illus; pbk

282 History of the club at the hundred & twentieth season. Sudbury: Wasps Football Club, 1987.
28p; pbk

283 Wasps in the Courage League 1987-1994 / John Gasson. 1994.
32p; pbk

   A statistical survey of the seven seasons prepared by the Wasps press officer and vice president.

Waterloo

284 Waterloo FC 1882-1982: an historical perspective centenary souvenir / Ian Hamilton Fazey. Liverpool: The Club, 1982.
37p; illus; pbk

West Hartlepool

285 West Hartlepool Rugby Football Club 1881-1981: centenary brochure / edited by Les Smith. Southwick: Inkerman, 1981?
92p; illus; pbk

286 West Hartlepool Rugby Football Club: the history up to 1981-2 / Steve Smith. West Hartlepool: The Club, 1982.
195p; illus

West Park

287 West Park RFC: the early years. 1983.
40p; pbk

Westcombe Park

288 The first fifty years: a history of Westcombe Park Rugby Football Club season 1904-05 to season 1953-54 / A. G. Offord. Orpington: The Orpington Press, 1953.
32p; illus; pbk

Weston-Super-Mare

289 Weston-Super-Mare Rugby Football Club centenary 1875 to 1975 / John Bailey.
71p; illus; pbk

Wigan

290 Official souvenir containing history, records and photographs 1879-1935. Wigan: Wigan Rugby Football League Club, 1935.

   Also covers the club's pre-league days 1879-95.

Wigan Old Boys

291   Wigan Old Boys Rugby Union Football Club jubilee bazaar. Wigan: The Club, 1935.

Wigton

292   A history of Wigton Rugby Union Football Club 1882/3-1982/3 / Walter Purdam and Michael Penrice; illustrated by Brian Campbell; foreword by Melvyn Bragg. 1982
47p; illus; pbk

Wilmslow

293   Wilmslow centenary 1884-1984 / edited by David Allaby.
52p; illus; pbk

Winscombe

294   1962-1987 the jubilee years: the history of the first 25 years of Winscombe Rugby Football Club / edited by Ernest Averis. Winscombe?: Clevedon Printing Company for The Club, 1987.
48p; illus; pbk

Worcester

295   Worcester Rugby Football Club: centenary history 1871-1971. Worcester: The Club, 1971.
24p; illus; pbk

Worthing

296   A history of Worthing Rugby Football Club 1920-1995 / Janet Rogers. Angmering: The Club, 1996.
120p; illus; pbk

York

297   York RUFC: golden jubilee 1928-78. York: The Club, 1978.
21p; illus; pbk

✻   'Wandering' Clubs

Barbarians

298   Barbarian records: a complete record of the Barbarian Football Club, 1890-1932 / compiled by E. De Lissa, with a foreword by O. L. Owen. London: Nicholson & Watson, 1933.
xxvi, 215p; illus   BL: X.449/909
☞   Subsequent ed. B299

299   Barbarian Football Club: history and complete record of results and teams, 1890-1955 / Emile De Lissa; brought up to date by A. Wemyss as editor, with historical foreword by O. L. Owen. London: Playfair Books, 1956.
275p; illus   BL: 7922.f.31
☞   Previous ed. B298

300   The Barbarians: the official history of the Barbarian Football Club / Nigel Starmer-Smith. London: Macdonald and Jane's, 1977.
240p; illus   ISBN: 0354085018
                         BL: X.629/11288

THE BARBARIANS
THE OFFICIAL HISTORY
OF THE BARBARIAN FOOTBALL CLUB

NIGEL STARMER-SMITH

MACDONALD AND JANE'S. LONDON

Luddites

301   Twenty one years of The Luddites RFC / K. T. Shaw. Yorkshire: The Club, 1994.
70p; illus; pbk
    A founding club playing schools such as Sedbergh. Originated in Huddersfield.

✳ *Schools*

Bishops Hereford School

302 Twenty five years of win and spin: to all who have worn the maroon and gold jersey, both in the good years and the not so good / compiled by J. F. Escott. Hereford: Bishops Hereford School, 1991.
49p; illus; pbk

> *Cover title: Twenty five years of win and spin: a silver jubilee of Bishops Hereford RFC*

Blundell's School

303 A hundred years of rugger at Blundell's / E. R. Crowe. Tiverton: Blundell's School, 1968.
71p; illus; pbk

Cheltenham College

304 Rugby football at Cheltenham College, 1844 to 1944/ E. Scott Skirving. Cheltenham: Darter's Bookshop, 1945.
39p; pbk

Colfe's School

305 The jubilee history / V. S. Anthony. London: Colfe's School Rugby Club, 1980?
19p; illus   BL: X.629/24942

The headmaster's report on the game which was first added to the school's curriculum in 1925.

Cornwall Public and Grammar Schools

306 Silver jubilee handbook: Cornwall Public and Grammar Schools Rugby Football Union. London: Pyramid, 1964.
31p   BL: X.449/209

Denstone College

307 Denstone rugby football, 1874-1947 / J. A. Adamson. Shrewsbury: Wilding, 1951.
121p; illus; index   BL: 7920.l.32

Durham School

308 Durham School RFC 1850-1975: souvenir brochure. Durham: Thomas Reed, 1975.
47p; illus; pbk

Eastbourne College

309 Eastbourne College rugby football 1900-1910 / Edward Carleton Arnold. Eastbourne: T. R. Beckett, 1910.
61p; illus   BL: 7919.b.32

King Henry VIII School

310 King Henry VIII RFC 1881-1981 / edited by G. P. C. Courtois. Coventry: The Club, 1981.
86p; illus; pbk

King's College School

311 Rugby football at King's College School 1864-1963 / D. G. Dalziel. Wimbledon: The School, 1963.
64p; pbk

Leicestershire Schools

312 Leicestershire Schools Rugby Union: centenary 1894-1994. Leicester?: 1994.
48p; illus; pbk

The main body of the history is given on pages 6-19. Three brief articles complete the history.

Queen Elizabeth Grammar School Wakefield

313 Queen Elizabeth Grammar School Wakefield: a history of school rugby, 1874-1987. Wakefield: The School, 1988.

Royal Grammar School, Newcastle upon Tyne

314 Royal Grammar School Newcastle upon Tyne Rugby Football Club 1877-1977 / edited by John Elders. Newcastle upon Tyne: The Club, 1977.
31p; illus; pbk

In a number of cases the form of football played was peculiar to the school and though rugby football was well on the way to becoming the accepted public school game in the 1850s, a number of schools, most notably Eton, Harrow, Winchester, Charterhouse and Westminster, preferred to retain their traditional games. For an account of the football played at these schools and a summary of the rules, see the series of articles by John D. Cartwright, and the resulting correspondence, in The Field, 487 (14 November 1863); 499 (21 November); 523 (28 November). A number of school histories chronicle the development of the football game through the games played. For example, A register of St. John's School, Leatherhead 1852-1937 (Croydon: Roffey & Clark, 1938) notes that in 1885 the school changed over from rugby to association football. A history of Shrewsbury School, 1552-1952 (Oxford: Basil Blackwell, 1952) describes the playing of douling or dowling, a game peculiar to the school and, later the association game. For further reading see The English public school by Vivian Ogilvie (London: Batsford, 1957) and Rise of the public schools by T. W. Bamford (London: Nelson, 1967).

Rugby School

315 Recollections of Rugby / 'An Old Rugbeian' (Charles
Henry Newmarch). London: Hamilton & Adams, 1848.
180p

BL: 732.a.9

Has a chapter devoted to 'Football' on pages 130-4.

316 The book of Rugby School: its history and its daily life.
Rugby: Privately printed, 1856.
252p; illus

BL: 8364.h.6

Although his name does not appear on the title page
or cover, the book was edited by Edward M. Goulburn.
E. W. Benson, Archbishop of Canterbury, contributed
the first three chapters and W. D. Arnold contributed
the chapter on football (pp. 147-69). The book was
not made available for sale.

317 Football records of Rugby School, 1823-1929 / collected
for the Old Rugbeian Society by a sub-committee
composed of Sir Alexander Gibb, K. McL. Marshall, F.
T. Dallin, C. P. Allen, H. C. Bradby, H. J. Kittermaster,
E. Satterthwaite, A. D. Stoop. Rugby: George Over,
1930.
119p; illus

BL: 7915.f.36

The rules of football as played at Rugby School,
September 1846, with revisions of 16th September
1847, are reproduced. There are also reports of the
first 'foreign' matches played by the school. The first
such game was against a team comprising Old
Rugbeians and residents in or near Rugby. The school
lost the match.

318 From Webb Ellis to World Cup: illustrations and
cuttings mainly of Rugby School / compiled and written
by David Ray. Rugby: Rugby School, 1991.
24p; illus

Written by the master in charge of football at Rugby
School. The text is secondary to the photographs
which chronicle the game at the school from the
middle of the eighteenth century through to the 1991
World Cup.

Sedbergh School

319 Sedbergh School Football Club: the record 1978-1983.
Sedbergh: The School, 1984.
24p; illus; pbk

Includes an outline of the club's tour to British
Columbia in 1984.

Sevenoaks School

320 From water into wine: a short history of Sevenoaks
School Rugby Football Club / edited by Mike Williams.
Sevenoaks: The School, 1986.
201p; illus; pbk

BL: YA.1994.b.7660

A full history of the school team interspersed with
contributions from guest writers and newspaper
reports.

Sherborne School

321 Rugby football at Sherborne School / Robert Hands.
Sherborne: The School, 1991.
192p; illus; index

Bibliography: p187

Warwick School

322 The development of the game of rugby football at
Warwick School over the past one hundred years, placed
within the context of the general history of the school /
compiled and edited by Martin Green. Warwick:
Warwick School, 1984.
95p; illus; pbk

From Water into Wine .....

**A Short History of Sevenoaks School
Rugby Football Club**

Edited by Mike Williams

✽ Regional Studies

323 Great rugger clubs / J. B. G. Thomas. London: Stanley
Paul, 1962.
206p; illus

BL: X.449/1196

The English clubs covered are: Barbarians, Bedford,
Birkenhead Park, Blackheath, Bristol, Cambridge
University, Coventry, Gloucester, Guy's Hospital,
Harlequins, Headingley, Leicester, Moseley,
Northampton, Old Merchant Taylors, Old Millhillians,
Oxford University, Plymouth Albion, Redruth,
Richmond, Rosslyn Park, Sale, Wasps, and Waterloo.

☞ Also listed at: B421, B494, B635

Avon

324   Combination: a review of the life and times of the Bristol
       Rugby Combination in memory of Charlie Humby /
       Derek Robinson. Bristol: Bristol & District Rugby
       Football Combination, 1986.
       96p; pbk   ISBN: 0951154508

Berkshire

325   Berkshire County Rugby Football Union 1931-1981:
       golden jubilee brochure / Keith D. Hellewell. Reading?:
       The Union, 1980.
       21p; illus; pbk

Cheshire

326   Rugby union in Lancashire and Cheshire / edited by
       Walter Bernard Croxford. Liverpool: Littlebury, 1952.
       127p; illus   BL: 7920.b.73
       ☞   Also listed at: B345

327   The history of Cheshire Rugby Football Union
       1876-1976. Cheshire: The Union, 1976.
       54p; illus; pbk

Cornwall

328   Rugby in the Duchy: Cornwall Rugby Football Union /
       edited by W. J. Robbins. Camborne: The Union, 1934.
       80p; illus; pbk

            Cover title: Cornwall Rugby Football Union jubilee,
            1884-1934: rugby in the Duchy
                      BL: Mic.A.10413(17) (microfilm copy)

329   1884-1959 rugby in the Duchy (rugby heritage): an
       official history of the game in Cornwall / Kenneth
       Pelmear. Camborne?: Cornwall RFU, 1960.
       x, 118p; illus; pbk

330   The first hundred years: the story of rugby football in
       Cornwall / Tom Salmon. Illogan: Cornwall RFU, 1983.
       vi, 150p; illus
                ISBN: 0946664005 (cased) • 0946664013 (pbk)
                                            BL: X.800/37325

331   Cornwall rugby champions / Colin Gregory. London:
       Transworld, 1991.
       103p; illus; pbk   ISBN: 1852251662

332   Cornwall Rugby Football Union: the path to the final
       1990-1991. Cornwall Rugby Football Union, 1991.
       37p; pbk

333   Tales of Twickenham / written and researched by Jerry
       Clarke and Terry Harry. Redruth: The authors, 1991.
       146p; illus

        'Reminiscences of Cornish people's day at Twickenham
        when Cornwall won the championship.'

334   Cornwall's rugby challenge: the glory years: Cornwall's
       county championship challenge from 1987 to 1994 /
       collated & published by Carole Monckton; all
       photographs by Phil Monckton. Penzance: The author,
       1994.
       88p; illus; pbk   ISBN: 0952498804
                                            BL: YK.1995.b.7823

Cumbria

335   South Cumbria Rugby Union centenary 1886-1986.
       Cumbria: The Union, 1986.
       27p; illus; pbk

        Previously known as Westmorland County Football
        Club.

Devon

336   The story of the Devon Rugby Football Union / F. A.
       Davey. 1964.
       208p; illus; pbk

Durham

337   Durham County Rugby Union: sixty years records of the
       County fifteen, 1876-1936 (including four unofficial
       matches played prior to the establishment of the Union,
       October 10th 1876) / C. Berkeley Cowell and E. Watts
       Moses. Newcastle upon Tyne: The Union, 1936.
       x, 244p; illus   BL: 07908.ff.25

338   Durham County Rugby Union: records of the county
       fifteen 1936-76 constituting a supplement to 'Sixty years
       records 1876-1936' published in 1936 / edited by W. J.
       R. Scott.
       110p; illus; pbk

East Midlands

339   Gleanings from the century 1897-1997 / P. Eads.
       Bedford?: East Midlands Rugby Union, 1997.
       160p; illus

Eastern Counties

340   The growth of a sporting venture: a history of the
       Eastern Counties Rugby Union / O. L. Owen.
       Dagenham: The Union, 1952.
       viii, 109p; illus   BL: 7920.b.84

341   A sporting venture continues / J. N. O'Neill. Eastern
       Counties RU, 1990.
       iv, 129p; illus; pbk

            Cover title: Eastern Counties Rugby Union 1890-1990: a
            sporting venture continues

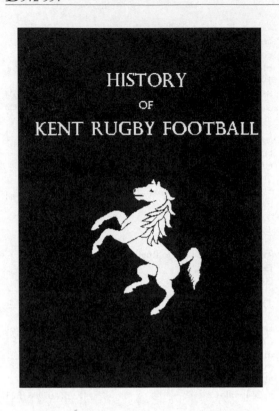

HISTORY
OF
KENT RUGBY FOOTBALL

Jersey

342 The Jersey Rugby Football Club: the story of rugby in Jersey / Gordon Young with Keith Goddard. Trinity, Jersey: Pedberry Press, 1992.
128p

Kent

343 History of Kent rugby football / John Paul Jordan. London: Purnell, 1949.
128p; illus   BL: X.629/24782

344 Kent County rugby football centenary 1880-1980. Kent: The Union, 1980.
53p; illus; pbk

Lancashire

345 Rugby union in Lancashire and Cheshire / edited by Walter Bernard Croxford. Liverpool: Littlebury, 1952.
127p; illus   BL: 7920.b.73
☞ Also listed at: B326

346 The history of rugby union in the Orrell district of Lancashire / D. L. Williams. University of Manchester, 1975. *Dissertation.*

347 Lancashire County Rugby Football Union centenary 1881-1981. Lancashire: The Union, 1981.
75p; illus; pbk

Leicestershire

348 Leicestershire Rugby Union: one hundred years of rugby development in the county 1887-1987 / S. I. 'Van' Hopkins. Leicester: The Union, 1986.
xl, 429p; illus; pbk   BL: YK.1989.b.2664

London

349 The London Society of Rugby Football Union Referees: the first one hundred years / edited by Tim Titheridge. London: The Society, 1988.
183p; illus

Middlesex

350 Middlesex County Rugby Football Union 1879-1979 / edited by E. V. Barnes. Castle Cary: Castle Cary Press, 1979.
103p; illus; pbk

> Cover title: MCRFU 1879-1979

Midlands

351 Midland rugby football / Gerald Holmes; foreword by Ivor Preece. Worcester: Worcester Press, 1950.
103p; illus

> Written by the Chief Librarian of the Birmingham Post and Mail. As well as the history of rugby in the Midlands there are brief chapters on twelve clubs in the area.

North Midlands

352 North Midlands rugby 1920-1970: a jubilee history of the North Midlands Football Union / Barry Bowker. 1970?
121p; illus; pbk

Northumberland

353 Northumberland Rugby Union centenary match souvenir programme and history 1880-1980: Northumberland v Derek Morgan's International XV, Wednesday October 1st 1980. The Union, 1980.
76p; illus   BL: X:629/25784

Oxfordshire

354 Oxford Rugby Football Union: golden jubilee 1932-1982. Oxfordshire: The Union, 1982.
40p; illus; pbk

Somerset

355   Somerset rugby football: a record of past seasons, with special reference to 1893-4 / George A. Roberts. Bath: Chronicle Office, 1894.
66p   BL: Mic.A.12569(16) (microfilm copy)

356   Seventy years of Somerset rugby 1875-1945. Somerset: The Union, 1945.
56p; illus; pbk

357   Somerset County Rugby Football Union Referees Society centenary 1889-1989: souvenir brochure. Taunton?: The Society, 1989.
23p; pbk

Surrey

358   Surrey County Rugby Football Union: records of the first sixty years, 1879-1939 / compiled by H. E. Steed and A. J. Trollope. London: Clowes, 1939.
56p; illus   BL: 7923.p.8

359   Surrey rugby: 100 years / edited by John Reed. London: Regency Press for the Surrey County Rugby Football Union, 1978.
160p; illus   BL: X.629/12124

Sussex

360   The Sussex County Rugby Football Union 1883-1983: one hundred years of Sussex rugby. Sussex: The Union, 1983.
48p; illus; pbk

Yorkshire

361   Fifty years' recollections of rugby football in Huddersfield and Yorkshire / W. Cosgrove. 1930?
24p; pbk

362   Yorkshire Rugby Union centenary 1869-1969 / edited by Philip Gaunt. Leeds?: The Union, 1970.
40p; illus   BL: X.611/5058

363   The origin and development of football in Leeds: a short study / compiled by Mike Green. Leeds: The author, 1992.
40p; illus, maps; pbk

'This short study takes the reader through from the first Leeds citizens meeting to play football on Woodhouse Moor in 1864 to the establishment of the leading Leeds clubs in the two codes of football that developed. This was almost completed by 1905.'

Scotland

The National Register of Archives (Scotland) was set up in 1946 to compile a record of papers of historical interest held in private hands in Scotland. The principal aim of the Register is 'to locate such papers, to offer advice on their care and to seek the owners' permission to allow information about their collections to be made available to researchers'. The NRA(S) is conducting a survey of the older rugby clubs in Scotland for information about their surviving records, e.g. minutes, annual reports, financial records, correspondence, membership records, fixture cards, match programmes, and photographs. These records are retained by the clubs but information about their existence is made available through the Register. To date the survey has covered Ardrossan Academicals, Buchan, Corstorphine, Dundee High School Former Pupils, Dunfermline, Duns, Edinburgh Northern, Gala, Garnock, Glasgow Academicals, Hamilton Academicals, Hawick PSA, Hawick Trades, Jed-Forest, Kelso, Lasswade, Lismore, Livingston, Madras College Former Pupils, Musselburgh, Peebles, Ross-Sutherland, Scottish Rugby Union, and Watsonians.

Aberdeenshire

364   Aberdeenshire Rugby Football Club 1875-1975. Aberdeen: The Club, 1975.
61p; illus; pbk

Aboyne

365   'Tell my wife I tried': Aboyne Rugby Club, the first ten years / compiled by Philip Strachan. Aboyne: The Club, 1987.
74p; illus; pbk

Ardrossan Academicals

366   Ardrossan Academicals Rugby Football Club 70th anniversary 1991-1992 / Leslie Callan. Ardrossan: The Club, 1991.
27p

Ayr

367   Pink and black: a history of Ayr Rugby Football Club / Ian Hay. Ayr: The Club, 1997.
195p; illus, maps; pbk   ISBN: 0907526721

Boroughmuir

368   Seventy-five years: a history of Boroughmuir Rugby
Football Club / Ian Nicholson. Edinburgh: The Club,
1996.
xi, 260p; illus   BL: YK.1997.b.2074

Clarkston

369   Making a mark: the story of Clarkston RFC, 1937-1977 /
G. A. McCready. Glasgow: The Club, 1977.
12, 140p; illus; pbk   BL: X.619/19532

Dundee High School Former Pupils

370   Dundee High School Former Pupils' Rugby Football
Club 1880-1980: centenary souvenir / D. L. Coutts.
Dundee: The Club, 1980.
71p; illus; pbk

   Cover title: DHSFP RFC centenary souvenir 1880-1980

Dunfermline

371   Dunfermline Rugby Football Club 1896-1986: a brief
history / William Keegan. Dunfermline: The Club, 1987.
80p; 1 coat of arms; pbk   BL: YK.1988.a.4715

Edinburgh Academicals

372   The Edinburgh Academical Football Club centenary
history: a history of the club and of football at the
Edinburgh Academy. Edinburgh: The Club, 1958.
165p; illus   BL: 7924.b.38

   A history of the club since the 1850s. Includes lists
   of office-bearers, internationals, 'blues', and inter-
   service players. About 40 pages are taken up with
   sponsors' advertising.

Edinburgh Borderers

373   Edinburgh Borderers Rugby Football Club seventy-fifth
anniversary, 1921-1996: the saga of a club / Adam
Robson. Edinburgh: The Club Committee, 1996.
xxix, 325p; illus   ISBN: 0952917505

Edinburgh Northern

374   Edinburgh Northern Rugby Football Club golden jubilee
1920-1970 / Tom Henderson. Edinburgh: The Club,
1970.
11p; illus; pbk

375   Edinburgh Northern Rugby Football Club: seventy-fifth
anniversary 1920-95. Edinburgh: The Club, 1995?
24p; illus; pbk

Edinburgh University Athletic Club

376   The story of Edinburgh University Athletic Club /
edited by C. M. Usher; foreword by Sir Edward
Appleton. Edinburgh: The Club, 1966.
xi, 439p; illus

   The Athletic Club controls all sports at Edinburgh
   University and this book marks its centenary. The
   chapter on rugby gives a full overview of the early days of
   Scottish rugby with original information on the many
   international players who attended the university.

Edinburgh Wanderers

377   Edinburgh Wanderers Football Club centenary
1868-1968. Edinburgh: The Club, 1968.
22p; illus; pbk

Fettesian-Lorettonians

378   The Fettesian-Lorettonian Club 1881-1931. Edinburgh:
The Club, 1931.
100p; illus

   This survey gives a general overview of the club during
   this period with details of the rugby football and
   cricket tours, lists of international rugby players and
   'blues', and results tables.

Gala

379   Gala Rugby Football Club / edited by Stuart Barton.
Gala: The Club, 1975.
183p; illus; pbk

   Cover title: The Gala story: 100 years 1875-1975

Glasgow Academicals

380   The Glasgow Academy: the first hundred years.
Glasgow: Blackie for the Glasgow Academy, 1946.
xvi, 277p; illus

   Includes a history of the Glasgow Academical Club by
   Tennant Sloan (pages 160-83), a list of office-
   bearers, a record of the first XV, and a list of rugby
   international players (pages 183-8).

381   Glasgow Academical Club: centenary volume
1866-1966. Glasgow: Blackie for the Club, 1966.
ix, 97p; illus

   Includes segments on: football, the early days; and,
   1900 to date.

Glasgow High School Former Pupils

382   Chocolate and gold: 100 years of rugby 1884-1984 /
Archie Jarvie. Glasgow: Glasgow High-Kelvinside
Rugby Football Club, 1984.
288p; illus

   The history of the club from its foundation in 1884
   and its amalgamation with Kelvinside Academicals in
   1982. Includes biographies of the international players.

Glasgow University

383   The history of Glasgow University Football Club
       1877-1995 / Donald Fergusson.

Glasgow University Athletic Club

384   Glasgow University Athletic Club: the story of the first
       hundred years / R. O. MacKenna. Glasgow: The Club in
       commemoration of the centenary of its foundation, 1981.
       128p; illus, 1 map; pbk   ISBN: 0852611706
                                                  BL: X.629/16850

Greenock Wanderers

385   Greenock Wanderers: the first hundred years 1873-1973
       / J. L. M. Forster. Scotland: The author, 1974?
       305p; illus   BL: X.622/13270

Haddington

386   The history of Haddington Rugby Football Club
       1911-1986 / F. D. Burnet and J. E. Jones. Haddington:
       The Club, 1986.
       72p; illus; pbk

Hawick

387   Fifty years football in Hawick 1873-1923. Hawick: James
       Edgar, 1923.
       111p; illus; pbk

388   The history of Hawick RFC 1873-1956 / Tom Paterson.
       Hawick: Scott & Paterson, 1956.
       120p; illus; pbk

389   100 years of Hawick rugby / edited by Bill McLaren.
       Hawick: The Club, 1972.
       112p; illus; pbk

Hawick Linden

390   Roots and branches 75 years: a history of Hawick Linden
       RFC. Hawick: The Club, 1996.
       64p; illus; pbk

Hawick PSA

391   Memories of a great club: PSA RFC 1919-1994, 75th
       anniversary brochure. Hawick: The Club, 1994.
       53p; illus; pbk

Hawick YM

392   'Once a redskin': 75th anniversary 1920-1995 Hawick
       YM RFC. Hawick: The Club, 1994.
       54p; illus; pbk

Heriot's School Former Pupils

393   Heriot rugby: (fifty years) / D. M. Clark. Edinburgh:
       George Heriot's Hospital School FP Rugby Club, 1948.
       133p; illus; pbk   BL: X.808/39046
         Includes full match reports for the club.

394   Heriot's!: a centenary history of George Heriot's School
       Former Pupils' Rugby Club / Douglas Middleton.
       Edinburgh: Sportsprint Publishing, 1990.
       x, 234p; illus; index

GREENOCK WANDERERS

THE FIRST HUNDRED YEARS

1873 – 1973

by

J. L. M. FORSTER

Holy Cross

395   A history of Holy Cross RFC to commemorate the
       diamond jubilee 1926-1986 / G. R. Whale. Edinburgh:
       The Club, 1986.
       28p; illus; pbk

Jed-Forest

396   Jed-Forest Rugby Football Club: centenary brochure /
       edited by Iain Mackenzie. Jedburgh: The Club, 1984.
       88p; illus; pbk
         Cover title: A hundred years at Riverside

Kelso

397 Kelso Rugby Football Club: (the Black and Whites 1876-1976). Kelso: The Club, 1976?
142p; illus; pbk

> *Cover title: A hundred years in 'black and white'*
> BL: X:629/23481

Kelso Harlequins

398 A history of the Kelso Harlequins to mark the fifty years of Kelso Harlequins / compiled by Arthur Hastie and Bill Forbes. Kelso: The Club, 1983.
11p; illus; pbk

> *Cover title: Kelso Harlequins Rugby Football Club 1982-1983: 50 years*

Kilmarnock

399 'More than a game': Kilmarnock Rugby Football Club a history, 1868-1973 / J. F. T. Thomson. Kilmarnock: The Club, 1973.
xx, 51p; illus; pbk

Kirkcaldy

400 Passes past and present: the centenary booklet of Kirkcaldy Rugby Football Club 1873-1973 / edited by G. H. Ballantyne and J. S. Methven. Kirkcaldy: The Club, 1973.
43p; illus; pbk

401 Kirkcaldy 88-89: up and away / J. S. Methven. Kirkcaldy: Kirkcaldy RFC, 1989.
26p; illus; pbk

Langholm

402 Langholm RFC 1871-1971 / Walter Bell. Langholm: The Club, 1971.
39p; illus; pbk

Linlithgow

403 The history of Linlithgow Rugby Club: 125 years of the Reds / Bruce A. Jamieson. Linlithgow: The Club, 1995.
164p; illus; pbk

> *Cover title: 'The Reds', Linlithgow Rugby Club: a history of Linlithgow Rugby Football Club 1870-1995*

Livingston

404 Livingston Rugby Football Club: Almond Park, twenty one years' history 1968-1989 / John P. Stewart and others. Livingston: The Club, 1989.
42p; illus; pbk

405 Livingston Rugby Football Club: silver jubilee 1968-1993 / J. P. Stewart. Livingston: The Club, 1993.
ii, 38p; illus; pbk

London Scottish

406 The first 100: a history of the London Scottish Football Club / Frank Morris. Richmond, Surrey: The Club, 1977.
199p; illus

Madras College Former Pupils

407 Golf isn't the only game you know: the story of Madras College Former Pupils' Rugby Football Club / Harry Smith. St Andrews: The Club, 1994.
131p; illus; pbk

Melrose

408 The story of the Melrose Rugby Football Club 1877-1952: 75th anniversary brochure / J. R. Frater. Melrose: The Club, 1952.
vii, 32p; illus; pbk

409 Melrose Rugby Football Club 1877-1977 / John Gilbert. Melrose: The Club, 1976.
x, 139p; illus; pbk

North Berwick

410 North Berwick RFC silver jubilee 1952-1977. Berwick: The Club, 1977.

411 North Berwick Rugby Football Club: the first forty years 1952-1992 / A. G. Seaton. North Berwick: The Club, 1992.
66p; illus; pbk

Panmure

412 Panmure Rugby Football Club 1880-1980. Panmure: The Club, 1980.
10p; illus; pbk

St Boswells

413 St Boswells Rugby Football Club: seventieth anniversary 1926-1996. St Boswells: The Club, 1997?
42p; pbk

Selkirk

414 Fifty years at Philiphaugh 1907-1957. Selkirk: Selkirk RFC, 1957.
36p; illus; pbk

Selkirk Youth

415 Selkirk Youth Rugby Club 75th anniversary: brief history 1921-1996. Selkirk: The Club?, 1996.
66p; illus; pbk

Stewart's College Former Pupils

416 The 'Daniels': a history of Stewart's College (FP) Football Club 1885-1973 / R. L. Sharp. Edinburgh: The Club, 1973.
54p

Walkerburn

417 Walkerburn Rugby Football Club centenary 1884-1984 official brochure / edited by John Smail. Walkerburn: The Club, 1984.
55p; illus; pbk

Watsonians

418 Watsonian Football Club centenary 1875-1975 / compiled by G. F. Anderson and others. Edinburgh: The Club, 1975.
88p; illus; pbk

West of Scotland

419 West of Scotland Football Club 1865-1965 / C. D. Stuart. Glasgow: The Club, 1965.
vi, 117p; illus

✲ *Schools*

Royal High School

420 Royal High School Rugby Football Club centenary 1868-1968 / compiled by R. Ironside and A. M. C. Thorburn. Edinburgh: The Club, 1968.
72p; illus; pbk

✲ *Regional Studies*

421 Great rugger clubs / J. B. G. Thomas. London: Stanley Paul, 1962.
206p; illus BL: X.449/1196

The Scottish clubs covered are: Aberdeen University, Edinburgh Academicals, Gala, Glasgow Academicals, Glasgow HS FP, George Heriot's FP, Hawick, Kelso, Langholm, London Scottish, Melrose, The Merchistonians FC, Royal HS FP, St. Andrew's University, Watsonians, The West of Scotland.

☞ Also listed at: B323, B494, B635

Borders

422 Border rugby recollections / 'Poynder' (W. D. Thomson). Kelso: Chronicle Printing Works, 1951.
64p

423 Rummle them up!: the Border rugby story / Walter Thomson; foreword by Bill McLaren. Edinburgh: Sportsprint, 1989.
vii, 87p; illus; index ISBN: 0859762874
BL: YK.1990.b.8952

The author is perhaps better known as 'Fly Half' in his role as match reporter for the *Sunday Post*.

Scottish Midlands

424 Midlands first and latest: a centenary year history of rugby in the Scottish Midlands / John Methven. Scotland: H. B. Rutherford, 1989.
xii, 99p; illus

Also includes the biographies of 27 players who were capped for Scotland.

Ireland

Ards

425 Ards Rugby Club 1928-78: the first fifty years, a commemorative jubilee magazine / edited by David Coffey. Newtownards: The Club, 1978.
72p; illus; pbk

Armagh

426 Try and try again: a centenary history of the City of Armagh Rugby Football Club / compiled by Seamus S. Duffy. Armagh: The Club, 1976.
76p; illus; pbk

Athlone

427 Athlone RFC 1951-1976. Athlone: The Club, 1976.
87p; illus; pbk

Athy

428 Athy Rugby Football Club 1880-1980. Athy: The Club, 1980.
67p; illus; pbk

Ballinasloe

429 Ballinasloe RFC 1875-1975: centenary souvenir programme / Tony D'Arcy. Ballinasloe: The Club, 1975.
32p; illus; pbk

Ballyclare

430 Ballyclare Rugby Football Club official opening of Clareview clubhouse: twenty-fifth anniversary of Ballyclare RFC, 1945/50-1974/75 / edited by E. W. Laird. Ballyclare: The Club, 1975.
45p; illus; pbk
   Contains the history of the club.

Ballymena

431 Ballymena Rugby Football Club centenary 1887-1987 / edited by George Burton. Ballymena: The Club, 1987.
xiv, 190p; illus; pbk

Ballymoney

432 Ballymoney RFC 21 anniversary 1952-1973. Ballymoney: The Club, 1973.
106p; illus; pbk

Bandon

433 Bandon Rugby Football Club, 1882-1982: a club history / John Merwick. Bandon: The Club, 1982.
104p; illus; pbk

Bangor

434 Bangor Rugby Football Club centenary 1885-1985 / Frank Humphreys and others. Bangor: The Club, 1985.
104p; illus; pbk

Bective Rangers

435 Bective Rangers Football Club: 75th anniversary 1881-1956. Blackrock: The Club, 1956.
67p; illus; pbk   BL: 7923.b.17

436 Bective Rangers Football Club centenary year 1981-1982. Dublin: The Club, 1981.
142p; illus; pbk

Blackrock College

437 Blackrock College RFC 1882/83-1982/83: the official history / Sean Diffley. Dublin: The Club, 1982.
96p; illus

Carrickfergus

438 Carrickfergus RFC: souvenir centenary programme. Carrickfergus: Universal Publishing, 1971.
24p; illus; pbk
   This is in effect a history of the club.

Clanwilliam

439 Clanwilliam Football Club 1879-1979: centenary history / Denis G. Marnane. Tipperary: The Club, 1979.
96p; illus; pbk

Clontarf

440 Clontarf Football Club centenary 1876-1976. Clontarf: The Club, 1976.
118p; illus; pbk

Cobh Pirates

441 Skull and cross-bones: the Cobh rugby story / John M. Kidney. Cobh: The author, 1990.
iii,187p; illus; pbk
   Cover title: A Cobh Pirates centenary publication

Coleraine

442 Coleraine Football Club: a history / Grant Cameron. Coleraine: D. and R. Promotions, 1988.
150p

Collegians

443 Collegians Rugby Football Club 1890-1990 / Pierre Paul Fry. Belfast: The Club, 1989.
iv, 144p; illus

Corinthians

444 Corinthians Rugby Football Club 1932-33 1981-82: 50 years a growin'. Dublin: Carlton, 1982.
64p; illus

Cork Constitution

445 100 years of Cork Constitution Football Club / Edmund Van Esbeck. Cork: The Club, 1993.
344p; illus

County Carlow

446 County Carlow Football Club rugby history 1873-1977 / edited by Thomas J. O'Brien. Carlow: The Club, 1977.
204p; illus; index

Delvin

447 Delvin Rugby Football Club history 1953-1993. Delvin: The Club, 1993.
104p; illus; pbk
   The club is situated near Drogheda.

Derry

448   City of Derry Rugby Football Club: centenary
1881-1981: a club history / edited by David Orr.
Londonderry: The Club, 1981.
108p; illus; pbk

Donaghadee

449   Donaghadee Rugby Football Club centenary 1885-1985.
Donaghadee: The Club, 1985.
43p; illus; pbk

Drogheda

450   Drogheda Rugby Football Club: 1880-1980 centenary
programme. Drogheda: The Club, 1980.
40p; illus; pbk

Dublin University

451   Dublin University Football Club 1854-1954. Dublin:
Montford Publications on behalf of the Committee of
Dublin University Football Club, 1954.
93p; illus; pbk

452   Dublin University Football Club 1866-1972: a pictorial
history. Dublin: The Club, 1973.
200p; illus

Dundalk

453   Dundalk Rugby Football Club: centenary year 1877-1977
/ Dermot Lavery. Dundalk: The Club, 1977.
44p; illus; pbk

Dungannon

454   Dungannon Football Club centenary 1873-1973: a club
history / compiled by J. E. Davidson. Dungannon: The
Club, 1973.
93p; illus; pbk

Ennis

455   Ennis Rugby Club / edited by Colm Walsh. Dublin:
Carlton, 1979?
40p; illus; pbk

Galway Corinthians

456   Galway Corinthians Rugby Football Club: 1977-78
yearbook / compiled by Jim Lydon. Dublin: Tara for the
Club, 1978.
60p; illus; pbk
   A history of the club.

Garryowen

457   Club history: Garryowen FC 1884-1984 / Charles
Mulqueen. Limerick: The Club, 1984.
116p; illus; pbk

Greystones

458   Greystones Rugby Football Club: record of half a
century / edited by Michael Flannery. Dublin: The Club,
1987.
164p; illus

Grosvenor

459   Grosvenor club rugby & hockey silver jubilee. Belfast:
The Club, 1979.
46p; illus; pbk

Guinness

460   Guinness Rugby Football Club 1942-1992: 50th
anniversary souvenir book. Dublin: The Club, 1992
48p; illus; pbk

Highfield

461   Fifty years of rugby: Highfield RFC 1930-1980 / edited
by Dermot Russell. Cork: Highfield RFC, 1980.
107p; illus; pbk

Instonians

462   Instonians 1919-1969: 50 years of fun and games / W.
Brownlow-White. Belfast: Instonians Rugby Club, 1969.
58p

Kinsale

463   Kinsale Rugby Football Club. Kinsale: The Club, 1985.
48p; illus; pbk

Lansdowne

464   The history of Lansdowne Football Club / compiled
and edited by Michael J. Connor. Dublin: Montford
Publications, 1951.
64p; illus; pbk

465   Lansdowne Football Club centenary 1872-1972: a club
history / edited by Garry Redmond. Dublin: The Club,
1972.
131p; illus; pbk

Malone

466   One hundred years of Malone RFC / compiled and
edited by Tom Russell. Belfast: The Club, 1992.
127p; illus; pbk

Monkstown

467   Monkstown Football Club: 1883-1983 / Edmund Van Esbeck. Monkstown, Co. Dublin: The Club, 1984?
78p; illus

Navan

468   Navan Rugby Football Club: programme to commemorate the formal opening of the extension to the pavilion by J. W. S. Irwin, President of the Irish Rugby Football Union on Sunday 21st December 1969. Armagh?: The Club, 1969
24p; illus; pbk

    Includes a brief two page history of the club.

Nenagh Ormond

469   Nenagh Ormond's century 1884-1984: a rugby history / Donal A. Murphy. Nenagh: Relay in association with Nenagh Ormond Rugby Football Club, 1984.
162p; illus; pbk   ISBN: 0946327033
                     BL: X.622/24002

North of Ireland

470   The North of Ireland Cricket & Football Club 1859-1959 / compiled by P. P. Fry. Belfast: Thos. Brough, Cox & Dunn, 1959.
137p; illus; pbk

Old Belvedere

471   Old Belvedere Rugby Football Club silver jubilee, 1930-1955. Dublin: The Club, 1955.
32p; illus; pbk

472   Old Belvedere Rugby Football Club: 1930-1980 golden jubilee. Dublin: The Club, 1980.
48p; illus

473   Ten out of fifty: a chronicle of Old Belvedere Rugby Football Club 1930-1980 / Edmund Van Esbeck. Dublin: The Club, 1980.
x, 94p; illus

Old Wesley

474   Old Wesley RFC, 1892-1954. Dublin: The Club, 1954.
72p; illus

475   Old Wesley Rugby Football Club: a centenary history / Edmund Van Esbeck. Dublin: The Club, 1991.
126p; illus; pbk

Portadown

476   Rugby football in Portadown, 1879-1979 / D. J. Gilpin. Portadown: The Club, 1981.
112p; illus; pbk

Nenagh Ormond's Century

1884   **1984**

A Rugby History

Donal A. Murphy

St. Mary's College

477   St. Mary's College RFC. Dublin: The Club, 1987?
19p; illus; pbk

Seapoint

478   A commemorative chronicle of Seapoint Rugby Football Club 1934-1984 / edited by Jerry White. Dublin: The Club, 1984.
72p; illus; pbk

Shannon

479   Shannon Rugby Football Club 1884-1984 / edited by Arthur Quinlan. Limerick: Limerick Leader, 1984.
208p; illus; pbk

    Cover title: Shannon Rugby Club centenary 1884-1984: club history

Terenure College

480   Terenure College RFC, 1940-1990 / edited by Michael Roche. Dublin: Terenure College, 1990.
48p; illus; pbk

Thomond

481 'Old Thomondgate, my native place': Thomond Rugby
Football Club golden jubilee season 1994/95 souvenir
book / compiled and edited by John Hartery.
Thomondgate: The Club, 1994.
121p; illus; pbk

Tralee

482 Tralee Rugby Football Club 1882-1982. Tralee: The
Club, 1982.
48p; illus; pbk

Trinity College

483 The bold Collegians: the development of sport in Trinity
College, Dublin / Trevor West. Dublin: The Lilliput
Press in association with DUCAC, 1991.
x, 150p; illus; index

> *Bibliography: p137-42*   ISBN: 0946640807
>   BL: YK.1994.a.12078

Making extensive use of material deposited in the
college library, Trevor West, a fellow of TCD, traces
the history of sport in the college, where rugby has
played a prominent role.

Tullamore

484 Tullamore Rugby Club: the story of fifty years 1937-87 /
Michael Byrne. Tullamore: The Club, 1987.
147p; illus

University College Cork

485 UCC RFC centenary history 1874-1974 / edited by
Dermot Russell. Cork: The Club, 1974.
xxii, 117p; illus; pbk

> *Cover title: University College Cork Rugby Football Club
> centenary history 1874-1974*

University College Dublin

486 University College Dublin Rugby Football Club
1910-1960 golden jubilee. Dublin: Domas, 1960.
61p; illus; pbk

Wanderers

487 Wanderers Football Club 1869/70-1969/70. Dublin:
The Club, 1969.
112p; illus; pbk

Westport

488 Westport Rugby Football Club official opening of
playing pitches & clubhouse, Sunday 14 Sept. 1986 /
edited by Stephen Breheny. Westport: The Club, 1986.
100p; illus; pbk

Contains the history of the club.

Young Munster

489 Young Munster RFC diamond jubilee yearbook
1901-1976 / edited by Peter Sheridan. Dublin: Tara for
The Club, 1976.
52p; illus; pbk

490 The story of Young Munster Rugby Football Club
1895/96-1995/96: a celebration of 100 years of football
/ compiled by Michael O'Flaherty; edited by Sean
Curtain. Limerick?: The Club, 1996?
351p; illus

✳ Schools

Leinster

491 Leinster Schools Senior Rugby Cup centenary
celebration 1886-1986 / D. M. MacCormack and Declan
Downs. Dublin: Director Publications, 1986.
x, 162p; illus; pbk

The Leinster Schools Senior Cup Final is played at
Lansdowne Road every year. Uniquely, the game lasts
for 70 minutes instead of the customary 80
minutes.

Methodist College

492 Methodist College Rugby Football Club / Paul Fry.
Belfast: The author, 1935.
40p   BL: 07908.h.6

A survey of the past sixteen years.

Royal Belfast Academical Institution

493 Rugby centenary: the Royal Belfast Academical
Institution. Belfast: William Sweeney, 1974.
62p; illus; pbk

✳ Regional Studies

494 Great rugger clubs / J. B. G. Thomas. London: Stanley
Paul, 1962.
206p; illus   BL: X.449/1196

The Irish clubs covered are: Bective Rangers,
Collegians, Cork Constitution, Dolphin, Dungannon,
Garryowen, Instonians, Lansdowne, London Irish,
North of Ireland, Old Belvedere, Queen's University
Belfast, and University College Dublin.

☞   Also listed at: B323, B421, B635

Connacht

495 Rugby in Connacht / Ralph O'Gorman. Galway?:
Connacht Rugby Union, 1996.
154p; illus   0906312450

Leinster

496 The history of the Association of Referees, Leinster
     Branch IRFU, 1902-1977 / Association of Referees,
     Leinster Branch IRFU. Dublin: The Branch, 1977?
     36p; illus; pbk   BL: X.629/14285
     Traces the birth of the Society of Rugby Referees for
     the province of Leinster at the Hibernian Hotel,
     Dublin, on 12 October 1902, attended by eight
     enthusiasts. Between 1926 and 1976, 58 matches
     at international level had been refereed by fifteen
     members of this Association.

497 Rugby in Leinster, 1879 to 1979 / edited by J. C.
     Conroy. Dublin: Centenary Sub-Committee of the
     Leinster Branch, Irish Rugby Football Union, 1980.
     xv, 105p; illus; pbk   ISBN: 095056642X
                                                                     BL: X.622/8111
     Relates the history of rugby at all levels in Leinster.

Limerick

498 Limerick's rugby history / C. N. Mulqueen. Limerick:
     The Limerick Leader, 1978.
     vii, 163p; illus; pbk

Munster

499 The Carling story of Munster rugby / Charles Mulqueen.
     Dublin: Mercier, 1983.
     160p; illus; pbk   ISBN: 0853427011
                                                                     BL: X.629/23558

Ulster

500 IRFU centenary match 1874-1974, Ulster v. The
     International Wolfhounds 12 September 1974, Sandel
     Lodge Park, Coleraine. Coleraine: The Union, 1974.
     70p; illus; pbk
     A comprehensive history of Ulster rugby by W. E.
     Crawford.

Wales

Aberaman

501 Aberaman Rugby Union Football Club: centenary
     1890-1990: the first 100 years. Aberaman: The Club,
     1990.
     39p; illus; pbk

Aberavon

502 Rugby and Aberavon: historical survey / edited by Bryn
     Thomas and D. B. Evans. Port Talbot: Aberavon Rugby
     Football Club, 1951.
     56p; illus; pbk
          Cover title: The Aberavon Rugby Football Club 1876-1951:
          its origins and evolution

503 Souvenir brochure: salute to rugby 1976 at the Avon
     Lido on February 26th. Aberavon: The Club, 1976.
     96p; illus; pbk

504 A concise history of Aberavon RFC / compiled by Alun
     Hussell. Bridgend: Chwarae, 1990.
     44p; pbk
     Comprises statistical tables.

Abercarn

505 Abercarn Rugby Football Club: centenary souvenir book
     / compiled by Tony Preece and Charles Huskings.
     Newbridge: The Club, 1995.
     viii, 84p; illus; pbk

Abergavenny

506 Abergavenny Rugby Football Club: centenary booklet
     1875-1975 / compiled by Alan Breeze. Abergavenny:
     The Club, 1975.
     57p; illus; pbk

Abertillery

507 Abertillery Rugby Football Club 1883-1983: the
     centenary book / Irene and Keith Thomas. Barry: The
     Club in conjunction with Stewart Williams Publications,
     1983.
     120p; illus   ISBN: 0900807571

Aberystwyth

508 Aberystwyth Rugby Football Club: an account of the
     first twenty-five years 1947-1972 / edited by Huw
     Spencer Lloyd. Aberystwyth: The Club, 1972.
     71p; illus; pbk

509   Aberystwyth RFC 1947-1997: 50th anniversary, or, Clwb
      Rygbi Aberystwyth: dathlu'r hanner canmlwyddiant /
      edited by Geoff Edwards. Aberystwyth: Clwb Rygbi
      Aberystwyth, 1997.
      88p; illus; pbk

      Includes 2 chapters in Welsh

Aberystwyth University See
      University College of Wales, Aberystwyth

Amman United

510   Amman United Rugby Football Club fiftieth anniversary
      1903-1953: a brief history of the club's progress / H.
      Slocombe. Carms.: The Club, 1952.
      32p; illus; pbk

Ammanford

511   Ammanford RFC: centenary 1887-1987 / Brian Fowler.
      Ammanford: The Club, 1987.
      42p; illus; pbk

Bangor

512   100 years of rugby football in Bangor, or, Canrif o rygbi
      ym Mangor / R. Wendell Edwards. Bangor: The Club,
      1980.
      100p; illus; pbk

      Text in Welsh and English.

Barry

513   Games of interchanging praise: a centenary history of
      rugby football in Barry 1887-1987 / Michael G. Bassett.
      Barry: Barry Rugby Football Club, 1988.
      256p; illus, coats of arms   ISBN: 0951366203
                                          BL: YK.1990.b.3274

Bethesda

514   Clwb rygbi Bethesda 1974-1984. Bethesda: The Club,
      1984.
      25p; illus; pbk
      Bilingual.

Blaenavon

515   Blaenavon Rugby Football Club centenary season
      1877-1977 / compiled by D. G. Jenkins. Blaenavon: The
      Club, 1977.
      124p; illus; pbk

Blaina

516   Blaina Rugby Football Club, 1875-1976: memories of
      Mutton Tump / Barbara M. Evans. Risca: Starling, 1976.
      137p; illus   ISBN: 0903434229
                                          BL: X.629/11035

Brecon

517   Brecon Rugby Football Club: one hundred years of
      rugby football 1879-1979 / Danny James, P. O. J.
      Rowlands. Brecon: The Club, 1979.
      70p; illus; pbk

Bridgend

518   Souvenir brochure to mark the 75th anniversary season
      of the Bridgend RFC 1879-1954 / edited by W. A. D.
      Lawrie. Bridgend: The Club, 1954.
      28p; illus; pbk

519   1878-1978 centenary gala. 1978.
      104p; illus

520   Bridgend Rugby Football Club: the first hundred years
      1878-1979 / W. A. D. Lawrie. Bridgend: The Club, 1979.
      216p; illus

521   Into the eighties: club history part 2 / W. A. D. Lawrie.
      Bridgend: The Club, 1985.
      157p; illus; pbk

Bro Ffestiniog

522   Clwb rygbi Bro Ffestiniog 1973-1994. Blaenau
      Ffestiniog: Y Clwb, 1994.
      41p; illus, 1 map; pbk
      Text in Welsh with a few items in English.

Builth Wells

523   Builth Wells Rugby Football Club centenary booklet
      1882-1982 / compiled by P. J. Morris and W. G.
      Probert. Builth Wells: The Club, 1982.
      41p; illus; pbk

Burry Port

524   Burry Port RFC centenary year 1980-1981. Llanelli:
      Michael Samuel, 1980.
      101p; illus; pbk

Bynea

525   1883 centenary year 1983 Bynea RFC. Llanelli: Michael
      Samuel, 1983.
      70p; illus; pbk

Cardiff

526   The Cardiff Rugby Football Club: history and statistics
      1876-1906 / compiled by C. S. Arthur. Cardiff: The
      Club, 1908.
      222p; illus

527   Cardiff Rugby Football Club: battle honours since 1876.
      Cardiff: South Wales Echo, 1970.
      12p

528 Cardiff Rugby Club: history and statistics, 1876-1975:
     'The greatest' / D. E. Davies. Cardiff: Cardiff Athletic
     Club, 1975.
     431p; illus
       ☞ Subsequent ed. B529

529 Cardiff Rugby Club: history and statistics, 1876-1975 /
     D. E. Davies. 2nd ed. Risca: Starling, 1976.
     435p; illus, 1 map   ISBN: 0903434245
                                           BL: X.629/11034
       ☞ Previous ed. B528

530 Cardiff Rugby Football Club centenary year 1976-77 /
     edited by J. B. G. Thomas. Cardiff: The Club, 1976.
     92p; illus; pbk

531 The statistical history of Cardiff Rugby Football Club
     1876-1984 / C. R. G. Harris. Cardiff: The Club, 1984.
     144p; illus; pbk   ISBN: 0950442119
       Gives the First XV results from 1876 to 1984 as well
       as notes for each decade.

Cardiff High School Old Boys

532 'The best and happiest team': a history of the Cardiff
     High School Old Boys Rugby Football Club 1929-1978
     / Gwyn Prescott. Cardiff: The Club, 1978.
     iv, 65p; illus; pbk

Carmarthen Athletic

533 Early in the morning: a history of Carmarthen Athletic
     Club / Neil Davies. Carmarthen: The Club, 1996.
     150p; illus; pbk

Carmarthen Harlequins

534 Carmarthen Rugby Football Club centenary year
     1874-1974 / compiled by T. L. Evans. Llandeilo: The
     Club, 1974.
     26p; illus; pbk
       The club adopted the name Harlequins in 1911.

Cefn Cribwr

535 Cefn Cribwr Rugby Club centenary 1888-1988 /
     compiled by David G. Hopkins. Cefn Cribwr: The Club,
     1988.
     55p; illus; pbk

Chepstow

536 The origin of Chepstow Rugby Football Club /
     compiled and edited by Bernard Jarvis. Chepstow: The
     Chepstow Society, 1978.
     48p; illus; pbk   ISBN: 0900278420
                                 BL: X.709/32340

       Match reports from 1878 to 1890; contains extracts
       from *The Chepstow Weekly Advertiser.* Also includes a
       pen portrait of Welsh international Edward Peake.

Cross Keys

537 100 years in black & white / Horace Jefferies.
     Pontypool: Griffin Press, 1985.
     205p; illus

Crynant

538 Stars on a Saturday afternoon: the story of Crynant
     Rugby Football Club / David Alexander. Crynant: The
     Club, 1990.
     64p; illus; pbk

Cwmbran

539 Cwmbran RFC: one hundred years of rugby / edited by
     Denis Gane. Cwmbran: The Club, 1980.
     iv, 116p; illus; pbk

Cwmtwrch

540 Tunnell o rygbi: hanes Clwb Rygbi Cwmtwrch
     1890-1990, or, A ton of rugby: the history of Cwmtwrch
     RFC / golygwyd gan Rod Rees. Cwmtwrch: The Club,
     1990.
     72p; illus; pbk

Dinas Powys

541 A history of Dinas Powys Rugby Football Club and its
     associations with the village, 1882-1982 / Anthony J.
     Moses & Brenda C. Moses. Risca: Starling, 1982.
     150p; illus
       Spine title: *Dinas Powys Rugby Football Club*
                                 ISBN: 0903434563
                                 BL: X.809/54300

Dunvant

542 Dunvant Rugby Football Club 1887-1987: 100 glorious
     years. Dunvant: The Club, 1987.
     60p; illus; pbk

Glais

543 The Glais rugby story 1896-1971: a brief history, 75
     years of rugby football / T. G. Cadwalladr. Clydach:
     Glais RFC, 1971.
     85p; illus; pbk

Glyncorrwg

544 Glyncorrwg Rugby Football Club 1880-1980: a brief
     summary of the first hundred years / edited by E.
     Thomas, V. T. White and others. Glyncorrwg: The Club,
     1980.
     46p; illus; pbk

Glynneath

545 Glynneath Rugby Football Club 1889/90-1989/90: the passing of a century / W. John Harries. Glynneath: The Club, 1990.
147p; illus

Gorseinon

546 Gorseinon Rugby Football Club 1883-1983. Gorseinon: The Club, 1983.
60p; illus; pbk

Gowerton

547 A history of the Gowerton Rugby Football Club / compiled by J. Hywel Rees. Gowerton: The Club, 1959.
108p; illus; pbk
   The history was produced to celebrate the 75th anniversary of the club.

548 The Gowerton Rugby Football Club 1884-1984: one hundred years on / J. Hywel Rees. Gowerton: The Club, 1983.
xviii, 187p; illus

Gwent College of Higher Education

549 75 years of college rugby: 1914/15-1989/90. Newport: Gwent College of Higher Education, 1990.

Hendy

550 Hendy Rugby Football Club: a brief history of the club's progress published to commemorate fifty years of affiliation to the Welsh Rugby Union 1907-57 / edited by H. Meurig Evans. Hendy: The Club, 1957.
18p; illus; pbk

551 Yr Hendy: the village and rugby club / compiled by Howard M. Jones and others. Hendy: Hendy RFC, 1993.
272p; illus, genealogical tables, maps

Kenfig Hill

552 A history of Kenfig Hill RFC: Welsh rugby union fiftieth anniversary 1922-23 to 1972-73 / Tony Lewis. Pyle: Picton, 1973.
xvi, 167p

Laugharne

553 Laugharne RFC centenary (1882-1993) / George Tremlett. Laugharne: The Club, 1993.
102p; illus; pbk

Llandaff

554 Llandaff RFC centenary 1876-1976. Llandaff: The Club, 1976.
10p; illus; pbk

Llandovery

555 Llandovery RFC centenary 1881-1981 / edited by Eifion Morgan. Llandovery: The Club, 1981.
35p; illus; pbk

Llandybïe

556 Llandebie Rugby Football Club 1901-1951 / T. H. Lewis. Llandebie: The Club, 1951.
23p; illus; pbk

557 Llandybïe RFC 1901/2-1976/7 / E. Noel Lewis. Llandybïe: The Club, 1976.
108p; illus; pbk

Llanelli

558 Into the eighties with Llanelli Rugby Club / compiled by Gareth Hughes. Llanelli: Llanelli and District Rugby Supporters' Club, 1979.
80p; illus; pbk
   A brief history of Llanelli RFC, profiles of the players and features by local historians and former players like Onllwyn Brace, Carwyn James and others.

559 One hundred years of scarlet / compiled by Gareth Hughes. Llanelli: The Club, 1983.
viii, 282p; illus   ISBN: 0950915904

560 The Scarlets: a history of Llanelli Rugby Football Club / Gareth Hughes; with illustrations by David Griffiths and Graham Howells. Llanelli: Llanelli Borough Council and Llanelli Rugby Football Club, 1986.
viii, 260p; illus; index   ISBN: 0906821053
   A supplement is published annually.

561 Son of scarlet fever / Les Williams. Llanelli: The author, 1993?
64p; illus; pbk
   Review of Llanelli RFC's 1992/93 season.

Llanelli Wanderers

562 Cyfeillach trwy grwydro: a history of the Llanelli Wanderers Rugby Club to 1982 / D. Roger Griffiths. Llanelli: The Club, 1982.
45p; illus; pbk

Llangennech

563 Bois y Llan: Llangennech RFC (1885-1985) / edited by Martin Rhys. Llangennech: The Club, 1987.
140p; illus; pbk

Llangwm

564 Llangwm RFC: a hundred years of rugby / Richard Howells. Llangwm: The Club, 1985.
64p; illus; pbk

London Welsh

565   The London Welsh at Old Deer Park: a souvenir to commemorate the partnership with the Richmond Cricket Club and the opening of the ground by the president The Right Hon. Viscount Tenby, September 21 1957. London: The Club, 1957.
58p; illus; pbk

    A history of the club.

566   Dragon in exile: the centenary history of London Welsh RFC / Paul Beken and Stephen Jones. London: Springwood, 1985.
318p; illus

Machen

567   Machen RFC 125 years, 1871-1996. Machen: The Club, 1996.
14p; illus; pbk

Maesteg

568   'The Old Parish', 100 not out 1882-1982: a history of Maesteg Rugby Football Club / Glyn Phillips and Gwyn James. Maesteg: The Club, 1982.
168p; illus

569   The Old Parish centenarians: Maesteg Rugby Football Club 1882-1982 / edited by Roy James. Maesteg: The Club, 1983.
68p; illus; pbk

Maesteg Celtic

570   Maesteg Celtic RFC: 50 glorious years 1925/26-1975/76 / edited by Islwyn Evans. Maesteg: The Club, 1975.
51p; illus; pbk

Mountain Ash

571   The first 100 years : the history of Mountain Ash Rugby Union Football Club, 1875-1975 / Ieuan Wyn Jones. Mountain Ash: The Club, 1975.
52p; illus; pbk

572   The Mountain Ash Rugby Football Club story: 'The old firm' volume 1: 1875-1950 / Emlyn Richards. Mountain Ash: The author, 1990?
64p; illus; pbk

Mumbles

573   100 years of Mumbles rugby / Alan Williams. Mumbles: The Club, 1987.
120p; illus; pbk

Narberth

574   One hundred years of rugby at Narberth / Dennis Irving. Narberth: The Club, 1982.
73p; illus; pbk   ISBN: 0850887879

Neath

575   Neath RFC 1871-1971: centenary year souvenir brochure / T. Dargavel. Neath: The Club, 1971.
58p; illus

576   The trail to triumph: Neath Rugby Football Club 1988/9 yearbook / edited by Rod Rees. Neath: The Club, 1989?
104p; illus; pbk

Neath Athletic

577   Neath Athletic: 50 years of rugby 1947-97 / Mike Price. Neath: The Club, 1997.
24p; illus; pbk

Newbridge

578   An illustrated history of Newbridge RFC / edited by Terry Powell. Risca: Starling, 1988.
255p; illus   ISBN: 0951393901
                                          BL: YK.1990.a.1824

Newport

579   Newport Rugby Football Club, 1875-1960 / Jack Davis. Newport: Newport Athletic Club, 1960?
128p; illus   BL: X.629/3797

    The author was senior correspondent for the South Wales Argus.

580   One hundred years of Newport rugby / Jack Davis. Risca: Starling, 1974.
283p; illus   ISBN: 0903434024
                                          BL: X.629/6979

581   Newport Rugby Football Club 1875-1975: 100 years of black and amber magic. Newport: The Club, 1975.
88p; illus; pbk

Newport Athletic

582   Newport Athletic Club: the record of half a century, 1875-1925 / compiled from various sources and edited by W. J. Townsend Collins. Newport: The Club, 1925.
206p; illus; pbk   BL: X.449/3055

    Although other sports are covered, rugby accounts for the greater part of the record. The British Library's copy was Collins' personal copy and contains his additional manuscript notes, and autograph.

583 Newport Athletic Club, 1875-1975. Newport: Starling, 1974.
184p; illus   BL: X.809/19745
> The club's rugby records compiled by Brian J. Jones are supplemented by short articles by divers hands including Rupert Cherry and J. B. G. Thomas.

Neyland

584 Neyland RFC 1885-1985 / Richard Howells. Haverfordwest: The Club?, 1985.
75p; illus

Ogmore Vale

585 Ogmore Vale Rugby Club 1879-1979: looking back 100 years / Glynne D. Lewis. Ogmore Vale: The Club, 1979.
33p; illus; pbk

Pembroke Dock Harlequins

586 Pembroke Dock Harlequins Rugby Football Club 1880-1980: centenary publication, 100 years of rugby football / edited by Michael Samuel. Pembroke Dock: The editor, 1981.
80p; pbk

Penarth

587 Penarth Rugby Football Club centenary season. Penarth: The Club, 1979.
35p; illus; pbk

588 The butcher boys of donkey island: an historical profile of Penarth RFC / John Musselwhite. Penarth: The Club, 1980.
183p; illus

Pentyrch

589 Pentyrch RFC: a club for all seasons 1883-1983 / Arthur and Don Llewellyn. Pentyrch: The Club, 1983.
140p; illus

Penybanc

590 Penybanc Rugby Football Club half centenary 1934/35-1984/85. Ammanford: The Club, 1984.
59p; illus; pbk

Penygraig

591 Penygraig RFC: 100 years of valley rugby 1877-1977. Penygraig: The Club, 1977.
63p; illus; pbk

Pontardawe

592 The history of Pontardawe RFC / J. R. Jones. Pontardawe: The Club, 1985.
128p; illus; pbk

Pontarddulais

593 Bont: the story of a village and its rugby club, Pontarddulais / Denver Evans. Pontarddulais: The Club, 1980.
343p; illus; index

Pontyberem

594 Dyddie dathlu: canmlwyddiant Clwb Rygbi Pontyberem a golwg ar y pentre / Arwel John; y lluniau a'r ffeithiau hanesyddol i gefndir y pentre wedi eu casglu gan Donald Williams. Pontyberem: Clwb Rygbi Pontyberem, 1995.
143p; illus; pbk

Pontyclun

595 Pontyclun Rugby Club 1896-1971: 75th anniversary season souvenir booklet. Pontyclun: The Club, 1971.
19p; illus; pbk

596 Hard kicks but good touches!: a celebration of 100 years of rugby at Pontyclun RFC, 1887-1987 / compiled by John David. Cowbridge: D. Brown, 1987.
95p; illus

Pontypool

597 Pontypool Rugby Football Club jubilee 1901-1951: 50 years of rugby history. Pontypool: Pontypool Rugby Supporters Club, 1951.
32p; illus; pbk
> The appointed editor, George H. Hoare, died before the booklet was completed. W. J. T. Collins ('Dromio') and others took over the reins.

598 Pontypool's pride: the official history of Pontypool Rugby Football Club 1868-1988 / Edward Donovan and others. Abertillery: Old Bakehouse Publications, 1988.
xii, 300p; illus; index
Bibliography: p290   ISBN: 0951218115

Pontypridd

599 Pontypridd RFC 1876-1976 / edited by Desmond T. Jones. Pontypridd: The Club, 1976.
68p; illus; pbk

600 100 years of rugby 1885-1985 / John R. Davies.
94p; illus

601 The Butchers Arms boys / Gareth Harris and Alan Evans. Neath: Rugby Unlimited, 1997.
91p; illus; pbk   ISBN: 095317140X

Porthcawl

602 Porthcawl RFC 1880/81-1980/81: the seaweeds / Alun Williams. Pyle: Picton, 1980.
248p; illus

Rhymney

603   One hundred years of Rhymney rugby: the centenary history of Rhymney RFC 1882-1982 / Philip T. Atkinson. Rhymney: The Club, 1982.
156p; illus

     Bibliography: p156

Risca

604   Risca Rugby days of glory / Jack Strickland. Newport: Starling, 1983.
85p; illus   ISBN: 0903434571
                     BL: X.629/20144

St. Peter's

605   One hundred years of the 'Rocks': the history of St. Peter's RFC 1886-1986 / D. F. Childs. Cardiff: The Club, 1986.
100p; illus; pbk

Senghenydd

606   Senghenydd: the village and its rugby club / William G. Boulton. Risca: Starling, 1982.
100p; illus   ISBN: 0903434539
                     BL: X.629/19450

Seven Sisters

607   Magnificent Seven: the centenary history of Seven Sisters Rugby Football Club, 1897-1997 / Hywel Francis. Seven Sisters: Seven Sisters Rugby Football Club, 1997.
54p; illus; pbk

    Welsh/English foreword.

South Wales Police

608   A century on the rugby beat: a history of 100 years of police rugby football in the South Wales Constabulary area / Gordon Westcott. Bridgend: South Wales Police Rugby Football Club, 1992.
xii, 212p; illus; pbk

Swansea

609   The Swansea story: a history of the Swansea Rugby Football Club 1874-1968 / Brinley E. Matthews. Swansea: Swansea Cricket and Football Club, 1968.
102p; illus   BL: X.449/3582

610   Swansea Cricket and Football Club 1874-1974: 100 glorious years / edited by Ron Griffiths. Swansea: The Club, 1973.
93p; illus; pbk

611   The life & times of Swansea RFC: the All Whites / David Farmer with contributions by David Price & Vernon Rees Davies. Swansea: DFPS, 1995.
xxii, 455p; illus; index   ISBN: 0952568004
                     BL: YK.1996.b.11859

Taffs Well

612   A view from the Garth: one hundred years of Taffs Well rugby 1887-1987 / Peter Thomas. Taffs Well: Taffs Well RFC, 1987.
104p; illus

Taibach

613   Taibach Rugby Football Club 1884-1984. Taibach: The Club, 1984.
64p; illus; pbk

Tonmawr

614   Tonmawr RFC 1897-1997: a century of passion / edited by Chris Thau. Tonmawr: The Club, 1997?
93p; illus; pbk

Tonna

615   Tonna Rugby Football Club centenary year / Andrew S. Jones. Tonna: The Club, 1987.
27p; illus; pbk

Treherbert

616   Treherbert Rugby Football Club centenary year 1874-1974. Treherbert: The Club, 1974.
37p; illus; pbk

Treorchy

617   Treorchy Rugby Football Club 1886-1986 / Vernon Davies and Cadfan Clayton. Treorchy: The Club, 1987.
139p; illus; pbk

Tycroes

618   Tycroes Rugby Football Club: souvenir brochure / compiled by T. E. Davies. Tycroes: The Club, 1979.
84p; illus; pbk

    Tour brochure to commemorate Tycroes RFC's 'first ever fixture abroad when the Club played against Club Rhodanien at Condrieu on the outskirts of Lyons, France, in April 1979'. Includes a history of the club.

    ☞   Also listed at: E108

619   Tycroes RFC 1911-1986 / D. Rees.
100p; illus

620   Tycroes RFC LXXV 1911-1986: 75th anniversary souvenir programme / edited by Terry Morgan. Tycroes: The Club, 1986.
91p; illus; pbk

Tylorstown

621 Tylorstown Rugby Football Club: 75th anniversary 1978-79 / edited by Selwyn Baber. Tylorstown: The Club, 1978.
40p; illus; pbk

University College of Wales Aberystwyth

622 UCW Aberystwyth CPC Clwb Rygbi/Rugby Club tymor canmlwyddiant 1986-1987 centenary season / edited by Meirion Derrick and others. Aberystwyth: University College of Wales Aberystwyth, 1987.

Contains 'Breathe on them, Aber!: the history of UCW rugby' by Gareth Williams.

Vardre United

623 Vardre United Rugby Football Club, 50th anniversary 1921-1971: 'from the twenties to the seventies' / Stanley Owen. Clydach: The Club, 1971.
illus; pbk

Waunarlwydd

624 Waunarlwydd Rugby Football Club 1900-1975 / compiled by Eldred Bayliss and Howard George. Waunarlwydd: The Club, 1975.
63p; illus; pbk

Ystalyfera

625 Ystalyfera RFC centenary year 1884-1984 brochure (100 years of rugby) / compiled by Gareth Williams and Noir James. Ystalyfera: The Club, 1984.
64p; illus; pbk

Ystradgynlais

626 Canmlwyddiant Ystradgynlais centenary / D. Mansel Jones. Ystradgynlais: The Club, 1992.
xv, 221p; illus   ISBN: 0951882007

✳ *'Wandering' Clubs*

Captain Crawshay's Welsh XV

627 50th anniversary Captain Geoffrey Crawshay's Welsh XV 1922-72: commemorative brochure / edited by J. B. G. Thomas. Cardiff: Captain Crawshay's RFC, 1972.
36p; illus; pbk

628 Crawshay's Welsh: clwb rygbi Crawshay / edited by Roy J. Thomas & Kelvin J. Bryon. Bridgend?: Crawshay's Welsh RFC, 1996.
48p; illus; pbk

✳ *Schools*

Amman Valley

629 Games in the primary schools: with reference to rugby at under-11 level in the Amman Valley and district / D. E. Thomas. University College of Wales, Aberystwyth, 1975. *Thesis.*

Six chapters: the aims and scopes of primary school games; the history of games; the uses of the playground; rugby at primary level in the Amman Valley; children's games in the playground; questionnaire to London Borough of Brent and Dyfed schools.

Christ College Brecon

630 Brecon football 1860-1880 / R. J. Boulton. Brecon: Brecknock Museum, 1969.
7p; illus; pbk

Traces the history of football, association in the early days, and rugby from 1874, at the school.

Grove Park

631 Forty years of rugby football at Grove Park / N. White. Wrexham: The author, 1988.
16p; pbk

Written by the former headmaster of Grove Park Grammar School for Boys.

Monmouth

632 Monmouth School Rugby Football Club: one hundred years / compiled by H. C. Toulouse. Newport: The School, 1973.
44p; illus; pbk

Pontllanfraith School

633 Scrum five: 50th anniversary Pontllanfraith School 1926-1976.

Swansea

634 Swansea Schools Rugby Union 1900-1975: 75th anniversary. Swansea?: The Union, 1975?
64p; illus; pbk

✳ *Regional Studies*

635 Great rugger clubs / J. B. G. Thomas. London: Stanley Paul, 1962.
206p; illus   BL: X.449/1196

The Welsh clubs are: Aberavon, Abertillery, Bridgend, Cardiff, Cross Keys, Ebbw Vale, Glamorgan Wanderers, Llanelli, London Welsh, Maesteg, Neath, Newbridge, Newport, Penarth, Pontypool, Pontypridd, and Swansea.

☞ Also listed at: B323, B421, B494

636 Club rugby: a visual celebration of the first-class club game in Wales / compiled by Paul Rees; introduction by Barry John. Cardiff: Oriel, 1985.
68p; illus; pbk   ISBN: 0946329176

The Welsh title is: Rygbi'r clybiau: cyflwyniad gweledol o'r gem clwb dosbarth cyntaf yng Nghymru; Welsh translation by Anne Howells. The Oriel Gallery displayed items borrowed from a number of Welsh clubs. Following a brief history of rugby in Wales, this bilingual work presents short histories of the 19 clubs which comprised the top tier in Wales. Also includes two poems, both in English, by Bob Reeves.

☞ Also listed at: H102

637 The rugby clubs of Wales / David Parry-Jones. London: Stanley Paul, 1989.
224p; illus, maps   ISBN: 0091738504
                                             BL: YK.1990.b.5701

Details the history of the major and minor clubs of Wales with maps of the grounds.

Pembrokeshire

638 Pembroke County Rugby Football Club. Pembrokeshire: Pembrokeshire County RFC, 1985.
22p; illus; pbk

Celebrates the 50th anniversary of the founding of Pembrokeshire County RFC.

South Wales

639 South Wales rugger souvenir / Emrys Evans. London: Findon, 1949.
40p; illus; pbk

Short histories of 16 clubs and 'a glance' at 6 others.

640 Record: history of rugby clubs in Amman, Dulais and Swansea valleys, 'the real backbone of Welsh rugby' / T. Graham Cadwalladr. Ystalyfera: South Wales Voice, 1966.
52p; pbk

Gives the history of seventeen clubs including, in each case, the year of foundation, when Welsh Union status was conferred, and the colours. Also includes a brief history of rugby in four schools.

South Africa

Albert

641 1878-1978 '100 not out': the story of the Albert Cricket Club and Albert Rugby Football Club, King William's Town, RSA / compiled and edited by Les Gardner. Cape Province, SA: The Club, 1978.
144p; illus; pbk

Bishops (Diocesan College, Rondebosch)

642 A history of rugby football and cricket at the Diocesan College / Malcolm Taylor. Cape Town, SA: The College, 1964.
iv, 23p; illus; pbk

643 Bishops rugby: a history / Paul Dobson. Cape Town, SA: Don Nelson, 1990.
288p; illus; index   ISBN: 1868060667

Buccaneers

644 The Buccaneers 1966-1986: 20 glorious sporting years / edited by Phil Whithair & Dick Quayle. Cape Town, SA: The Club, 1986.
45p; illus; pbk

Crusaders

645 The Crusader Rugby Club centenary 1887-1987: souvenir brochure. Port Elizabeth, SA: The Club, 1987.
75p; illus; pbk

De Beers

646 De Beers rugby 100: 1894-1994 / Steve Lunderstedt. Kimberley, SA: Kimberley Marketing and Promotions, 1994.
40p; illus; pbk   ISBN: 0620184442
Text in Afrikaans and English.

Gardens

647 Tuine Rugbyklub: 75e jubileum, or, Gardens Rugby
Football Club: 75th anniversary. Cape Town, SA: The
Club, 1954.
32p; illus
   Text in English and Afrikaans.

648 Tuine Rugbyklub 1879-1979, or, Gardens Rugby Club.
Cape Town, SA: Centenary Festival Committee of the
Gardens Rugby Club, 1978.
47p; illus   ISBN: 0620040394

Kimberley

649 Kimberley Club / Constance Warner. Kimberley, SA:
Kimberley Marketing and Promotions, 1994.
40p; pbk

Maritzburg College

650 Jimeloyo-Ji!: a history of the Maritzburg College first XV
/ Skonk Nicholson and Tony Wiblin. Pietermaritzburg,
SA: MC Publications,1990.
vii, 126p; illus; pbk

Olympics

651 Olympic Rugby Football Club 75th anniversary /
compiled and edited by Douglas N. Fox. Port Elizabeth,
SA: The Club, 1956.
52p; illus; pbk   BL: 7923.cc.7

652 1881-1981 Olympic Football Club: 100th anniversary
souvenir brochure. Port Elizabeth, SA: The Club, 1981.
95p; illus; pbk
   Text in Afrikaans and English.

Quaggas

653 Quagga Rugby Football Club: 21, 1955-1976, or,
Kwagga Rugby-Voetbal Klub. Johannesburg, SA: The
Club, 1976.
71p; illus; pbk

Queen's College, Queenstown

654 Queen's College golden jubilee rugby brochure
1924-1974. Queenstown: The College, 1974.
42p; illus; pbk

St. Andrew's College Grahamstown

655 The history of rugby football at St. Andrew's College
Grahamstown / N. M. Kunhardt, R. G. Ross.
Grahamstown, SA: The College, 1966.
53p; illus; pbk

Somerset West

656 Golden jubilee, or, Goue jubileum, 1904-1954. Somerset
West, SA: Somerset West Rugby Football Club, 1954.
104p; illus
   Text in Afrikaans and English.

South African College Schools

657 Rugby at SACS / co-ordinated by Willi Wighard. Cape
Town, SA: The School, 1996.
82p; illus; pbk

Swifts

658 Swifts RFC: 75 years 1891-1966, or, Swifts RVK: 75 jare
/ edited by W. P. Sellick. Uitenhage, SA: The Club, 1966.
110p; illus; pbk

659 1891-1981 Swifts RFC 90 years, or, Swifts RVK 90 jare.
Uitenhage, SA: The Club, 1981.
16p; illus; pbk

660 1891-1991: Swifts Rugby Voetbal Klub eenfeesuitgawe,
or, Rugby Football Club centenary issue / compiled by
Albert Timms. Uitenhage, SA: The Club, 1991.
55p; illus; pbk
   Text in Afrikaans and English.

Union High, Graaff-Reinet

661 A history of rugby football at Union High, Graaff-Reinet
/ John Wegerhoff. Graaff-Reinet, SA: The School, 1977.
74p; illus; pbk

University of Cape Town

662 The varsity spirit: the story of rugby football at the
University of Cape Town, 1883-1963 / Louis Babrow
and Richard K. Stent. Cape Town, SA: Johnston &
Neville, 1963.
x, 174p; illus   BL: X.441/1062

663 University of Cape Town Rugby Football Club
centenary 1882-1982 / edited by Louis Babrow. Cape
Town, SA: The Club, 1982.
95p; 1 coat of arms; pbk

Villagers

664 100 years of rugby: the story of the Villager Football
Club / R. K. Stent. Cape Town, SA: The Club, 1976.
vi, 147p; illus

665 The Villager rugby magazine 1995-Brookside experience:
the home of the Villager Football Club. Claremont, SA:
The Club, 1995.
32p; illus; pbk
   Nine authors write the history of the club.

666 History of the founding of Villager Football Club / Ian
     Fraser. Cape Town, SA: The Club, 1996.
     8p; pbk

Wanderers (Johannesburg)

667 Old gold: the history of the Wanderers club / Thelma
     Gutsche. Cape Town, SA: Howard Timmins, 1966.
     206p; illus

Young Stars

668 Young Stars souvenir brochure 1997 / edited by Hashim
     Sale and M. Rafiek. Cape Town, SA: The Club, 1997.
     64p; illus

❋ Regional Studies

669 Top South African rugby playing schools: a guide to
     South African rugby playing schools / compiled and
     edited by Chris Dutton and Michael Collins.
     Johannesburg, SA: M. Collins, 1997.
     78p; illus   ISBN: 1875065067
     Information on 26 schools.

Eastern Cape

670 Rugby down the years: an Eastern Cape and Border
     Schools' rugby history / S. G. Dugmore. Grahamstown,
     SA: The Schools, 1978.
     317p; illus; pbk
     Presents the history of twelve schools.

671 'N eeu van OP rugby, 1888-1988 / saamgestel deur
     Willie Muller, or, A century of EP rugby, 1888-1988 /
     compiled by Willie Muller. Port Elizabeth, SA: OPRU,
     1988.
     188p; illus   ISBN: 0620122978
                                          BL: YA.1996.b.5142
     A history of rugby in the Eastern Province in English
     and Afrikaans.

672 Border rugby history 1891-1991 / compiled and edited
     by Percy Owen. East London, SA: Border Rugby
     Football Union, 1991.
     69p; illus; pbk

Pretoria

673 Senior rugby in Pretoria, 1938-1988 / Ignatius Philippus
     Wilhelm Pretorius. University of South Africa, 1990.
     Master's thesis.

Kwazulu-Natal

674 The history of Natal rugby 1870-1964 / edited by C. O.
     Medworth. Cape Town, SA: Howard Timmins, 1964.
     184p; illus

675 The Natal rugby story / Alfred Herbert; edited by Reg
     Sweet. Pietermaritzburg, SA: Shuter & Shooter in
     conjunction with the Natal Rugby Union, 1980.
     444p; illus   ISBN: 0869854895
                                          BL: X.622/13051

676 Natal 100: centenary of Natal rugby union / Reg Sweet.
     Durban, SA: Natal Rugby Union, 1990.
     ix, 468p; illus   ISBN: 0620135689

Transvaal

677 Northern Transvaal rugby 50 / edited by M. C. van Zyl.
     Pretoria, SA: Northern Transvaal Rugby Union, 1988.
     433p; illus; index
            Translated from the Afrikaans
            Bibliography: p405-7   ISBN: 0620115416

678 Transvaal Rugby Football Union: 100 years / Jannie
     Ferreira. Johannesburg, SA: The Union, 1989.
     256p; illus   ISBN: 0620133007

Western Cape

679 Western Province rugby football season 1904 / C.
     Hodson. Cape Town, SA: Western Province RFU, 1904.
     24p; illus; pbk

680 Jubilee programme 1883-1933 / Western Province
     Rugby Football Union. Cape Town, SA: The Union,
     1933.
     Contains a detailed account of the early history of
     the Newlands ground.

681 W. P. rugby: centenary 1883-1983 / A. C. Parker.
     Newlands, SA: Western Province Rugby Football Union,
     1983.
     320p; illus   ISBN: 0620065559

682 Charity rag: extract from the history of the Western
     Province Rugby Union. Cape Town, SA: Cultural
     History Museum, 1995.
     8p; illus; pbk
     (SACHM pamphlet; no. 4)
            Bibliography: p7   ISBN: 1875045074

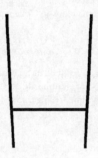

New Zealand

Albion

683   100 years of rugby with the Albion Rugby Football Club / prepared by Henry Tilson. Christchurch, NZ: The Club, 1985.
112p; illus; pbk

Alexandra

684   History of the Alexandra Rugby Football Club. Alexandra, NZ: The Club, 1990.
148p; illus; pbk
   Covers 1890-1990

Alhambra

685   Boots of the Bamas: the history of the Alhambra Rugby Football Club, 1884-1984 / Carole Hendry. Dunedin, NZ: Kerr, 1984.
51p

Awatere

686   75th jubilee Awatere Rugby Football Club, 1906-81. Seddon, NZ: The Club, 1981.
90p; illus; pbk

687   Awatere sportsview '81. Seddon, NZ: Awatere Rugby Football Club, 1981.
28p; illus; pbk
   Supplement to '75th jubilee Awatere Rugby Football Club, 1906-81'

Bombay

688   The struggle to the top: history of the Bombay Rugby Football Club, 1888-1988 / Rex Warwood; with guest chapters by Dave Hunt, Ian Brice, John Holmes; foreword by Andy Dalton. Bombay, NZ: The Club, 1988.
148p; illus

Centurions

689   Halfway: the first 50 years of Centurions rugby / William Alfred Brien. Wellington, NZ: Civic Press, 1990.
201p; illus; pbk

Christchurch

690   'Give 'em the axe': the first hundred years of Christchurch Football Club / Dick Brittenden. Christchurch, NZ: The Club, 1963.
93p; illus
   Cover title: Christchurch Football Club 1863-1963
   A short account of rugby in Canterbury and a history of the club.

Clifton

691   Clifton Rugby Football Club centennial, 1880-1980 / Sidney A. C. Summers. New Plymouth, NZ: Taranaki Newspapers, 1980.
127p; illus

Clutha

692   Forward, threequarters, and all: a centennial history of the Clutha Rugby Football Club Inc. / compiled by Ken Jones. Balclutha, NZ: The Club, 1976.
96p; illus

College Rifles

693   College Rifles 1897-1972: 75th jubilee / edited by Max Smith. Auckland, NZ: The Club, 1972.
64p; illus

Collingwood

694   Collingwood Rugby Football Club 1889-1994: a history / M. H. Strange. Collingwood, NZ: The author, 1994.
48p; illus; pbk

Crescent

695   Crescent Rugby Football Club: a century of rugby at Kaitangata, 1877-1977 / compiled by Ken Jones. Kaitangata, NZ: The Club, 1977.
80p; illus
   Variant title: The coal boys: a century of rugby at Kaitangata

Cromwell

696   A century of rugby, 1888-1988: Cromwell, Bannockburn, Lowburn / W. H. Perriam. Cromwell, NZ: Cromwell Rugby Football Club, 1988.
44p; illus; pbk

Dannevirke

697   75th jubilee, Dannevirke Old Boy's Rugby Football Club Inc. 1910-1985: Queen's birthday weekend 1985, official souvenir booklet. Dannevirke, NZ: The Club, 1985.
48p; illus; pbk

Drummond

698   Three score and more, 1920-1980: a history of the Drummond (and associated) rugby football clubs / compiled by Vincent Gregory Boyle. Drummond, NZ: Drummond Rugby Football Club, 1980.
104p; illus

History of the Drummond, Calcium-Isla Bank, Otahuti, Heddon Bush and Tarangitura rugby clubs, which combined as the Drummond Rugby Football Club in the 1920s.

Drury

699   Drury Rugby Football Club celebrations: 75 years plus / compiled by Marie F. Chitty. Papakura, NZ: The Club, 1980.
73p; illus; pbk

Eltham

700   Eltham Rugby Football Club centennial, 1888-1988 / edited by Joy Urbahn. Eltham, NZ: The Club, 1988.
120p; illus; pbk

701   Saturday's warriors: the building of a rugby stronghold / Piet de Jong. Palmerston North, NZ: Massey University, 1991.
iv, 70p; illus; pbk

   Bibliography: p65-70   ISBN: 090866561X
Social history of rugby in Eltham.

Excelsior

702   Excelsior centennial, 1888-1988 / compiled by Harry J. Barnett; edited by Anne Hore. Oamaru, NZ: Excelsior Rugby Football Club, 1988.
57p; illus; pbk

Feilding

703   Yellow yarns: Feilding Rugby Football Club, 1982. Feilding, NZ: The Club, 1982.
15p; illus; pbk

Gimmerburn-Patearoa

704   Gimmerburn-Patearoa jubilee: 1907-1982. Dunedin, NZ: Gimmerburn-Patearoa Rugby Football Club Jubilee Committee, 1982.
43p; illus

Gladstone

705   Gladstone Football Club jubilee souvenir 1902-1952. Gladstone, NZ: The Club, 1952.
48p; illus; pbk

Green Island

706   The history of the Green Island Rugby Football Club Inc.: 1884-1984 / written and compiled by Gordon Brown. Green Island, NZ: The Club, 1984?
128p; illus

   Bibliography: p126

Greytown

707   The golden years of rugby, 1876-1976: a history of the Greytown Rugby Club's first 100 years / M. J. Greathead and H. A. McPhee. Greytown, NZ: Greytown Rugby Football Club Centennial Book Committee, 1976.
92p; illus

Hastings Celtic

708   Hastings Celtic Rugby Football Club Inc.: 75th jubilee 1910-1985, Queen's birthday weekend, June 1985. Hastings, NZ: The Club, 1985.
56p; illus; pbk

Heriot

709   Heriot Rugby Football Club Inc.: centennial history, 1885-1985 / edited by Alistair McMurran. Heriot, NZ: The Club, 1985.
104p; illus; pbk

Invercargill

710   A ton of time: Invercargill Rugby Football Club 1874-1974 / N. R. Lines. Invercargill, NZ: The Club, 1974?
143p; illus

Irwell

711   Irwell Rugby Football Club 1883-1983: a century of Irwell rugby, 25th, 26th, 27th March 1983 / compiled by John and Lyndsay Lay. Irwell, NZ: The Club, 1983.
13p; pbk

Kaiapoi

712   Kaiapoi Rugby Football Club 100 years, 1883-1983: a history of 100 years with the Kaiapoi Rugby Club. Kaiapoi, NZ: The Club, 1982.
48p; illus; pbk

Kaierau

713   Kaierau RFC history / Vaughan A. Brookie. 1966?

Kaikorai

714   Kaikorai Rugby Football Club centennial: 1884-1984. Dunedin, NZ: The Club, 1984.
72p; illus; pbk

Kaipara Flats

715   Kaipara Flats Rugby Football Club, 1889-1989 / historians, Mark Ryburn and Anne Dickson. Warkworth, NZ: The Club, 1989.
104p; illus; pbk

   Also covers the history of tennis and cricket.

Kaiwaka

716 Kaiwaka RFC, 1891-1991. Kaiwaka, NZ: The Club, 1991.
112p; illus, maps; pbk ISBN: 0473012232

Kiwi

717 Kiwi Rugby Football Club, Hokitika, 1910-1985: 75th
jubilee / prepared by John Bateman and others.
Hokitika, NZ: The Club, 1985.
40p; illus; pbk

Lawrence

718 Lawrence, 1884-1984: 100 years of rugby in Lawrence /
prepared by Christine Searle. Lawrence, NZ: Lawrence
Football Club, 1984.
61p; illus; pbk

Levin Wanderers

719 Levin Wanderers Rugby Football Club Inc. 90th jubilee,
1898-1988: souvenir record of 90 years of achievement /
W. C. Shilton. Levin, NZ: The Club, 1988.
112p; illus; pbk

Lincoln College

720 Rugby football in the life of Lincoln College: a centennial
history, 1881-1980 / I. D. Blair. Lincoln, NZ: Lincoln
College Rugby Football Club, 1982.
112p; illus; pbk

Linwood

721 One hundred years of green and black / edited by Dion
Crooks from information supplied by George Stove.
Christchurch, NZ: Clarity, 1986.
88p; illus; index; pbk

Marist (Greymouth)

722 Marist Rugby Football Club Incorporated, established
1934: golden jubilee celebrations, Queen's birthday
weekend, June 1st, 2nd, 3rd 1984. Greymouth, NZ: The
Club, 1984.
38p; illus; pbk

Marist (Wanganui)

723 Marist Rugby Football Club celebrates 75th jubilee,
1917-1992; Marist Netball Wanganui, celebrates 55th
jubilee, 1937-1992. Wanganui, NZ: Marist Rugby
Football Club and Marist Netball Wanganui, 1992.
68p; illus; pbk

Martinborough

724 The Martinborough Rugby Football Club (Incorporated)
celebrate the 75th birthday, 1904-1979 / William G.
Byers. Martinborough, NZ: The Club, 1979.
14p; illus; pbk

Matakanui-Valley

725 Matakanui-Valley and districts: 100 years of rugby /
Willie Donnelly. Omakau, NZ: Matakanui-Valley Rugby
Club, 1987.
104p; illus; pbk

   Cover title: 100, 1887-1987

Mataura

726 Long time passing: centennial publication of the Mataura
Rugby Football Club Inc. / edited by D. C. W. Muir.
Mataura, NZ: The Club, 1986.
120p; illus; pbk ISBN: 0473003376

Maungaturoto

727 Maungaturoto Rugby Football Club: centennial,
1886-1986, 28th-29th March 1986 / compiled by
Margaret Massey. Maungaturoto, NZ: The Club, 1986.
24p; illus; pbk

Merivale-Papanui

728 Merivale-Papanui Rugby Football Club 1882-1982: a
centennial history. Christchurch, NZ: The Club, 1982.
68p; illus, 1 coat of arms; pbk

Methven

729 Methven rugby: 100 years. Ashburton, NZ: Methven
Rugby Football Club, 1996.
64p; illus

Napier Marist Brothers Old Boys

730 The Napier Marist Brothers Old Boys Rugby Football
Club Inc.: the first 75 years: a souvenir booklet. Napier,
NZ: The Club, 1983.
48p; illus; pbk

Nelson

731 100 years of rugby: the birth and evolution of our
national game / W. A. (Bill) Reed in collaboration with
Arthur C. Swan. Nelson, NZ: Nelson Rugby Football
Club, 1969.
190p; illus; pbk

   *Cover title: The story of Nelson Rugby Football Club
   1870-1969*

New Plymouth High School Old Boys

732 Old Boys for ever: the New Plymouth High School Old Boys' Rugby Football Club: the first 75 years (1919-1994). New Plymouth, NZ: The Club, 1994.
102p; illus; pbk

North Dunedin/Alhambra

733 125 years 1872-1997. New Zealand: The Club, 1997.
12p; illus; pbk
   The two clubs have amalgamated.

North Shore

734 C'mon Shore!: the first one hundred years of the North Shore Rugby Football Club 1873-1940 / Earnest J. Eyre; 1940-1972 / collation of miscellaneous data by Selwyn H. Speight. Auckland, NZ: The Club, 1973.
197p; illus; pbk

Nuhaka

735 Nuhaka celebrates 110 years of Nuhaka rugby: 90 years of Nuhaka schooling / edited by Huia (Christy) Koziol. Nuhaka, NZ: Nuhaka School & Nuhaka Rugby Club, 1988.
48p; illus; pbk

Oamaru

736 ARFC Athletic Oamaru, 1886-1986: centennial souvenir / compiled by T. R. Collett. Oamaru, NZ: Oamaru Mail, 1986.
64p; illus; pbk

Oamaru Old Boys

737 Oamaru Old Boys Rugby Football Club Inc.: 75th anniversary, 1911-1986 / compiled by Leo Breen. Oamaru, NZ: The Club, 1986.
32p; illus; pbk

Ohaeawai

738 Ohaeawai Rugby Football Club Incorporated: the first one hundred years, 1888-1988. Kaikohe, NZ: The Club, 1988.
51p; illus; pbk

Okaiawa

739 Centennial Okaiawa RFC 1896-1996 / compiled and written by Linda Megaw. Okaiawa, NZ: The Club, 1996.
29p; illus; pbk

Onslow

740 '50 years of Onslow rugby' / compiled by Bruce Heather. Wellington, NZ: Onslow Rugby Football Club, 1975.
105p; illus

Opawa

741 Golden jubilee of the Opawa Football Club Inc., 1906-1956. Marlborough, NZ: The Club, 1956.
22 leaves

Otago University

742 Otago University Football Club jubilee, 1936: history of the club / Arthur R. Andrew and W. S. Robertson. Dunedin, NZ: Otago Daily Times and Witness Newspapers, 1936.
67p

743 Otago University Rugby Football Club 1886-1969 / David Hay. Dunedin, NZ: Light Blues Association, 1969.
112p; illus

Oxford

744 Oxford Rugby Football Club centennial, 1883-1983 / Gavin Inch and Max Henderson. Oxford, NZ: The Club, 1983.
56p; illus; pbk

Palmerston North HSOB

745 Palmerston North High School Old Boys: 75th anniversary. Palmerston North, NZ: The Club, 1996.
24p; illus; pbk

Petone

746 Petone RFC: 75th jubilee souvenir 1885-1959 / W. H. W. Sweeney and I. E. Burrows. Petone, NZ: The Club, 1959.
77p; illus

747 Petone Rugby Football Club Inc., 1885-1975: 90th jubilee souvenir / records compiled by P. J. Gallagher, J. S. Grace, A. R. Harding; New Zealand photographs by Bob Palamountain and others. Petone, NZ: The Club, 1975.
70p; illus; pbk

748 'True blue': the first 100 years of the Petone Rugby Football Club Incorporated, 1885-1985 / Don Griffin and Peter Gallagher. Petone, NZ: The Club, 1985.
176p; illus; pbk

Pioneer

749 A brief history of the Pioneer Rugby Football Club compiled to mark the 75th anniversary, 1904-1979 / J. F. McArthur. Gore, NZ: The Club, 1981.
56p; illus; pbk

Pirates (Dunedin)

750 Pirates Football Club, Dunedin Inc.: centennial,
1882-1982 / Stephen Davie. Dunedin, NZ: The Club,
1982.
75p; illus; pbk

Pirates (Invercargill)

751 One hundred years of Pirates rugby, 1883-1983 /
compiled by J. C. Hardy. Invercargill, NZ: Pirates Rugby
Football Club, 1983.
95p; illus   ISBN: 0473001373

Pirates (Taihape)

752 Pirates Rugby Football Club Taihape Incorporated, 75th
jubilee, 1909-1984: Taihape June 1st to 4th 1984.
Taihape, NZ: The Club, 1984.
32p; illus; pbk

Pleasant Point

753 True grit: a century of Pleasant Point rugby / written and
edited by T. G. Broughton. Pleasant Point, NZ: Pleasant
Point Rugby Football Club Centennial Committee, 1989.
96p; illus; pbk

Poneke

754 A willing band of youths: the history of the Poneke
Football Club. Wellington, NZ: The Club, 1984.
118p; illus, 1 genealogical table   ISBN: 0473002760

Ponsonby District

755 Ponsonby District Rugby Football Club (Inc.) centennial
album 1874-1974 / edited by Birke Lovett. Ponsonby,
NZ: The Club, 1974.
62p; illus; pbk

Porirua

756 Porirua Rugby Football Club Inc.: 75th jubilee
programme, 1910-1985. Porirua, NZ: The Club, 1985.
20p; illus; pbk

Port Chalmers

757 A century of rugby at Port Chalmers 1883-1983 /
Harold A. Roberts and W. M. Innes. Port Chalmers, NZ:
The Club?, 1983.
42p; pbk

Rakaia

758 Rakaia Rugby Football Club (Incorporated): centennial
celebrations, 1876-1976: souvenir programme.
Ashburton, NZ: The Club, 1976.
32p; illus

Rangiuru

759 The Rangiuru Sports Club centennial story. Te Puke,
NZ: The Club, 1993.
84p; illus; pbk

Redwood

760 Redwood Rugby Club's first 25 years / compiled by club
founder Ron Thorn. Blenheim, NZ: The Club, 1991.
35p; illus; pbk

Ross

761 Looking back, 1890-1990 / compiled by the Ross
Centennial Committee. Ross, NZ: Ross RFC, 1990.
32p; illus; pbk

> Cover title: *Looking back: a history of Ross Rugby Football
> Club 1880-1980*

Ruahine

762 The first fifty years: a brief record of the Ruahine Rugby
Football Club's activities since its formation in 1914 /
Ronald Yelverton Sinclair. 1964?

763 Ruahine 1914-1989, Rugby Football Club: 75th jubilee /
compiled by B. D. & M. A. Stephenson. Dannevirke,
NZ: Dannevirke Publishing, 1989.
36p; illus; pbk

> Supplement to: The first fifty years.

Sheffield

764 Sheffield Rugby Club 1896-1996: centennial booklet
containing a brief history of the club, historical
photographs & other memorabilia. Sheffield, NZ: The
Club, 1996.
43p; illus; pbk

Southern (Dunedin)

765 The history of the Southern Rugby Football Club,
1884-1984 / Winston Cooper; with a foreword by C. K.
Saxton. Dunedin, NZ: The Club, 1984.
vii, 208p; illus; pbk

> Bibliography: p207-8

Southern (Te Kopuru)

766 Southern (Te Kopuru) Football Club Incorporated,
1884-1984: centennial booklet. Te Kopuru, NZ: The
Club, 1984.
110p; illus; pbk

Star (Invercargill)

767   Star Rugby Football Club 1886-1986: centennial souvenir / J. W. Stead and others; records compiled by B. A. Mahoney, J. R. Bell and L. P. Bell; edited by A. V. Keast, J. G. Smith, and G. R. Latta. Invercargill, NZ: The Club, 1986.
96p; illus; pbk

> Cover title: NZ Invercargill Star Rugby Club centennial, 1886-1986

Stokes Valley

768   Stokes Valley Rugby Football Club Inc. 1949-1989 / compiled by E. D. Marino and O. D. Davies. Wellington, NZ: The Club, 1989.
51p; illus; pbk

Sumner

769   Sumner Rugby Football Club Inc.: a historical journey / Gordon J. L. Mitchell. Christchurch, NZ: The Club, 1997.
92p; illus; pbk

Sydenham

770   Sydenham Rugby Football Club 1882-1982. Sydenham, NZ: The Club, 1982?
88p

Taieri

771   Taieri Rugby Football Club, 1883-1983 / Bruce Mitchell. Mosgiel, NZ: The Club, 1983.
75p; illus; pbk

Takapau

772   Takapau Rugby Club 1886-1986 centennial. Hastings, NZ: The Club?, 1986.
40p; illus; pbk

Takapuna

773   Takapuna Rugby Football Club Incorporated: golden jubilee, 1934-1984. Auckland, NZ: The Club, 1984.
16p; illus; pbk

Temuka

774   A century of rugby in Temuka: a record of the Temuka Rugby Football Club in the last 100 years / D. S. Kelman. Temuka, NZ: The Club, 1975.
102p; illus

Thistle

775   Thistle AFC: a history of the Thistle Association Football Club's first 50 years, 1936-1986 / K. M. Fallow, author; G. R. Latta, editor. Invercargill, NZ: The Association, 1986.
16 leaves; illus

Timaru Old Boys

776   Timaru Old Boys' Rugby Football Club: golden jubilee history, 1919-1969 / Jack Clemens. Timaru, NZ: Timaru Herald, 1969.
102p; illus

Titahi Bay

777   History of the Titahi Bay Rugby Football Club from 1954 to 1979 / V. J. Moroney and A. J. Youle. Titahi Bay, NZ: Titahi Bay Rugby Football Club Silver Jubilee Committee, 1979.
104p; illus

Tukapa

778   Tukapa Rugby Football Club, New Plymouth, 1892-1992: 100 glorious years. New Plymouth, NZ: The Club, 1992.
128p; illus

Union

779   A century of club rugby: Union Rugby Football Club (Inc.) / R. I. Douglas. Dunedin, NZ: Coulls Somerville Wilkie, 1972.
43p; pbk

University of Canterbury

780   University of Canterbury RFC diamond jubilee 1883-1958. Canterbury, NZ: The Club, 1958?
54p; illus

Upper Hutt

781   Fifty golden years, 1920-1970 / compiled by D. G. Hercock. Upper Hutt, NZ: Upper Hutt Rugby Football Club, 1970.
137p; illus

Victoria University of Wellington

782   Victoria University of Wellington Rugby Football Club: the story of the green and golds, 1902-1987 / John Andersson. Wellington, NZ: The Club, 1988.
271p; illus; pbk

Waihou

783 The Waihou one hundred: 1880 to 1980 / researched by
E. J. Tynan; prepared by Peter Reilly. Waihou, NZ:
Waihou Rugby Football Club Centennial Committee,
1980.
72p; illus

Waitohi

784 Waitohi Rugby Football Club: centennial booklet,
1885-1985 / edited by Norma Herd. Picton, NZ: The
Club, 1985.
22p; illus; pbk

Wellington

785 A century of rugby: a history of the Wellington Football
Club's first hundred years / R. Veysey. Wellington, NZ:
The Club, 1970.
72p; illus

Westport

786 Westport Rugby Football Club, 1886-1986 centennial
jubilee 28th, 29th, 30th March 1986: 1886-1986
Westport Rugby Football Club Incorporated centenary /
compiled and written by R. W. (Wongi) White; historical
records by Robert Hutt. Westport, NZ: The Club, 1986.
134p; illus; pbk

   Cover title: 100th anniversary, 1886-1986

Winton

787 Winton Rugby Football Club centennial celebrations,
1882-1982, Queen's birthday weekend, 4th, 5th, 6th
June: souvenir programme. Winton, NZ: The Club, 1982.
8p; pbk

Wyndham

788 Chasing the leather: a brief history on the first 75 years
of the Wyndham Rugby Football Club 1901-1976 / L. B.
Leitch. Southland, NZ: The Club, 1976.
40p; illus

789 Wyndham Rugby Club 90th jubilee celebrations
1901-1991: souvenir pamphlet, including Wyndham
rugby history supplement. Wyndham, NZ: The Club,
1991.
19p; pbk

Zingari-Richmond

790 Zingari-Richmond Football Club (Inc.) centennial
publication / edited by Jeff Holloway. Dunedin, NZ:
The Club, 1978.
48p

❋ Regional Studies

Auckland

791 1883-1933: fifty years' record of rugby in Auckland /
compiled by A. J. Billington. Auckland, NZ: Auckland
Rugby Football Union, 1933.
92p; illus; pbk
   ☞ See also: B792; B793

792 Rugby in Auckland, 1883-1967: official history of the
Auckland Rugby Football Union Inc. Auckland, NZ:
The Union, 1968.
235p; illus

   *Incorporates material first published in: 1883-1933: fifty
   years' record of rugby in Auckland*   BL: X.611/5188
   ☞ See also: B791

793 100 years, Auckland rugby: official history of the
Auckland Rugby Football Union Inc. Auckland, NZ:
The Union, 1983.
318p; illus

   *Includes and updates 1883-1933: fifty years' record of rugby
   in Auckland*
   ☞ See also: B791

794 Blue & white: an illustrated record of Auckland's
glorious Ranfurly Shield era, 1985-1988 / Lindsay
Knight. Auckland, NZ: Rugby Press, 1988.
96p; illus; pbk

Bay of Plenty

795 Bay of Plenty Rugby Union Inc.: diamond jubilee
1911-1971. Bay of Plenty, NZ: The Union, 1972.
32p; illus; pbk

Canterbury

796 Canterbury Rugby Football Union jubilee, July 1879-
1929: fifty years' history: also origin of rugby football,
football in the province prior to 1879, South Canterbury
football / W. G. Garrard. Christchurch, NZ: New
Zealand Newspaper, 1929.
80p

797 Rugby football in Canterbury 1929-1954 / J. K. Moloney.
Christchurch, NZ: Canterbury Rugby Football Union, 1954.
116p; illus; pbk

798 Mid-Canterbury Rugby Football Union (formerly the
Ashburton County Rugby Union) golden jubilee
1927-1977 / compiled by J. W. Smith and others.
Ashburton, NZ: The Union, 1977.
72p; illus

   *Cover title: 50 years first class rugby in Ashburton county
   and mid-Canterbury, 1927-1977.*

799 The Canterbury rugby history, 1879-1979 / Larry
     Saunders. Christchurch, NZ: Canterbury Rugby Football
     Union, 1979.
     144p; illus; pbk

800 The origins and development of rugby in Christchurch
     1860-1885 / Phil Murray. University of Canterbury, NZ,
     1983. *Master's thesis.*

801 Red & black: a permanent record of Canterbury rugby,
     1983. Christchurch, NZ: South Island Sports, 1983.
     256p; illus; pbk

802 Glory days: Alex Wyllie and the Canterbury Ranfurly
     Shield team 1982-85 / Kevin McMenamin.
     Christchurch, NZ, London: Whitcoulls, 1986.
     238p; illus   ISBN: 0723307954
                                          BL: YK.1987.a.3732

803 100 years of South Canterbury rugby / edited & written
     by Rex Bowden, Lyndsay Nixon; illustrations by Rowena
     Norton. Timaru, NZ: SCRFU, 1988.
     132p; illus; pbk

        *Cover title: Men in all weather: 100 years of South
        Canterbury rugby; Bibliography: p3*

804 One for the ref!: a centennial history of the Canterbury
     Rugby Referees' Association 1894-1994 / Roy Cairns and
     Alan Taylor. Christchurch, NZ: The Association, 1994.
     164p; illus; pbk

Counties

805 Counties '79: rugby champions of New Zealand / Rex
     Warwood. Pukekohe, NZ: Franklin County News, 1979.
     64p; illus

Gisborne

806 Rugby in Poverty Bay 1878-1964, commemorating the
     75th jubilee of the Union / Arthur C. Swan. Poverty
     Bay: Poverty Bay Rugby Football Union, 1965.
     127p; illus; pbk

        The club was founded in 1890.

Hawke's Bay

807 1884-1984 Hawke's Bay Rugby Union centenary special
     feature. Napier, NZ: The Tribune, 1984.
     15p; illus

        Supplement to: The Hawke's Bay Herald-Tribune,
        Thursday May 31st 1984

808 History of Hawkes Bay rugby / Stuart Hills. Hawkes
     Bay, NZ: The Hawkes Bay Union, 1995.

King Country

809 Pinetree country: a pictorial record of King Country's
     50th jubilee year (1972) / compiled and written by Ron
     Cooke & Ian Pilkington. Taumarunui, NZ: R. L. Cooke,
     1973.
     140p; illus; pbk   ISBN: 0908724047

Manawatu Wanganui

810 Horowhenua Rugby Football (Incorporated): 75 years of
     rugby 1893-1968. Horowhenua, NZ: Horowhenua
     Rugby Football Union, 1968.
     169p; illus; pbk

811 Social aspects of rugby football in Manawatu from 1878
     to 1910 / Neal Swindells. Massey University, NZ, 1978.
     Doctoral thesis.

812 Manawatu rugby 1886-1980: a statistical record of the
     Manawatu Rugby Union, its matches and representatives
     in first class rugby: includes the Manawhenua Rugby
     Union 1925-1932 / compiled by Clive A. Akers. Opiki,
     NZ: The author, 1981.
     116p; pbk

813 Manawatu rugby: the first 100 years, 1886-1986 / Clive
     Akers. Palmerston North, NZ: Manawatu Rugby
     Football Union, 1986.
     247p; illus; pbk

814 Blue and black: bruised but unbowed: 100 years of
     Wanganui rugby / Peter Johnston. Wanganui, NZ:
     Wanganui Rugby Football Union, 1989.
     224p; illus, coats of arms; pbk

815 In Jacob's shadow: the centennial history of the
     Horowhenua Rugby Football Union 1893-1993 / Clive
     Akers. Horowhenua: The Union, 1993.
     201p; illus; pbk

Marlborough

816 Rugby in Marlborough: a souvenir booklet published to
     mark the centennial of the Marlborough Rugby Union
     Football Union 1888-1988 / Harry Turvey. Blenheim,
     NZ: The Union, 1988.
     96p; illus; pbk

        Bibliography: p3

Northland

817 North Auckland Rugby Football Union Inc. golden
     jubilee 1920-1970. Whangarei?, NZ: The Union, 1970.
     116p; illus; pbk

818 100 years of Whangarei rugby: the centennial booklet of the Whangarei & Districts Rugby Sub-Union / compiled by Murray Dunn and Gary Frew with the assistance of the Sub-Union Centennial Committee and the Whangarei clubs. Whangarei, NZ: The Union, 1995. 120p; illus; pbk

Otago

819 The history and development of rugby football in Dunedin, 1871-1881 / Grant D. Connon and Stephen M. Haycock. University of Otago, NZ, 1977. *Thesis.*

820 The pride of southern rebels on the occasion of the Otago Rugby Football Union centenary 1881-1981 / Sean O'Hagan. Dunedin, NZ: Pilgrims South Press, 1981. 224p; illus   BL: X.622/21895

821 Otago 17 - Southland 11: a social history of Otago rugby in the 1940s / Anthony Lunch. University of Otago, NZ, 1984. *Thesis.*

822 Rugby in blue and gold / Dave McLaren. Corrected ed. Dunedin, NZ: Hanmade, 1993. 1 vol. (unpaged); spiral

    Previous ed.: 1992   ISBN: 0473017237

Southland

823 Southland Rugby Football Union: jubilee souvenir, 1887-1936 / edited and compiled by A. V. Keast. Invercargill, NZ: Southland Times Print, 1936? 56p; illus

824 Something to crow about: the centennial history of the Southland Rugby Football Union / Lynn McConnell. Invercargill, NZ: Craig Printing, 1986. 356p; illus; index   ISBN: 0908629206

825 Southland Rugby Referees' Association: 1894-1994 centennial / M. Tipa. Invercargill, NZ: The Association, 1994. 72p; illus; pbk   ISBN: 047302926X

Taranaki

826 1885-1960: 75 years of rugby in Taranaki. Taranaki, NZ: The Union, 1960. 40p; illus; pbk

827 100 years of Taranaki rugby, 1885-1985. New Plymouth, NZ: Taranaki Rugby Union 1985. 95p; illus; pbk

Tasman

828 Rugby in the Buller / Arthur C. Swan and Norman Crawshaw. Westport, NZ: Buller Rugby Football Union, 1993. 95p; illus; pbk

    Running title: Buller rugby centenary

Waikato

829 Waikato Rugby Football Union (Incorporated): golden jubilee 1921-1971 / Winston Hooper. Hamilton, NZ: The Union, 1971. 143p; illus; pbk

830 Mooloo magic / Winston Hooper; pictures by Kirby Wright. Hamilton, NZ: The author, 1980. 48p; illus; pbk

831 The might of Mooloo: the history of the fourth Waikato Rugby Union 1921-1996 / Winston Hooper; statistical information supplied by Geoff Miller. Hamilton, NZ: The Union, 1996. 208p; illus; pbk   ISBN: 0473042320

832 Waikato RFU jubilee. 1996. 200p

    Limited edition

THE
PRIDE
OF

SOUTHERN
REBELS

on the occasion of the
Otago Rugby Football Union Centenary 1881-1981

Sean O'Hagan

Pilgrims South Press
Dunedin, New Zealand

Wellington

833 Records of Wairarapa Union 1886-1946 / H. J. McKenzie. Carterton, NZ: The Union, 1946.
108p; illus; pbk

> *Cover title: Wairarapa Rugby Football Union jubilee issue 1886-1946*

834 Wellington's rugby history, 1870-1950 / Arthur C. Swan and Gordon F. W. Jackson. Wellington, NZ: Reed, 1952.
195p; illus; pbk

835 Wellington's rugby history, 1951-1979: part II the completion of 100 years / compiled by Alex Veysey and Bob Fox with the assistance of Paul Elenio, Joseph Romanos and Ian Gault from the records of the Wellington Rugby Football Union by Gordon Jackson and Albert Butterworth. Wellington, NZ: The Union, 1979.
169p; illus; pbk

836 A history of the playing of rugby union football in the Foxton district, 1880-1980 / edited by A. N. Hunt. Foxton, NZ: Foxton Rugby Club Centennial Committee, 1980.
63p; illus

> Covers Foxton, Awahou, Moutoa, Foxton-Moutoa, Albion, Moutoa Estate, Fire Brigade, Crusaders, Old Boys, Foxton ATC, Foxton State School, Foxton DHS, and Manawatu College clubs.

837 Wairarapa Bush centennial 1886-1986: a historical record of the Wairarapa Bush Rugby Football Union / A. J. McKenzie. Carterton, NZ: Roydhouse for Wairarapa Rugby Football Union, 1987.
242p; illus; pbk

838 The 31st man: 100 years of the Wellington Rugby Referees' Association / compiled by Scott Sargentina. Wellington, NZ: The Association, 1994.
107p; illus; pbk

West Coast

839 Rugby in retrospect: 21 years of post-war rugby on the West Coast / Albert Watkin in association with Kevin Bell. Greymouth, NZ: West Coast Rugby Union, 1966.
56p; illus; pbk

840 Rugby west of the alps, 1875-1990: marking the centennial of the West Coast Rugby Football Union Inc. / compiled by B. J. (Bernie) Guerin. Greymouth, NZ: The Union, Centennial Committee, 1990.
96p; illus; pbk

Australia

Brisbane Grammar School

841 One hundred years of grammar rugby / Peter James. Bowen Hills, Aust.: Boolarong, 1988.
xi, 163p; illus   ISBN: 0864390637

Canberra Royals

842 Canberra Royals Rugby Football Club 1949-1989: 40th anniversary commemorative booklet. Weston, Aust,: The Club, 1989.
28p; illus; pbk

Croydon-Maroondah

843 Croydon-Maroondah Rugby Union Football Club: the first twenty-five years, 1971-1996 / compiled and edited by Bryn Jones. Croydon, Aust.: The Club, 1997.
90p; illus

Easts

844 Easts rugby story 1900-1975 / Eddie Kann. Orange, Aust.: Chandler, 1975.
197p; illus; pbk

Eastwood

845 Those magnificent men: 50 years of Eastwood rugby / Allan Wilson. Eastwood, Aust.: Eastwood Rugby Club, 1997.

Gordon

846 The Highlanders: the first 50 years of the Gordon Rugby Football Club / Phil Wilkins. Sydney, Aust.: The Club in association with Ayres & James Heritage Books, 1986.
xii, 180p; illus

> *Also issued in a limited commemorative edition*
> ISBN: 0949256064

Gosford

847 Gosford Rugby Club, 21st anniversary, 1975-1995.
Gosford, Aust.: The Club, 1995.
76p; illus

Mosman

848 Two blues: 100 years of Mosman rugby / Jeff Hewitt.
Cremorne, Aust.: Team Creative Services, 1996.
198p; illus; pbk

Bibliography: p198   ISBN: 0646278363

Northern Suburbs

849 Norths: a history of the first fifty years of the Northern
Suburbs Rugby Union Football Club Inc., Canberra
ACT: the Galloping Greens. Belconnen, Aust.: The
Club, 1988.
xi, 104p; illus

Cover title: Norths, the first fifty years

Prince Alfred Old Collegians

850 Prince Alfred Old Collegians Football Club, 1925-1985 /
Mervyn Wyke Evans. Kent Town, Aust.: The Club, 1985.
112p   ISBN: 0959011102

St. Joseph's College, Sydney

851 The tradition: 100 years of rugby at St. Joseph's College
/ James Gray. Sydney, Aust.: Phillip Mathews Publishers
for The College, 1994.
vii, 154p; illus

University of Western Australia

852 The green and golden era: a history of the University of
Western Australia Rugby Football Club 1929 to 1994: 65
years of rugby / Rick Wolters. Nedlands, Aust.: The
University, 1994.
105p; illus

Walcha

853 Memories from scrum and ruck: a history of the Walcha
Rugby Union Football Club, 1894-1994 / Graham
Croker. Walcha, Aust.: The Club, 1994.
266p; illus

> Limited to an edition of 1,000 copies, the book
> chronicles the achievements of the club. Because no
> minute books exist and two fires, in 1928 and 1932,
> destroyed a number of the files belonging to two local
> newspapers, the early history of the club was difficult
> to research. The author pieced together the story
> after the Second World War by drawing on his own
> recollections as well as club and media records.

✱ Regional Studies

New South Wales

854 The game for the game itself!: the development of
sub-district rugby in Sydney in remembrance of every
person who has administered, played for or supported a
sub-district rugby club / Tom Hickie. St. Ives, Aust.:
Sydney Sub-District Rugby Union, 1983.
234p; illus; pbk   ISBN: 095919410X

> Examines how sub-district rugby developed. Its belief
> in the amateur distinguishes it from the district
> player.

855 Sporting spectacles: cricket and football in Sydney
1890-1912 / Martin Sharp. Australian National
University, 1986. *Doctoral thesis.*
viii, 475 leaves

856 The origins of rugby football in Sydney to 1880 /
Thomas Vincent Hickie. University of New South
Wales, Aust., 1992. *Doctoral thesis.*

> Evaluates a number of past interpretations of the
> pre-1880 period and compares them with the
> material revealed from a detailed examination of the
> Sydney newspapers of that time. When football began
> to be played on a continual basis from the 1860s,
> private gentlemen's clubs, the university and the
> schools provided the clubs to enable the sport to
> survive and eventually prosper. In addition, they were
> able to obtain use of public open space in Sydney on
> more than an occasional basis. Consideration is also
> given to the rival codes of Australian rules and
> soccer and the threat they posed.

Queensland

857 The marauding maroons: the rise of Queensland rugby /
Bret Harris. Cammeray, Aust.: Horwitz, 1982.
117p; illus

> *Cover title: The rise of Queensland rugby*

ISBN: 072551342X

858 Maroon: highlights of one hundred years of rugby in
Queensland 1882-1982 / edited by W. H. Bickley.
Brisbane, Aust.: Queensland Rugby Union, 1982.
169p; illus   ISBN: 0959310509

859 A history of rugby football in Queensland 1882-1891 /
Peter A. Horton. University of Queensland, Aust., 1989.
Doctoral thesis.

860 Red! red! red!: the history of Queensland rugby / Ian
Diehm. Caringbah, Aust.: Playright, 1997.
296p; illus   ISBN: 0949853593

Canada

James Bay

861 JBAA: the first 100 years / Lewis G. Madley. Victoria,
Can.: James Bay Athletic Association, 1986.
vi, 215p; illus

> *Cover title: James Bay Athletic Association 1886-1986*
> ISBN: 0969275005

✳ Regional Studies

Alberta

862 A history of rugby football in Edmonton / Patrick
Lamb. Edmonton, Can.: The author, 1986.
83p; illus; pbk

> *Bibliography: p69-75*

863 A history of rugby football in Edmonton (Alberta) / Patrick
Lamb. University of Alberta, Can., 1990. *Master's thesis.*
123p

Covers the period 1891-1986.

Nova Scotia

864 The origin and early development of rugby in Nova Scotia /
Ralph M. Davies. Dalhousie University, Can., 1978. *Thesis.*

865 A history of rugby in Nova Scotia / Ralph M. Davies.
Dalhousie University, Can., 1979. *Master's thesis.*

866 The decline of English rugby and the rise of Canadian
football in Halifax 1930 to 1954 / Robert Stephen Kossuth.
University of Windsor, Can., 1996. *Master's thesis.*
152p

Describes how the introduction of football by the Royal
Canadian Navy during the Second World War coupled
with the English rugby administrators' inability to
promote the game resulted in the decline of rugby.

Ontario

867 The Ontario Rugby Football Union 1904. Toronto,
Can.: Hambly, 1904.
64p   BL: D

Includes: Constitution, rules of championship
competition, and rules of the game.

Saskatchewan

868 Saskatchewan rugby: a history / David W. Brown.
Regina, Can.: Saskatchewan Rugby Union, 1993.
142p; illus; pbk

> *Bibliography: p123-42*   ISBN: 0969631839

✳ Additional References

869 Sports and games in Alberta before 1900 / J. E. Reid.
University of Alberta, Can., 1969. *Master's thesis.*

Information on a number of rugby tournaments
played in the Edmonton area.

870 The development of sports in Alberta 1900-1918 / C.
Blackburn. University of Alberta, 1974. *Master's thesis.*

Has a section on the development of rugby.

Rest of the World

Kenya ~ Nondescripts

871 Fifty years of Nondies / edited by John Lloyd and
others. Kenya, 1972.
44p; illus; pbk

Latvia

872 Regbija Federacija Latvija, or, Latvia in Rugby World
Cup Sevens '93. Riga, Latvia: Latvian RU, 1993.
33p; illus; pbk

Text in Latvian and English. Contains a brief history
of rugby in Latvia.

☞ Also listed at: D62

Malta ~ Overseas

873   Overseas Rugby and Sports Club (1946-1982): the
       history of the club / compiled by Norman Morgan.
       Scarborough: The compiler, 1978.
       2 vols; illus; pbk   BL: X.622/9866
          A detailed history of the club first set up as a rugby
          club in 1946. Cricket, soccer, and hockey sections
          were added later.

USA ~ New York

874   New York Rugby Football Club 1930-1979: its founding
       and early days / Albert Woodley. New York, US: The
       author, 1979.
       96p; illus; pbk

USA ~ University of California

875   California football history / Brick Morse. Berkeley, US:
       Gillick Press, 1937.
       223p; illus
            Author is Clinton Ralza Morse   BL: X.622/20122
          The history of rugby at the University from 1880 to
          1937.

Zimbabwe ~ Hartsfield

876   Hartsfield, after fifty years / Robert Prentice. Bulawayo:
       Matabeleland Rugby Football Board, 1988.
       24p; illus; pbk

CALIFORNIA
FOOTBALL
HISTORY

BY

BRICK MORSE, PH. B., DOC. F.*
ATHLETIC HISTORIAN, A. S. U. C

PRINTED BY THE GILLICK PRESS, BERKELEY, CALIFORNIA

*President Tully Knoles of The College of the Pacific Conferred on Mr. Morse the Degree of
Doctor of Football, the only degree of its kind in the world

Chapter C

Personalities

Contents

Biographies & Autobiographies

Allen, 'Bull' (New Zealand)

1   Little Bull / written & illustrated by Peter Harold. New Plymouth, NZ: Taranaki Rugby Football Union, 1994.
20p; chiefly illus; pbk   ISBN: 0473029154
    For children.

Andrew, Rob (England)

2   A game and a half: an autobiography / Rob Andrew. London: Hodder & Stoughton, 1994.
186p; illus   ISBN: 0340624817
          BL: YK.1995.b.14983

    ☞ Subsequent ed. C3

3   A game and a half: an autobiography / Rob Andrew. London: Hodder & Stoughton, 1995.
viii, 275p; illus; index; pbk   ISBN: 0340666889
          BL: YK.1996.a.14929

    'Fully updated to include the high drama of the 1995 Rugby World Cup.'
    ☞ Previous ed. C2

Armstrong, Gary (Scotland)

4   Jethart's here!: the Gary Armstrong story / Gary Armstrong and Derek Douglas; foreword by Bill McLaren. Edinburgh: Mainstream, 1995.
187p; illus   ISBN: 1851587276
          BL: YK.1996.b.12407

Barnes, Stuart (England)

5   Smelling of roses: a rugby life / Stuart Barnes. Edinburgh: Mainstream, 1994.
206p; illus   ISBN: 1851586407
          BL: YK.1995.b.10432

Batchelor, Denzil

6   Babbled of green fields / Denzil Batchelor. London: Hutchinson, 1961.
223p   BL: 10818.pp.20

    Sports editor of *Picture Post* and sports correspondent, Batchelor includes among his sporting memories a chapter on rugby.

Batty, Grant (New Zealand)

7   Grant Batty: a biography / Bob Howitt; foreword by J. J. Stewart. Auckland, NZ: Rugby Press, 1977.
255p; illus   ISBN: 0959755306

Beaumont, Bill (England)

8   Thanks to rugby / Bill Beaumont. London: Stanley Paul, 1982.
207p; illus   ISBN: 0091507502
          BL: X.629/19350

9   Billy Beaumont: the lion of winter / Sean Pryor. London: Star, 1983.
188p; illus; pbk   ISBN: 0352312335
          BL: X.629/20359

Bennett, Phil (Wales)

10   Everywhere for Wales / Phil Bennett and Martyn Williams. London: Stanley Paul, 1981.
175p; illus   ISBN: 0091463106
          BL: X.629/16714

Berry, John (England)

11   Buff Berry and the Mighty Bongers / Michael Latham. Chorley: Mike RL Publications, 1995.
96p; illus; pbk   ISBN: 0951609858

    John Berry (1866-1930) played rugby for Kendal Hornets, Tyldesley, Lancashire and England. Joining Tyldesley in 1888 he remained with the club until 1901, seven years after it became a member of the then Northern Union. Berry was also instrumental in forming a Westmorland county club. The biography was published in a limited edition of 500 copies.

Blakeway, Phil (England)

12   Rubbing shoulders: the story of a rugby prop / Phil Blakeway with Chris Ducker. London: Stanley Paul, 1985.
147p; illus   ISBN: 0091628601
          BL: X.629/27574

Botha, Naas (South Africa)

13   Naas / Edward Griffiths. Pretoria, SA: Leo Publishers, 1989.
256p; illus; index   ISBN: 0620132248

14   Naas Botha: rugby's golden boy / Chris Greyvenstein, A. C. Parker and T. Shnaps. Cape Town, SA: Don Nelson, 1989.
48p; illus   ISBN: 1868060624

Brewer, Mike (New Zealand)

15   Mike Brewer: the authorised biography with Phil Gifford. Auckland, NZ: Rugby Publishing, 1995.
208p; illus   ISBN: 0908630530

Brooke, Zinzan (New Zealand)

16   Zinny: the Zinzan Brooke story with Alex Veysey. Auckland, NZ: Rugby Publishing, 1995.
232p; illus; pbk   ISBN: 0908630549

17   Zinzan Brooke. Auckland, NZ: Hodder Moa Beckett, 1997.
70p; illus
(Awesome)   ISBN: 1869585267
   For children.

Brooke-Cowden, Mark (New Zealand)

18   All Black: what's it like to be Mark Brooke-Cowden? / text by Judith Holloway from the transcript of an interview with Mark Brooke-Cowden by Liz Brook; photographs by Peter Bush, Liz Brook and others. Petone, NZ: Price Milburn, 1987.
32p; illus
(Top people)   ISBN: 0705513467
   For children.

Brown, Gordon (Scotland)

19   Broon from Troon: an autobiography / Gordon Brown. London: Stanley Paul, 1983.
219p; illus   ISBN: 0091502608
                                                     BL: X.629/20916

Bruce, J. Alex (New Zealand)

20   Alex the Bruce / Bob Luxford. Palmerston North, NZ: Rugby Museum Society of New Zealand, 1994.
32p; illus; pbk
   Bruce played for New Zealand in 1913/14 and was a prominent cricketer for Wellington.

Bunce, Frank (New Zealand)

21   Midfield liaison: the Frank Bunce, Walter Little story / Bob Howitt. Auckland, NZ: Rugby Publishing, 1996.
237p; illus   ISBN: 090863059X
   ☞ Also listed at: C138

22   Frank Bunce. Auckland, NZ: Hodder Moa Beckett, 1997.
69p; illus
(Awesome)   ISBN: 186958533X
   For children.

Burrows, James (New Zealand)

23   Pathway among men / J. T. Burrows. Christchurch, NZ: Whitcombe and Tombs, 1974.
212p; illus   ISBN: 0723303789
                                                     BL: X.800/10185

   Autobiography of a distinguished soldier and sportsman — university boxing champion, cricketer at provincial level, rugby player for Canterbury and New Zealand in South Africa in 1928 and national selector and coach.

Burton, Mike (England)

24   Never stay down: an autobiography / Mike Burton and Steve Jones. London: Queen Anne Press, 1982.
186p; illus   ISBN: 0356085651
                                                     BL: X.800/33012

Campese, David (Australia)

25   On a wing & a prayer: the autobiography of David Campese / David Campese with Peter Bills. London: Queen Anne Press, 1991.
175p; illus   ISBN: 0356179583
                                                     BL: YK.1991.b.7141

26   David Campese / co-ordinated by David Clark. Sydney, Aust.: Macmillan, 1996.
113p; illus
(Ironbark legends)   ISBN: 0732908507

Carling, Will (England)

27   Captain's diary, 1989-1991 / Will Carling. London: Chatto & Windus, 1991.
161p; illus   ISBN: 0701136529
                                                     BL: YK.1992.b.4526

28   Carling: a man apart / Peter Bills. London: Witherby, 1993.
254p; illus; index   ISBN: 0854932305
                                                     BL: YK.1993.b.14074

   ☞ Subsequent ed. C32

29   Will Carling / Andrew Ward; designed by Ness Wood. London: Hippo, 1993.
48p; illus; pbk
(Sports shots)   ISBN: 059055185X
                                                     BL: YK.1994.a.10571

   Written for children.

PATHWAY AMONG MEN

❊❊❊❊❊❊❊❊

J. T. Burrows

30 Will Carling: the authorised biography / David Norrie. London: Headline, 1993.
viii, 312p; illus; index
    Bibliography: p vii
                        ISBN: 0747209022
                        BL: YK.1994.b.867

☞ Subsequent ed. C31

31 Will Carling: the authorised biography / David Norrie. 2nd ed. London: Headline, 1994.
ix, 403p; illus; index   ISBN: 0747242852

☞ Previous ed. C30

32 Carling: a man apart / Peter Bills. New ed. London: Gollancz, 1996.
352p; illus; index; pbk
    Bibliography: p339
                        ISBN: 0575062606
                        BL: YK.1996.a.6325

☞ Previous ed. C28

Carson, Bill

33 W. N. Carson: footballer and cricketer / A. H. Carman. Wellington, NZ: Sporting Publications, 1947.
68p; illus; pbk

Chilcott, Gareth (England)

34 Cooch, Mr Chilcott to you: the experiences of Gareth Chilcott / Gareth Chilcott with Tony Ferrand. London: Johnsons, 1990.
74p; illus   ISBN: 1873304005
                        BL: YK.1992.a.9691

Christie, Kitch

35 Kitch: triumph of a decent man / Edward Griffiths. Johannesburg, SA: CAB, 1997.
vi, 151p; illus   ISBN: 0620217715
  Kitch Christie coached South Africa up to the 1995 World Cup.

Claassen, Wynand (South Africa)

36 More than just rugby / Wynand Claassen, with Dan Retief. Johannesburg, SA: Strydom, 1985.
318p; illus   ISBN: 0947025022
☞ Subsequent ed. C37

37 More than just rugby: the final chapter / Wynand Claassen with Dan Retief. 2nd ed. Durban North, SA: Rugby 15 International, 1995.
324p; illus; pbk   ISBN: 0620194936
  Chronicles events in South African rugby after 1985: the rebel tour of the country by a New Zealand XV, negotiations with the ANC in 1989, the formation of the SARFU in 1992, and finally, the Rugby World Cup final in Johannesburg in 1995.

☞ Previous ed. C36

Clarke, Don (New Zealand)

38 The boot / Don Clarke and Pat Booth. Wellington, NZ: Reed, 1966.
194p; illus
  Don Clarke played full-back for New Zealand.

Cleaver, Hylton

39 Before I forget / Hylton Reginald Cleaver. London: Hale, 1961.
190p; illus; index   BL: 10765.d.10
  The sports broadcaster and author of school stories and plays illustrates his autobiography with a number of rugby events: law changes, the British Lions, Cardiff Arms Park and its singing, the vagaries of selectors.

Collis, Robert (Ireland)

40 The silver fleece: an autobiography / Robert Collis; decorated by T. G. Wilson. London: Nelson, 1936.
290p   BL: 010822.g.21
  Robert Collis, MD, specialised in paediatrics. In his memoirs he recalls early childhood in Ireland, attending Rugby School and the universities of Cambridge and Yale and King' s College Hospital where he continued and completed his medical studies. He won two rugby blues, supplementing these with games for Harlequins and Surrey and seven appearances for Ireland in 1924 and 1925. He records that 'the winter of 1924-25 was for me the most successful in my whole [rugby] football career ... to be fit, to play continually before large, cheering crowds, to be recognized and pointed out in the street, to be rung up by the evening papers and asked your opinion on problems of the day, and see yourself quoted with the Archbishop of Canterbury, Tallulah Bankhead, Jack Dempsey, Marie Stopes, or Mr Baldwin, is very gratifying to one's personal vanity'.

41 To be a pilgrim / Robert Collis; foreword by Christy Brown. London: Secker and Warburg, 1975.
ix, 244p; illus; index   ISBN: 0436105616
                        BL: X.320/10044
  Nearly 40 years after the publication of his memoirs, Collis has updated his lifestory. Covering the same ground, academic and sporting prowess in Ireland and England, he continues with an account of his life from before the Second World War: the war years – helping the survivors of Belsen; a period in Nigeria; and, finally, his discovery and treatment of Christy Brown who had cerebral palsy. Through his experience as a playwright and author, Collis encouraged Christy Brown to become a writer. During a rugby career of 22 years Collis captained or led every side he played for, except Ireland. We are told that Collis 'learned more self-discipline through rugby football than in any other way'.

Cotton, Fran (England)

42 Fran: an autobiography / Fran Cotton. London: Queen
Anne Press, 1981.
192p; illus; index   ISBN: 0362005826
                                      BL: X.622/11684

Cowley, Gavin (South Africa)

43 Having a ball / G. Cowley. Port Elizabeth, SA: Sporting
Publications, 1983.
108p; illus; index; pbk   ISBN: 0620071869
   A member of a distinguished sporting family, Cowley
   represented Eastern Province in cricket and rugby.

Craven, Danie (South Africa)

44 A life in rugby / Ted Partridge. Johannesburg, SA:
Southern Book Publishers, 1991.
xiii, 161p; illus   ISBN: 1868123553

45 Doc: the life of Danie Craven / Paul Dobson. Cape
Town, SA: Human & Rousseau, 1994.
297p; illus; index
     Bibliography: p272-7   ISBN: 0798133147

46 The Craven tapes: Doc tells all / Keith Clayton and
Chris Greyvenstein. Cape Town, SA: Human &
Rousseau, 1995.
192p; illus   ISBN: 0798134143

Cullen, Christian (New Zealand)

47 Christian Cullen. Auckland, NZ: Hodder Moa Beckett,
1997.
70p; illus
(Awesome)   ISBN: 1869585402
   For children.

Dallaglio, Lawrence (England)

48 Diary of a season / Lawrence Dallaglio. London: Virgin,
1997.
ix, 230p; illus   ISBN: 1852276746

David, Tommy (Wales)

49 Tommy David / edited by Dan O'Neill. Cardiff:
Thomson Media, 1983.
91p; illus   ISBN: 0950404225

Davies, Dai

50 Man of Amman: the life of Dai Davies / Phil Melling.
Llandysul: Gomer, 1994.
xi, 135p; illus; index; pbk
     Also contains: Surfing the hurricane ISBN: 1859020836
                                      BL: YK.1996.a.5892

Davies, Gareth (Wales)

51 Gareth Davies standing off: my life in rugby / Gareth
Davies with Terry Godwin. London: Macdonald, 1986.
176p; illus   ISBN: 0356121577
                                      BL: X.622/26021

Davies, Gerald (Wales)

52 Gerald Davies: an autobiography. London: Allen and
Unwin, 1979.
xv, 160p; illus; index   ISBN: 0047960523
                                      BL: X.629/14443

Davies, Jonathan (Wales)

53 Jonathan: an autobiography / Jonathan Davies with
Peter Corrigan. London: Stanley Paul, 1989.
224p; illus   ISBN: 0091741874
                                      BL: YK.1990.b.982

54 Jonathan Davies: code breaker / Jonathan Davies with
Peter Corrigan. London: Bloomsbury, 1996.
vii, 216p; illus; index   ISBN: 074752551X
                                      BL: YK.1997.b.5621

Number 8
─────────────────

Mervyn Davies
with David Parry-Jones

foreword by John Dawes

  PELHAM BOOKS

Davies, Mervyn (Wales)

55 Number 8 / Mervyn Davies with David Parry-Jones;
foreword by John Dawes. London: Pelham, 1977.
208p; illus   ISBN: 0720709806
                                      BL: X.629/11344
   Traces Davies' journey from London Welsh 3rd XV to
   the Welsh international side.

De Villiers, H. O. (South Africa)

56 H. O.: a biography of courage / Neville Leck. Cape
Town, SA: Nelson, 1977.
227p; illus

> *Bibliography: p227*　　　ISBN: 090923826X

Deans, Colin (Scotland)

57 You're a hooker, then: an autobiography / Colin Deans.
Edinburgh: Mainstream, 1987.
208p; illus; index　　　ISBN: 1851580794
BL: YK.1989.b.2805

Doble, Sam (England)

58 Sam: a man for all seasons / edited by M. Blair. Midlands
Sports Magazines, 1977.
32p; illus; pbk

Dooley, Wade (England)

59 The tower and the glory: the Wade Dooley story / Wade
Dooley with Gerry Greenberg. Edinburgh: Mainstream,
1992.
192p, illus　　　ISBN: 1851584617
BL: YK.1993.b.13711

Doyle, Mick (Ireland)

60 Doyler / Mick Doyle. Dublin: Gill and Macmillan, 1991.
xi, 194p; illus　　　ISBN: 0717118541
BL: YK.1992.a.8891

Duckham, David (England)

61 Dai for England: the autobiography of David Duckham
/ foreword by Bill McLaren. London: Pelham, 1980.
223p; illus; index　　　ISBN: 0720712793
BL: X.629/14629

Dunlop, Edward (Australia)

62 Weary: the life of Sir Edward Dunlop / Sue Ebury.
Harmondsworth: Viking, 1994.
709p; illus, maps; index

> *Bibliography: p682-7*　　　ISBN: 0670847607
BL: YC.1994.b.4922

'Weary' Dunlop played for Australia in two matches,
both against New Zealand, in 1932 and 1934. A
pharmacist and surgeon, Dunlop took his expertise
into the Australian Imperial Force at the outbreak of
the Second World War. Captured by the Japanese in
Java, he was incarcerated for three years. He stood
up for the well-being of the men in his command in the
face of the Japanese enemy. On returning to
Australia he became a national hero, and he
dedicated his life to caring for former prisoners-of-
war.

Dwyer, Bob

63 Bob Dwyer: the winning way / Phil Derriman. London:
Lennard, 1992.
198p; illus; index　　　ISBN: 1852915250

Edwards, Gareth (Wales)

64 Gareth / Gareth Edwards. London: Stanley Paul, 1978.
176p; illus　　　ISBN: 0091348005
BL: X.629/12197

Ella Gary, Glen & Mark (Australia)

65 Ella, Ella, Ella / Bret Harris. Windlesham: Springwood,
1984.
128p; illus　　　ISBN: 0862541220
BL: X.622/22570

> Biographies of the Ella brothers who played for
> Australia.

Evans, Ieuan (Wales)

66 Bread of heaven / Ieuan Evans and Peter Jackson.
Edinburgh: Mainstream, 1995.
224p; illus; index　　　ISBN: 1851587861
BL: YK.1996.b.10288

☞　Subsequent ed. C67

67 Bread of heaven / Ieuan Evans and Peter Jackson.
Updated ed. Edinburgh: Mainstream, 1997.
256p; illus; index　　　ISBN: 1840180080

> Updated to include the 1995 World Cup.

☞　Previous ed. C66

Farr-Jones, Nick (Australia)

68 Nick Farr-Jones: the authorised biography / Peter
FitzSimons. Milsons Point, Aust., London: Random
House Australia, 1993.
viii, 285p; illus; index
ISBN: 0091785413 • 0091827582 (Australia)
BL: YK.1994.b.2842

Fatialofa, Peter (Western Somoa)

69 Fats: Peter Fatialofa and the Manu Samoa story / Peter
Fatialofa with Phil Gifford. Auckland, NZ: Rugby
Publishing, 1996.
191p; illus　　　ISBN: 0908630611

Finnane, Steve (Australia)

70 The game they play in heaven: Australian rugby from the
inside / Steve Finnane. Sydney, Aust.: McGraw-Hill,
1979.
vii, 168p; illus　　　ISBN: 0070935599

Fitzpatrick, Sean (New Zealand)

71   Fronting up: the Sean Fitzpatrick story / Steven
O'Meagher. Auckland, NZ: Moa Beckett, 1994.
240p; illus   ISBN: 1869581105

The biography of Sean Fitzpatrick, the New Zealand
hooker and captain since 1992.

72   Sean Fitzpatrick. Auckland, NZ: Hodder Moa Beckett,
1997.
72p; illus
(Awesome)   ISBN: 1869585232

For children.

Fox, Grant (New Zealand)

73   The game the goal: the Grant Fox story / Alex Veysey.
Auckland, NZ: Rugby Press, 1992.
215p; illus   ISBN: 0908630395

Fraser, Bernie (New Zealand)

74   Ebony & ivory: the Stu Wilson, Bernie Fraser story as
told to Alex Veysey. Poole: Blandford, 1984.
271p; illus   ISBN: 0713716320
                                          BL: X.622/25267

☞   Also listed at: C235

French, Ray (England)

75   My kind of rugby: union and league / Ray French;
foreword by Dick Jeeps. London: Faber & Faber, 1979.
xvi, 139p; illus   ISBN: 0571114229
                                          BL: X.629/12660

Having played both union and league at international
level, French recalls the moments he relished in the
two games. He also explores the relationship of the
two codes.

Fry, C. B.

76   Mr C. B. Fry / Albert Craig. London?: Wright, 1906.
A card folded in 4; illus

77   C. B. Fry: the man and his methods / A. W. Myers; with
a preface by G. H. R. Dabbs. Bristol: J. W. Arrowsmith,
1912.
xi, 189p   BL: 010854.de.31

C. B. Fry is one of sport's best known 'all-rounders'.
An unfortunate bout of flu prevented him from adding
a rugby cap to his list of honours.

78   Life worth living: some phases of an Englishman / C. B.
Fry. London: Eyre & Spottiswoode, 1939.
423p; illus   BL: 10859.d.5

79   C. B. Fry / Denzil Batchelor. London: Phoenix House,
1951.
64p; illus
(Cricketing lives)   BL: X.629/3574(3)

80   C. B.: the life of Charles Burgess Fry / Clive Ellis.
London: Dent, 1984.
x, 294p; illus; index
Bibliography: p277-8   ISBN: 0460046543
                                 BL: X.950/34764

81   The captain's lady / Ronald Morris. London: Chatto &
Windus, 1985.
178p; illus; index
Bibliography: p167   ISBN: 0701129468
                                 BL: X.800/41837

The biography of C B's wife, Beattie Fry.

Gainsford, John (South Africa)

82   Nice guys come second / John Gainsford as told to
Neville Leck, with a review of the Lions tour. Cape
Town, SA: Nelson, 1974.
256p; illus   ISBN: 0909238049

The final three chapters review the 1974 British and
Irish Lions in South Africa.

Gallagher, John (New Zealand)

83   John Gallagher: what is it like to be an All Black? / text
by Kevin Boon from the transcript of an interview with
John Gallagher by Liz Brook. Petone, NZ: Nelson Price
Milburn, 1990.
32p; illus; pbk
(Top people)   ISBN: 0705514951

For the younger reader.

84   John Gallagher: the world's best rugby player? / John
Gallagher with Chris Brown, Alan McColm. Harrogate:
R & B, 1991.
188p; illus

*Subsequently published as: John Gallagher: the million dollar
fullback. Auckland, NZ: Rugby Press, 1991*
                                 ISBN: 1873668503
                                 BL: YK.1992.b.3989

Gerber, Danie (South Africa)

85   Danie Gerber: maestro of the midfield / Chris
Schoeman. Cape Town, SA: Sable Media, 1995.
208p; illus; index
Bibliography: p201-3   ISBN: 0958406251

Tells the story of one of the best centres to appear
on a rugby field. From the age of 22 to 34 Gerber
played in 24 matches for South Africa, scoring 19
tries.

Gerrard, Major R. A. (England)

86 Men of a stout countenance / D. Crichton-Miller.
Abertillery: Dp, 1976.
143p; illus; pbk

Gibson, Alan

87 A mingled yarn / Alan Gibson. London: Collins, 1976.
222p   ISBN: 000216115X
                                         BL: X.809/40653

As well as chronicling his days as President of the
Union at Oxford, BBC producer, Liberal Party
politician, and member of the BBC's 'Round Britain'
quiz, the author describes cricket and rugby matches
he has witnessed as broadcaster and journalist.

Going, Sid (New Zealand)

88 Super Sid: the story of a great All Black / Bob Howitt.
Auckland, NZ: Rugby Press, 1978.
288p; illus   ISBN: 0959755314

Gravell, Ray (Wales)

89 Grav / Lyn Jones a Ray Gravell. Llandysul: Gomer, 1986.
186p; illus; pbk   ISBN: 0863832636
                                         BL: YK.1987.a.1207

Written in Welsh.

Greenwood, J. E. (England)

90 A cap for Boots: an autobiography / J. E. Greenwood.
London: Hutchinson Benham, 1977.
xvii, 254p; illus, 1 genealogical table; index
                                         ISBN: 0091288908
                                         BL: X.529/31626

Greenwood was a director of Boots Company Limited
– hence the title of his autobiography.

A CAP FOR BOOTS

AN AUTOBIOGRAPHY
J. E. GREENWOOD

HUTCHINSON BENHAM
LONDON

Gronow, Ben

91 An appreciation of a great footballer 1904 to 1924 / Ben
Gronow. Huddersfield: The author, 1924?
34p; illus; pbk

Guscott, Jeremy (England)

92 At the centre / Jeremy Guscott with Stephen Jones.
London: Pavilion, 1995.
247p; illus   ISBN: 1857930843
                                         BL: YK.1996.b.1252

Gwynn, Stephen

93 Experiences of a literary man / Stephen Gwynn.
London: Butterworth, 1926.
312p; index   BL: 010856.d.47

The author of over twenty books and brother of
Lucius Gwynn who played rugby for Ireland in the
1890s, and Arthur Gwynn, who also represented
Ireland on the rugby field – one cap in 1895. Gwynn
comments on his brothers' sporting skills: 'Neither he
[Arthur] nor Lucius had great weight or speed to
account for his prowess on the football field; I should
say each of them was about five feet nine and eleven
stone – Arthur much the more sturdily built.... But it
was often noticed at the time that whereas either of
them would break away from other notable backs
opposed to them, men two or three stone heavier, yet
if Lucius or Arthur got his hands to these bigger,
faster men, down they went'. Gwynn also notes
Lucius' intellectual side: 'Later on, when he was
reading for fellowship in T.C.D. (Trinity College, Dublin),
he gave up football, and I asked him why he did not
play just to keep fit; the loss of time would be only a
couple of hours twice a week or so. He told me that it
would take him off his work: in other words, if he
played at all, his mind, when it was not definitely
bidden to do something else, would fall automatically
to working out permutations and combinations of
play, inventing stratagems of passing and methods
of attack'. One wonders what Gwynn's observations
would be were he alive today. Even before the recent
introduction of professionalism, it is some time since
a player of international rugby has had to think of
sacrificing the game in order to pursue a career in his
chosen profession.

Haden, Andy (New Zealand)

94 Boots 'n all! / Andy Haden. Auckland, NZ: Rugby Press,
1983.
247p; illus; index

Subsequently reprinted: Poole: Blandford, 1984
                        ISBN: 0908630131 • 0713714921 (Blandford)
                                         BL: X.622/23186

95 Lock, stock 'n barrel / Andy Haden. Auckland, NZ:
Rugby Press, 1988.
232p; illus   ISBN: 090863028X

Hardy, Norman

96 Sole practice: the personal and professional experiences of a rugby playing chartered accountant / Norman Hardy; edited by M. G. Robertson. Collaroy, Aust.: The author, 1991.
99p; illus, maps
   Hardy played rugby for Easts.

Hare, Dusty (England)

97 Dusty / Dusty Hare with David Norrie; foreword by Bill McLaren. London: Queen Anne Press, 1985.
208p; illus   ISBN: 0356106373
                                 BL: X.622/23368

Hart, John

98 Straight from the Hart: the career and philosophy of a rugby revolutionary / Paul Thomas. London: Lennard/Queen Anne Press, 1993.
280p; illus   ISBN: 1852915331

99 Change of Hart / Paul Thomas. Auckland, NZ: Hodder Moa Beckett, 1997.
305p; illus   ISBN: 1869585712

Hastings, Gavin (Scotland)

100 High balls and happy hours: an autobiography / Gavin Hastings with Clem Thomas. Edinburgh: Mainstream, 1994.
192p; illus   ISBN: 1851586458
                                 BL: YK.1995.b.14901

Hastings, Scott (Scotland)

101 Great Scott!: the autobiography of Scotland's most capped player / Scott Hastings and Derek Douglas. Edinburgh: Mainstream, 1996.
190p; illus   ISBN: 1851588930
                                 BL: YK.1997.b.4373

Hawthorne, Phil (Australia)

102 Until the final whistle: Phil Hawthorne's life in football / Mike Jenkinson. Sydney, Aust.: Ironbark, 1996.
261p; illus; pbk   ISBN: 0330357166

Hearn, Danny (England)

103 Crash tackle / Danny Hearn with Ross Reyburn. London: Arthur Barker, 1972.
168p; illus   ISBN: 0213993791
                                 BL: X.629/4288

Heatlie, Barry (South Africa)

104 The first three generations of Heatlies in South Africa / Charles Hugo Heatlie. Worcester, SA: Boland Agricultural Museum, 1981.
135p; illus; pbk   ISBN: 0620050659
   A biography of Barry Heatlie is given on pages 68-72.

Hewson, Allan (New Zealand)

105 For the record: the Allan Hewson story / Ian Gault. Auckland, NZ: Rugby Press, 1984.
240p; illus   ISBN: 0908630158

Holmes, Terry (Wales)

106 My life in rugby / Terry Holmes. London: Macmillan, 1988.
viii, 181p; illus   ISBN: 0333402294
                                 BL: YK.1988.a.2818

Horan, Tim (Australia)

107 Perfect union: the parallel lives of Wallaby centres Tim Horan and Jason Little / Michael Blucher. Sydney, Aust.: Macmillan, 1995.
300p; illus; index   ISBN: 0732908140
   ☞ Also listed at: C137

Hore, Jack (New Zealand)

108 Jack Hore, a Southern man: the story of Jack Hore 1928-36 All Black, from Otago's Southern Club / Dave McLaren and Bob Luxford. Palmerston North, NZ: Rugby Museum Society of New Zealand, 1995.
32p; illus; pbk   ISBN: 0473035839

Howard, Peter (England)

109 Peter Howard: life and letters / Anne Wolrige Gordon. London: Hodder & Stoughton, 1969.
318p; illus   ISBN: 0340108401
                                 BL: X.100/6998

   Written by Howard's daughter. Chronicles his life: Millhill, Oxford; rugby for England; member of the British bobsleigh team that broke the world record in the 1939 World Championship; rugby correspondent, later political correspondent for the Sunday Express and other newspapers; devoted rest of life to the work of moral re-armament.

Humphreys, Jonathan (Wales)

110 Capten Cymru / Jonathan Humphreys ac Androw Bennett. Talybont: Y Lolfa, 1996.
172p; pbk   ISBN: 0862433991
   Captain of Wales — a personal diary by Jonathan Humphreys during his time as captain of Wales.

Irvine, Andy (Scotland)

111 Andy Irvine: an autobiography / Andy Irvine with Ian Robertson. London: Stanley Paul, 1985.
212p; illus   ISBN: 0091622700

James, Carwyn (Wales)

112 Carwyn un o 'fois y pentre' / golygydd John Jenkins. Llandysul: Gwasg Gomer, 1983.
196p; illus; pbk   ISBN: 0863830862
     BL: X.950/36236

Includes some contributions in English; also, a poem written by Dic Jones in strict metre to the memory of Carwyn James.

☞ See also: H140

113 Carwyn: a personal memoir / Alun Richards. London: Michael Joseph, 1984.
ix, 165p; illus; index   ISBN: 0718124200
     BL: X.629/24444

John, Barry (Wales)

114 The Barry John story / Barry John. London: Collins, 1974.
190p; illus   ISBN: 0002160110
     BL: X.629/6042

Jones, Frank

115 A schoolmaster looks back / Frank Jones. Birmingham: Norman Tiptaft, 1949.
96p; illus   BL: 10863.de.7

Jones was first secretary of Aston Old Edwardians in 1889, and then president for fifty years until his death in 1961. Writes about rugby, and much else, in this work.

Jones, Ian (New Zealand)

116 Ian Jones. Auckland, NZ: Hodder Moa Beckett, 1997.
71p; illus
(Awesome)   ISBN: 1869585321
    For children.

Jones, Lewis (Wales)

117 King of rugger: an autobiography / Lewis Jones. London: Stanley Paul, 1958.
192p; illus   BL: 7943.fff.9

Jones, Michael (New Zealand)

118 Iceman: the Michael Jones story / Robin McConnell. Auckland, NZ: Rugby Press, 1994.
268p; illus   ISBN: 0908630441

119 Michael Jones. Auckland, NZ: Hodder Moa Beckett, 1997.
71p; illus
(Awesome)   ISBN: 1869585259
    For children.

Jones, Paul

120 War letters of a public school-boy / Paul Jones, with a memoir by his father Harry Jones. London: Cassell, 1918.
vi, 280p; illus; index   BL: 010905.f.11

Jones joined the Army in April 1915 and while on service he penned a number of letters before he was killed in action near Ypres in July 1917. His father supplies a memoir in the first 118 pages of the book. A chapter entitled 'Football' chronicles Jones' rugby career at Dulwich College.

Jones, Peter (New Zealand)

121 'It's me, Tiger': the Peter Jones story / as told to Norman Harris. Wellington, NZ: Reed, 1965.
77p; illus

Kirk, David (New Zealand)

122 Black & blue / David Kirk. Auckland, NZ: Hodder Moa Beckett, 1997.
207p; illus   ISBN: 186958581X

Kirkpatrick, Ian (New Zealand)

123 Kirky / Lindsay Knight. Auckland, NZ: Rugby Press, 1979.
240p; illus   ISBN: 0959755357
     BL: X:950/31517

Kirwan, John (New Zealand)

124 Running on instinct: the John Kirwan story / Paul Thomas. Auckland, NZ: Moa Beckett, 1992.
272p; illus   ISBN: 1869471075

Kronfeld, Josh (New Zealand)

125 Josh Kronfeld. Auckland, NZ: Hodder Moa Beckett, 1997.
69p; illus
(Awesome)   ISBN: 1869585348
    For children.

Laidlaw, Chris (New Zealand)

126 Mud in your eye: a worm's eye view of the changing world of rugby / Chris R. Laidlaw. Wellington, NZ: Reed, 1973.
198p; illus

Subsequently reprinted: London: Pelham, 1974
     ISBN: 072070720X
     BL: X.629/6417

Laidlaw, Roy (Scotland)

127 Rugby partnership / John Rutherford and Roy Laidlaw
with Norman Mair. London: Stanley Paul, 1988.
176p; illus   ISBN: 0091727030
                                               BL: YK.1989.a.4849

☞ Also listed at: C195

Le Roux, Johan (South Africa)

128 Biting back / Johan Le Roux with Jan De Koning.
Wilropark, SA: De Koning, 1995.
85p; illus; pbk   ISBN: 062019376X

Lewis, Dai (Wales)

129 America bid me welcome: the autobiography of Dai H.
Lewis. Buffalo, US: The author, 1943.
iv, 151p; illus

   Lewis became the managing director of the
   Automobile Club of Buffalo. In his memoirs he
   recounts his days in Cardiff, where his sporting
   prowess won him two caps for Wales in 1886. Later
   that year, aged 19, Lewis emigrated to America where
   he remained until his death in 1943.

Lewis, Tony

130 Playing days / Tony Lewis. London: Stanley Paul, 1985.
251p; illus; index   ISBN: 0091622808
                                               BL: X.629/27807

   Though described as a 'cricket autobiography', the
   author makes mention of his rugby days at Cambridge
   University where he won a blue, and in Wales.

Lewis, Wally

131 King Wally: the story of Wally Lewis / Adrian
McGregor. St Lucia, Aust., London: University of
Queensland Press, 1987.
viii, 247p; illus; index; pbk   ISBN: 070222037X
                                               BL: YK.1988.a.3373

   Before becoming a star in rugby league, Lewis played rugby
   union at a very exciting level. He was one of the stars
   of the Aussie schoolboys side to the UK in the 1980s.

Liddell, Eric (Scotland)

132 Eric Liddell: the making of an athlete and the training of
a missionary / D. P. Thomson. Glasgow: Eric Liddell
Memorial Committee, 1945.
40p; illus; pbk   BL: 10857.a.15
   Written by a friend and former colleague.

133 Scotland's greatest athlete: the Eric Liddell story / David
P. Thomson. Crieff: Research Unit, 1970.
240p   SBN: 900867043
                                               BL: X.708/6923

☞ Subsequent ed. C134

134 Eric H. Liddell, athlete and missionary / David P.
Thomson. Revised ed. of 'Scotland's greatest athlete: the
Eric Liddell story'. Crieff: Research Unit, 1971.
xxx, 230p; illus   BL: X.200/4812
   Includes a chapter 'Scottish rugby internationalist'.
☞ Previous ed. C133

135 The flying Scotsman / Sally Magnusson. London:
Quartet, 1981.
191p; illus; pbk   ISBN: 0704333791
                                               BL: X.629/15426

   Includes brief coverage of Liddell's rugby achievements.

136 Eric Liddell: born to run / Peter Watkins; illustrated by
Gavin Rowe. London: MacRae, 1983.
42p; illus
(Blackbird books)   ISBN: 086203129X
                                               BL: X.808/38900

   For children

Little, Jason (Australia)

137 Perfect union: the parallel lives of Wallaby centres Tim
Horan and Jason Little / Michael Blucher. Sydney, Aust.:
Macmillan, 1995.
300p; illus; index   ISBN: 0732908140
☞ Also listed at: C107

Little, Walter (New Zealand)

138 Midfield liaison: the Frank Bunce, Walter Little story /
Bob Howitt. Auckland, NZ: Rugby Publishing, 1996.
237p; illus   ISBN: 090863059X
☞ Also listed at: C21

Lochore, Brian (New Zealand)

139 Lochore: an authorised biography / Alex Veysey, Gary
Caffell, Ron Palenski. Auckland, NZ: Hodder Moa
Beckett, 1996.
271p; illus   ISBN: 1869583035

Lockhart, Robert H. Bruce (Scotland)

140 My Scottish youth / Sir Robert Hamilton Bruce
Lockhart. London: Putnam, 1937.
372p; index   BL: 10824.k.41

141 Friends, foes and foreigners / Sir Robert Hamilton
Bruce Lockhart. London: Putnam, 1957.
286p; index   BL: 010604.b.32

142 Giants cast long shadows / Sir Robert Hamilton Bruce
Lockhart. London: Putnam, 1960.
253p; index   BL: 10799.s.31

   Includes a biographical account of K. G. McLeod who
   played for Scotland.

Lomu, Jonah

143 Jonah Lomu / photography by Photosport & Sally Tagg;
text by Jonah Lomu and Phil Kingsley-Jones. London:
Hodder & Stoughton, 1997.
108p; chiefly illus; pbk ISBN: 0340713232

Louw, Rob (South Africa)

144 For the love of rugby / Rob Louw with John
Cameron-Dow. Melville, SA: Hans Strydom, 1987.
225p; illus ISBN: 0947025162

Loveridge, Dave (New Zealand)

145 Loveridge, master halfback / Ron Palenski. Auckland,
NZ: Moa, 1985.
263p; illus; index ISBN: 0908570988

Lynagh, Michael (Australia)

146 Noddy: the authorised biography of Michael Lynagh /
Andrew Slack. Port Melbourne, Aust.: Heinemann, 1995.
xi, 276p; illus; index ISBN: 0855615710

McBride, Willie John (Ireland)

147 Willie John: the autobiography of Willie John McBride as
told to Edmund Van Esbeck. Dublin: Gill and
Macmillan, 1976.
160p; illus; index ISBN: 0717108031
BL: X.629/10881

Willie John

**The Autobiography of
Willie John McBride
as told to
Edmund Van Esbeck**

GILL AND MACMILLAN

MacCarthy, Winston

148 Listen…! it's a goal / Winston MacCarthy. London:
Pelham, 1973.
175p; illus, maps; index ISBN: 0720705355
BL: X.629/5476

Autobiography of the New Zealand broadcaster. He
covers a number of sports and, as he is known as 'the
voice of New Zealand rugby', a great deal of rugby.

McCormick, William Fergus (New Zealand)

149 Fergie / Alex Veysey. Christchurch, NZ, London:
Whitcoulls, 1976.
194p; illus ISBN: 0723304696
BL: X.629/10572

McKechnie, Brian (New Zealand)

150 McKechnie, double All Black: an autobiography / Brian
McKechnie with Lynn McConnell. Invercargill, NZ:
Craigs, 1983.
181p; illus; index ISBN: 0908629109
McKechnie played rugby and cricket for New Zealand.

McLaren, Bill

151 Talking of rugby: an autobiography / Bill McLaren.
London: Stanley Paul, 1991.
226p; illus; index ISBN: 009173875X
BL: YK.1991.b.7347

McLauchlan, Ian (Scotland)

152 Mighty Mouse: an autobiography / Ian McLauchlan
with Ian Archer. London: Stanley Paul, 1980.
149p; illus ISBN: 0091433908
BL: X.629/15980

McLean, Paul (Australia)

153 Paul McLean / Malcolm McGregor. St Lucia, Aust.,
London: University of Queensland Press, 1985.
xiii, 217p; illus; index ISBN: 0702218855
BL: YK.1986.a.1495

Mains, Laurie (New Zealand)

154 Laurie Mains / Bob Howitt and Robin McConnell.
Auckland, NZ: Rugby Publishing, 1996.
224p; illus ISBN: 0908630700

Marshall, Justin (New Zealand)

155 Justin Marshall. Auckland, NZ: Hodder Moa Beckett,
1997.
68p; illus
(Awesome) ISBN: 1869585356
For children.

Mayne, Robert Blair (Ireland)

156　Rogue warrior of the SAS: Lt. Col. 'Paddy' Blair Mayne, DSO (3 bars), Croix de guerre, Legion d'honneur / Roy Bradford and Martin Dillon; foreword by David Stirling. London: Murray, 1987.
xiv, 256p; illus; index

　Bibliography: p245　　　　ISBN: 0719544300
　　　　　　　　　　　　　　BL: YC.1987.a.10907

　Mayne made six appearances for Ireland and three for the British Isles in the late thirties.

Meads, Colin (New Zealand)

157　Colin Meads, All Black / Alex Veysey. Auckland, NZ, London: Collins, 1974.
256p; illus

　　　　　　　　　　　　　　ISBN: 0002111829
　　　　　　　　　　　　　　BL: X.629/10153

Mehrtens, Andrew (New Zealand)

158　Andrew Mehrtens. Auckland, NZ: Hodder Moa Beckett, 1997.
71p; illus
(Awesome)　　　　　　　　ISBN: 1869585364

　For children.

Meredith, Vincent

159　A long brief: recollections of a crown solicitor / Vincent Meredith. Auckland, NZ: Collins, 1966.
213p

　Memoirs of Sir Vincent Meredith, QC (1877-1965), Crown Solicitor for 31 years. He played rugby in Wellington and managed the New Zealand rugby teams in Australia in 1910 and the British Isles in 1935.

Messenger, Herbert Henry (Australia)

160　The master: the story of H. H. 'Dally' Messenger and the beginning of Australian rugby league / Dally R. Messenger. London: Angus & Robertson, 1982.
94p; illus; pbk　　　　　ISBN: 0207147310
　　　　　　　　　　　　　　BL: X.622/23169

Mexted, Murray (New Zealand)

161　Mexted: pieces of eight / Murray Mexted with Alex Veysey. Auckland, NZ: Rugby Press, 1986.
232p; illus　　　　　　　ISBN: 0908630255

Miller, Gerrit Smith

162　Gerrit Smith Miller: an appreciation / edited by Winthrop S. Scudder. Dedham, US: Noble and Greenough School, 1924.
30p; illus　　　　　　　　BL: 010881.k.36

　The introduction suggests that as Gerrit Smith Miller organised the Oneida Football Club of Boston in 1862, it would be appropriate to erect a tablet in his honour, similar to the one at Rugby School in honour of William Webb Ellis. The idea for the American version was prompted by an article written for the Boston Transcript of 3 March 1923 by G. F. Philip Bussy of the Westminster Gazette. Bussy's article outlined the history of rugby and a version of this 'history of rugby football in England' is produced in this booklet.

Mobbs, Edgar (England)

163　The Mobbs' Own: the 7th Battalion, the Northamptonshire Regiment / David Woodall. Spratton: R. Frisby in association with D. Woodall, 1994.
168p; illus; pbk　　　　　ISBN: 0952447509
　　　　　　　　　　　　　　BL: YK.1996.a.3595

　Though this is the history of Mobbs the soldier and the 7th Battalion, the Northamptonshire Regiment, it also contains biographical details of the man.

Moore, Brian (England)

164　Brian Moore: the autobiography / Brian Moore with Stephen Jones. London: Partridge, 1995.
371p; illus; index　　　　ISBN: 1852252340
　　　　　　　　　　　　　　BL: YK.1996.a.21825

Moran, Herbert M. (Australia)

165　Viewless winds: being the recollections and digressions of an Australian surgeon / Herbert M. Moran. London: Peter Davies, 1939.
352p　　　　　　　　　　　BL: 10859.bb.12

　Though only capped once for his country, Moran skippered the first Wallabies to England and Wales in 1908. He captures his rugby-playing days in chapter 2, pages 33-79: 'Men, rough men and rugby'.

Morgan, Cliff (Wales)

166　Cliff Morgan: the autobiography: beyond the fields of play / Cliff Morgan with Geoffrey Nicholson. London: Hodder & Stoughton, 1996.
246p; illus　　　　　　　ISBN: 0340657413

Mourie, Graham (New Zealand)

167　Graham Mourie captain: an autobiography with Ron Palenski. Auckland, NZ: Moa, 1982.
285p; illus; index

　Subsequently reprinted: London: Arthur Barker, 1983
　　　　　　　　　　　　　　ISBN: 0213168510
　　　　　　　　　　　　　　BL: X.622/15439

Muller, Hennie (South Africa)

168　Tot siens to test rugby / Hennie Muller. Cape Town, SA: Howard Timmins, 1953.
211p; illus

　The author played rugby for South Africa.

Nepia, George (New Zealand)

169   I, George Nepia: the golden years of rugby / George
Nepia and Terry McLean. London: Herbert Jenkins,
1963.
207p; illus
BL: X.449/32

170   George Nepia / Kevin Boon. Wellington, NZ: Kotuku,
1994.
24p; illus; pbk
(Famous New Zealand men)
ISBN: 0908947135

O'Connor, Michael (Australia)

171   The best of both worlds: the Michael O'Connor story /
Bret Harris. Sydney, Aust.: Pan Macmillan, 1991.
214p; illus
ISBN: 07329-07454

Offiah, Martin

172   Martin Offiah: a blaze of glory / David Lawrenson.
London: Methuen, 1993.
184p; illus

   Spine title: Offiah
ISBN: 0413359018
BL: YK.1993.b.14699

173   Offiah: my autobiography / Martin Offiah with David
Lawrenson. London: CollinsWillow, 1997.
256p; illus; index
ISBN: 0002187787
BL: YK.1998.b.2283

O'Reilly, Tony (Ireland)

174   Oh really O'Reilly: a biography of Dr A. J. F. O'Reilly /
C. H. Walsh. Blackrock, Co. Dublin: Bentos, 1992.
360p; illus; index
ISBN: 1872184057
BL: YK.1993.b.7989

175   The player / Ivan Fallon. London: Hodder & Stoughton,
1994.
xi, 360p; illus; index

   Bibliography: p359-60
ISBN: 0340583215
BL: YK.1996.b.2916

   Today Tony O'Reilly is an international tycoon —
   mention Kerrygold, Heinz, and the vast newspaper
   empire and O'Reilly's name comes to mind. Before
   trading in his rugby boots for the boardroom, O'Reilly
   played in 39 international games, 29 for Ireland and
   10 for the British Lions. Fallon concentrates on
   O'Reilly the businessman, but fulfils the duty of a
   biographer by not omitting his background: family,
   schooling, sporting prowess (especially rugby) and
   friends.

176   Life of O'Reilly: the authorised biography / Tom
Rubython; illustrated by Grant Robertson. London:
Cleveland Press, 1995.
xiii, 273p; illus
ISBN: 0952471809

Osborne, Glen (New Zealand)

177   Glen Osborne. Auckland, NZ: Hodder Moa Beckett,
1997.
72p; illus
(Awesome)
ISBN: 1869585399
   For children.

Osler, Bennie (South Africa)

178   The Bennie Osler story as told to Chris Greyvenstein.
Cape Town, SA: Howard Timmins, 1970.
163p; illus
BL: X.629/4572

THE
BENNIE OSLER
STORY

as told to
Chris Greyvenstein

with special tributes by
Stanley Osler, Dr. Danie Craven and George Manuel

HOWARD TIMMINS
CAPE TOWN
1970

Parry-Jones, David

179   Action replay: a media memoir / David Parry-Jones.
Llandysul: Gomer, 1993.
199p; illus; pbk
ISBN: 185902016X
BL: YK.1994.a.4682

   The author was, for many years, a rugby
   commentator on BBC Wales. He is now a freelance.

Pell, Albert

180   The reminiscences of Albert Pell, sometime MP for
South Leicestershire / edited, with an introduction, by
Thomas Mackay. London: John Murray, 1908.
lii, 370p; illus
BL: 010827.ee.12

   Albert Pell (1820-1907), old Rugbeian, entered Trinity
   College, Cambridge at the age of eighteen. Noticing
   that a number of students, like himself, were too

heavy to hunt or row, or were too poor, he recruited a few 'university men' and set about teaching them the rudiments of the game he knew from his days at Rugby. The first 'puntabout' took place on Parker's Piece and soon their subsequent exploits attracted a fair crowd. Although the description of this event is brief (pages 71-2) and no indication is given that the initial event led to regular games against opponents similarly versed in the rules of the game, Pell is recognised as the instigator of the game of rugby at Cambridge.

Pilecki, Stan (Australia)

181 Stan the man: the many lives of Stan Pilecki / Max Howell, Lingyu Xie, Peter Horton. Auckland, NZ: Celebrity Books, 1997.
208p; illus; index; pbk   ISBN: 0958364419
'A tribute to one of the great characters of Australian rugby. Also presents the inside story on players, coaches and managers.'

Poidevin, Simon (Australia)

182 For love not money: the Simon Poidevin story / Jim Webster. Crows Nest, Aust.: ABC Books, 1990.
205p; illus   ISBN: 0733300499

Popplewell, Nick (Ireland)

183 Poppy: time to ruck and roll / Nick Popplewell with Liam Hayes. Dublin: Hero Books, 1995.
viii, 220p; illus; pbk   ISBN: 0952626004

Portus, Garnet (England)

184 Happy highways / G. V. Portus. Carlton, Aust.: Melbourne University Press, 1953.
x, 294p; illus; index   BL: 10864.aa.3
Born and raised in Australia, Garnet Portus spent a few years in England on a Rhodes Scholarship. As well as playing rugby at Oxford University, Portus turned out for Blackheath and England (two caps in 1908). His autobiography recalls 'the stimulation and satisfaction of an unusually varied career, from cadetship in the NSW Dept. of Mines to the Chair of Political Science and History in the University of Adelaide... by way of ordination in the Anglican Ministry...'. Moreover, he has been a lifelong sports enthusiast. And what more natural than his subsequent experiences as coach, Australian Rugby Union selector, and referee?

Poulton, Ronnie (England)

185 The life of Ronald Poulton / his father Edward Bagnall Poulton. London: Sidgwick & Jackson, 1919.
viii, 410p; illus; index   BL: 010855.d.4

Price, Graham (Wales)

186 Price of Wales / Graham Price written with Terry Godwin. London: Willow, 1984.
160p; index   ISBN: 0002180669
                         BL: X.629/25803

Price, Ray (Australia)

187 Perpetual motion / Ray Price with Neil Cadigan. North Ryde, Aust.: Angus & Robertson, 1987.
192p; illus   ISBN: 0207156948
Ray Price played for Australia before switching to rugby league.

Probyn, Jeff (England)

188 Upfront: the Jeff Probyn story / Jeff Probyn and Barry Newcombe. Edinburgh: Mainstream, 1993.
191p; illus   ISBN: 1851585540
                         BL: YK.1995.b.1550

Richards, Dean (England)

189 Deano / Dean Richards with Peter Bills. London: Gollancz, 1995.
220p; illus; index   ISBN: 0575061103
                                BL: YK.1996.b.2152

Risman, Gus

190 Rugby renegade: autobiographical reminiscences / Gus Risman. London: Stanley Paul, 1958.
142p   BL: 7924.b.14

Rives, Jean-Pierre (France)

191 Jean-Pierre Rives: a modern Corinthian / Peter Bills; translations by Averil Craven. London: Allen & Unwin, 1986.
192p; illus, 1 map
    Includes translations from the French   ISBN: 0047961236
                                               BL: X.622/26081

Robbie, John (Ireland)

192 The game of my life / John Robbie. London: Pelham, 1989.
195p; illus   ISBN: 0720719364
                         BL: YK.1993.a.4306

Robbins, Peter (England)

193 Life at one hundred miles an hour: a biography of P. G. D. Robbins / Michael Blair. Ludlow: G & A Publishing, 1987.
123p; illus

Roberts, G. D. (England)

194 Without my wig / G. D. Roberts; with a foreword by A. P. Herbert. London: Macmillan, 1957.
xi, 286p; illus; index   BL: 10864.k.39

'Khaki' Roberts, Q.C., educated at Rugby and Oxford University, won two rugby and two tennis blues. As well as playing rugby for Devon, he represented England while still an undergraduate. This autobiography reveals a full life on the playing fields but it is only a brief interlude in a distinguished legal career. Evidence of this is given in his account of the trial of German major war criminals at Nuremberg in 1945-46, where he was a member of the British prosecuting delegation.

Rutherford, John (Scotland)

195 Rugby partnership / John Rutherford and Roy Laidlaw with Norman Mair. London: Stanley Paul, 1988.
176p; illus   ISBN: 0091727030
                               BL: YK.1989.a.4849

☞ Also listed at: C127

Samuel, Bill

196 Rugby body and soul / Bill Samuel. Llandysul: Gomer, 1986.
155p; illus; index   ISBN: 086383289X
                               BL: YK.1988.a.2586

Welsh rugby can be thankful to Bill Samuel for teaching Gareth Edwards to develop his obvious natural athletic ability. This autobiography tells the story of their relationship. And there is more: the importance of Welsh culture to Bill Samuel — the language, the people, and the sport.

Scott, Bob (New Zealand)

197 The Bob Scott story / R. W. H. Scott and T. P. McLean. London: Herbert Jenkins, 1956.
x, 209p; illus; index   BL: 7922.f.28

Sewell, E. H. D.

198 The log of a sportsman / E. H. D. Sewell. London: Fisher Unwin, 1923.
247p; illus; index   BL: 7911.bb.25

Reminisces on playing rugby during his schooldays; it includes a chapter, 'Concerning rugby'. The rest of the book is taken up with a number of other sports.

199 An outdoor wallah / E. H. D. Sewell. London: Stanley Paul, 1945.
136p   BL: 10861.bb.27

Chapter 17: 'A rugby reverie'.

Shelford, Wayne (New Zealand)

200 Buck: the Wayne Shelford story as told to Wynne Gray. Huddersfield: Springfield, 1990.
215p; illus   ISBN: 094765593X

Shrewsbury, Arthur

201 'Give me Arthur': a biography of Arthur Shrewsbury / Peter Wynne-Thomas. London: Arthur Barker, 1985.
xi, 163p; illus   ISBN: 0213169258

☞ Also listed at: E11

Smith, J. V. (England)

202 'Good morning, President': rugby from the top / J. V. Smith. London: Allen & Unwin, 1985.
xvi, 173p; illus, 1 map   ISBN: 004796104X
                               BL: X.622/25173

Smith, Steve (England)

203 The scrum half of my life: an autobiography / Steve Smith with Geoff Green. London: Stanley Paul, 1984.
205p; illus   ISBN: 0091592208
                               BL: X.629/25958

Sole, David (Scotland)

204 Heart and Sole: a rugby life / David Sole with Derek Douglas; foreword by Ian McGeechan. Edinburgh: Mainstream, 1992.
253p; illus   ISBN: 1851584935
                               BL: YK.1993.b.10236

Spencer, Carlos (New Zealand)

205 Carlos Spencer. Auckland, NZ: Hodder Moa Beckett, 1997.
71p; illus
(Awesome)   ISBN: 1869585372

Stanley, Joe (New Zealand)

206 Smokin' Joe / Phil Gifford. Auckland, NZ: Rugby Press, 1990.
205p; illus   ISBN: 090863031X

Stoddart, Andrew E. (England)

207 'My dear victorious Stod': a biography of A. E. Stoddart / David Frith. New Malden: The author, 1970.
199p; illus; index   SBN: 950183709
                               BL: X.629/3464

Sullivan, Clive

208 Hard road to the top / Joe Latus. Hull: Boulevard Stadium Publications, 1973.
110p; illus   ISBN: 0903751003
                               BL: X.629/5529

Thomas, J. B. G.

209 Rugger in the blood: fifty years of rugby memoirs / J. B.
G. Thomas. London: Pelham, 1985.
256p; illus; index   ISBN: 0720716217
BL: X.809/65691

Thomas, Watcyn (Wales)

210 Rugby-playing man / Watcyn Thomas; foreword by
Vivian Jenkins. London: Pelham, 1977.
102p; illus; index   ISBN: 0720709520
BL: X.629/11089

Thorburn, Paul (Wales)

211 Kicked into touch: an autobiography / Paul Thorburn.
London: Stanley Paul, 1992.
vii, 183p; illus   ISBN: 0091749670
BL: YK.1992.a.3318

Thornett, Ken (Australia)

212 Tackling rugby / Ken Thornett with Tom Easton.
London: Lansdowne Press, 1966.
166p; illus   BL: X.449/2587
Thornett recalls his pre-rugby league days in rugby
union.

Tindill, Eric (New Zealand)

213 Eric Tindill / Kevin Boon. Wellington, NZ: Kotuku,
1996.
24p; illus
(Famous New Zealanders)   ISBN: 0908947178
For children.

Todd, A. W. P. (Ireland)

214 Caught in the act: the story of my life / Richard Todd.
London: Hutchinson, 1986.
302p; illus, 1 map; index   ISBN: 0091638003
BL: YC.1986.a.5454
Richard Todd, the actor, is the son of A. W. P. Todd
who appeared at full-back for Ireland in 1913-14. Todd
junior illustrates his father's background.

Troup, Major W.

215 Sporting memories: my life as Gloucestershire County
cricketer, rugby and hockey player, and member of
Indian police service / Major W. Troup. London:
Hutchinson, 1924.
x, 312p; illus   BL: 7904.ff.8
Although Troup played rugby for Clifton, Bristol and
Gloucestershire and was a trialist for England in
1888, there is very little rugby content in this
autobiography.

Tuigamala, Va'aiga (New Zealand)

216 Inga the winger / Bob Howitt. London: Queen Anne
Press, 1993.
224p; illus   ISBN: 1852915439

Underwood, Rory (England)

217 Flying wing: an autobiography / Rory Underwood with
David Hands. London: Stanley Paul, 1992.
x, 181p; illus   ISBN: 0091750741
BL: YK.1993.b.7071

Uttley, Roger (England)

218 Pride in England: a rugby autobiography / Roger Uttley
with David Norrie. London: Stanley Paul, 1981.
189p; illus   ISBN: 0091463203
BL: X.629/17017

Wakelam, Henry

219 Half-time: 'the mike and me' / Henry B. T. Wakelam.
London: Nelson, 1938.
343p; illus   BL: 10857.c.6
The former Harlequin and broadcaster recalls many
sporting occasions. There is much rugby, including the
first broadcast of a rugby International – England
and Wales at Twickenham in January 1927.

Ward, Tony (Ireland)

220 The good the bad and the rugby: the official biography
of Tony Ward / John Scally. Dublin: Blackwater Press,
1993.
374p; illus; pbk   ISBN: 0861214633

Watkins, David (Wales)

221 The David Watkins story / David Watkins and Brian
Dobbs. London: Pelham, 1971.
154p; illus   SBN: 720704553
BL: X.629/3250

222 David Watkins: an autobiography / David Watkins;
edited by David Parry-Jones. London: Cassell, 1980.
234p; illus; index   ISBN: 0304306924
BL: X.629/17785

Weaving, Stuart

223 Ambassador of friendship: an autobiography. Stuart
Weaving with F. Cleary. Kimberley, SA: Bisby Services,
1990.
217p; illus   ISBN: 0620147997
BL: YK.1993.a.6200

FLANNELLED FOOL
AND MUDDIED OAF

The Autobiography of

Peter West

W.H. ALLEN · LONDON
1986

West, Peter

224 Flannelled fool and muddied oaf: the autobiography of
Peter West. London: W.H. Allen, 1986.
256p; illus

ISBN: 0491038925
BL: YC.1987.b.6995

Peter West has been a broadcaster on television and
radio for over 35 years. In the summer he covered
cricket and the tennis championships while in the
winter he worked as a rugby commentator. He
supplemented the latter with a column on rugby in
The Times and, later, the *Daily Telegraph*.

Wheeler, Peter (England)

225 Rugby from the front / Peter Wheeler. London: Stanley
Paul, 1983.
215p; illus

ISBN: 0091546605
BL: X.629/23195

☞ Subsequent ed. C226

226 Rugby from the front / Peter Wheeler. Rev. ed. London:
Panther, 1984.
240p; illus; pbk

ISBN: 0586062939
BL: YK.1989.a.4046

☞ Previous ed. C225

Whetton Alan & Gary (New Zealand)

227 Brothers in arms: the Alan & Gary Whetton story with
Paul Lewis. Auckland, NZ: Moa, 1991.
256p; illus

Published in association with Television New Zealand
ISBN: 1869470818

Williams, Bleddyn (Wales)

228 Rugger, my life / Bleddyn Williams. London: Stanley
Paul, 1956.
192p; illus

BL: 7923.i.2

Williams, Bryan (New Zealand)

229 Beegee: the Bryan Williams story / Bob Howitt.
Auckland, NZ: Rugby Press, 1981.
288p; illus

ISBN: 095975539X

Williams, Chester (South Africa)

230 Chester: South Africa's favourite rugby son / Paul
Dobson. Cape Town, SA: Sable Media, 1995.
63p; illus; pbk

*Includes a folded poster. Spine title: Chester Williams, a
South African hero*
ISBN: 095840626X

Williams, Ian (Australia)

231 In touch: rugby, life worth living / Ian Williams.
London: Kingswood, 1991.
213p; illus

ISBN: 0413646602
BL: YK.1991.b.6651

Williams, J. P. R. (Wales)

232 JPR: an autobiography / J. P. R. Williams. London:
Collins, 1979.
254p; illus; index

ISBN: 0002160382
BL: X.629/12480

Wilson, Jeff (New Zealand)

233 Jeff Wilson: the natural / Pat Booth. Auckland, NZ:
Moa Beckett, 1994.
96p; illus; pbk

ISBN: 1869580907

234 Jeff Wilson. Auckland, NZ: Hodder Moa Beckett, 1997.
71p; illus
(Awesome)

ISBN: 1869585380

Wilson, Stu (New Zealand)

235 Ebony & ivory: the Stu Wilson, Bernie Fraser story as
told to Alex Veysey. Poole: Blandford, 1984.
271p; illus

ISBN: 0713716320
BL: X.622/25267

☞ Also listed at: C74

Woods, S. M. J. (England)

236   My reminiscences / Samuel M. J. Woods; with personal
      appreciations by P. F. Warner and G. L. Jessop. London:
      Chapman & Hall, 1925.
      211p   BL: 7904.df.43

237   Sammy: the sporting life of S. M. J. Woods / Clifford
      Jiggens. Bristol: Sansom, 1997.
      160p; illus; index   ISBN: 1900178850

Wooller, Wilf (Wales)

238   Wickets, tries and goals: reviews of play and players in
      modern cricket, rugby and soccer / John Arlott, Wilfred
      Wooller, Maurice Edelston. London: Sampson Low,
      Marston, 1949.
      x, 236p   BL: 7917.f.22

      Covers sport in general. Wilf Wooller includes an
      autobiographical segment in the piece on rugby.

239   The skipper: a biography of Wilf Wooller / Andrew
      Hignell. Litlington: Limlow, 1995.
      224p; illus; index

         Bibliography: p219-220   ISBN: 1874524122
                                             BL: YK.1996.b.854

      Wooller was a fine sportsman – rugby for Cambridge
      University and Wales; cricket for Glamorgan; soccer
      for Cardiff City and squash for Wales.

Wyllie, Alex (New Zealand)

240   Grizz, the legend / Phil Gifford. Auckland, NZ: Rugby
      Press, 1991.
      248p; illus   ISBN: 0908630360

Collective Biographies

241   Famous footballers and athletes / edited by C. W.
      Alcock and R. Hill. London: Hudson & Kearns,
      1895-1896.
      14 parts; illus   BL: Mic.A.9439(1) (microfilm copy)
      ☞ See also: C242; C307

242   Famous footballers 1895-1896 / edited by C. W. Alcock
      and Rowland Hill. London: Hudson & Kearns, 1897?
      224p; illus; index

      Originally published in weekly parts with sixteen
      photographs in each issue, the book contains 224
      individual photographs of association and rugby
      football players. Each photograph of an individual has
      a text. Photographs of teams bear the name of each
      person.
      ☞ See also: C241; C307

243   Rugby football Blues: biographical record of those who
      have taken part in the Oxford v. Cambridge rugby
      football matches 1872-1911 / compiled by George B.
      Routledge. London: Merritt & Hatcher, 1911.
      viii, 154p; pbk

      There is a copy of this extremely scarce book in the
      National Library of Ireland.

244   The rugby football internationals roll of honour / E. H.
      D. Sewell. London, Edinburgh: T. C. & E. C. Jack, 1919.
      vii, 237p; illus   BL: 10803.h.17

      Biographies of rugby internationals killed in World War
      One.

245   Rugby players who have made New Zealand famous /
      R. A. Stone. Auckland, NZ: Scott & Scott, 1938.
      100p; illus; pbk

246   They played for New Zealand: a complete record of
      New Zealand rugby representatives 1884-1947 and their
      matches / Arthur C. Swan. Wellington, NZ: Reed for
      Sporting Publications, 1947.
      96p
      ☞ See also: C253; C258; C265

247   Unicorn rugby register: 1947 secondary rugby records /
      edited by R. Melgund Thomson. Christchurch, NZ:
      Coulls Somerville Wilkie, 1947.
      24p; pbk

248   Giants of South African rugby with a report on the
      'Lions' / Arthur C. Parker. Cape Town, SA: Howard
      Timmins, 1955.
      xii, 275p; illus

         Also published: Wellington, NZ: Reed, 1955
                                                 BL: 7920.g.49

      Book one, chapters 1-11: biographies of eleven giants
      of South African rugby. Book two, chapters 1-15:
      reports on the 24 matches played by the 1955 Lions
      in South Africa.

249   Great rugger players, 1900-1954 / J. B. G. Thomas; with
      a foreword by Rhys T. Gabe. London: Stanley Paul, 1955.
      192p; illus   BL: 7920.g.48

      The achievements in the game of 32 internationals.

250 The Springboks talk: interviews with members of the
Springboks rugby union team / Maxwell Price. Cape
Town, SA: Howard Timmins, 1955.
196p; illus   BL: 7922.m.1
   Profiles of South African players.

251 Great men of New Zealand rugby / H. Tillman.
Christchurch, NZ: Lancaster Press, 1957.
110p; illus

252 Great contemporary players / J. B. G. Thomas. London:
Stanley Paul, 1963.
174p; illus   BL: 7926.w.36

253 They played for New Zealand, volume 2: 1884-1963 /
Arthur C. Swan. Wellington, NZ: Sporting Publications,
1963.
139p
  ☞ See also: C246; C258; C265

254 Centenary history of the Rugby Football Union / Uel
Addison Titley and Alan Ross MacWhirter. London:
Rugby Football Union, 1970.
216p; illus; maps; index   BL: X.625/50
  Includes a biographical section containing the 62
  presidents of the RFU (1871-1970/71), the 11
  vice-presidents of the RFU, the 13 honorary
  treasurers of the RFU, the 11 secretaries of the RFU
  and the 999 players who have played for England
  from 1871 to 1971.
  ☞ Also listed at: A79

GREAT RUGGER PLAYERS

1900 - 1954

by

J. B. G. THOMAS
Author of "On Tour", etc.

With a Foreword by
RHYS T. GABE

With 32 Illustrations

STANLEY PAUL AND CO. LTD
London Melbourne Sydney Auckland
Bombay Cape Town New York Toronto

255 Rugby: the great ones / edited by Cliff Morgan. London:
Pelham, 1970.
136p; illus   SBN: 720703077
                   BL: X.629/2894

256 Football is fifteen / Gordon Slatter. Christchurch, NZ:
Whitcombe & Tombs, 1972.
190p; illus   ISBN: 0723303371
  The author has profiled the players who, in his opinion,
  are the best to represent the greatest New Zealand
  XV.

257 They made headlines / Chris Greyvenstein. Cape Town,
SA: Don Nelson Enterprises and Tafelberg Uitgewers,
1972.
172p; illus
   Bibliography: p172   ISBN: 0624003329
  Profiles twelve Springboks.
  ☞ See also: C278

258 They played for New Zealand, volume 3 / Arthur C.
Swan. Wellington, NZ: New Zealand Rugby Football
Union, 1973.
166p; pbk
  'A complete record of New Zealand rugby
  representatives 1884-1972 and their matches.'
  ☞ See also: C246; C253; C265

259 New Zealand rugby greats / Bob Howitt. Auckland,
NZ: Moa in association with Dominion Breweries, 1975.
320p; illus   ISBN: 0908570457
  ☞ See also: C266; C310; C311

260 Army rugby union international honours: players who
have gained international honours whilst serving in the
Army / J. S. McLaren. Army Rugby Union, 1978.
15p; pbk

261 Men in black / R. H. Chester & N. A. C. McMillan.
London: Pelham, 1978.
390p; illus
   Bibliography: p387-90   ISBN: 0720711223
                   BL: X.622/6652

262 A century of Welsh rugby players / Wayne Thomas.
Birmingham: Ansells Brewery, 1979.
199p; illus; pbk   BL: X.629/12949

263 Great rugby players / David Norrie. London: Hamlyn,
1980.
176p; illus   ISBN: 0600371913
                   BL: X.622/8474

264 The encyclopedia of New Zealand rugby / compiled by
R. H. Chester & N. A. C. McMillan. Auckland: Moa in
association with Dominion Breweries, 1981.
446p; illus

    Bibliography: p443-6   ISBN: 0908570392

New Zealand representatives 1884-1980; selected
for New Zealand but did not play; players unlucky not
to represent New Zealand; New Zealanders capped
overseas; services internationals; All Blacks who
excelled at other sports; international referees;
leading rugby administrators; New Zealand selectors;
men of the media.

   ☞ Subsequent ed. C274

265 They played for New Zealand: a complete record of
New Zealand rugby representatives 1884-1981 and their
matches, volume 4 / Arthur H. Carman. Tawa, NZ:
Sporting Publications, 1981.
163p; illus

   ☞ See also: C246; C253; C258

266 New Zealand rugby greats, volume 2 / Bob Howitt.
Auckland, NZ: Moa in association with Dominion
Breweries, 1982.
383p; illus

    Variant title: Rugby greats   ISBN: 0908570473

Details on 25 rugby players prominent since World
War Two.

   ☞ See also: C259; C310; C311

267 Enwogion byd y bêl / golygwyd gan W. J. Jones.
Aberystwyth: Gwasg Cambria, 1983.
176p; illus; index; pbk
(Cyfres enwogion y byd; 4-6)   ISBN: 0900439122
                           BL: X.950/36516-36518

Gareth Williams contributes biographies on: Arthur
Gould, Bleddyn Williams, Lewis Jones, Barry John,
Gerald Davies and Gareth Edwards (Wales); Michael
Gibson (Ireland); Lucien Mias (France); George Nepia
(New Zealand).

268 Australian rugby union: the game and the players / Jack
Pollard; foreword by Sir Nicholas Shehadie. North Ryde,
Aust.: Angus & Robertson in association with Australian
Broadcasting Corporation, 1984.
xiii, 945p; illus

    Bibliography: p943-5   ISBN: 0207150060
   ☞ Also listed at: A220; subsequent ed.: C295

269 Who's who in international rugby / data compiled by
Tony Bodley; additional material from Ian Morrison;
revised by Terry Cooper; copy edited by Terry Mahan.
London: Queen Anne Press, 1984.
128p; illus; pbk
(Who's who in sport series)

    Series editor: David Emery   ISBN: 0356104346
                           BL: X.629/27325

270 Ciarán Fitzgerald agus foireann rugbaí na hÉireann /
Breandán Ó hEithir. Baile Átha Cliath: Coisciim, 1985.
vi, 149p; illus; pbk

'Ciarán Fitzgerald and the Irish rugby team.'

271 Gary Knight, Andy Dalton, John Ashworth: the
geriatrics / Lindsay Knight. Auckland, NZ: Moa, 1986.
269p; illus   ISBN: 090857004X

The trio earned the title 'The Geriatrics' during the
1983 tour against the Lions.

272 Gone north: Welshmen in rugby league, volume 1 /
Robert Gate. Ripponden: The author, 1986.
ix, 173p; illus; pbk   ISBN: 0951119001
                           BL: YK.1987.a.740

Before becoming rugby league players, the Welshmen
in this study had played rugby union. The work
examines their career in rugby league and their
contribution to the game in Wales.

   ☞ See also: C279

273 The complete who's who of international rugby / Terry
Godwin. Poole: Blandford, 1987.
447p

    Bibliography: p447   ISBN: 0713718382
                           BL: YK.1987.b.1859

274 The encyclopedia of New Zealand rugby / compiled by
R. H. Chester, N. A. C. McMillan, R. A. Palenski. 2nd
ed. Auckland, NZ: Moa, 1987.
359p; illus   ISBN: 0908570163
   ☞ Previous ed. C264

275 Gareth Edwards' 100 great rugby players. London:
Macdonald, 1987.
224p; illus   ISBN: 0356142000
                           BL: YK.1987.b.7399

276 Makers of champions: famous New Zealand coaches /
Joseph Romanos. Lower Hutt, NZ: Mills, 1987.
234p; illus

277 New Zealand rugby legends: 15 reflections / T. P.
McLean. Auckland, NZ: Moa, 1987.
206p; illus   ISBN: 186947015X

'T. P. McLean has wandered down memory lane and
selected fifteen personalities who have had the
greatest impact on the game in the years before the
Second World War.'

278 20 great Springboks, 1949-1987 / Chris Greyvenstein.
2nd ed. Cape Town, SA: Nelson, 1987.
255p; illus; pbk

    Bibliography: p254-5   ISBN: 1868060314

Updates the author's earlier work, 'They made
headlines', 1972.

   ☞ See also: C257

279 Gone north: Welshmen in rugby league, volume 2 /
Robert Gate. Ripponden: The author, 1988.
x, 182p; illus; pbk   ISBN: 0951119036
                        BL: YK.1990.a.259

     Before becoming rugby league players, the Welshmen
in this study had played rugby union.

   ☞   See also: C272

280 Doc Craven's tribute: the legends of Springbok rugby
1889-1989 / edited by K. Clayton. Howard Place, SA:
KC Publications, 1989.
xvi, 232p; illus; index   ISBN: 062014176X

281 Famous fullbacks / Joseph Romanos. Auckland, NZ:
Rugby Press, 1989.
208p; illus   ISBN: 0908630298

282 British Lions / John Griffiths. Swindon: Crowood, 1990.
224p; illus   ISBN: 1852235411
                  BL: YK.1991.b.2394

     Chronicles the tours of South Africa and the
Antipodes by the British and Irish Lions. Each section
has biographies of a number of the players.

   ☞   Also listed at: E7

283 Famous flankers / Joseph Romanos. Auckland, NZ:
Rugby Press, 1990.
208p; illus   ISBN: 0908630301

284 Giants of post-war Welsh rugby / edited by Clive
Rowlands & David Farmer. Swansea: Malcolm Press,
1990.
144p; illus   ISBN: 0951657003
                BL: YK.1993.b.10390

     28 leading rugby figures choose their greatest player.

Who's Who of
Welsh International Rugby Players

John M Jenkins, Duncan Pierce, Timothy Auty

Bridge Books, Wrexham, Clwyd

285 Gloucester RFC: players 1990. Gloucester: The Club,
1990.
52p

286 Kick off: New Zealand rugby special / text by John
Lockyer; photographs by Fotopacific; artwork by Paul
Rogers and Andrew Tristram. Auckland, NZ:
Heinemann Reed, 1990.
111p; illus; pbk   ISBN: 0790001276

     Profiles of Wayne Shelford, Grant Fox, John Kirwan
and other All Blacks.

287 Rugby characters / caricatures by John Ireland, text by
Cliff Morgan. London: Stanley Paul, 1990.
92p; illus   ISBN: 0091745845

     Profiles 36 international players from England,
Scotland, Ireland, Wales and France, divided into
full-backs (5), threequarters (6), half-backs (8),
forwards (17), as well as a referee, two coaches and a
commentator.

288 The rugby union who's who / compiled and edited by
Alex Spink. London: CollinsWillow, 1990-1996?

        Published annually;
        Variant title: The Save & Prosper rugby union who's who
                     ISSN: 1357-0234
                     BL: ZK.9.a.1793

     The first two editions covered the home countries
only; for the 3rd edition coverage was extended to
include Australia, New Zealand and South Africa.

289 100 great rugby characters / Joseph Romanos and Grant
Harding; illustrations by Murray Webb. Auckland, NZ:
Rugby Press, 1991.
208p; illus   ISBN: 0908630344

290 They led the All Blacks / Lindsay Knight. Auckland,
NZ: Rugby Press, 1991.
178p; illus   ISBN: 0908630379

     Covers: Early leaders; Fred Allen; Bob Stuart; Wilson
Whineray; Brian Lochore; Ian Kirkpatrick; Andy Leslie;
Graham Mourie; Andy Dalton; David Kirk; Wayne
Shelford as well as Ronnie Dawson and John Dawes
who captained the British and Irish Lions; Statistics.
The work is 'an attempt to background those who had
significant captaincy tenures', concentrating
'essentially with All Black rugby since World War II'. So
the book 'if not exactly by design, has become a
detailed history of All Black rugby since 1945. The
various captains have become the common, linking
focus...'.

291 Who's who of Welsh international rugby players / John
M. Jenkins, Duncan Pierce, Timothy Auty. Wrexham:
Bridge Books, 1991.
191p; illus

        Bibliography: p191
                     ISBN: 1872424104
                     BL: YK.1992.b.5

292   The complete who's who of England rugby union
      internationals / Raymond Maule. Derby: Breedon
      Books, 1992.
      200p; illus

         Bibliography: p200   ISBN: 187362610X
                                              BL: YK.1993.b.12597

      Relies heavily on Godwin's 'The complete who's who of
      international rugby', 1987. It is strange, therefore,
      that this work is not credited in the bibliography, and
      at least four biographies are missing.

293   Great All Black wingers / Lindsay Knight. Auckland,
      NZ: Rugby Press, 1992.
      175p; illus   ISBN: 09086300409

294   The great number tens / Frank Keating; foreword by
      Barry John. London: Partridge, 1993.
      ix, 271p; illus   ISBN: 1852251921
                                             BL: YK.1994.b.13180

295   Australian rugby: the game and the players / Jack
      Pollard; edited by David O'Neil. Rev., enlarged updated
      ed. Chippendale, Aust.: Ironbark, 1994.
      712p; illus   ISBN: 0330356194

      Like the previous 1984 edition this work details the
      history of rugby in Australia, biographies of players,
      tours from and to Australia.

      ☞   Also listed at: A225; previous ed.: C268

296   The famous XV: Scotland's all time rugby greats / Kevin
      Ferrie. Edinburgh: Scottish Rugby Magazine, 1994.
      xi, 204p; illus   ISBN: 1899564004
                                             BL: YK.1996.a.364

      In the foreword by Matthew Gloag (of Matthew Gloag
      & Son, sponsors of the Scottish rugby team) it is
      claimed that this book 'charts the rugby careers of
      fifteen of Scotland's finest and most celebrated
      players'. The selection of the players spanning the
      years 1964-1994, was chosen by Norman Mair, rugby
      correspondent of *The Scotsman*, Bill McMurtrie,
      rugby reporter of *The Herald*, and Ian MacGregor
      chairman of the Scotland selectors in the 1984
      Grand Slam season.

297   Fifty rugby stars describe my greatest game / edited by
      Bob Holmes and Chris Thau. Edinburgh: Mainstream,
      1994.
      191p; illus   ISBN: 1851586342
                                             BL: YK.1996.b.43

298   The great little All Black signature book / compiled by
      Margot Butcher. Auckland, NZ: Rugby Press, 1994.
      72p; illus
      (Great little signature book service)
                                             ISBN: 0908630468

      Biographical sketches with blank pages designed for
      autographs.

299   Real men wear black / Trevor McKewen. Auckland,
      NZ: Rugby Press, 1994.
      244p; illus   ISBN: 090863045X

      Profiles a number of New Zealand rugby international
      players in both union and league.

      ☞   Subsequent ed. C301

300   Newport rugby greats / Alan Roderick; with original
      illustrations by Bozena Roderick. Newport, Gwent:
      Handpost, 1995.
      xiii, 231p; illus; index; pbk

         Bibliography: p211   ISBN: 0951521357
                                              BL: YK.1996.a.13874

      Pen portraits of over 300 players who played for
      Newport.

301   Real men wear black / Trevor McKewen. Rev. ed.
      Auckland, NZ: Rugby Press, 1995.
      244p; illus   ISBN: 090863045X

      Profiles a number of New Zealand rugby international
      players in both union and league.

      ☞   Previous ed. C299

302   South African rugby test players, 1949-1995 / Graham
      K. Jooste. London: Penguin, 1995.
      xiii, 158p; index; pbk

         Variant title: South African rugby teams 1949-1995
                                             ISBN: 0140250174
                                             BL: YA.1995.a.28699

303   30 super Springboks / Paul Dobson. Cape Town, SA:
      Human & Rousseau, 1995.
      232p; illus

         Bibliography: p229-32   ISBN: 0798134119

      The thirty biographical portraits are not merely fact
      files – date and place of birth and death, education,
      rugby career and occupation. The sketches tell the
      story of rugby in South Africa from 1891 to 1894; the
      position of the game in South African society;
      relations with opponents; touring; and the characters
      who have graced the game: Japie Krige, Bennie Osler,
      Boy Louw, Danie Craven, Hennie Muller, Doug
      Hopwood, John Gainsford, Danie Gerber and Chester
      Williams.

304   The Famous Grouse who's who of South African rugby
      1996 / edited by Wynand Claassen and Chris Schoeman.
      Durban, SA: Rugby 15 International, 1996.
      vi, 229p; illus; pbk   ISBN: 062020463X

      A who's who of provincial players in South Africa. It
      was originally planned to update the information and
      issue the publication annually at the start of each
      rugby season.

305   The giants of Irish rugby / John Scally. Edinburgh:
      Mainstream, 1996.
      224p; illus   ISBN: 1851588345
                                             BL: YK.1997.b.4149

306 Wallaby greats / Max Howell and Lingyu Xie. Glenfield, Aust.: Rugby Publishing, 1996.
190p; illus; pbk   ISBN: 0908630603

307 Famous rugby footballers 1895. Harefield: Yore, 1997.
120p; illus
(Byegone gem reprint)

> *Facsimile of part of: Famous footballers 1895-1896;*
> *Limited ed. of 250 copies*   ISBN: 1874427429
> BL: LB.31.c.9102

☞ See also: C241; C242

308 A homage: Maccabi South Africa pays tribute to Springbok rugby / Keith Clayton. Howard Place, SA: 1997.
33p; illus; index; pbk

> Biographies of the ten Jewish players who have represented the Springboks.

309 International rugby Hall of Fame / edited by Alan Evans. Auckland, NZ: The International Rugby Hall of Fame Trust, 1997.
16p; illus; pbk

> Brief biographies of the fifteen players inducted to the Rugby Hall of Fame.

310 New Zealand rugby greats: volume 3 / Bob Howitt. Auckland, NZ: Hodder Moa Beckett, 1997.
344p; illus

> *Variant title: Rugby greats*   ISBN: 1869584783
> Covers 25 players: John Ashworth, Graeme Bachop, Robin Brooke, Zinzan Brooke, Olo Brown, Frank Bunce, Andy Dalton, Sean Fitzpatrick, Grant Fox, John Gallagher, Craig Green, Ian Jones, Michael Jones, John Kirwan, Jonah Lomu, Andrew Mehrtens, Murray Mexted, Mark Shaw, Wayne Shelford, Wayne Smith, Joe Stanley, Warwick Taylor, Alan Whetton, Gary Whetton, and Jeff Wilson.

☞ See also: C259; C266; C311

311 New Zealand rugby greats / Bob Howitt. Auckland, NZ: Hodder Moa Beckett, 1997.
3 vols. (1,030p); illus   ISBN: 1869584732

> Considers 75 of the greatest All Blacks. Volumes 1 and 2 have been updated.

☞ See also: C259; C266; C310

312 A sporting century 1863-1963: athletics, rugby, cricket / Anne Pallant. Kingsbridge: The author, 1997.
192p; illus; pbk   ISBN: 0953018903

> The story of a family's participation in three sports over a period of a century, focusing mainly on the author's father, E. G. Butcher, who played rugby for Plymouth, Devonport Albion, Plymouth Albion, Devon, and Barbarians, was an England trialist and RFU committee member (1939-63).

313 Who's who of South African rugby / Chris Schoeman. Cape Town, SA: Don Nelson, 1997-

✳ *Additional References*

314 The sportfolio: portraits and biographies of heroes and heroines of sport & pastime. London: George Newnes, 1896.
140p; illus; index   BL: Cup.1253.d.18

315 Sport and pastime in the Transvaal: including biographical sketches of Transvaal sportsmen / edited by E. J. L. Platnauer. Johannesburg, SA: Weenderlich/Wunderlich, 1908.
256p; illus

> Rugby appears on pages 61-98.

316 The bond of sacrifice: a biographical record of all British officers who fell in the Great War: vol. 1 Aug.-Dec., 1914 / military editor, L. A. Clutterbuck, in association with W. T. Dooner; naval editor, C. A. Denison. London: Anglo-African Publishing Contractors, 1916.
xlvii, 459p; illus

> *No more published*   BL: 9083.h.37
> To claim that this work contains a biographical record of all British officers who were killed in the Great War is an exaggeration. It includes a number of rugby players who played at international and first class level: C. E. Wilson (England); J. L. Huggan, L. Robertson and R. F. Simson (Scotland); A. B. Read (Army, Richmond, Barbarians); E. F. Boyd (Oxford Blue, Army, Blackheath); W. S. Yalland (Clifton).

317 Who's who in the sporting world: rugby. Johannesburg, SA: CNA, 1933.
92p; illus   BL: P.P.2579.cde

> Part of a series covering all sports.

318 Rhodesian sports profiles 1907-1979 / Glen Byrom; illustrated by Henk van Rooyen. Bulawayo: Books of Zimbabwe Publishing, 1980.
256p; illus

> Nine rugby players are profiled.

319 Quest for gold: the encyclopedia of American Olympians / Bill Mallon & Ian Buchanan with Jeffrey Tishman. New York, US: Leisure Press, 1984.
495p; illus; pbk   ISBN: 0880112174

> Includes biographies of the players who represented the United States rugby teams in the Olympic Games of 1920 and 1924.

320 Great sporting eccentrics / David Randall. London: Allen, 1985.
192p; illus; pbk   ISBN: 0491030045

> A highly entertaining list of eccentric personalities from all sports, including the rugby player called up by mistake to play for his country, and the one-handed Irish rugby international. Contains unique coverage.

321 Moments of greatness, touches of class / Simon Barnes; edited by Andrew Longmore. London: Kingswood, 1991. x, 310p; illus; pbk   ISBN: 0413653609
BL: YK.1991.a.6314

Stephen Jones' contribution, 'Hop and Gerald: images of brilliance' looks at Hop Maddocks and Gerald Davies both of whom were prolific try scorers and Welsh international wingers. David Hands in 'Robert Norster: king of the jungle' profiles Robert Norster, the Welsh international lock. In addition, 'A match lost but a spirit found' by Chris Thau chronicles success in Romanian rugby.

322 Fyffes dictionary of Irish sporting greats / John Gleeson; foreword by Jimmy Magee. Chapelizod: Etta Place, 1993. 503p; illus   ISBN: 095218270X
BL: YK.1994.a.852

Covers all sports with rugby well represented.

323 The Guinness international who's who of sport / Peter Matthews, Ian Buchanan, Bill Mallon. Enfield: Guinness, 1993. 730p; index; pbk   ISBN: 0851129803
BL: YK.1994.b.1366

Includes biographies of 125 rugby players from Britain, Ireland, France, South Africa, New Zealand and Australia.

324 Auld acquaintance: great Scots characters I have known / Ben Coutts. Edinburgh: Mercat, 1994. 112p; illus; pbk   ISBN: 1873644302
BL: YK.1996.a.9039

Pages 46-52 are devoted to Lord Bannerman of Kildare. A Gaelic enthusiast and patriot, he also played rugby for Scotland as J. M. Bannerman, winning 37 caps between 1921 and 1929.

325 The all-time greats of British and Irish sport / Peter Matthews and Ian Buchanan. Enfield: Guinness, 1995. 474p; index; pbk   ISBN: 0851126782
BL: YK.1996.b.984

Biographies of over 2,000 sports personalities. Includes 171 rugby union players.

326 Black diamonds: the Aboriginal and Islander sports hall of fame / Colin & Paul Tatz. St Leonards, Aust.: Allen & Unwin, 1996. xvi, 20, 127p

Documents the 127 indigenous Australians – Aborigines, Tours Strait and South Sea Islanders – elected to the Hall of Fame. 'Membership is confined to those who have represented Australia, or their state or territory…. A further criterion was the person's contribution to Aboriginal identity at the time of his or her career, or later'. The earliest reference to an Aboriginal playing representative rugby is to Frank Ivory who played centre and full-back for Queensland in two matches against New South Wales in 1893 and 1894. Includes the rugby international players Gary, Glen and Mark Ella, Lloyd McDermott and Lloyd Walker.

327 Limerick lives / edited by Mary Fennelly; photography by Michael Martin. Limerick: EuroPRomotions for the Samaritans of Limerick and Tipperary, 1996. 160p; illus   ISBN: 0952905809

Limerick lives is 'a Samaritans' fund-raising project, published as a contribution to Limerick's 800th Charter celebrations'. Rugby is represented by: Philip Danaher, John Fitzgerald, Pat Murray, Brian O'Brien, and Pat O'Donnell.

328 Modern Irish lives: dictionary of 20th century Irish biography / edited by Louis McRedmond. Dublin: Gill and Macmillan, 1996. 328p   ISBN: 0717121984

Among the rugby players are: Ciarán Fitzgerald, Mike Gibson, Tom Kiernan, Jackie Kyle, Karl Mullen, Tony O'Reilly and Willie John McBride.

329 Great sporting eccentrics: weird and wonderful characters from the world of sport / Geoff Tibballs. London: Robson, 1997. ix, 245p

   Bibliography: p143-5   ISBN: 1861051220
Rugby is covered on pages 177-86.

Chapter D

Competitions

Contents

Domestic Competitions

❋ Five Nations ~ General

1 A souvenir book of Scottish rugby international matches, containing the programmes of rugby football internationals from 1934 to 1939. Edinburgh: R. W. Forsyth, 1945.
128p; illus

 A limited edition containing 19 match programmes: Scotland v. Wales, Scotland v. Ireland 1934-39, and Scotland v. New Zealand 1935.

2 Irish Rugby Football Triple Crown souvenir: a review from 1899-1949. Dublin: The Irish Annuals Press, 1949?
92p; illus; pbk

3 A souvenir book of Scottish rugby international matches, containing the programmes of rugby football internationals from 1946 to 1950. Edinburgh: R. W. Forsyth, 1951.
164p; illus

 A limited edition comprising 23 match programmes: Scotland v. Wales 1946 (twice) -50, France 1947-50, Ireland 1946-50, England 1946-50, New Zealand (Army) 1946, and Australia 1947.

4 Welsh Triple Crown souvenir 1893-1952 / J. B. G. Thomas. 1952.
48p; pbk

5 The International Rugby Championship 1883-1983 / Terry Godwin. London: Willow, 1984.
498p; illus   ISBN: 000218060X
                   BL: X.622/20037

 A well-researched account of rugby internationals from Scotland v. England in 1871 to Ireland v. England in 1983. Includes match reports, statistics, and a full list of players for each country.

6 The Five Nations championship, 1947-1993 / John Griffiths. London: Methuen, 1994.
176p; illus; pbk   ISBN: 0413359611
                      BL: YK.1994.b.3979

 Profiles of 100 players from the international teams of England, Scotland, Ireland, Wales and France between 1947 and 1993. Also lists all the players who appeared in the Five Nations matches since 1947 with dates of birth and death and the number of caps won in the series.

7 Rugby: the Five Nations Championship magazine. London: Stonehart Sports Magazines, 1996-

 Published annually   ISSN: 1361-5203
                             BL: ZK.9.b.9285

☞ Also listed at: I202

❋ Five Nations ~ Specific Competitions

8 Rugby in a sea of mud: impressions of a memorable struggle / Nichevo. Dublin: The Irish Times, 1927.
16p; illus; pbk

 A report of the Ireland v. Scotland match at Lansdowne Road, Dublin on 26 February 1927, reprinted from The Irish Times, 28 February 1927.

9 Irish rugby review Triple Crown souvenir: a survey of the games and competitions of 1948-49 with records for the years 1925-49 / F. J. Murphy. Dublin: The author, 1949?
48p; illus; pbk

10 Y Gamp Lawn: golwg ar y tîm a'r tymor / R. Gerallt Jones, Huw Llewelyn Davies, Carwyn James. Talybont: Y Lolfa, 1978.
64p; illus; pbk   ISBN: 0904864685
                      BL: P.441/871

 'The Grand Slam: a look at the team and season'. In 1978 Wales won the Triple Crown for the third year in succession and the second Grand Slam in three years. This is an account of the season. In Welsh.

11 Book of the Triple Crown. Dublin: Libra House, 1982.
47p; illus; pbk

 Variant title: Benson and Hedges book of the Triple Crown
                      ISBN: 0904169189
                      BL: X.629/19120

 Four rugby correspondents chronicle Ireland's progress in the 1982 Five Nations Championship. Though thwarted by France from achieving the Grand Slam, Ireland won the Triple Crown. All players and the coach, Tom Kiernan, are profiled. A results sequence against fellow home country opponents to 1982 completes the record. Includes an introduction by Lord Killanin.

12 Triple Crown champions / edited by John Redmond. Dublin: Swift, 1982.
60p; illus; pbk

 Cover title: Souvenir magazine of Ireland's historic triumph: Triple Crown champions 1982

13 Scotland: the crowning glory: the story of the Triple Crown triumph, 1984 / Bill McLaren. Edinburgh: Studioscope in conjunction with Mainstream, 1984.
44p; illus; pbk   ISBN: 0906391660

14 Scotland's Grand Slam '84 / Ian McLauchlan and Chris Rea. London: Stanley Paul, 1984.
94p; illus   ISBN: 0091592100
                 BL: X.622/21554

15   The year of the thistle: Scotland's grand slam 1983-84 /
      Norman Mair. London: Collins, 1984.
      197p; illus   ISBN: 0002181509
           Another account of Scotland's victory of that year.

16   Ireland's Triple Crown / Karl Johnston. Dublin: Gill and
      Macmillan, 1985.
      184p; illus; pbk   ISBN: 0717114279
                                                     BL: X.629/28131

      A souvenir of Ireland's historic triumph.

17   The flowering of Scotland: Grand Slam '90 / compiled
      by Derek Douglas; foreword by David Sole. Edinburgh:
      Mainstream in conjunction with the Glasgow Herald,
      1990.
      190p; illus   ISBN: 1851583076
                                                     BL: YK.1991.b.2443

18   Scotland's Grand Slam 1990 / Ian McGeechan, David
      Sole and Gavin Hastings with Ian Robertson and Mick
      Cleary. London: Stanley Paul in association with the
      Royal Bank of Scotland, 1990.
      127p; illus   ISBN: 0091746493
                                                     BL: YK.1990.b.9122

19   The Save & Prosper book of England's Grand Slam
      1991 / Rob Andrew and Dean Richards with Ian
      Robertson and Mick Cleary. London: Stanley Paul, 1991.
      123p; illus   ISBN: 009175173X
                                                     BL: YK.1991.b.3457

20   The year of the rose: England's Grand Slam '91 / edited
      by Barrie Fairall; foreword by Bill Beaumont. Edinburgh:
      Mainstream, 1991.
      189p; illus
           At head of title page: The Daily Telegraph
                                                     ISBN: 1851584412
                                                     BL: YK.1991.b.8031

21   5 Nations '96 / Richard Bath. 1996.
      114p; illus; pbk
           Previews the 1996 season.

22   Five Nations '96 / edited by Glyn Wilmshurst; foreword
      by Mike Catt. London: Absolute Sports, 1996?
      98p; illus; pbk
      (World sporting classics series)   BL: YK.1996.b.8817

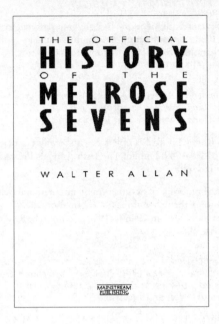

THE OFFICIAL
HISTORY
OF THE
**MELROSE
SEVENS**

WALTER ALLAN

MAINSTREAM
PUBLISHING

✳ *Melrose Sevens*

23   The official history of the Melrose Sevens / Walter
      Allan. Edinburgh: Mainstream, 1994.
      185p; illus, 1 map   ISBN: 1851586601
                                                     BL: YK.1996.b.9

Olympic Games

Rugby has appeared in four Olympic Games – 1900, 1908, 1920 and 1924. France, Germany and Great Britain took part in the 1900 event with France winning the gold, and Germany the silver. The team representing Britain were, in the main, from clubs in the Birmingham area.
The 1908 Games saw Australia and Cornwall contesting the medals. Australia, who were on tour in the United Kingdom, secured the gold medal beating the British team 32-3. The Anglo-Welsh tourists to New Zealand were the original choice to represent Great Britain, but they never received their letter of invitation and Cornwall, who were the English county champions in the preceding 1907-08 season, were asked to step in.
The 1920 Games, held in Antwerp, saw the USA defeat France in the final. D. B. Carroll, who had played in the winning Australian XV in 1908, was a member of the victorious American team.
In the Paris Games of 1924 France, Romania and the USA were the competing nations with France succumbing to the

Americans in the final.

Rugby was a demonstration sport in the Berlin Olympics in 1936. The four countries taking part were Germany, France, Italy and Romania. France defeated Germany 19-14 in the final, and in the play-off for third and fourth place Italy beat Romania 8 points to 7.

24   Report of the American Olympic Committee Seventh Olympic Games. Antwerp: 1920.

Includes a chapter by C. L. Tilden, manager of the United States rugby team, 'Winners in a foreign game-rugby football'. He describes the selection of the American team from the universities and clubs on the Pacific coast, the only area in the country playing rugby.

World Cup

25   Kickoff!: Rugby World Cup ... review. Bristol: IRFB Services, 1993-   BL: ZK.9.b.9203

☞ Also listed at: I191

26   The World Cups / Kevin Boon; edited by Allan R. Kirk. Wellington, NZ: Kotuku, 1993.
24p; illus; pbk
(The story of the All Blacks; 12)   ISBN: 0908947062
For children.

27   Rugby disunion / Derek Wyatt. London: Victor Gollancz, 1995.
224p; illus; index   ISBN: 0854932410
BL: YK.1996.b.13325

The story behind three World Cups.

✻ *1987 Tournament ~ Australia & New Zealand*

28   BBC Rugby Special featuring a review of the World Cup / Nigel Starmer-Smith & Ian Robertson. London: BBC Books, 1987.
112p; illus   ISBN: 0563206217
BL: YK.1988.b.4350

29   A guide to the rugby union World Cup 1987 / Andrew Thomas. Swansea: Christopher Davies, 1987.
127p; illus, maps, plans; pbk   ISBN: 0715406833
BL: YK.1988.a.1577

Includes: a brief history of the game; the International Rugby Football Board; rugby at the Olympic Games; the sixteen countries competing; World Cup grounds in New Zealand and Australia; basics of the game and guide to positions.

30   Rugby World Cup 1987: ABC guide / Gerwyn Williams; edited by Norman Tasker. Sydney, Aust.: ABC Enterprises for the Australian Broadcasting Corporation, 1987.
64p; illus   ISBN: 064252775X

31   World Cup rugby: the Wallabies versus the world / Phil Jarratt; foreword by Sir Nicholas Shehadie. North Ryde, Aust.: Angus & Robertson, 1987.
52p; illus   ISBN: 0207155925

✻ *1991 Tournament ~ British Isles & France*

32   1991 rugby union World Cup special / Rob Bonnet. Manchester: World International, 1991.
64p; illus; pbk   ISBN: 0749803991

33   Carling's England: the making of the World Cup team / Barry Newcombe. London: Harvill, 1991.
249p; illus   ISBN: 0002721309
BL: YK.1993.a.10767

34   The Daily Telegraph rugby union World Cup guide 1991 / edited by Chris Jones. London: Sidgwick & Jackson, 1991.
272p; illus; pbk   ISBN: 0283060743
BL: ZK.9.a.2247

A country-by-country analysis of the participants and all the statistics necessary to enjoy the event.

35   England World Cup '91. London: Centrepoint Colour under licence to the Rugby Football Union, 1991.
80p; illus; pbk   BL: ZK.9.b.6258

All the facts and figures presented in advance of the tournament.

36   ITV Sport's Rugby World Cup / edited by Mick Cleary
     and Hugh McIlvanney. London?: Newton Wells/Rococo
     Group, 1991?
     338p; illus, maps; pbk   BL: YK.1994.b.4407
     *A magazine type publication carrying a high
     proportion of advertising.*

37   News of the World Rugby World Cup 1991 / edited by
     Chris Dighton and Brendan Gallagher. London:
     Invincible, 1991.
     63p; illus; pbk   BL: ZK.9.a.1910
     *A lavishly illustrated magazine type publication
     issued in advance of the competition.*

38   The official book of the Rugby World Cup, 1991 /
     edited by Ian Robertson. London: Stanley Paul, 1991.
     191p; illus   ISBN: 009174881X
                                              BL: YK.1993.b.3504

39   Rugby World Cup weekly. Windsor: Burlington, 1991-
                                              ISSN: 0963-6870
                                              BL: ZK.9.d.684

     ☞   Also listed at: J188

40   The Wallabies' World Cup! / Greg Growden with Spiro
     Zavos, Simon Poidevin, Evan Whitton and an
     introduction by John Huxley; World Cup photographs
     by Bob Thomas. East Melbourne, Aust.: Text Publishing
     in association with the Sydney Morning Herald, 1991.
     112p; illus   ISBN: 1863722238

41   World champions / photography: Ross Land & Ross
     Setford; text by Richard Becht. Canberra, Aust.:
     Meadowset Graphics and Fotopacific, 1991.
     128p; chiefly illus   ISBN: 0949742333
     *Over 200 colour photographs from the 1991 World
     Cup.*

42   Rugby World Cup '91 / David Guiney; edited by Mark
     Herbert. Dublin: Sportsworld, 1992?
     ii, 130p; illus; pbk   BL: YK.1993.a.10391

43   SA Sports Illustrated Rugby World Cup: the ultimate
     fan's guide / Edward Griffiths. Vlaeberg, SA: Touchline
     Media, 1992.
     159p; illus; pbk   ISBN: 0620190639

✱ *1995 Tournament ~ South Africa*

44   1995 rugby World Cup review / Paul Dobson. Cape
     Town, SA: Sable Media, 1995.
     80p; illus; pbk   ISBN: 1868258645
     *Gives the results, pool-by-pool, to the final on 24
     June 1995. Also has statistics.*

45   Carling's men / Mick Cleary. London: Weidenfeld &
     Nicolson, 1995.
     92p; illus   ISBN: 0297835319
                                              BL: LB.31.b.11859

46   The complete book of the Rugby World Cup 1995 /
     edited by Ian Robertson, with Mick Cleary and Steve
     Bale. London: Hodder and Stoughton, in association
     with Scottish Life, 1995.
     192p; illus   ISBN: 0340649534
                                              BL: YK.1996.b.10594

47   Flying Springbok Rugby World Cup 1995 / edited by
     Deon Viljoen. Sandton, SA: ABBM, 1995.
     200p; illus; pbk

48   Lessons from & the impact of Rugby World Cup 1995 /
     James Seymour. Pretoria, SA: Satour, 1995.
     16 leaves; pbk   ISBN: 0864855443
     *Assesses the impact of the tournament on the
     tourist trade in South Africa.*

49   Phil Kearn's World Cup diary / Phil Kearns and Peter
     Jenkins. Sydney, Aust.: Pan Macmillan, 1995.
                                              ISBN: 0330357018
     Kearns played hooker for Australia.

50   Rugby World Cup '95 / Richard Bath. London: Aurum
     Carlton, 1995?
     80p; illus; pbk   ISBN: 1854103482
                                              BL: YK.1996.b.744

51   Rugby World Cup 1995. Sandton, SA: Ideadata Pretoria,
     1995?
     344p; illus; pbk

52   Rugby World Cup '95: in association with Scottish Life /
     edited by Ian Robertson. London: Hodder & Stoughton,
     1995.
     192p; illus   ISBN: 0340649534

53   Rugby World Cup 1995: souvenir booklet and TV
     viewers World Cup guide. South Africa: Republican
     Press, 1995.
     96p; illus; pbk

54   Rugby World Cup review / David Guiney. Dublin:
     Sportsworld, 1995.
     46p; illus; pbk
          'Match by match reports' – cover   ISBN: 1900110016
                                              BL: YK.1996.b.15638

55   SA Sports Illustrated road to victory: world champions
     1995: the Springboks' story / edited by Peter Davies.
     Vlaeberg, SA: Touchline Media, 1995.
     80p; illus; pbk   ISBN: 1919707018

56   World Cup 1995 / edited by Peter Bills. London:
     Hamlyn, 1995.
     80p; illus; pbk   ISBN: 0600585859
                                              BL: YK.1995.b.11458

57   World Cup 1995: the definitive guide / Paul Dobson.
     Cape Town, SA: Sable Media, 1995.
     72p; illus; pbk   ISBN: 1919695028

58 World Cup '95 diary / Rob Andrew; edited by Philip
Evans. Leicester: Independent UK Sports, 1995.
135p; illus; pbk   ISBN: 1899429042
                                    BL: YK.1996.b.11792

59 In search of Will Carling: an epic journey through Africa
to the Rugby World Cup / Charles Jacoby. London:
Simon & Schuster, 1996.
343p; illus, maps   ISBN: 0684816733
                                    BL: YK.1996.b.16089

60 The story of the Rugby World Cup, South Africa 1995 /
text by Paul Dobson and Nick Cain with additional copy
by Nelson Mandela and others. Cape Town, SA:
Royston Lamond International, 1996?
1 vol.; illus, maps

Also issued in a special leather-bound edition
                ISBN: 0958392986 (cased) • 0958392978 (pbk)
                                    BL: YA.1996.b.2639

World Cup Sevens

61 Doping control programme, Rugby World Cup Sevens
Tournament, 12-18 April 1993: competitors and official
guidelines. Edinburgh: Scottish Sports Council, 1993.

A guide to the categories of drugs prohibited for use
by sports people and the drug testing procedures
undertaken at the Rugby World Cup Sevens
Tournament.

62 Regbija Federacija Latvija, or, Latvia in Rugby World
Cup Sevens '93. Riga, Latvia: Latvian RU, 1993.
33p; illus; pbk

Text in Latvian and English. Contains a brief history of
rugby in Latvia.

☞ Also listed at: B872

63 World Cup 7's / edited by Fintan Nicholls. London:
Rugby Publications, 1993.
111p; illus; pbk

ITV Sport publication   ISBN: 0947700607

64 Rugby World Cup Sevens: divine intervention / edited
by John Blondin. Potts Point, Aust.: National
Publishing, 1997.
122p; illus

Overseas Competitions

❋ *Bell's Touch Rugby*

65 Bell's Touch Rugby classic tournament. 1993?-

❋ *Bledisloe Cup*

66 Tooheys official Bledisloe Cup book 1987. Pymble,
Aust.: Playbill, 1987.
60p; illus

67 Bledisloe magic / Max Howell, Lingyu Xie and Peter
Horton. Auckland, NZ: Rugby Publishing, 1995.
228p; illus; pbk   ISBN: 0908630522

Written by two former Australian rugby international
players both of whom are currently university
teachers, and a Chinese-born sports historian at the
University of Queensland. Through interviewing New
Zealand and Australian players, managers, and
coaches, and consulting scrapbooks and writings, the
authors have fashioned the story of the Bledisloe
Cup since its birth in 1931 to the game at Sydney
Football Stadium on 17 August 1994. The team
line-ups and the scoring sequence are given, but the
final score is not easy to find and the name of the
referee and the actual date of each game are
omitted.

68 The gold & the black: the rugby battles for the Bledisloe
Cup, New Zealand vs Australia 1903-94 / Spiro Zavos.
St. Leonards, Aust.: Allen & Unwin, 1995.
viii, 196p; illus; pbk

Bibliography: p194-5   ISBN: 1863739041

✳ *Currie Cup*

69   The Currie Cup story / Brian M. Crowley. Cape Town, SA: Don Nelson, 1973.

70   Road to glory: a pictorial record of Natal's Currie Cup triumph / John Bishop in conjunction with Craig Jamieson and Ian McIntosh. Pietermaritzburg, SA: Natal Witness, 1990.
71p; illus, coats of arms; pbk   ISBN: 0620153571

✳ *Hong Kong Sevens*

71   The Hong Kong Sevens: a book to celebrate the glorious years of rugby sevens in Hong Kong / Kevin Sinclair. Hong Kong: Arden, 1985.
147p; illus   ISBN: 9622650015

72   Hong Kong: the Sevens celebrating 20 years / John Blondin. Potts Point, Aust.: National Publishing Group in association with the Hong Kong Rugby Football Union, 1995.
112p; illus   ISBN: 064623675X

73   Hong Kong Sevens. Highbury House Communications, 1996-

   Spine title: Cathay Pacific HongKong Bank Sevens
          BL: ZK.9.b.9972

✳ *National Provincial Championship*

74   Fields of glory: NPC 21 years, 1976-1996 / Steven J. Garland; foreword by Sir David Beattie. Auckland, NZ: HarperCollins, 1997.
viii, 408p; illus   ISBN: 1869502337

✳ *Ranfurly Shield*

75   The log 'o wood: complete history of the Ranfurly Shield / Arthur C. Swan. Christchurch, NZ: Whitcombe & Tombs, 1960.
152p; illus   BL: 7925.l.22

76   Ranfurly Shield rugby: the complete book of match reports, comments, teams, photographs and records / A. H. Carman. Wellington, NZ: Reed, 1960.
256p; illus   BL: X.449/35
   ☞ Subsequent ed. D80

77   The Ranfurly Shield story / J. K. Moloney. Auckland, NZ: Ronault House, 1960.
140p; illus

78   Forever amber: souvenir Ranfurly Shield record 1958-64. New Plymouth, NZ: Taranaki Newspapers, 1964?
56p; illus; pbk

79   The Leopard history of Ranfurly Shield rugby / compiled by Arthur C. Swan. Hastings, NZ: Leopard Brewery, 1967.
96p; illus

80   Ranfurly Shield rugby: the complete book of match reports, comments, teams, photographs and records / A. H. Carman. 2nd ed. Wellington, NZ: Reed, 1967.
281p; illus
   ☞ Previous ed. D76

81   Shield fever / Lindsay Knight. Auckland, NZ: Rugby Press, 1980.
299p; illus   ISBN: 0959755381
   ☞ Subsequent ed. D82

82   Shield fever: the complete Ranfurly Shield story / Lindsay Knight. Rev. ed. Auckland, NZ: Rugby Press, 1986.
315p; illus   ISBN: 0908630220
   ☞ Previous ed. D81

✳ *Ross Shield*

83   Wattie's '84 Ross Shield tournament, Hastings: centenary 1884-1984. Hastings, NZ: Hastings Ross Shield Committee, 1984.
58p; illus; pbk

Chapter E

The Tours

Contents

Touring

1   No prisoners: a background to rugby touring / David
    Frost. London: Pelham, 1978.
    143p; illus; index   ISBN: 0720710375
                                          BL: X.629/12064

2   The visitors: the history of international rugby teams in
    New Zealand / R. H. Chester & N. A. C. McMillan.
    Auckland, NZ: Moa, 1990.
    671p; illus

    *'A limited edition of 1200 numbered copies, featuring 1300
    illustrations, was published in a hand-bound volume
    measuring 535mm x 382mm' – t.p. verso*
                                          ISBN: 1869470605

British Isles & Irish Tourists

3   Pride of the Lions / Reg Sweet. London: Bailey &
    Swinfen, 1962.
    231p; illus   BL: 7926.h.41

    An account of the international rugby football
    matches between South Africa and the British Isles
    since 1891.

4   The Lions / Wallace MacDonald Reyburn. London:
    Stanley Paul, 1967.
    203p; illus   BL: X.449/2687

5   Rugby in black and red / J. B. G. Thomas. London:
    Pelham Books, 1968.
    240p; illus

    The All Blacks in Britain and France 1967. Also
    reviews British Isles tours in the Antipodes and
    South Africa from 1888 to 1962.

    ☞   Also listed at: E253

6   The Irish Lions 1896-1983 / Barry Coughlan. Dublin:
    Ward River Press, 1983.
    247p; illus; pbk   ISBN: 0907085679

    This work provides an overview of the Irish involvement
    with the [British] Lions since their foundation, to the
    tour of New Zealand in 1983. Appendix D lists the
    Irish tourists.

7   British Lions / John Griffiths. Swindon: Crowood, 1990.
    224p; illus   ISBN: 1852235411
                                          BL: YK.1991.b.2394

    ☞   Also listed at: C282

8   The history of the British Lions / Clem Thomas.
    Edinburgh: Mainstream, 1996.
    269p; illus; pbk   ISBN: 1851588698
                                          BL: YK.1997.b.5051

    ☞   Subsequent ed. E10

9   Glory, glory Lions: the taming of South Africa / Chris
    Dighton & Iain Spragg; foreword by Cliff Morgan.
    London: Bookman, 1997.
    96p; illus   ISBN: 1840430052

10 The history of the British Lions / Clem Thomas. New
    ed. updated by Greg Thomas. Edinburgh: Mainstream,
    1997.
    288; illus; pbk   ISBN: 1840180005

    Updated by the author's son to include the Lions'
    1997 tour to South Africa.

    ☞   Previous ed. E8

British Isles & Irish Tourists ~ Specific Tours

❋ 1888 to New Zealand & Australia

11   'Give me Arthur': a biography of Arthur Shrewsbury /
Peter Wynne-Thomas. London: Arthur Barker, 1985.
xi, 163p; illus   ISBN: 0213169258

> Gives an account of the cricket and rugby tours to
> Australia. Relates how the tour of the Antipodes was
> arranged for the British Isles rugby tourists in 1888.

> ☞ Also listed at: C201

❋ 1891 to South Africa

12   Memoir of the visit of the British football team to South
Africa, 1891. Cape Town, SA?: 1891.
vi, 56p; illus; pbk

> Pen portraits of the players, reports of all the
> matches, and a summary of results.

❋ 1896 to South Africa

13   The book of the English rugby football team in South
Africa 1896: portraits and biographies / compiled by H.
G. C. 3rd ed. Cape Town, SA: 1896.
32p; illus

> *Previous eds. untraced*

❋ 1903 to South Africa

14   South African rugby & association football guide &
handbook of the English touring teams. Cape Town, SA:
W. Preston Buchanan, 1903.
128p   BL: 07905.de.8

> 'It is hoped to make the handbook an annual…' – only
> one edition appeared however.

❋ 1904 to New Zealand

15   Sketcher's cartoons, caricatures & photos: the British
football team: Britain v. Otago & Southland, August
10th, 1904 / F. R. Rayner. Dunedin, NZ: J. Wilkie?, 1904.
36p; illus

> *'Sketcher' was the pseudonym of Frederick Richard Rayner*

16   Souvenir of twenty years' football published in
connection with the visit of the British team to New
Zealand, August 1904: illustrations and records of
English, Australian and New Zealand teams since 1884.
Christchurch, NZ: Walter E. Knott under authority of
the Otago Rugby Football Union, 1904.
32p; illus; pbk

A series of photographs of New Zealand teams and
visiting teams to New Zealand, interspersed with
advertisements.

❋ 1908 to New Zealand

17   Practical imperialism: the Anglo-Welsh rugby tour of
New Zealand, 1908 / G. T. Vincent. University of
Canterbury, NZ, 1996. *Master's thesis.*

> Following the successful tour of the 1905 All Blacks
> to the UK, Ireland and France, and the 'Professional'
> All Black tour to Britain in 1907, the RFU organised a
> tour to New Zealand in 1908. Aware of the threat of
> professionalism to rugby in New Zealand, the RFU
> decided it was timely to counter the threat with a
> 'rescue effort' in the form of an Anglo-Welsh side (the
> Scots and Irish had refused to become involved). The
> venture proved to be a failure as there was great
> disparity between the two football cultures.

18   Sketcher souvenir: fifty photographic records and
sketches of the Anglo-Welsh and New Zealand teams.
Wellington, NZ: Fred R. Rayner, 1908.

19   Souvenir & official programme of the British rugby
football team in New Zealand 1908. Wellington, NZ:
Ferguson & Hicks for the Imperial Advertising and
Theatrical Agency, 1908?
40p; illus; pbk

20   With the British rugby team in Maoriland / R. A. Barr.
Dunedin, NZ: Otago Daily Times & Witness, 1908.
168p; illus

❋ 1910 to South Africa

21   The British Rugby Football team in South Africa 1910:
portraits and biographies of the team and of leading South
African players and officials: official list of fixtures, etc.,
past history and records of the game in South Africa: the
official handbook of the tour for the Transvaal Rugby
Football Union / edited by I. D. Difford. Johannesburg,
SA: Union Publicity Association, 1910.
226p; illus; pbk

22   My recollections and reminiscences / William A. Millar.
Cape Town, SA: Juta, 1926.
xiii, 106p

> South African rugby tours of Britain, Ireland and
> France in 1906 and 1912, and the return tour of
> South Africa in 1910.

> ☞ Also listed at: E158; E164

23   Official souvenir of the British rugby and association football tours: records of the games and souvenir of the British teams' visit to South Africa, 1910 / compiled by Leslie A. Cox and Francis G. Pay. Cape Town, SA: The authors, 1910.
111p; illus; pbk

> *Cover title: Souvenir of the British rugby and association football tours 1910*   BL: D
>
> Issued under the patronage and with the authority of the South African Rugby Board and the South African Football Association.

✱ *1924 to South Africa*

24   Official souvenir of British rugby tour, 1924. Cape Town, SA: Johnson, Hopkins & McKowen, 1924.
96p; illus

> The fifth British and Irish tour to South Africa.

25   Souvenir: British rugby tour, 1924. Cape Town, SA: Hortors, 1924.
40p; illus

> Sponsored by United Tobacco Companies (South) Ltd.

✱ *1930 to New Zealand*

26   With the British rugby team in New Zealand / G. T. Alley. Christchurch, NZ: Simpson & Williams, 1930.
180p; illus

✱ *1938 to South Africa*

27   'Our rugby Springboks': souvenir of the visit of the British rugby team to South Africa and Southern Rhodesia, 1938 / Ivor D. Difford. Johannesburg, SA: Published under the authority and with the approval of the South African Rugby Football Board by the Central News Agency, 1938.
104p; illus; pbk   BL: 7915.t.5

> 'A complete history of all South Africa's rugby international matches (1891-1937) and of Springbok tours to Britain, Australia and New Zealand, and of those countries to South Africa'.

☞ Also listed at: E147

✱ *1950 to New Zealand & Australia*

28   1950, the year of the Lions: a history of the British Isles rugby union team in New Zealand and Australia during the winter of 1950 / D. J. Williams. Hamilton, NZ: The author, 1988.
xiv, 242p; illus; index; pbk   ISBN: 0473007002

✱ *1955 to South Africa*

29   The Lions on trek / J. B. G. Thomas. London: Stanley Paul, 1956.
207p; illus   BL: 7922.f.24

30   Lions rampant: the British Isles rugby tour of South Africa, 1955 / Vivian Jenkins. London: Cassell, 1956.
275p; illus   BL: 7923.aa.4

✱ *1959 to Australia, New Zealand & Canada*

31   The 1959 Lions in New Zealand & Australia / Frederick W. Boshier. Wellington, NZ: Blundell Brothers, 1959.
96p; illus; pbk

32   Kings of rugby: the British Lions' 1959 tour of New Zealand / Terry McLean. London: Bailey & Swinfen, 1960.
247p; illus   BL: 7925.k.18

33   Lions courageous / J. B. G. Thomas. London: Stanley Paul, 1960.
223p; illus   BL: 7925.b.89

34   Lions down under: the British Isles rugby tour of Australia and New Zealand, 1959 / Vivian Jenkins. London: Cassell, 1960.
xvi, 288p; illus   BL: 7925.b.74

✱ *1962 to South Africa*

35   The British Lions tour of South Africa 1962 / 'Rugby Football Correspondent of The Times'. London: Times Publishing, 1962.
97p; illus   BL: 7923.ttt.37

36   Lions among the Springboks / J. B. G. Thomas. London: Stanley Paul, 1963.
199p; illus   BL: 7926.h.18

> The 1962 British Isles tour of South Africa is described, highlighting the exciting moments on the field and the interesting events encountered on their trek across the country.

✱ *1966 to New Zealand, Australia & Canada*

37   The '66 Lions in New Zealand: a pictorial record of the 1966 Lions rugby touring in New Zealand / Francis Quinn Goldingham. Palmerston North, NZ: Viscount, 1966.
64p; all illus

38   The Lion tamers / T. P. McLean. Wellington, NZ: Reed, 1966.
260p; illus

     272p; illus

39   Lions at bay / J. B. G. Thomas. London: Pelham Books, 1966.
     231p; illus   BL: X.449/2304

40   Lions at bay / John W. Waters. New Plymouth, NZ: Taranaki News-papers, 1966.
     56p; illus; pbk

❋ *1968 to South Africa*

41   The 1968 Lions: the British Isles tour of South Africa / John Reason. London: Eyre & Spottiswoode, 1968.
     260p; illus   SBN: 413262400
                        BL: X.449/3423

42   Die Britse Leeus in Suid-Afrika 1968, or, The British Lions in South Africa 1968 / edited by G. J. Kotze. South Africa: 1968.
     32p; illus; pbk

43   The Lion tamers / A. C. Parker. London: Bailey & Swinfen, 1968.
     215p; illus   BL: X.449/3461

44   On trek again: an account of the rugby tour in Southern Africa by the 1968 Lions / J. B. G. Thomas. London: Pelham, 1968.
     192p; illus   BL: X.449/3370

45   Springboks on trial / L. Wilson. Cape Town, SA: Buren, 1968.
     127p; illus

❋ *1971 to New Zealand & Australia*

46   Britain's finest Lions / Lindsay Knight. 1971.
     132p; illus

47   British Lions 1971 / Clem Thomas.
     50p; illus

48   Dewi Bebb yn Seland Newydd gyda Llewod '71. Llandybie: Llyfrau'r Dryw; Caerdydd: HTV Cymru/Wales, 1972.
     118p; illus; pbk

       Foreword by Carwyn James   ISBN: 0853391092

     Pen portraits of the Welsh players in the squad. Bebb reported in Welsh on the games for HTV Cymru/Wales.

49   How the Lions won: the stories and skills behind two famous victories / edited by Terry O'Connor. London: Collins, 1975.
     253p; illus   ISBN: 0002113643
                        BL: X.629/10266

     The first famous victory was that of 1971.

    ☞ Also listed at: E57

50   Lions rampant: the Lions tour in New Zealand 1971 / T. P. McLean. Wellington, NZ: Reed, 1971.
     268p; illus   ISBN: 0589007165

51   The Lions' share / Gabriel David and David Frost. Auckland, NZ: Hicks, Smith; London: Eyre and Spottiswoode, 1971.
     x, 205p; illus   ISBN: 0456009604

52   The Lions speak / Carwyn James and others; edited by John Reason. London: Rugby Books, 1972.
     152p; illus; pbk   ISBN: 0723303592

     Papers delivered at an international players' conference held at the Polytechnic of North London in July 1971.

53   The mighty Lions 1971 tour of New Zealand / John Reason. Christchurch, NZ: Whitcombe & Tombs, 1971.
     206p; illus   ISBN: 0723303282

54   The roaring Lions / J. B. G. Thomas. London: Pelham, 1971.
     179p; illus   SBN: 720705452
                        BL: X.629/3870

55   The victorious Lions: the 1971 British Isles rugby union tour of Australia and New Zealand / John Reason. London: Rugby Books, 1971.
     249p; illus   BL: X.629/4007

❋ *1974 to South Africa*

56   The greatest Lions: the story of the British Lions tour of South Africa, 1974 / J. B. G. Thomas; with a foreword by Willie John McBride. London: Pelham Books, 1974.
     175p; illus   ISBN: 0720707862
                        BL: X.629/6383

57   How the Lions won: the stories and skills behind two famous victories / edited by Terry O'Connor. London: Collins, 1975.
     253p; illus   ISBN: 0002113643
                        BL: X.629/10266

     Covers the tours of 1971 and 1974.

    ☞ Also listed at: E49

58   The unbeaten Lions: the 1974 British Isles rugby union tour of South Africa / John Reason. London: Rugby Books, 1974.
     258p; illus   ISBN: 0903194023
                        BL: X.629/10007

✼ *1977 to New Zealand & Fiji*

59   Heroes to a man: a pictorial account of the 1977 British Lions tour of New Zealand including their match against Fiji on their way home and against the Barbarians in the jubilee match at Twickenham in the presence of HRH Prince Charles / Terry Godwin. London: Colorsport and the International Sportswriters' Club, 1977.
64p; illus; pbk

60   Life with the Lions: the inside story of the 1977 New Zealand tour / John Hopkins. London: Stanley Paul, 1977.
x, 158p; illus, 1 map; index   ISBN: 0091317401
                                      BL: X.620/17253

61   Lions '77 full NZ tour coverage: highlights in colour / edited by Graeme Douglas and Rob Tucker; photographs by New Zealand Herald staff; photographers Ross Wiggins and others. Auckland, NZ: Wilson and Horton, 1977.
96p; chiefly illus; pbk

      Cover title: Tour of New Zealand by Lions rugby team
                                      ISBN: 0868640255

62   Lions 77 on tour in New Zealand / Keith Quinn. London: Eyre Methuen, 1977.
194p; illus   ISBN: 0413388506
                                      BL: X.629/11908

63   Lions down under: the 1977 British Isles rugby union tour of New Zealand and Fiji / John Reason. London: Rugby Books, 1977.
3, 202p; illus   ISBN: 0903194031
                                      BL: X.629/11909

64   The long lost tour: Lions '77 / Barry John, Graham Thorne. Swansea: Christopher Davies, 1977.
135p; illus; pbk   ISBN: 0715404326
                                      BL: X.619/17991

65   Rugby 77: the British Lions in New Zealand / edited by Robin Charteris. Dunedin, NZ: Otago Daily Times, 1977.
48p; illus

66   Trial of strength: the 1977 British Lions in New Zealand / J. B. G. Thomas. London: Pelham, 1977.
176p; illus   ISBN: 0720709679
                                      BL: X.629/12111

67   Winter of discontent: the 1977 Lions in New Zealand / T. P. McLean. Wellington, NZ: Reed, 1977.
211p; illus
      The British Isles team in New Zealand and Fiji 1977.

✼ *1980 to South Africa*

68   Backs to the wall: the 1980 rugby union tour of South Africa by the British Isles and Ireland / John Reason. London: Rugby Football Books, 1980.
218p; illus   BL: 81/2611

69   British Lions 1980 / John Hopkins; statistics by Michael Nimmo; photographs by David Rogers. Kingswood: World's Work, 1980.
15, 234p; illus, 1 map; index   ISBN: 043706851X
                                      BL: X.629/14167

70   Injured pride: the Lions in South Africa / Carwyn James and Chris Rea; edited by Rupert Cherry. London: Arthur Barker, 1980.
vii, 206p; illus, 1 map   ISBN: 0213167824
                                      BL: X.629/14571

      Former international players, James of Wales and Rea of Scotland, followed the British Lions tour of South Africa in 1980. They analyse the 18 matches played, team selection, tactics, individual performances. As well as a look at the lighter side of the tour, the authors examine the political situation in the country and conclude that while the tour may not have helped the move towards integration, the presence of the Lions in South Africa did no harm.

71   The South African trip / R. M. Court. Bognor Regis: New Horizon, 1984.
197p; illus   ISBN: 071250205X
                                      BL: X.629/24523

      A detailed supporter's diary of the 1980 British Lions tour of South Africa right down to the menu for lunch. Includes the words of two rugby songs in Afrikaans with parallel English translations.

72   Springbok triumph: Lions tour of South Africa / photographed by John Rubython and Miles Bishop. Cape Town, SA: Howard Timmins, 1980.
160p; illus   ISBN: 0869781820

73   Springboks under siege: the New Zealand tour, pioneering in America, Irish in South Africa, Beaumont's Lions: an illustrated record of Springbok rugby in 1980 and 1981 / edited by Colin Bryden & Mark Colley; foreword by Wynand Claassen. Hillbrow, Johannesburg, SA: Now Publications, 1981.
160p; illus

      A record of the 15 tests played by South Africa between April 1980 and September 1981; the tour of New Zealand and the United States; the tour of South Africa by Ireland and the British Isles.
      ☞ Also listed at: E192

74   Wounded Lions and other 1980 rugby / J. B. G. Thomas. London: Pelham, 1981.
vii, 168p; illus   ISBN: 0720713099
                                      BL: X.629/15087

✻ *1983 to New Zealand*

75   1983 British Lions rugby tour. Auckland, NZ: TVNZ
     Enterprises, 1983.
     50p; illus; pbk

76   Lions '83 on tour in New Zealand through the lens of
     Peter Bush. Poole: Blandford, 1983.
     143p; illus   ISBN: 0713714360
                                                BL: YK.1988.b.898

77   Lions 83: the New Zealand tour / David Frost. London:
     Pelham, 1983.
     v, 161p; illus, 1 map   ISBN: 0720714796
                                                BL: X.629/22738

78   The Lions in winter: the British and Irish Lions in New
     Zealand, 1983 / Karl Johnston. London: Allen &
     Unwin, 1983.
     193p; illus   ISBN: 0047960809
                                                BL: X.629/22588

79   Lions' tour of N.Z. '83 / Paul Elenio, Ian Gault; pictures
     supplied by Ian Mackley and others. Wellington. NZ:
     Wellington Newspapers, 1983.
     128p; illus; pbk

     Cover title: 1983 Lions in New Zealand

80   On the Lions' trail / Don Cameron. Auckland, NZ:
     Rugby Press, 1983.
     240p; illus   ISBN: 0908630123

81   Two sides to the argument: All Blacks v. Lions '83 /
     Terry McLean with Andy Dalton and Ian Robertson
     with Bill Beaumont. London: Stanley Paul, 1983.
     174p; illus   ISBN: 0091545005
                                                BL: X.529/61980

82   A wounded pride: the 1983 Lions in New Zealand /
     Keith Quinn. Auckland, NZ: Methuen, 1983.
     187p; illus; pbk   ISBN: 0456032304
     Also covers the All Blacks v. Australia.

✻ *1993 to New Zealand*

83   So close to glory: the Lions in New Zealand 1993 / Ian
     McGeechan with end of tour reflections from Gavin
     Hastings. Harpenden: Queen Anne in association with
     Scottish Life, 1993.
     96p; illus; pbk   ISBN: 1852915323
                                                BL: YK.1995.b.321

✻ *1997 to South Africa*

84   Arolwg o daith y Llewod '97 / N. E. Griffiths. Elim, SA:
     Stamford, 1997.
     iv,48p; illus; pbk

85   Best seat in the house / Miles Harrison; foreword by
     Gavin Hastings. London: Aurum, 1997.
     xi, 176p; illus   ISBN: 1854105345
                                                BL: YC.1998.b.2442

86   Gavin Hastings' British Lions 97 / edited by Gavin
     Hastings. London, EMP, 1997?
     66p; illus, 1 map; pbk
        Includes a poster   BL: YK.1997.b.7075

87   Heroes all: the official book of the Lions in South Africa
     1997 / Ian McGeechan with Mick Cleary; introduction
     by Willie John McBride; photographs by Colin Elsey and
     Stuart Macfarlane; additional photographs from Reuters.
     London: Hodder & Stoughton, 1997.
     140p; illus   ISBN: 0340707402
                                                BL: YK.1998.b.1230

88   The Lions diary / Jeremy Guscott and Nick Cain.
     London: Michael Joseph, 1997.
     187p; illus   ISBN: 0718143132
                                                BL: YK.1998.b.3831

89   Lions in Africa: the official SARFU Lions tour souvenir
     programme / edited by James Lewis. Cape Town, SA:
     Montgomery-Scott International, 1997.
     192p; illus; pbk

        Cover title: SARFU's official guide to the 1997 Lions' tour
        of South Africa: a press record of the tour

90   The Lions raw: a captain's story, South Africa 1997 /
     Martin Johnson with Howard Johnson. Edinburgh:
     Mainstream, 1997.
     188p; illus   ISBN: 1840180234

91   Lions uncaged / John Bentley with Phil McNeill.
     London: Chameleon, 1997.
     128p; illus

        Jacket subtitle: A British Lion's inside view of the
        triumphant tour of South Africa   ISBN: 0233993444
                                                BL: YK.1998.b.6138

92   My pride of Lions: the British Lions tour of South Africa
     1997 / Fran Cotton. London: Ebury, 1997.
     192p; illus; index   ISBN: 0091854229

93   Rugby World presents the definitive guide to the 1997
     Lions tour: a free souvenir handbook to commemorate
     the first professional tour by the Lions. London: IPC
     Magazines, 1997.
     106p; illus; pbk

        Spine title: Rugby world's definitive guide to the 1997 Lions
        tour

Other British & Irish Sides

94 Ireland v. New Zealand: 100 years of international rugby / David Guiney. Dublin: PR Books, 1989.
112p; illus

> *Cover title: Ireland v. New Zealand 100 years of rugby football*

> ISBN: 1872553001
> BL: YK.1994.a.3308

☞ Also listed at: E284

95 Red dragons of rugby: Welsh-All Black encounters from 1905-1969, including the 1969 Welsh rugby tour of New Zealand, Australia and Fiji / Terry McLean. Wellington, NZ: Reed, 1969.
150p; illus

96 Musselburgh Rugby Football Club: Canada tour, August 1952. Musselburgh: The Club, 1952.
24p; illus, map, coat of arms

97 Manager's report on the Cambridge University Rugby Football Club's tour of Japan 1953 / S. V. Perry. Cambridge: Cambridge University RFC, 1953.
11p; pbk

> Eight matches played in Japan. The report gives the names of the touring party, a summary of results, and an outline of the refereeing, travel arrangements, and comments on the Japanese play.

98 Manager's report on the Oxford and Cambridge Universities rugby union tour of British Columbia and California 1955 / P. W. Kininmonth. The Union, 1955.
15p; pbk

> The combined team played a dozen matches in British Colombia and California in March and April 1955. The report summarises: refereeing; styles of play; grounds, gates, etc.; climate; results and names of players (11 Oxford and 10 Cambridge Blues). Also provides a brief history of the British Columbia and the Northern and Southern California Rugby Unions.

99 Manager's report on the combined Oxford and Cambridge Universities Rugby Football Clubs tour to Argentina, Chile and Uruguay 1956 / J. M. Williams. The Clubs, 1956.
23p; pbk

> Thirteen matches plus a seven-a-side tournament were played in Argentina, Chile and Uruguay in August and September 1956. The party consisted of 24 players, seven of whom were internationals, a referee and a player-manager. The report logs their progress, the standard of refereeing, hospitality and arrangements, and a history of the three Unions. During the Peron regime rugby in Argentina 'stood out against the pressure from the Government and the Secret Police and all manners of persecution in the endeavour to keep the game amateur and non State-controlled. Cuba University was the backbone of the students' resistance, and on three occasions Peron disbanded the Rugby Club in an effort to stamp out this core of resistance.'

100 Report on the combined Oxford and Cambridge rugby tour of Ceylon, Malaya, Thailand and Japan, August to October 1959 / A. J. Herbert and J. S. M. Scott. Oxford and Cambridge Universities RFU, 1959.
10p; pbk

> The party of 24 and A. J. Herbert, the player-manager, took part in 15 matches — five in Ceylon, one in Malaya (played under floodlights), two in Thailand, and seven in Japan — between 20 August and 4 October 1959. The report outlines the tour.

101 The Ambassadors / John L. T. Dawson. Hawick: Tweedale, 1967.
80p; illus; pbk

> This is an account of the Scottish Border Club tour to South Africa in May 1967. As well as contributions from South African writers, the final section of the book gives an overview of rugby in the Borders.

102 All Blacks in Wales / John Billot. Rhondda: Ron Jones Publications, 1972.
239p; illus   ISBN: 0950162310

> Includes coverage of the Welsh tour of New Zealand in 1969.

☞ Also listed at: E262

103 Wales in New Zealand / Alex Veysey. London: Dominion & Sunday Times, 1968.
80p

104 Greystones Rugby Football Club USA tour 1974. Greystones: The Club, 1974.
24p; illus; pbk

> Six match tour in May 1974.

105 Bective Rangers Football Club West Indies tour 1976. Dublin: The Club, 1976.
58p; illus; pbk

> Six match tour during August 1976.

106 Dublin University Football Club USA rugby tour 1977. Dublin: The Club, 1977.

107 Old Belvedere RFC American tour 1978, 5th-21st May. Dublin: The Club, 1978.
54p; illus; pbk

> Three match tour and tournament.

108 Tycroes Rugby Football Club: souvenir brochure / compiled by T. E. Davies. Tycroes: The Club, 1979.
84p; illus; pbk

Tour brochure to commemorate Tycroes RFC's 'first ever fixture abroad when the club played against Club Rhodanien at Condrieu on the outskirts of Lyons, France, in April 1979'. Includes a brief history of the club.

☞ Also listed at: B618

109 Stewart's-Melville Former Pupils' Rugby Football Club Canadian tour 1980. Edinburgh: The Club?, 1980.
91p; illus

110 Wanderers FC tour of USA, May 22-June 8, 1980: souvenir programme. Dublin: The Club, 1980.
88p; illus; pbk

Four matches and tournament.

111 Bohemian RFC 1981 tour brochure. Limerick: The Club, 1981.
64p

112 Greystones Rugby Football Club 1981 tour of Zimbabwe 28 April-17 May. Greystones: The Club, 1981.
88p; illus; pbk

Six match tour, the first to Zimbabwe by a senior Irish club.

113 St. Mary's College RFC Dublin, Ireland Canadian tour 1981 August 1-14 - September 4. Dublin: The Club, 1981.
20p; illus; pbk

Five match tour.

114 Greenock Wanderers RFC: America 1982. Greenock: The Club, 1982.
64p; illus; pbk

115 Twickenham RFC USA 1984 tour guide. Twickenham: The Club, 1984.

116 University College Dublin Australian tour. Dublin: University College Dublin Rugby Club, 1984.
80p; illus

117 Edinburgh University Rugby Football Club: Brazil tour 1986. Edinburgh: The Club, 1986.
32p; illus; pbk

118 Leicester Football Club world tour 1987. Leicester: The Club, 1987.
64p; illus; pbk

Over a period of six days in August 1987 the club played in four matches in Australia, one in New Zealand and one in Singapore.

119 Leicestershire Rugby Union tour to Italy. Leicester: Leicestershire Rugby Football Union, 1987.
20p; illus; pbk

The tour took in three matches between 17 and 23 May 1987.

120 Gaeaf gwyn a hafau duon: tim rygbi Cymru, Mai 1987-Mehefin 1988 / Thomas Davies. Capel Garmon: Gwasg Carreg Gwalch, 1988.
150p; illus; pbk   ISBN: 0863811124
                                    BL: YK.1989.a.5081

Details the record of the Welsh rugby XV from May 1987 to June 1988 when it participated in two trips to New Zealand, the first for the inaugural World Cup, and the second for an eight match tour.

121 Llantrisant RFC centenary tour Florida 1989. Llantrisant: The Club, 1989.
33p; illus; pbk

Club tour of Florida, May/June 1989.

122 Tour to Canada 1989. Pontypridd: Pontypridd RFC, 1989.
32p; illus

123 Welsh Rugby Union tour of Namibia: official souvenir programme issued by the NRU. Windhoek: Namibia Rugby Union, 1990.
16p; illus; pbk

Wales played six matches in Namibia in May and June 1990.

124 Leicestershire Rugby Union Holland tour 1991. Leicester: The Union?, 1991.
48p; illus; pbk

Three matches were played from 3 to 5 May 1991.

125 California 92: Clwb Rygbi Pwllheli. Pwllheli: Clwb Rygbi Pwllheli, 1992.
19p; illus; pbk

Pwllheli RFC toured California in October and November 1992.

126 Musselburgh Rugby Football Club: Canada tour, August 1992. Musselburgh: The Club, 1992.
24p; 1 map, coat of arms; pbk

127 Wesley College Zimbabwe tour 1992. Dublin: The College, 1992.
80p; illus; pbk

128 Leicestershire Rugby Union Ontario Canada tour. Leicester: The Union?, 1995.
57p

A 3-match tour took place from 8-12 May 1995.

✳ *Schools*

129 WSSRU South African tour 1956 / compiled by Alan Evans. Tamworth: The author, 1995.
21p; pbk

The Welsh Secondary Schools Rugby Union eight match tour of South Africa in 1956.

130 Australia-New Zealand RFSU 1979 tour report / compiled by J. MacG. Kendall-Carpenter. Rugby Football Schools' Union, 1980.
32p; illus; pbk

Report of the tour of Australia (11 matches) and New Zealand (2 matches) in August and September 1979.

131 The Leys School rugby tour to Australia 1992.
31p; pbk   BL: YK.1994.a.519

132 Rugby School Antipodean tour 1992 / compiled by David Ray. Rugby: Rugby School, 1992.
48p; illus

The school played two matches in Australia, five in New Zealand, and one in Fiji. The brochure contains pieces by old boys, extracts from school chronicles and newspapers, and messages from the headmaster, the presidents of Barbarians RFC, and the chairman of the Rugby World Cup 1991.

133 Blackheath rugby under 14 Italy tour 1993, Abruzzo region April 7 - April 14: souvenir programme. Blackheath: The Club, 1993.
46p; illus; pbk

134 King Edward's School Birmingham Rugby Club South African tour 1995 / edited by Keith Phillips. Birmingham: The School, 1995.
27p; illus; pbk

Eighteen day, six match tour of South Africa, August 1995.

135 Radley College RUFC South Africa tour 1995. Abingdon: The School, 1995.
48p; illus; pbk

Six matches in August 1995.

136 The Windsor Boys' School tour 1995 South African souvenir programme. Windsor: The School, 1995.
39p; illus; pbk

Six matches played in July and August 1995.

137 The John Cleveland College Rugby Football Club Canada tour July 1996: souvenir brochure. Leicester: The Club?, 1996.
30p; illus; pbk

The school played five matches plus one sevens tournament.

French Tourists

✱ *1958 to South Africa*

138 The great fight of the French fifteen / Denis Lalanne, translated by E. J. Boyd-Wilson. Wellington, NZ: Reed, 1960.
174p; illus

Translation of: *Le grand combat du quinze de France*
BL: X.449/1086

✱ *1961 to New Zealand & Australia*

139 Cock of the rugby roost: the 1961 French tour of New Zealand / T. P. McLean. Wellington, NZ: Reed, 1961.
215p; illus

140 La mêlée fantastique: the French rugby tour of New Zealand 1961 / Denis Lalanne; translated by E. J. Boyd-Wilson. Wellington, NZ: Reed, 1962.
207p

Covers French tours during 1959 to 1961, with emphasis on the tour of New Zealand and Australia 1961.

✱ *1967 to South Africa*

141 Franse in Suid-Afrika 1967, or, French in South Africa: tournée de l'équipe de France en Afrique du Sud, 1967. Johannesburg, SA: Springbok Sport, 1967.
29p; illus; pbk

In Afrikaans and English. Covers France's 13 match tour of South Africa in July and August 1967.

142 Ruffled roosters / A. C. Parker. Cape Town, SA: Howard Timmins, 1967.
175p; illus

The French tour of South Africa 1967.

✱ *1968 to New Zealand & Australia*

143 All Black power: the story of the 1968 All Blacks in Australia and Fiji and the 1968 French team in New Zealand and Australia / T. P. McLean. Wellington, NZ: Reed, 1968.
262p; illus
☞ Also listed at: E255

144 France in New Zealand / Alex Veysey. London: Dominion & Sunday Times, 1968.
80p

✳ *1979 to New Zealand*

145 All Blacks, retreat from glory / Don Cameron.
Auckland, NZ: Hodder & Stoughton, 1980.
178p; illus

   Reviews the All Blacks in Australia, England, Scotland
   and Italy in 1979, and the French and Argentinian
   tours of New Zealand in the same year.

   ☞ Also listed at: E275; E312

✳ *1993 to South Africa*

146 Tour le France: the official SA Rugby Football Union
brochure for the 1993 French rugby tour to South Africa
/ edited by Simon Lewis, Gary Owen & Trevor Quelch
in co-operation with Jonathan Goslett. Claremont, SA:
T.P. Publications, 1993.
30p; illus; pbk   ISBN: 0620175095

South African Tourists

147 'Our rugby Springboks': souvenir of the visit of the British
rugby team to South Africa and Southern Rhodesia, 1938 /
Ivor D. Difford. Johannesburg, SA: Published under the
authority and with the approval of the South African
Rugby Football Board by the Central News Agency, 1938.
104p; illus; pbk   BL: 7915.t.5

   'A complete history of all South Africa's rugby
   international matches (1891-1937) and of Springbok
   tours to Britain, Australia and New Zealand, and of
   those countries to South Africa'.

   ☞ Also listed at: E27

148 Springbok annale: internasionale toere na en van Suid-
Afrika, or, Springbok annals: international tours to and
from South Africa 1891-1958 / compiled by D. H. Craven.
Johannesburg, SA: issued by the Publications Committee on
instructions of the South African Rugby Board, 1958.
400p; illus

   In Afrikaans and English.

149 Springbok and silverfern: the great tests since 1921 / Reg
Sweet; foreword by Dr. D. H. Craven. Cape Town:
Howard Timmins, 1960.
200p; illus

   The story of the test matches between South Africa
   and New Zealand.

   ☞ Also listed at: E198

150 Springbok annale: internasionale toere na en van
Suid-Afrika, or, Springbok annals: international tours to
and from South Africa 1891-1964 / compiled by D. H.
Craven. Johannesburg, SA: issued by the South African
Rugby Board as part of their jubilee celebrations, 1964.
636p; illus

   In Afrikaans and English.

151 Good-bye Newlands farewell Eden Park / Fred
Labuschagne. Cape Town, SA: Howard Timmins, 1974.
242p; illus   ISBN: 0869780883

   Observation of events in the South African-New
   Zealand rugby relationship. Records highlights from
   the tours between the two nations. As the author
   died before completion of the book Chris Greyvenstein
   has added two chapters.

   ☞ Also listed at: E199

152 Springboks in Wales / John Billot. Rhondda: Ron Jones
Publications, 1974.
311p; illus   ISBN: 0950162337

153 Giants in green and gold: Springboks versus Wallabies
1921-1993 / Ian Diehm. Bowen Hills, Aust.: Boolarong
Press, 1994.
vi, 263p; illus   ISBN: 0864391730

   Chronicles the tours from South Africa to Australia
   (1921, 1937, 1956, 1965, 1971), and from Australia to
   South Africa (1933, 1953, 1961, 1963, 1969). And as
   world champions in South Africa in 1992, the
   Wallabies beat the Springboks in only the second
   international match on South African soil since the
   return of South Africa into the international rugby
   arena post-apartheid.

   ☞ Also listed at: E291

154 Rugby's greatest rivalry: South Africa vs New Zealand,
1921-1995 / Paul Dobson. Cape Town, SA: Human &
Rousseau, 1996.
301p; illus, maps   ISBN: 0798136200

   Tells the history of the South Africa-New Zealand
   rivalry from its inception in 1921. As well as the
   characters (players, coaches, referees, and so on),
   there are the pre- and post-apartheid days, the
   political demonstrations and the rebel tours.

   ☞ Also listed at: E207

155 A score to settle: a celebration of All Black-Springbok rugby 1921-1996 / Graham Hutchins; illustrated by Rodger McLaren with additional sketches by Henry Nicholas. Wellington, NZ: Grantham House, 1997. 152p; illus; pbk

> *Bibliography: p152*   ISBN: 1869340639

☞ Also listed at: E208

156 Winters of revenge: the bitter rivalry between the All Blacks and the Springboks / Spiro Zavos. Auckland, NZ: Viking, 1997. 264p; illus; pbk   ISBN: 0670875740

☞ Also listed at: E209

South African Tourists ~ Specific Tours

✽ 1906 to British Isles & France

157 The Carolin papers: a diary of the 1906/07 Springbok tour / compiled and edited by Lappe Laubscher and Gideon Nieman. Pretoria, SA: Rugbyana, 1990. 235p; illus; index

ISBN: 0620145005 • 0620145013 (de luxe edition)

H. W. 'Paddy' Carolin was selected as vice-captain of the South African party to tour the four home unions and France in 1906. Carolin recorded events on the tour and matches in letters to L. A. Cox, the sports editor of the *Cape Times*. These letters form the basis of the Carolin papers. As well as annotating the writings of Carolin, the editors provide a biography of Carolin, and additional information about the tour.

158 My recollections and reminiscences / William A. Millar. Cape Town, SA: Juta, 1926. xiii, 106p

South African rugby tours of Britain, Ireland and France in 1906 and 1912.

☞ Also listed at: E22; E164

159 The South Africans' rugby tour, 1906: souvenir album containing the photos and biographical sketches. Cardiff: Rees' Electric Press, 1906. 20p; illus; pbk

160 Souvenir of the South African rugby football team. Cape Town, SA: Cape Times, 1907. 20p; illus; pbk   BL: D

Biographical sketches of the members of the South African side which toured Britain, Ireland and France in 1906, with a list of fixtures.

161 The Springbokken tour in Great Britain: souvenir of the first tour of a South African rugby team in Great Britain during the season 1906/7 / edited by E. J. L. Platnauer. Johannesburg, SA: G. Wunderlich, 1907. 237p; illus   BL: Cup.1262.l.30

Includes biographies of the players on pages 171 to 216.

162 The 'Springboks': history of the tour 1906-07 / F. Neville Piggott. London: The Cricket Press, 1907. 140p; illus

163 With the Springboks in England 1906-07 / C. V. Becker. Johannesburg, SA: Wallach & Sinclair, 1907? 192p; illus; pbk

Coverage of all 28 matches and the game against Stade Racing in Paris is reproduced from the British national and local newspapers.

✽ 1912 to British Isles & France

164 My recollections and reminiscences / William A. Millar. Cape Town, SA: Juta, 1926. xiii, 106p

☞ Also listed at: E22; E158

165 Souvenir of the South African rugby football team / Leslie A. Cox. Cape Town, SA: Cape Times, 1912. 24p; illus; pbk

> *Cover title: S.A. rugby tour of 1912: the team and its prospects, photographs of the players*   BL: D

✽ 1921 to New Zealand

166 Pounding battle: match report Canterbury v South Africa played at Lancaster Park, Christchurch, 30 July 1921. Christchurch, NZ: Nag's Head Press, 1995. 39p   ISBN: 0908784732

Match report reprinted from *The Sun*, Christchurch, issues 30 July and 1 August 1921, published in an edition of 150 numbered copies. The New Zealand side defeated South Africa by 6 points to 4, the first defeat of a South African side on its first tour of New Zealand. The occasion is of great importance in the annals of New Zealand rugby.

✱ *1931 to British Isles*

167   Illustrated souvenir of the Springboks tour 1931/1932 /
compiled and edited by Francis G. Richings. London: C.
Mitchell, 1932.
64p; illus; pbk

> *Cover title: Illustrated souvenir of the Springboks South
> African rugby team tour 1931-1932, England, Ireland,
> Scotland, Wales*

> Articles, fixture lists, group photographs, pen
> pictures of the players, and sheet music. Ivor D.
> Difford contributes an article on 'The history of the rugby
> football game in South Africa'; preface by Paul Roos.

✱ *1937 to New Zealand & Australia*

168   South Africa's greatest Springboks / John E. Sacks.
Wellington, NZ: Sporting Publications, 1938.
208p; illus; pbk

> This is the 'complete story of the historic 1937 tour',
> as well as the South African and New Zealand final
> trials, and unofficial and official matches in Australia
> and New Zealand. Sacks, the sports editor of the
> *Rand Daily Mail* and the *Sunday Times*, Johannesburg,
> travelled as special correspondent with the team to
> New Zealand. The book also contains comments from
> New Zealand observers.

169   Taranaki rugby almanac: published in commemoration
of the visit to New Zealand of the Springbok rugby team
July, August, September, 1937 / 'Poster'. Taranaki, NZ:
Hawera Star Publishing, 1937.
illus; pbk

> Covers the itinerary and profiles the South African
> players. Also contains match records of New Zealand
> provinces, New Zealand results overseas, British
> teams results in New Zealand and South African
> results in Great Britain. The author was the rugby
> critic of the *Hawera Star*.

✱ *1951 to British Isles & France*

170   The 1951-52 Springbok rugby tour of the British Isles
and France: commemorative booklet 1991 / edited by
Keith Clayton. Howard Place: Clayton, 1991.
47p; illus; pbk

> The booklet was prepared for a reunion of the 1951-52
> Springbok party at the Carlton, Johannesburg on 15
> November 1991. A number of contributors recount the
> international matches and a few personalities.

171   The fourth Springboks, 1951-1952 / Richard Kenneth
Stent. London: Longmans, Green, 1952.
ix, 212p; illus   BL: 7921.bb.35

172   Springbok story 1949-1953 / D. H. Craven. Cape Town,
SA: K. Beerman Publishers, 1954.
200p; illus

In three parts: Part 1 deals with the 1949 All Blacks
in South Africa; Part 2 describes the Springboks in
Britain, Ireland and France in 1951-52; Part 3 is an
account of the 1953 Australian tour of South Africa.

☞   Also listed at: E234; E295

✱ *1956 to New Zealand & Australia*

173   The 1956 Springboks in New Zealand: the complete
history of a momentous tour / edited by John Fairbairn.
Auckland, NZ: A. D. Organ, 1956.
114p; illus; pbk

174   The battle for the rugby crown / Terry McLean.
Wellington, NZ: Reed, 1956.
238p; illus

☞   Subsequent ed. E175

175   The battle for the rugby crown / T. P. McLean. 2nd ed.
Wellington, NZ: Reed, 1957.
239p; illus   BL: 7923.m.30

☞   Previous ed. E174

176   The Kiwis conquer / Reg Sweet. Cape Town, SA:
Howard Timmins, 1956.
xx, 216p; illus

> *Also published: Wellington, NZ: Reed, 1956*
> BL: 7923.ff.20

177   'The mighty Springboks': souvenir of the 1956 South
African rugby tour including the story of the first and
second Springboks in New Zealand and Australian and
other interesting tours / Sid Nicholls. Sydney, Aust.:
Tomalin & Wigmore, 1956.
80p; illus; pbk

THE BATTLE FOR THE
RUGBY CROWN

By
TERRY McLEAN

WELLINGTON
A. H. & A. W. REED

178 Old heroes: the 1956 Springbok tour and the lives beyond / Warwick Roger. Auckland, N.Z., London: Hodder & Stoughton, 1991.
222p; pbk
ISBN: 0340554851
BL: YK.1994.a.12984

179 Springboks at bay! / Maxwell Price. London: Longmans, Green, 1956.
viii, 213p; illus
BL: 7923.i.8

✳ *1960 to British Isles & France*

180 Springbok glory / J. B. G. Thomas. London: Stanley Paul, 1961.
224p; illus
BL: 7925.g.1

181 Springboks in the Lion's den / Maxwell Price. London: Bailey & Swinfen, 1961.
225p; illus
BL: 7925.c.103

The fifth South African tour to the British Isles and France 1960-61.

✳ *1965 to Australia & New Zealand*

182 The Bok busters: the 1965 Springboks in Australia and New Zealand / Terry McLean. Wellington, NZ: Reed, 1965.
211p; illus

THE KIWIS CONQUER

by

REG. SWEET

A. C. PARKER

NOW IS THE HOUR

The 1965 'Boks in Australia and New Zealand

BAILEY BROS. & SWINFEN
LONDON EC 4
1965

183 The fourth Springbok tour of New Zealand / R. J. Urbahn & D. B. Clarke. Wellington, NZ: Hicks Smith, 1965.
199p; illus

184 Now is the hour: the 1965 'Boks in Australia and New Zealand / A. C. Parker. London: Bailey & Swinfen, 1965.
xii, 258p; illus
BL: X.449/1752

The fourth Springbok tour to Australia and New Zealand 1965.

✳ *1969 to British Isles*

185 Springbok invasion / J. B. G. Thomas. London: Pelham Books, 1970.
199p; illus
SBN: 720704200
BL: X.629/2599

The sixth South African tour to the British Isles 1969-70.

186 There was also some rugby: the sixth Springboks in Britain / Wallace MacDonald Reyburn. London: Stanley Paul, 1970.
182p; illus
SBN: 091044708
BL: X.629/3158

✳ *1971 to Australia*

187 Die Onoorwinlikies: Springbokke in Australia / G. Hattingh. Johannesburg, SA: de Skrywer, 1972.

Two editions, Afrikaans and English, of the tour of Australia in 1971 by the Springboks.

188   The unbeatables: Springboks in Australia / Kim Shippey;
      photographs Gert Hattingh. Pretoria, SA: Die
      Transvaaler, 1971.
      144p; illus

*   *1981 to New Zealand & America*

189   1981: the tour / Geoff Chapple. Wellington, NZ: Reed, 1984.
      xi, 327p; illus   ISBN: 0589015346

190   Counting the cost: the 1981 Springbok tour in
      Wellington / student contributors, Anna Aitken and
      others; editors, David Mackay and others. Wellington,
      NZ: Victoria University, 1982.
      75p
      (Occasional papers; no.1)

191   Springboks in New Zealand, 1981 / Ian Gault; pictures
      by Barry Durrant and others; colour pictures by Peter
      Bush; edited by James Curran. Wellington, NZ:
      Wellington Newspapers Limited, 1981.
      128p; illus; pbk

      Cover title: The 1981 Springboks in New Zealand

192   Springboks under siege: the New Zealand tour,
      pioneering in America, Irish in South Africa, Beaumont's
      Lions: an illustrated record of Springbok rugby in 1980
      and 1981 / edited by Colin Bryden & Mark Colley;
      foreword by Wynand Claassen. Hillbrow, Johannesburg,
      SA: Now Publications, 1981.
      160p; illus

      A record of the 15 tests played by South Africa
      between April 1980 and September 1981; the tour of
      New Zealand and the United States; the tour of
      South Africa by Ireland and the British Isles.

      ☞ Also listed at: E73

193   Storm out of Africa: the 1981 Springbok tour of New
      Zealand / Richard Shears, Isobelle Gidley. Northcote, NZ:
      Macmillan, 1981.
      154p; illus   ISBN: 0333301374

Other South African Sides

194   The South African Universities rugby tour of Kenya.
      Nairobi, 1930?
      illus; pbk

      Edward Grigg the Governor of Kenya contributed a
      foreword to the booklet commemorating the first
      visit to Kenya of a South African rugby team. The
      team left Lourenco Marques on 18 December 1929
      and departed for home on 8 February 1930 after a 13
      match tour including three clashes with Kenya,
      described as tests. A series of brief articles
      highlights the officials and clubs affiliated to the
      Rugby Football Union of Kenya in 1929; the growth of
      rugby in the country; a tour itinerary and brief
      biographies of the South African players and an
      overview of rugby in South Africa.

195   Diocesan College 1993: rugby tour to the United
      Kingdom / editor Duncan Cruickshank. Rondebosch,
      SA: Diocesan College School, 1993.
      28p; illus; pbk

      Produced by the school for a tour of England and
      Scotland in November and December 1993, the
      brochure highlights the achievements of the school in
      rugby. Apart from former pupils who have worn the
      green jersey of South Africa, four have played for
      England, four for Scotland, one for Wales, and one
      each for Sri Lanka, Canada and Zimbabwe.

196   Shandelier/SA Technikon rugby tour to Netherlands,
      UK & France '94. Braamfontein, SA: SA Technikon
      Rugby Committee, 1994.
      32p; illus, 1 map; pbk   ISBN: 0620191155

New Zealand Tourists

197 Fifty years of the All Blacks: a complete history of New Zealand rugby touring teams in the British Isles, 1905-1954 / compiled by Wilfred Wooller & David Owen; with contributions by Rhys T. Gabe and others; foreword by Sir Wavell Wakefield. London: Phoenix House, 1954.
272p; illus   BL: 7921.b.63

198 Springbok and silverfern: the great tests since 1921 / Reg Sweet; foreword by Dr. D. H. Craven. Cape Town: Howard Timmins, 1960.
200p; illus

   The story of the test matches between South Africa and New Zealand.

   ☞ Also listed at: E149

199 Good-bye Newlands farewell Eden Park / Fred Labuschagne. Cape Town, SA: Howard Timmins, 1974.
242p; illus   ISBN: 0869780883

   Observation of events in the South African-New Zealand rugby relationship. Records highlights from the tours between the two nations. As the author died before completion of the book Chris Greyvenstein has added two chapters.

   ☞ Also listed at: E151

200 All Blacks versus Springboks / Graeme Barrow. Auckland, NZ: Heinemann, 1981.
159p; illus, 1 map   ISBN: 0868633763
                                                 BL: X.629/16352

   ☞ Subsequent ed. E201

201 All Blacks versus Springboks: a century of rugby rivalry / Graeme Barrow. Rev. ed. Auckland, NZ: Reed, 1992.
216p; illus, 1 map; pbk   ISBN: 0790002787
   ☞ Previous ed. E200

202 Grand slam / Kevin Boon; edited by Allan R. Kirk. Wellington, NZ: Kotuku, 1993.
24p; illus; pbk
(The story of the All Blacks; 10)   ISBN: 090894702X
   For children.

203 Kiwis & Lions / Kevin Boon; edited by Allan R. Kirk. Wellington, NZ: Kotuku, 1993.
24p; illus, 1 map; pbk
(The story of the All Blacks; 4)
   For children.

204 Kiwis & Springboks / Kevin Boon; edited by Allan R. Kirk. Wellington, NZ: Kotuku, 1993.
24p; illus, 1 map; pbk
(The story of the All Blacks; 5)
   For children.

205 Kiwis and Wallabies / Kevin Boon; edited by Allan R. Kirk. Wellington, NZ: Kotuku, 1993.
24p; illus, 1 map; pbk
(The story of the All Blacks; 6)
   For children.

206 Springbok fever / Kevin Boon; edited by Allan R. Kirk. Wellington, NZ: Kotuku, 1993.
24p; illus, pbk
(The story of the All Blacks; 8)   ISBN: 0908947011
   For children.

207 Rugby's greatest rivalry: South Africa vs New Zealand, 1921-1995 / Paul Dobson. Cape Town, SA: Human & Rousseau, 1996.
301p; illus   ISBN: 0798136200

   Tells the history of the South Africa-New Zealand rivalry from its inception in 1921. As well as the characters (players, coaches, referees, and so on), there are the pre- and post-apartheid days, the political demonstrations and the rebel tours.

   ☞ Also listed at: E154

208 A score to settle: a celebration of All Black-Springbok rugby 1921-1996 / Graham Hutchins; illustrated by Rodger McLaren with additional sketches by Henry Nicholas. Wellington, NZ: Grantham House, 1997.
152p; illus; pbk

   Bibliography: p152   ISBN: 1869340639
   ☞ Also listed at: E155

209 Winters of revenge: the bitter rivalry between the All Blacks and the Springboks / Spiro Zavos. Auckland, NZ: Viking, 1997.
264p; illus; pbk   ISBN: 0670875740
   ☞ Also listed at: E156

New Zealand Tourists ~ Specific Tours

❋ *1888 to British Isles, Australia & New Zealand*

210 Forerunners of the All Blacks: the 1888-89 New Zealand native football team in Britain, Australia and New Zealand / Greg Ryan. Canterbury, NZ: University Press, 1993.
152p; illus; index
      ISBN: 0908812302 (cased) • 0908812353 (limited ed.)

Based on a master's thesis in history at the University of Canterbury, but written for a general readership, the book recounts the forming of the team before embarking on a 107 match tour commencing in Napier on 23 June 1888 and ending in Auckland on 24 August 1889. In between the team played 74 games in Britain and Ireland and 16 games in Australia. The relationship between the native team and the New Zealand rugby authorities is examined as well as other social issues.

    ☞ See also: E212

211 The forgotten expedition: aspects of the native team's tour of New Zealand, Australia and Britain, June 23 1888 to August 24 1889 / E. G. Bolger. University of Auckland, NZ, 1986. *Master's thesis.*
96 leaves; illus

212 The Originals: the 1888-89 New Zealand native football team in Britain, Australia and New Zealand / G. J. Ryan. University of Canterbury, NZ, 1992. *Master's thesis.*
    ☞ See also: E210

213 Rugby football (past and present) and the tour of the native team / compiled by T. Eyton in Great Britain, Australia, & New Zealand in 1888-89; also hints to clubs and young players, &c. by G. A. Williams, J. A. Warbrick, and H. Wynyard. Palmerston North, NZ: William Hart, Caxton Printing Works, 1896.
128p; illus

The compiler was a promoter of the tour. Profiles of the 26 players and the matches they played in Great Britain, 74 in 6 months, are recounted. Also, a chapter on the prospect of a future tour to New Zealand.

❋ *1903 to Australia*

214 Souvenir of New Zealand football, in connection with the visit of the New Zealand team to Australia 1903. Sydney, Aust.?: Walter E. Knott, 1903.
18p; chiefly illus; pbk
(RNB sports series)

❋ *1905 to British Isles*

215 Missionaries of empire: the 1905 All Black tour / Timothy N. W. Buchanan. University of Canterbury, NZ, 1981. *Master's thesis.*
ii, 64 leaves; illus

216 The New Zealand football team souvenir of the visit to Wales December 1905. Cardiff: A M'Lay, 1905.
12p; illus; pbk

217 Souvenir of the New Zealand rugby football team, 1905. Christchurch, NZ: New Zealand Rugby Union, 1905.
28p; illus; pbk

    Facsimile edition published: Wellington, NZ: Athletic Rugby Football Club; Colonial Associates, 1981

218 The triumphant tour of the New Zealand footballers, 1905: an illustrated record / from notes by George H. Dixon. Wellington, NZ: Geddis & Blomfeld, 1906.
xv, 176p; illus

219 The Wales test 1905: match reports & commentary on the first Wales v. New Zealand rugby test played at Cardiff Arms Park, 16 December 1905 / R. S. Gormack. Hand-set ed. Christchurch, NZ: Nag's Head, 1983.
73p

    Jacket subtitle: Wales 3, All Blacks 0;
    limited ed. of 300 copies

Press reports from the South Wales Echo and the Lyttelton Times.

220 Why the 'All Blacks' triumphed!: secret of our success / the New Zealand Captain. London: Associated Newspapers, 1906.
99p   BL: D

David Gallaher's story of the tour as presented by the Daily Mail.

❋ *1924 to Australia, British Isles, France & Canada*

221 Heroes of the Silver Fern: All Blacks tour 1924-25. Christchurch, NZ: Edward H. Marriner, 1925.
88p; illus

222 The triumphant tour!: the All Blacks in England, Ireland and Wales, 1924-1925: an interesting account of all matches played; English comments and criticism; photographs of team and players; Welsh memories of 1905; with a history of the game in New Zealand. Wellington, NZ: L. T. Watkins, 1925.
176p; illus; pbk

223 With the All Blacks in Great Britain, France, Canada and
     Australia 1924-25 / Read Masters. 2nd ed. Christchurch,
     NZ: Christchurch Press, 1928.
     166p; illus

     1st ed. untraced

✳ *1928 to South Africa*

224 All Blacks NZ. 1928: souvenir / sketches by P. G. Reid;
     cartoons by A. S. Paterson. Wellington, NZ: Coulls,
     Somerville Wilkie, 1928.
     48p; illus

225 Official souvenir programme of the All Blacks South
     African tour, 1928: records and photographs of the
     games and teams from 1891-1928 / compiled by S. S.
     Strauss. Cape Town, SA: Townsend, Taylor & Snashall
     for the author, 1928.
     52p; illus; pbk

226 With the All Blacks in Springbokland 1928: the book of the
     great rugby tour: an interesting account of all matches played
     / M. F. Nicholls. Wellington, NZ: L.T. Watkins, 1928.
     200p; illus

     *Coverage of all the matches played; South African
     comments and criticism; photographs of teams and
     players; pithy pars; international opinions; South
     African play and players; the inside history of this
     famous rugby tour; rugby records.*

✳ *1935 to British Isles & Canada*

227 The All Blacks of jubilee year 1935: an interesting
     account of all the matches played in the United Kingdom,
     with comments and criticism of the play and players,
     photographs of teams, records of players, matches, etc. /
     L. T. Watkins. Wellington, NZ: The author, 1936.
     135p; illus; pbk

228 Reciprocal trade and the history of All Black-British
     rugby tour 1935-1936 / compiled and edited by B. M.
     Turner. London: L. H. Mills, 1936.
     95p; illus

229 The tour of the third All Blacks, 1935 / C. J. Oliver and
     E. W. Tindill; edited by A. H. Carman, A. C. Swan and
     Read Masters. Wellington, NZ: Wright and Carman, 1936.
     200p; illus; pbk

230 Wales v New Zealand / Wilf Wooller. Taunton: R.
     Walsh, 1995.
     illus

     Limited ed. of 150 copies
     *A reprint of Wooller's contribution from 'I was there'
     (London: Collins, 1966) in which he reminisces on the
     game between Wales and New Zealand at Cardiff on 21
     December 1935. Normally a centre, Wooller played on
     the wing in this match.*

✳ *1946 to British Isles, France & New Zealand*

231 Broadcasting with the Kiwis / Winston McCarthy.
     Wellington, NZ: Reed for Sporting Publications, 1947.
     142p; illus; pbk

     *An account of the Second NZEF (Kiwi) tour to the
     British Isles, France and New Zealand in 1946.*

✳ *1949 to South Africa*

232 The All Blacks on trek again / Winston McCarthy.
     Wellington, NZ: Sporting Publications, 1950.
     222p; illus

233 Guide to Africa tour, 1949: the All Black team /
     Graham Beamish. Matamata, NZ: Beamish and Murray,
     1949.
     52p; illus; pbk

234 Springbok story 1949-1953 / D. H. Craven. Cape Town,
     SA: K. Beerman Publishers, 1954.
     200p; illus

     *In three parts: Part 1 deals with the 1949 All Blacks
     in South Africa; Part 2 describes the Springboks in
     Britain, Ireland and France in 1951-52; Part 3 is an
     account of the 1953 Australian tour of South Africa.*

     ☞ Also listed at: E172; E295

✳ *1953 to British Isles, France & North America*

235 All Black tours 1953-54 and the story of our famous All
     Blacks in their five main tours / Sydney Nicholls.
     Auckland, NZ: Graham Beamish, 1953.
     80p; illus

236 Bob Stuart's All Blacks: an account of the New Zealand
     rugby football team's tour of the British Isles, 1953-54 /
     T. P. McLean. Wellington, NZ: Reed, 1954.
     216p; illus   BL: 7921.e.108

237 The fourth All Blacks, 1953-54 / John Hayhurst.
     London: Longmans, Green, 1954.
     xi, 267p; illus   BL: 7922.b.19

238 On tour: the story of the rugby visitors to the British
     Isles: details of exciting matches, incidents and great
     players / J. B. G. Thomas. London: Stanley Paul, 1954.
     192p; illus   BL: 7921.b.53

239 Round the world with the All Blacks: the story of the
     New Zealand tour to the British Isles, France, Canada
     and America, 1953-54 / Winston McCarthy. Wellington,
     NZ: Sporting Publications, 1954.
     166p; illus

✻ *1960 to South Africa*

240 All Blacks in South Africa / F. W. Boshier. Wellington, NZ: Blundell, 1960.
130p; illus

241 The All Blacks juggernaut in South Africa / A. C. Parker; with a foreword by Jack Sullivan. Cape Town, SA: Tafelberg-Uitgewers, 1960.
254p; illus

> *Also published: Christchurch, NZ: Whitcombe & Tombs, 1960*
> BL: 7925.c.52

242 All Blacks mysterious / G. Armour. Auckland, NZ: F. Hinton, 1960.
64p; illus
The All Blacks in South Africa 1960.

243 The battle of the giants: on rugby football / C. O. Medworth. Cape Town, SA: Howard Timmins, 1960.
xi, 202p; illus   BL: 7925.l.39
The New Zealand tour of South Africa 1960.

244 Beaten by the 'Boks: the 1960 All Blacks in South Africa / Terry McLean. Wellington, NZ: Reed, 1960.
262p; illus   BL: X.449/637

245 Trek out of trouble: the South African tour of the 'All Blacks' rugby team, 1960 / Noel Holmes; with a summary of the tour by Tom Pearce. Christchurch, NZ: Whitcombe & Tombs, 1960.
230p; illus, 1 map   BL: 7925.l.34

✻ *1963 to British Isles, France & Canada*

246 All Blacks tour, 1963-1964: a complete record of the tour, Great Britain, France, Ireland / Andrew Mulligan. London: Souvenir Press, 1964.
191p; illus

247 The fifth All Blacks / J. B. G. Thomas. London: Stanley Paul, 1964.
181p; illus   BL: X.449/66

248 Whineray's All Blacks / Richard R. I. Evans. London: Pelham Books, 1964.
235p; illus   BL: X.629/6259

249 Whineray's men / Morrie Hill. 1964.
70p; illus
A pictorial record of the tour.

250 Willie away: Wilson Whineray's All Blacks of 1963-64 / T. P. McLean. London: Herbert Jenkins, 1964.
302p; illus   BL: X.449/937

✻ *1967 to British Isles & France*

251 All Black magic: the 1967 tour / T. P. McLean. Wellington, NZ: Reed, 1968.
183p; illus

252 The All Blacks, 1967: tour of the British Isles and France / David Brough James Frost. London: Wolfe Publishing; Christchurch, NZ: Whitcombe & Tombs, 1968.
168p; illus   BL: X.449/2970

253 Rugby in black and red / J. B. G. Thomas. London: Pelham Books, 1968.
240p; illus
Also reviews British Isles tours in the Antipodes and South Africa from 1888 to 1962.
☞ Also listed at: E5

254 The unsmiling giants: the sixth All Blacks / Wallace Reyburn. London: Stanley Paul, 1968.
170p; illus   ISBN: 009086980X

✻ *1968 to Australia & Fiji*

255 All black power: the story of the 1968 All Blacks in Australia and Fiji and the 1968 French team in New Zealand and Australia / T. P. McLean. Wellington, NZ: Reed, 1968.
262p; illus
☞ Also listed at: E143

✻ *1970 to South Africa*

256 All Black-ed out / F. Labuschagne. Wellington, NZ: Reed, 1970.
166p; illus

257 All Blacks in South Africa 1970 with Alex Veysey. Wellington, NZ: Dominion & Sunday Times, 1970.
2 vols: 120p; 92p; illus; pbk

258 Die All Blacks in Suid-Afrika 1970, or, The All Blacks in South Africa 1970. South Africa: 1970.
32p; illus; pbk

259 Battling the Boks / T. P. McLean. Wellington, NZ: Reed, 1970.
261p; illus

260 The greatest series: South Africa versus New Zealand 1970 / illustrations and text by Rufus Papenfus. Cape Town, SA: John Malherbe, 1970.
68p; illus
Mostly illustrations. Also published in Afrikaans.

261   Rugby and be damned / Gabriel R. David. Wellington, NZ: Hicks, Smith, 1970.
219p; illus
SBN: 456009108
BL: X.629/3189

❋ *1972 to British Isles, France & North America*

262   All Blacks in Wales / John Billot. Rhondda: Ron Jones Publications, 1972.
239p; illus
ISBN: 0950162310

Includes coverage of the Welsh tour of New Zealand in 1969.

☞   Also listed at: E102

263   The avenging All Blacks: the story of the All Blacks' tour of the British Isles, 1972-73 / J. B. G. Thomas; with a foreword by Carwyn James. London: Pelham, 1973.
180p; illus
ISBN: 0720706785
BL: X.629/5277

264   Scarlet fever. Llanelli?: Llanelli RFC, 1973?
57p; illus; pbk

An account of Llanelli's victory over the All Blacks at Stradey Park, Llanelli on 31 October 1972.

265   They missed the bus: Kirkpatrick's All Blacks of 1972/73 / Terry McLean. Wellington, NZ: Reed, 1973.
322p; illus
ISBN: 0589008005

266   The winter men: the seventh All-Blacks tour / Wallace Reyburn. London: Stanley Paul, 1973.
149p; illus
ISBN: 0091163501

❋ *1974 to British Isles, Australia & Fiji*

267   All Blacks come back: Terry McLean looks at New Zealand and world rugby / T. P. McLean. London: Pelham, 1975.
165p; illus
ISBN: 0720708443
BL: X.629/10019

☞   Also listed at: A191

Describes the two tours made by the All Blacks in 1974: the first to Australia and Fiji in May and June, and the second to Ireland, Wales and England in November.

❋ *1976 to South Africa*

268   '76 All Blacks in South Africa / Alex Veysey and Ian Mackley. Wellington, NZ: Dominion Sunday Times, 1976.
2 vols; illus

269   All Blacks in Africa: a pictorial record of the New Zealand Rugby Union team's tour of South Africa, July to September, 1976 / photographs by Ross Ellis Wiggins. Auckland, NZ: Wilson and Horton, 1976.
96p; illus; pbk
ISBN: 0868640123

270   Goodbye to glory: the 1976 All Black tour of South Africa / Terry McLean. Wellington, NZ: Reed, 1976.
vii, 176p; illus

Subsequently published: London: Pelham, 1977
ISBN: 0720709970 (UK)
BL: X.629/11452

271   One in the eye: the 1976 All Blacks in South Africa / Barry Glasspool. Cape Town, SA: Howard Timmins, 1976.
166p; illus
ISBN: 0869781413
BL: X.629/22386

Includes a 10 page who's who listing of All Blacks.

❋ *1978 to British Isles*

272   After the final whistle: Mourie's 'grand-slam' All Blacks, and the controversies, personalities and tactics of post-war New Zealand rugby / Spiro Zavos. Wellington, NZ: Fourth Estate Books, 1979.
243p; illus
ISBN: 0908593058

273   Grand slam All Blacks / Keith Quinn. Wellington, NZ: Methuen, 1979.
160p; illus

274   Mourie's All Blacks: the team that found itself / Terry McLean. Auckland, N.Z., London: Hodder and Stoughton, 1979.
ix, 184p; illus
ISBN: 0340242175
BL: X.629/12793

❋ *1979 to British Isles, Australia & Italy*

275   All Blacks, retreat from glory / Don Cameron. Auckland, NZ: Hodder & Stoughton, 1980.
178p; illus

Reviews the All Blacks in Australia, England, Scotland and Italy in 1979, and the French and Argentinian tours of New Zealand in the same year.

☞   Also listed at: E145; E312

276   Guesswork and gumption: the '79 All Blacks in England and Scotland / Peter J. Reilly. Berwick-upon-Tweed: Tweedale, 1980.
120p; illus

277   Mourie's men: the eighth All Blacks in the British Isles / Wallace Reyburn; photographs by Peter Bush. London: Cassell, 1979.
204p; illus
ISBN: 0304304654
BL: X.629/12702

✽ *1980 to British Isles, Australia, Fiji &*
North America

278 1980 All Blacks in Wales / Ian Gault; photographs by
Peter Bush assisted by Hedley Mortlock. Wellington,
NZ: Wellington Newspapers, 1980.
72p; illus; pbk

279 Rugby triumphant: the All Blacks in Australia and Wales
/ Don Cameron. London: Hodder and Stoughton, 1981.
205p; illus   ISBN: 0340269502

280 Tour of the century: the All Blacks in Wales 1980 /
Keith Quinn. Auckland, NZ: Methuen, 1981.
176p; illus; pbk   ISBN: 0456028803

> Two tours by the All Blacks in 1980: Australia and
> Fiji, and North America and Wales.

✽ *1981 to France & Romania*

281 All Blacks in Romania, France, 1981 / Alex Veysey,
Peter George Bush. Wellington, NZ: Wellington
Newspapers, 1981.
96p; illus; pbk

> *Cover title: 1981 All Blacks in France and Romania*

✽ *1992 to South Africa*

282 All Black attack: the official S.A. Rugby Football Union
brochure for the 1992 New Zealand rugby tour to South
Africa. Claremont: T.P. Publications, 1992.
46p; illus; pbk   ISBN: 0620169230

Other New Zealand Sides

283 Northern tour of the Dunedin Football Club, 1877 / S.
E. Sleigh. Dunedin, NZ: R. T. Wheeler, 1877.
30p; pbk

> The team played against other New Zealand sides:
> Christchurch, Auckland, Nelson, Wellington, Temuka,
> and Timaru.

284 Ireland v. New Zealand: 100 years of international rugby
/ David Guiney. Dublin: PR Books, 1989.
112p; illus

> *Cover title: Ireland v. New Zealand 100 years of rugby*
> *football*   ISBN: 1872553001
>   BL: YK.1994.a.3308

☞ Also listed at: E94

285 The New Zealand Maori rugby tour, 1926-1927, New
Zealand, Australia, Ceylon, France, England, Wales,
Canada from the 'rugby diary' of the late T. P. (Tom)
Robinson of Little River / D. J. C. Pringle. Akaroa, NZ:
Akaroa Mail, 1971.
80p; illus

> Written when the author was in his early twenties and
> published posthumously.

286 Rugby versus Rommel: 2 NZEF rugby reunion, 1961 /
Paul Patrick Donoghue. Wellington, NZ: The Rugby
Reunion Committee, 1961.
78p; illus

> 'This publication ... recalls of the rugby achievements
> of members of the 2NZEF in England in 1940 and in
> the Middle East from 1940-1944.'

287 Five seasons of Services rugby: the history of the New
Zealand Services team in Great Britain, Ireland and
France, 1941-1946 / Arthur C. Swan and Arthur H.
Carman (in collaboration with Eric Grant and Ray
Dalton, and with the assistance of several members of
the side). Wellington, NZ: Sporting Publications, 1946.
48p; illus; pbk

288 West out West / Peter J. Reilly. Paeroa, NZ: The Club,
1977.
128p; illus; pbk

> Tour of California and Hawaii, 1977, by the Paero West
> RFC.

289 Cavaliers in South Africa 1986 / text by Doug Laing and
Kip Brook; compiled by Richard Reid; photography by
Wessel Oosthuizen. Auckland, NZ: South Sea Visuals,
1986.
80p; illus; pbk   ISBN: 0473003848

> The New Zealand Cavaliers twelve match tour of
> South Africa. Contains match reports and player
> interviews.

290 Neath Rugby Football Club: one day in October, the
story of Neath versus New Zealand, The Gnoll,
Wednesday 25 October 1989 / compiled and edited by
Rod Rees. Neath: The Club, 1990.
14p; illus; pbk

Australian Tourists

291 Giants in green and gold: Springboks versus Wallabies 1921-1993 / Ian Diehm. Bowen Hills, Aust.: Boolarong Press, 1994.

vi, 263p; illus   ISBN: 0864391730

> Chronicles the tours from South Africa to Australia (1921, 1937, 1956, 1965, 1971), and from Australia to South Africa (1933, 1953, 1961, 1963, 1969). And as world champions in South Africa in 1992, the Wallabies beat the Springboks in only the second international match on South African soil since the return of South Africa into the international rugby arena post-apartheid.

☞ Also listed at: E153

292 With the Wallabies / Greg Growden. Sydney, Aust.: ABC Books, 1995.

viii, 198p; illus; index   ISBN: 0733304206

> Growden, the chief rugby writer for two Sydney newspapers, chronicles the exploits of the Australian team on and off the field in a number of countries in the period 1984-1994.

Australian Tourists ~ Specific Tours

✷ 1913 to New Zealand

293 Souvenir of the first Australian team to visit New Zealand, under the auspices of the Australian Bowling Council. Sydney, Aust.: Batson, 1914.

28p; illus

✷ 1947 to British Isles, France & North America

294 The 1947/8 Wallaby tour: the one that nearly got away: the story of the 3rd Wallaby tour of Great Britain, Ireland, France, Canada and USA / compiled by Malcolm Spark. Darley: The author, 1989.

iii, 258p; illus; pbk

> *Limited ed. of 700 copies*   ISBN: 0951539302
>   BL: YK.1990.a.5646

✷ 1953 to South Africa

295 Springbok story 1949-1953 / D. H. Craven. Cape Town, SA: K. Beerman Publishers, 1954.

200p; illus

> In three parts: Part 1 deals with the 1949 All Blacks in South Africa; Part 2 describes the Springboks in Britain, Ireland and France in 1951-52; Part 3 is an account of the 1953 Australian tour of South Africa.

☞ Also listed at: E172; E234

✷ 1963 to South Africa

296 Ringside view / A. C. Parker. Cape Town, SA: Howard Timmins, 1963.

256p; illus   BL: X.629/6987

> Also looks at other sports.

THE 1947/8 WALLABY TOUR

THE ONE THAT NEARLY GOT AWAY

COMPILED BY MALCOLM SPARK

✱ 1969 to South Africa

297 Die Wallabies in Suid-Afrika 1969, or, The Wallabies in South Africa 1969. South Africa: 1969.
32p; illus; pbk

298 Wallabies without armour: tour of South Africa 1969 / Maxwell Price. Cape Town, SA: Howard Timmins, 1969.
208p; illus

> *Also published: Wellington, NZ: Reed, 1970*
> ISBN: 0589070681

✱ 1972 to New Zealand

299 The Wallabies '72: the Australian rugby team in New Zealand, 1972 / Lindsay Knight; edited by Brian O'Brien. Wellington, NZ: A.B.D.Clark, 1972.
64p; illus

✱ 1975 to British Isles

300 Wallabies' walkabout: the story of the Australian tour of the British Isles, 1975-76 / J. B. G. Thomas. London: Pelham, 1976.
183p; illus   ISBN: 0720708990
BL: X.629/10565

✱ 1984 to British Isles

301 Victorious Wallabies UK tour 1984 / Terry Cooper; compiled by Peter A. Murray; foreword by Mark Ella. Waterloo, Aust.: Waterloo Press, 1985.
104p; chiefly illus   ISBN: 0725703148

✱ 1992 to South Africa

302 Wizards from Oz: the official S.A. Rugby Football Union brochure for the 1992 Australian rugby tour to South Africa / edited by Ian Gault and others. Claremont, SA: T.P. Publications, 1992.
38p; illus; pbk   ISBN: 0620169249

✱ 1996 to British Isles & Italy

303 Tour guide: Italy, UK, Ireland 1996. Potts Point, Aust.: Australian Rugby Union, 1996.
34p; illus; pbk

Other Australian Sides

304 The football tour of the New South Wales team through New Zealand 1901 / J. R. Henderson. 1902?
41p; pbk

> Originally published in the *Referee* and the *Sunday Times* by the special correspondent of the tour which took place between August 17 and September 7 1901. Of the seven matches played, the visitors won one and lost six.

305 For the sake of the game: 1927/28 Waratahs / Peter Fenton. Crows Nest, Aust.: Little Hills Press, 1996.
192p; illus   ISBN: 1863150870

> The Waratahs from New South Wales played 31 matches in their tour of England, Wales, Scotland, Ireland and France between 17 September 1927 and 28 January 1928. They also played games in Colombo, Ceylon (Sri Lanka) and Vancouver, Canada on their way to and from the United Kingdom and France. Using the official tour report, newspaper reports and sports journals, the author pieces together the story of the tour.

306 Report of the tour of the New South Wales Rugby Union representative team, the Waratahs, 1927-1928: presented to the Council on Friday, 27th March 1928. Sydney, Aust.: The Union, 1928.
19p; illus; pbk

307 Australian schoolboys tour 1977/78 report: England, Wales, Ireland, Japan, Holland, France / Australian Schools Rugby Union. Canberra, Aust.: The Union, 1978.
83p; illus

> The report of the tour was written by the Tour Manager, B. Wallace, St. Edmunds College, Canberra.

308 The Australian Rugby Football Schools' Union versus the New Zealand Rugby Football Schools' Union in the presence of His Excellency the Governor Rear Admiral Peter Sinclair: Saturday 29th September 1990. Canberra, Aust.: Australian Schools' Rugby Union, 1990.
28p; illus; pbk

309 1994 Wesley College rugby union tour of the UK. Perth, Aust.: Wesley College, 1994.
25p; illus; pbk

Between December 3 and 22, 1994, Wesley College played six games against schools in England, Scotland and Wales. The articles in the brochure serve as an appetiser for the tour. A couple of articles look at the relationship of Wesley College with two of the schools on the tour: Mill Hill School and Daniel Stewart's and Melville College. Four pages are devoted to pen portraits of the boys in the touring squad.

310   Hale School and Perth College (Australia) 1996 United Kingdom and Hong Kong tour. Perth, Aust.: 1996.
23p; illus; pbk

Tour brochure commemorating the participation of the rugby, netball and hockey teams of the two schools in England, Scotland, Wales and Hong Kong during December 1996.

311   St. Patrick's College, Strathfield first XV 1996 South African tour souvenir programme. Strathfield, Aust.: The School, 1996.
32p; illus; pbk

Five match tour of South Africa June/July 1996.

Tourists from the Rest of the World

❋ *Argentinian Tourists*

312   All Blacks, retreat from glory / Don Cameron. Auckland, NZ: Hodder & Stoughton, 1980.
178p; illus

Reviews the All Blacks in Australia, England, Scotland and Italy in 1979, and the French and Argentinian tours of New Zealand in the same year.

☞ Also listed at: E145; E275

❋ *Canadian Tourists*

313   Balmy Beach Rugby Club 25th anniversary Western Canada tour programme. Toronto: The Club, 1980.
30p; illus; pbk

❋ *Fijian Tourists*

314   Fiji Rugby Union Australian tour 1980. Suva: Fiji Rugby Union, 1980.
16p; illus; pbk

315   Llanelli 31 Fiji 28: this is the story of the Llanelli Rugby Club's fight back to defeat the Fijians at Stradey Park on Tuesday 5th November, 1985 / compiled by Glyn Walters. Llanelli: The author, 1986?
37p; illus; pbk

The game is recalled from match reports.

❋ *Japanese Tourists*

316   Japan Rugby Union Football Union UK tour 1976. The Union, 1976.
28p; illus; pbk

The side played four matches in England and Scotland in September and October 1976.

317   Superman RFC 10th anniversary 1975-1985 Wales & England tour 13-23rd Sept. 1985. Tokyo: The Club, 1985.
13p; illus; pbk

The Japanese side played three matches on their short tour: Bridgend Athletic, Glyncorrwg and Old Paulines. The brochure includes pen portraits of the players.

❋ *United States Tourists*

318   Manhattan Rugby Football Club tour de France 1975. Manhattan, US: The Club, 1975.
16p; illus; pbk

Four matches and a sevens tournament.

319   The University of Kansas and the City of Lawrence Rugby Football Club Celtic tour – 79: Scotland and Ireland December 29, 1978-January 13, 1979. Kansas, US: The Club, 1978.
57p; illus; pbk

320   Grizzlies New Zealand tour 1984. California, USA: Pacific Coast Rugby Football Union, 1984.
24p; illus; pbk

321   Baylor-Strickers RFC 1982 tour: Ireland, Wales, England. Houston, US: The Club, 1992.
34p; illus; pbk

Two matches in Ireland, one each in Wales and England.

Theory & Practice

Contents

Refereeing & Laws of the Game

1   Football rules: the following rules were sanctioned by a levee of the Sixth, on the 28th of August 1845, as the laws of football played at Rugby School. Rugby: J. S. Crossley, 1846?

   This was the earliest attempt to set down the rules of the game. They were then regularly amended and re-issued over the next few years and were to form the basis of the official RFU rules.

2   The laws of football founded on the rules of the game as played at Rugby School. London: 1866.   BL: D

3   The laws of football as played at Marlborough College. Marlborough: G. Perkins, 1867.

4   The laws of football, as played at Magdalene College School. Oxford: The School, 1871.
   18p; pbk

5   The Foot Ball Association of Canada, organized 1873: rules, rugby union. Montreal?: The Association, 1876.
   8p

6   The laws of the Rugby Union. London: The Cricket Press, 1879.
   26p   BL: 7908.a.16
   ☞ Subsequent ed. F8

7   The two codes of football. London: The Cricket Press, 1879.
   41p; pbk   BL: D
   ☞ Subsequent ed. F10

8   The laws of the Rugby Union. London: The Cricket Press, 1880.
   23p   BL: Mic.A.8892(7) (microfilm copy)
   ☞ Previous ed. F6; subsequent ed. F12

9   Rules of the rugby union game of football as adopted by the Canadian Rugby Football Union, September 14th 1880. Ottawa, Can.: Canadian Rugby Football Union, 1880.
   11p; pbk

10 The two codes of football. London: The Cricket Press, 1880.
   82p; pbk   BL: D
   ☞ Previous ed. F7; subsequent ed. F11

11 The two codes of football. London: The Cricket Press, 1881.
   36p; pbk   BL: D
   ☞ Previous ed. F10

12 The laws of the Rugby Union. London: The Cricket Press, 1882.
   26p   BL: Mic.A.8892(9) (microfilm copy)
   ☞ Previous ed. F8

13 Constitution and laws of the game. Ottawa, Can.: Canadian Rugby Football Union, 1884.
   16p; pbk

14 Rules & bye-laws, results of matches, hints to players. Christchurch, NZ: Printed by Lyttelton Times for East Christchurch Football Club, 1884.
   31p

15 The laws of the Football Association and of the Rugby Union: corrected to the present time. Sheffield: Hurst, 1885.   BL: 7908.a.57

16 The laws of the Rugby Union. London: Wright, 1888.
                                                    BL: D

17 The Rugby Football Union: bye-laws of the game. Greenwich: H. Richardson, published by authority, 1888.
   72p   BL: D

18 Guide to football, containing the rugby and association rules. London: Fortey, 1890.
                      BL: Mic.A.7635(8) (microfilm copy)

19 Football: its laws, rules & definition of terms; also bye-laws of the rugby union and association; lacrosse: laws of the game; the game of rounders. Manchester: Heywood, 1891-1895.
                      BL: Mic.A.7131(7) (microfilm copy)

20 Boot's football guide, 1891-92 / James Anderson Peddie. London: A. Boot, 1892.
   45p; pbk

   Contains diagrams of the fields, rugby and association rules
                                                    BL: D

21 The laws of football: the rugby union game revised to date. London: 'Pastime' Office, 1894.
   29p; pbk   BL: D
   ☞ Subsequent ed. F22

22 The laws of football: the rugby union game revised to date. London: 'Pastime' Office, 1895.
   29p; pbk   BL: D
   ☞ Previous ed. F21

23 Rhodesia Rugby Football Union bye-laws of the game for 1897. Bulawayo: The Union, 1897.
   62p

24   Constitution, rules of championship competition, and
     rules of the game / Ontario Rugby Football Union.
     Toronto, Can.: G. Soole, 1903.
     64p; pbk   BL: D

25   The laws of football as played at the New School,
     Abbotsholme, Derbyshire. Abbotsholme: Abbotsholme
     School, 1906.
     1 folded sheet   BL: 7911.b.18

26   The Vancouver Rugby Football Union: by-laws and laws
     of the game 1906-1907. Vancouver, Can.: Art
     Emporium, 1906.
     48p; pbk

27   The Rugby Football Union: bye-laws and laws of the
     game, list of secretaries and addresses, 1910-1911.
     Twickenham: The Union, 1910.
     117p   BL: Mic.A.12567(6) (microfilm copy)

28   The South African Rugby Football Board: articles of
     association, regulations and bye-laws, and laws of the
     game for 1912. Cape Town, SA: Sid P. Cowen Printers,
     1911.
     126p; illus

29   The game of rugby football: analysis of laws and some
     don'ts for players and referees / Gil Evans. Birmingham:
     Cornish Bros, 1923.
     46p; pbk   BL: Mic.A.6906(18) (microfilm copy)
     The author was an international referee.

30   Reflections of a rugby referee / G. E. Dunn. London:
     Lowe & Brydone, 1925.
     76p

31   R.U. & R.L. rugby rules. Edinburgh: Thornton's, 1930?
     48p; pbk
     (The sports trader series)

32   Elementary rugby / T. H. Boswate. Sydney, Aust.: New
     South Wales Rugby Union, 1944.
     16p; illus; pbk

33   Bye-laws and laws of the game. Twickenham: Rugby
     Football Union, 1946-   BL: P.P.2489.wie
     *Includes lists of rugby clubs with secretaries'
     addresses.*

34   Why the whistle went: notes on the laws of rugby
     football for innocent new players, knowledgeable old
     players and spectators of all descriptions / Humphrey F.
     Ellis. Twickenham: The Rugby Football Union, 1948.
     38p; illus; index; pbk   BL: 7919.aaa.28
     ☞ Subsequent ed. F35

35   Why the whistle went: notes on the laws of rugby
     football for innocent new players, knowledgeable old
     players and spectators of all descriptions / Humphrey F.
     Ellis. Rev. ed. Twickenham: The Rugby Football Union,
     1948.
     38p; illus; index; pbk   BL: 7922.b.37
     ☞ Previous ed. F34; subsequent ed. F39

36   The history of the laws of rugby football / prepared by
     Sir Percy Royds. Twickenham: Walker, 1949.
     iii, 241p; index   BL: 7920.g.45

37   Rugby union football. London: Educational
     Productions, 1951.
     48p; illus; pbk
     (Know the game)   BL: W.P.3073/12
     *Prepared with the Rugby Football Union. Explains the
     laws and basic principles of rugby.*
     ☞ Subsequent ed. F56

38   Rugby referees' right rulings / J. J. de Kock. Cape Town,
     SA: Maskew Miller, 1951.
     viii, 76p; pbk   BL: 7922.aa.83

39   Why the whistle went: notes on the laws of rugby
     football for innocent new players, knowledgeable old
     players and spectators of all descriptions / Humphrey F.
     Ellis. 2nd revision. Twickenham: The Rugby Football
     Union, 1951.
     38p; illus; index; pbk   BL: 7922.b.38
     This is actually the third edition.
     ☞ Previous ed. F35; subsequent ed. F43

40　Case laws. Twickenham: Rugby Football Union, 1954.
96p; pbk　　　　　　　　　　　　　　BL: 7922.a.2
☞　Subsequent ed. F45

41　Handbook of the New Zealand Rugby Referees'
Association: by-laws and rules of the game of rugby
football together with a summary of infringements and
penalties. Wellington, NZ: New Zealand Rugby Football
Union, 1954.
70p; illus

42　The Rugby Football Union: laws of the game and notes
for the guidance of referees. Twickenham: Walker, 1954-
　　Various editions published　　　　BL: W.P.4232

43　Why the whistle went: notes on the laws of rugby
football for innocent new players, knowledgeable old
players and spectators of all descriptions / H. F. Ellis.
4th ed. Twickenham: The Rugby Football Union, 1954.
45p; illus; index; pbk　　　　　　　BL: 7922.b.39
☞　Previous ed. F39; subsequent ed. F47

44　The art of refereeing: a handbook for rugby union
referees / edited by H. F. Ellis and illustrated by
Fougasse. Twickenham: The Rugby Football Union,
1956.
70p; illus; pbk
　　Most of the text is written by Alan S. Bean　　BL: 7923.g.16

45　Case laws. 2nd ed. Twickenham: Rugby Football Union,
1956.
110p　　　　　　　　　　　　　　　BL: 7923.de.1
☞　Previous ed. F40; subsequent ed. F48

46　The spectator's handbook: an aid to the appreciation of
athletics, boxing, cricket, association and rugby football
and lawn tennis / John Barclay Pick. London: Phoenix
Sports Books, 1956.
144p; illus　　　　　　　　　　　　BL: 7922.ee.23
　　One chapter for each of the named sports. The rugby
　　union chapter begins by acknowledging 'the basic
　　oddity of rugby' and concludes with advice on 'how to
　　distinguish a good team from one less good'.

47　Why the whistle went: notes on the laws of rugby
football for innocent new players, knowledgeable old
players and spectators of all descriptions / Humphrey
Francis Ellis. 5th ed. Twickenham: Rugby Football
Union, 1956.
45p; illus; index; pbk　　　　　　　BL: 7923.i.18
☞　Previous ed. F43; subsequent ed. F52

48　Case laws. 3rd ed. Twickenham: Rugby Football Union,
1957.
109p　　　　　　　　　　　　　　　BL: 7923.p.5
☞　Previous ed. F45; subsequent ed. F49

RUGBY FOOTBALL UNION

Case Laws

TWICKENHAM

49　Case laws. 4th ed. Twickenham: Rugby Football Union,
1958.
80p　　　　　　　　　　　　　　　BL: 7924.a.2
☞　Previous ed. F48; subsequent ed. F53

50　The laws of the game of rugby football and notes on the
laws of the game as framed by the International Rugby
Football Board and adopted by the Australian Rugby
Football Union. Sydney?, Aust.: The Australian Rugby
Football Union, 1958-
　　Various editions published

51　New rugby laws explained / J. J. de Kock. Cape Town,
SA: Vacuum Oil Company of South Africa, 1958.
vi, 58p; pbk

52　Why the whistle went: notes on the laws of rugby
football for innocent new players, knowledgeable old
players and spectators of all descriptions / H. F. Ellis.
6th ed. Twickenham: The Rugby Football Union, 1958.
46p; illus; index; pbk　　　　　　　BL: 7924.aa.29
☞　Previous ed. F47; subsequent ed. F57

53　Case laws. 5th ed. Twickenham: Rugby Football Union,
1961.
82p　　　　　　　　　　　　　　　BL: X.449/1979
☞　Previous ed. F49

54　The ABC of rugby / J. J. de Kock. Johannesburg, SA:
Shirley Cooper, 1962.
69p; pbk

55 Laws of the game of rugby football as framed by the International Rugby Football Board, with notes on the laws as approved by the Board. Masterton, NZ: New Zealand Rugby Football Union, 1962?
99p; pbk

56 Rugby union football. New ed. Wakefield: EP, 1965.
48p; illus; pbk
(Know the game)

Produced in collaboration with the Rugby Football Union

ISBN: 0715801287

☞ Previous ed. F37; subsequent ed. F61

57 Why the whistle went: notes on the laws of rugby football / H. F. Ellis. 7th ed. Twickenham: Rugby Football Union, 1966.
47p; illus; index; pbk

☞ Previous ed. F52

58 Instant rugby: a 5 minute guide to the laws most players have trouble with. Twickenham: Rugby Football Union, 1969.
8p; illus; pbk   BL: X.619/10172

59 Instructions and notes for guidance of referees. Bristol?: International Rugby Football Board, 1970.
27p; pbk

60 Rheolau rygbi / golygwyd gan Howard Lloyd. Caerdydd: Undeb Rygbi Cymru, 1970?
39p; pbk
Rules published by the Welsh Rugby Union.

61 Rugby union football. New ed. Wakefield: EP Publishing, 1972.
48p; illus; pbk
(Know the game)

Produced in collaboration with the Rugby Football Union

☞ Previous ed. F56; subsequent ed. F68

62 The history of the laws of rugby union football 1949-1972 / prepared by C. H. Gadney for the Rugby Football Union. Twickenham: Rugby Football Union, 1973.
83p; index; pbk

63 Rules, by-laws, regulations / Franklin & Districts Football Association Incorporated. Auckland, NZ: The Association, 1975.
88p; index

64 Play the whistle: a practical guide to rugby refereeing / Paul Akon with caricatures by Rodney Hayes. Sydney, Aust.: Australian Society of Rugby Referees, 1976.
63p; illus; pbk

65 Mini rugby. Ottawa, Can.: Canadian Rugby Union, 1979?
15p; illus; pbk
Rules.

66 Rugby law: a player's guide / J. J. Stewart. Petone, NZ: John Paul Productions, 1980.
48p; pbk   ISBN: 0908585047

67 Referee / Humphrey Rainey. Dunedin, NZ: McIndoe, 1982.
152p; illus; pbk

Cover title: Referee, referee, referee   ISBN: 0868680400

The author's experiences as a rugby union referee.

68 Rugby union football. New ed. Wakefield: EP Publishing, 1982.
48p; illus; pbk
(Know the game)

Produced in collaboration with the Rugby Football Union
Bibliography: p47-8   BL: WP.3073/157

☞ Previous ed. F61; subsequent ed. F73

69 Laws of the game of rugby football and instructions and notes on the laws as framed by the International Rugby Football Board. Auckland, NZ: New Zealand Rugby Football Union, 1983.
131p; illus; index

70 The principles of rugby football: a manual for coaches and referees based on papers delivered at the Welsh Rugby Union centenary international conference for coaches and referees. London: Allen & Unwin, 1983.
x, 189p; illus, maps   ISBN: 0047960671
BL: X.629/20603

☞ Also listed at: F307

71 What every rugby player should know: laws for the player, or, Wat elke rugbyspeler behoort te weet: reëls vir die speler / Justus R. Potgieter. Uniedal, SA: Stelsport, 1983.
20p; illus; pbk   ISBN: 0620066679
Text in English and Afrikaans.

72 The golden rules of rugby / Ian Heath. London: Corgi, 1984.
47p; chiefly illus; pbk   ISBN: 0552125911
BL: X.629/25998

☞ Also listed at: J74

73 Rugby union / produced in collaboration with the Rugby Football Union. New ed. London: A. & C. Black, 1984.
48p; illus; index; pbk
(Know the game)

☞ Previous ed. F68; subsequent ed. F78

74 Rugby union laws illustrated / Clive Norling with Terry Godwin. London: Pelham, 1985.
107p; illus   ISBN: 0720716225
BL: X.629/27740

75 Variations to the laws of the game of rugby football and instructions and notes on the laws applicable to all Australian domestic football under the age of 19 years: as adapted by the Australian Rugby Football Union Ltd with the approval of the International Rugby Football Board. Australia: The Union, 1985.
111p; illus; index

76 New image rugby manual. Auckland, NZ: ASB TrusteeBank in association with the New Zealand Rugby Union, 1986.
25 leaves; illus; pbk

77 Rheolau rygbi / cyfieithwyd o'r Saesneg gan Thomas Davies. Caerdydd: Undeb Rygbi Cymru, 1986.
66p; index; pbk

   Rules translated by Thomas Davies and published by the Welsh Rugby Union.

78 Rugby union / produced in collaboration with the Rugby Football Union. New ed. London: A. & C. Black, 1986.
48p; illus; index; pbk
(Know the game)   ISBN: 0713656301
                                           BL: WP.3073/180

   ☞ Previous ed. F73; subsequent ed. F81

79 World Cup rugby, 1987. Wellington, NZ: New Zealand Referees' Association and International Rugby Football Board, 1987.
2 vols.: 135, 41p; illus

   Spine title: Laws of the game of rugby football & consolidated rulings   ISBN: 0908793006 (vol. 1) • 0908793014 (vol. 2)

80 Laws of the game of rugby football (as framed by the International Rugby Football Board), instructions and notes on the laws for guidance of referees. Cape Town, SA: International Rugby Football Board, 1988-

   Issued annually
   Parallel English and Afrikaans text.

81 Rugby union / produced in collaboration with the Rugby Football Union. New ed. London: A. & C. Black, 1989.
32p; illus; pbk
(Know the game)   ISBN: 071365659X
   ☞ Previous ed. F78; subsequent ed. F88

82 Rugby union laws explained / Jim Fleming & Brian Anderson; foreword by Bill McLaren. Moffat: Lochar, 1991.
191p; illus; index   ISBN: 0948403624
                                           BL: YK.1991.b.5530

   ☞ See also: F84

83 Coaches and players guide to the laws of rugby football: incorporating IRFB changes effective from 7 June 1992. Wellington, NZ: New Zealand Rugby Football Union, 1992.
56p; illus; pbk

84 The new rugby union laws explained / Jim Fleming & Brian Anderson. Australian ed. Sydney, Aust.: ABC Enterprises for the Australian Broadcasting Corporation, 1992.
xv, 174p; illus; index; pbk   ISBN: 0733301886
   ☞ See also: F82

85 The official international revised laws to the game of rugby football. Randburg, SA: Kevan Thompson, 1992.
28p; illus; pbk   ISBN: 0620169397
   Parallel English and Afrikaans text.

86 Big Aussie rules book / Jim Main. Auckland, NZ: Rugby Press, 1994.
128p; illus; pbk   ISBN: 0908630476

87 The laws in plain English. Bristol: International Rugby Football Board, 1994.
190p; illus; index; pbk   ISBN: 0952373505
   Includes a section on referee signals.

88 Rugby union. New ed. London: A & C Black, 1994.
48p; illus, plans; index; pbk
(Know the game)
   Produced in collaboration with the Rugby Football Union
                                           ISBN: 0713636777
                                           BL: YK.1994.a.4769

   ☞ Previous ed. F81; subsequent ed. F105

89 A study of the leisure time exercise habits of rugby union referees from the Bristol and Gloucester Referees' Societies / G. Bulstrode. University of Bristol, 1994.
Master's thesis.

90 USA rugby handbook of the laws of the game 1994-1995 / United States of America Rugby Football Union. San Diego, US: USA Rugby, 1994.

   Also includes national committees and members, territorial and local area union committees and members, and a directory of named members.

91 101 decisions: basic laws for referees, coaches, players and spectators / Justus Potgieter & Freek Burger. Uniedal, SA: Stelrek, 1995.
104p; illus; index; pbk

92 Rugby: a player's guide to the laws / Derek Robinson. London: CollinsWillow, 1995.
160p; illus; pbk   ISBN: 0002187000

93 Rugby and cricket for mums: a brief introduction to rugby and cricket for mums and all other supporters new to the game / A. Sue Porter; illustrations by Amanda Stiby. London: Souvenir Press, 1995.
103p; illus

ISBN: 0285633023
BL: YK.1996.a.20921

The positions and the laws are explained in simple terms for the benefit of spectators who are completely new to rugby.

94 The 'team of three' touch judging: minimum standards. 2nd ed. Twickenham: Rugby Football Union, 1995.
16p; illus; pbk

1st ed. untraced

An official video accompanies this work.

95 United rugby rules / David Adams. 1995.
pbk

Rules for both the league and union games.

96 The complete referee / Jeremy G. Turner; edited by Richard S. Podmore. Colorado Springs, US: USA Rugby, 1996.
143p; illus

Examines the role of the referee.

97 Fair play codes for people in rugby. Twickenham: Rugby Football Union, 1996.
12p; pbk

98 Instant rugby: a 5 minute guide to the laws. Twickenham: Rugby Football Union, 1996.
11p; pbk

99 Instant rugby: a 5 minute guide to the laws: under-19 version. Twickenham: Rugby Football Union, 1996.
11p; pbk

100 Rugby: a referee's guide / Ed Morrison and Derek Robinson. London: CollinsWillow, 1996.
191p; illus; index; pbk

ISBN: 000218754X
BL: YK.1996.a.23436

101 Rugby continuum: rules of play: with effect from 17th August 1996. Twickenham: Rugby Football Union, 1996.
12p; pbk

102 Rugby law explained: a down-to-earth guide to the laws of rugby union / Mike Mortimer; illustrated by Tony Harding. Leicester: Kairos, 1996.
56p; illus; pbk

ISBN: 1871344077

☞ Subsequent ed. F104

103 The RFU rugby union referee's manual / Richard Greensted. London A. & C. Black, 1997.
vii, 120p; illus; pbk

ISBN: 0713646144
BL: YK.1998.b.1111

104 Rugby law explained: a down-to-earth guide to the laws of rugby union / Mike Mortimer; illustrated by Tony Harding and Roger Fairbrother. 2nd ed. Leicester: Kairos, 1997.
80p; illus; pbk

ISBN: 187134414X

☞ Previous ed. F102

105 Rugby union. New ed. London: A & C Black, 1997.
48p; illus, plans; index; pbk
(Know the game)

Produced in collaboration with the Rugby Football Union

ISBN: 0713647205

☞ Previous ed. F88

106 Rugby union rules / Eddie Knights. London: Ward Lock, 1997.
80p; illus; index
(A player's guide)

ISBN: 0706375602 (cased) • 0706375599 (pbk)
BL: YK.1998.a.980

Coaching, Tactics & Training

107 Rugby football, and how to excel in it / Dr Irvine. 1887.
(The boy's own bookshelf; vol. 2)

BL: 4419.o.30/2

108 How to play football: association and rugby / by 'An Old Player'. Manchester: Heywood, 1891.
24p; pbk

BL: Mic.A.7802(2) (microfilm copy)

109 The rugby union game / C. J. B. Marriott; The association game / C. W. Alcock. London: Routledge, 1894.
120p; illus
(The 'Oval' series of games)

BL: D

History and instructional text.

☞ Also listed at: A12; subsequent ed. F114

110   Rugby football / B. Fletcher Robinson; edited by Max
      Pemberton. London: A. D. Innes, 1896.
      x, 338p; illus
      (The Isthmian Library; no. 1)   BL: 7920.ff.1/1
         Covers the development of the game; positional play;
         the role of the referee and captain; training; the
         nurseries of the game in England and Scotland; and,
         rugby abroad.

111   Football, hockey and lacrosse / J. H. C. Fegan, Tinsley
      Lindley, H. F. Prevost Battersby and J. C. Isard. London:
      T. Fisher Unwin, 1900.
      xiv, 189p; illus
      (The sports library)   BL: 07912.ee.75/2
         The opening section on rugby football is by Fegan.

112   The art of rugby football: with hints and instructions on
      every point of the game / Thomas Rangiwahia Ellison.
      Wellington, NZ: Geddis & Blomfield, 1902.
      80p; illus
         A solicitor before becoming a barrister, Ellison was
         the first Maori to be admitted to the bar. He was a
         member of the New Zealand Native team of 1888-89
         which toured New Zealand, the UK and Australia and,
         in 1893, the captain of the first official New Zealand
         team.

113   How to play rugby football: the theory and practice of the
      game / Harry Alexander. Uppingham: John Hawthorn, 1902.
      52p
      BL: 07905.ee.28

114   Football: the rugby union game / Charles J. B. Marriott;
      The association game / C. W. Alcock. 2nd ed. London:
      Routledge, 1903.
      127p; illus
      (The 'Oval' series of games)
         Pages 1-54: Rugby union football; pages 91-117: Rugby
         union and the laws of rugby union football.
      ☞ Also listed at: A28; previous ed. F109

115   Rugby union football / Philip Trevor 'Dux'; with
      illustrations by Ernest Prater, Max Cowper, C. M.
      Padday, S. T. Dadd, etc. London: Chapman & Hall, 1903.
      278p; illus
                                                  BL: 07905.g.46

116   Rugby football / Jerome J. Rahilly. London: Pearson, 1904.
      122p   BL: 7912.i.32
         After a brief retrospect, the qualifications and duties
         of each position on the field are then considered with
         tips for the referee on what to wear and how to make
         himself heard.

117   The complete rugby footballer on the New Zealand system
      / D. Gallaher and W. J. Stead. London: Methuen, 1906.
      xxiv, 322p; illus; index   BL: 2271.c.5
         'In the following pages we have told for the first time
         all about our game that there is to tell. One of the
         signatories [Gallaher] to these remarks acted as the

captain of the team during the tour and the other
one [Stead] as the vice-captain...'. The tour referred
to was of the British Isles and France in 1905.

118   Letters to young rugby football players / XVIth Man.
      London: Blackie, 1907.
      112p   BL: Mic.A.9046(3) (microfilm copy)

119   Modern rugby football: New Zealand methods, points
      for the beginner, the player, and the spectator / A. H.
      Baskerville. London: Gordon & Gotch, 1907.
      128p; illus   BL: D

120   Rugby guide and how to play rugby / 'Old International'.
      London: British Sport Publishing, 1907.
      139p; illus
      (Spalding's athletic library)   BL: 07908.i.14/22

121   The modern rugby game and how to play it / E. Gwyn
      Nicholls. London: 'Health & Strength', 1908.
      86p; illus

122   Hints on rugby football / W. A. Symcox. London: 1911.
      22p; illus   BL: Mic.A.7747(14) (microfilm copy)

123   Modern rugby football / John E. Raphael; illustrations
      from photographs by G. Beldam. London: Grafton, 1918.
      xv, 296p; illus   BL: 07911.e.13

124   Rugby in South Africa: hints to players and rules of the
      game / C. V. Becker. Johannesburg, SA: Football and
      Sports Publications, 1919?
      155p

125   Rugby football: how to succeed / H. B. T. Wakelam.
      London: Evans, 1920.
      ☞ Subsequent ed. F162

126   Rugby football in theory and practice and especially
      from the point of view of school football /
      'Alleyniensis.' 2nd ed. London: W. A. Symcox, 1921.
      60p
         Previous ed. untraced   BL: D

127   First steps to rugby football / 'Alleyniensis' (W. D.
      Gibbon). London: Mills & Boon, 1922.
      128p; illus   BL: 07911.de.80

128   Modern rugby tactics: a handbook for school players /
      'Touch Flag'. London: Simpkin, Marshall, Hamilton,
      Kent, 1922.
      viii, 79p; pbk   BL: D

129   Notes on rugby football / G. S. Conway. Cambridge:
      Faber & Tyler, 1922.
      24p; pbk
      (Cambridge review 'New Blue' series; no. 2)
                                                  BL: W.P.6930/2
         Coaching. Reprinted from *The Cambridge Review* of
         18th & 25th November and 2nd December 1921, and
         20th & 27th January 1922.

130 Rugby football / D. R. Gent. London: George Allen & Unwin, 1922.
220p; illus
(British sports library; vol. 1)   BL: 07908.e.22(1)

131 Rugby football & how to play it / J. M. B. Scott. London: Chatto & Windus, 1922.
xix, 108p; illus   BL: 07911.e.58

132 Rugby football for beginners / E. M. Johnstone. London: Grant Richards, 1922.
87p   BL: 7911.aaa.54
    Junior rugby.

133 The rugby game and how to play it / by six internationals; edited by C. J. B. Marriott. London: Athletic Publications, 1922.
127p; illus; pbk   BL: Mic.A.10606(8) (microfilm copy)

134 Rugby football / W. J. A. Davies. London: Webster's, 1923.
254p; illus   BL: 07911.eee.42
See also: F149

135 Rugby union football / Philip Trevor. London: Heinemann, 1923.
viii, 248p   BL: 07911.e.72

136 Hints to rugby players / Basil Scholefield. East London, SA: Daily Dispatch, 1924.
15p; pbk
    Reprint of articles published by the Daily Dispatch, South Africa, on training, coaching, tactics, passing, heeling, etc.

137 Modern rugby football / C. J. B. Marriott, with chapters on forward and back play, captaincy, and refereeing by A. D. Stoop, F. C. Potter-Irwin, R. Cove Smith, D. R. Gent; and a foreword by Rowland Hill. London: G. Bell, 1924.
vi, 138p; illus   BL: 7904.de.18

138 Modern rugby football / L. R. Tosswill. London: Renwick of Otley, 1924.
97p
(Spalding's athletic library; no. 24)
      BL: Mic.A.16571(20) (microfilm copy)

139 A manual of rugby football for public schools / Robert M. Rayner. London: Andrew Melrose, 1925.
140p   BL: 7904.ee.21
    A textbook for schoolboys. On the subject of clothing the schoolboy is warned that 'putting on a dirty smelly jersey makes you feel "cheap" at the very start of the proceedings', and 'always wear your jersey inside your shorts. You will then minimise the risk of being tackled by it, or getting it torn'.

140 Rugby football / H. H. Lund. King William's Town, SA: King Printing Co., 1925.
65p; illus; pbk

141 Rugby football / R. Cove Smith. London: Methuen, 1925.
xi, 144p; illus; index   BL: 7904.ee.26

142 Rugby football: hints on how to play it / L. R. Tosswill. London: Harrap, 1925.
127p; illus
(Masters of sports)   BL: 7920.aaa.11/4

143 A lecture on rugby football / P. C. Adams. Birmingham: Cornish Bros, 1926.
39p; pbk   BL: D
    A brief coaching book.

144 'Rugger' / A. T. Young. London: Foulsham, 1926.
88p; illus; pbk
(Foulsham's sports library; no. 8)   BL: X.629/6605(8)

145 A text book on rugby football / I. M. B. Stuart. London: Athletic Publications, 1926.
x, 135p; illus   BL: 07912.f.71

146 Rugby: the game / 'Ompax'; foreword by K. G. McLeod. Glasgow: Hedderwick, 1927.
152p; index   BL: 07905.ee.71
    The elementary principles of the game are explained: its development; the field of play; the ball; backs and forwards in attack; tackling; backing-up. Deals with the theory of the game, the practice of it, the spirit of it, its history, and even the way it should be watched.

147 Rugger / W. W. Wakefield and H. P. Marshall. London: Longmans, 1927.
xi, 491p; illus; index   BL: 7908.g.31
    Divided into 3 parts, the first being the rugby reminiscences of Wakefield from his school days up to the date of publication. There then follows a treatise on the theory and practice of rugby. Finally comes a section on records.
    ☞ Subsequent ed. F153

148 Rugger!: the greatest game / Hylton Cleaver. London: Christophers, 1927.
39p; pbk   BL: Mic.A.10336(12) (microfilm copy)

149 Rugby football / W. J. A. Davies. Abridged ed. London: Webster's, 1928.
160p   BL: 07906.g.45
    ☞ See also: F134

150 Rugby football / W. Livingstone Irwin. London: Warne, 1928.
64p; illus; pbk
(Warne's recreation books)   BL: X.629/6699(12)

151   Rugby football: place-kicking / Robert Alexander
      Chrystal. London: Herbert Jenkins, 1928.
      15p   BL: Mic.A.10397(9) (microfilm copy)

152   New Zealand rugby football: some hints and criticisms /
      Irwin Hunter. Auckland, NZ: Whitcombe & Tombs,
      1929.
      128p; illus; index   BL: D

      *Written by an English born New Zealand doctor, the
      book is a mixture of a little history and how to play
      rugby.*

153   Rugger / W. W. Wakefield and H. P. Marshall. New and
      cheaper ed. London: Longmans, 1930.
      xi, 509p; illus; index   BL: 07906.i.33

      ☞ Previous ed. F147; subsequent ed. F160

154   The theory of modern rugby football / I. M. B. Stuart.
      London: Macmillan, 1930.
      xiv, 198p   BL: 07911.ee.55

155   Twickenham calling: a book for players and spectators of
      rugby football / Capt. Henry B. T. Wakelam with a
      foreword by Adrian Stoop. London: G. Bell, 1930.
      ix, 165p; illus   BL: 7916.a.26

      *The author was rugby correspondent for the Morning
      Post and running commentator for the BBC. In
      addition to a general description of the game, there
      are notes on the role of each position, technical
      terms, tactics, and a brief run down on specific
      players and teams of distinction.*

156   Rugby football to-day / Edward H. D. Sewell. London:
      John Murray, 1931.
      xii, 352p; illus; index   BL: 7916.aa.23

157   Rugby football / D. R. Gent. London: Eyre &
      Spottiswoode, 1932.
      224p; illus
      (Aldin series)   BL: 7921.f.28(5)

      ☞ See also: F158

158   The Aldin book of outdoor games: rugby football by D.
      R. Gent; golf by H. Cotton; lawn tennis by J. H. Doeg
      and Allison Danzig; cricket by M. D. Lyon. London:
      Eyre & Spottiswoode, 1933.
      xv, 695p; illus

      *A reissue in one volume of the editions previously published in
      the 'Aldin series'*

                                        BL: 7904.b.31

      ☞ See also: F157

159   How to play rugby football / W. J. A. Davies. London:
      Constable, 1933.
      xxi, 163p; illus   BL: 7916.aaa.38

160   Rugger, and how to play it / Sir William Wavell
      Wakefield and Howard Percival Marshall. New and
      revised ed. of Part II of 'Rugger'. London: Longmans
      Green, 1935.
      xiii, 194p; illus   BL: 07908.de.7

      ☞ Previous ed. F153

161   Rugby football / H. B. T. Wakelam. London: Dent, 1936.
      xi, 223p; illus
      (Modern sports)   BL: X.629/6646(1)

162   Rugby football: how to succeed / H. B. T. Wakelam;
      with a foreword by J. E. Greenwood. London: Evans,
      1936.
      32p; illus; pbk   BL: 7915.s.10

      ☞ Previous ed. F125; subsequent ed. F181

163   Rugby football / Clifford W. Jones. London: Pitman,
      1937.
      xviii, 174p; illus; index
      (Games and recreations)   BL: W.P.11671/10

      *Includes a chapter on 'Three-Quarter Play' by Wilfred
      Wooller.*

      ☞ Subsequent ed. F166

164   Rugger practice and tactics / Harry F. MacDonald and
      John Idwal Rees. London: Arnold, 1938.
      141p   BL: 7908.eee.54

165   Schoolboy rugby football: an address / William John
      Hoare. London: National Union of Teachers, 1938.
      9p   BL: D

      *An address delivered to the meeting of teachers
      interested in school sports, at the Margate
      Conference of the National Union of Teachers, 1938.*

166   Rugby football / Clifford W. Jones. 2nd ed. London:
      Pitman, 1939.
      xvii, 170p; illus; index
      (Games and recreations)

      ☞ Previous ed. F163; subsequent ed. F175

167   Rugger / G. S. Conway, C. A. Kershaw, and G. V.
      Stephenson. London, Glasgow: Blackie, 1939.
      x, 179p; illus   BL: Mic.A.12488(1) (microfilm copy)

168   Rugby football for the learner-player / O G;
      introduction by Wilfred Wooller. London: Universal
      Publications, 1940.
      iv, 76p; illus; pbk   BL: 07907.ee.7

      Aimed at the junior and schools markets.

169   Football fundamentals: illustrating the basic principles of
      rugby / Ray Norman. Sydney, Aust.: Halstead, 1941.
      62p; illus

170   Rugby football drill and games for performance in the
      playground / Ray Norman. Sydney, Aust.: Halstead, 1943.
      32p; illus

171   Rugby football / A. E. Mitchell. Sydney, Aust.: NSW
      Rugby Union, 1945.
      80p; illus

172   Rugby football for schools / John T. Hankinson.
      London: Allen & Unwin, 1946.
      xii, 181p; illus   BL: 7918.aa.89
      Designed for use by both coaches and players.
      Photographs and diagrams are used to illustrate
      different aspects of the game.
      ☞   Subsequent ed. F199

173   Rugger: do it this way: learn your rugger from
      photographs / Mark Sugden and Gerald Hollis;
      photographs by John Barlee. London: John Murray,
      1946.
      viii, 44p; illus   BL: 7916.f.48
      ☞   Subsequent ed. F207

174   Rugger's an attacking game / Peter Lawless. London:
      Sampson Low, Marston, 1946.
      xi, 116p   BL: 7917.aa.47
      Neat, well articulated observations on rugby and how
      it should be played, by a former Richmond and
      Barbarian player. Lawless, a war correspondent
      attached to the American Forces during World War II,
      was killed crossing the Rhine.

      RUGBY FOOTBALL

      FOR THE

      LEARNER-PLAYER

      By

      O G

      Introduction by
      WILFRED WOOLLER
      (The Welsh International)

      LONDON
      UNIVERSAL PUBLICATIONS, LTD.
      FANN STREET, ALDERSGATE STREET, E.C.1

175   Rugby football / Clifford Jones. 3rd ed. London:
      Pitman, 1949.
      xvii, 170p; illus; index
      (Games and recreations)   BL: W.P.11671/33
      ☞   Previous ed. F166

176   A short-cut to rugby: a book for the spectator and the
      player / C. K. Friedlander and Patrick Tebbutt. Cape
      Town, SA: Central News Agency, 1949.
      163p; illus; pbk   BL: 7921.b.9
      Looks at different playing positions, captaincy, the
      referee, and the radio commentator. Lively anecdotes
      by present and past participants in the game in
      South Africa.

177   How to play rugby football / 'John Mainwaring'.
      London: Foyle, 1950.
      102p; illus
      Author's real name is O. L. Owen   BL: 7921.aa.12

178   Let's talk rugger / Basil H. Travers. London: Eyre &
      Spottiswoode, 1950.
      xvi, 246p; illus   BL: 7917.f.30
      Details the planning, both strategic and tactical,
      that goes into a game.
      ☞   Subsequent ed. F186

179   Rugby: some do's and don'ts. Newcastle: Newcastle
      Journal and North Mail, 1950-1951.
      Continued as: Rugby digest
      ☞   See also: F189

180   Rugby football / Haydn Tanner. London: Nicholas
      Kaye, 1950.
      150p; illus   BL: 7917.de.145

181   Rugby football: how to succeed / Henry B. T. Wakelam.
      New ed. London: Evans, 1950.
      32p; illus   BL: 7919.ee.28
      Covers: dress and keeping fit; the idea, the game, and
      purpose of its players; details of play; the plan and
      actions of the game; coaching.
      ☞   Previous ed. F162

182   Steps to first-class rugger / Geoffrey De la Condamine;
      with a foreword by Sir Wavell Wakefield. London:
      Herbert Jenkins, 1950.
      154p; illus   BL: 7920.bb.3
      Well illustrated with photographs, this coaching book
      sets out to raise the standard of schoolboy rugby to
      its pre-war level.

183   Teach yourself rugby football / F. N. S. Creek. London:
      English Universities Press, 1950.
      196p; illus
      (Teach yourself books)   BL: W.P.706/110
      ☞   Subsequent ed. F215

184 Start the right way: cricket and rugby football for the junior boy and his coach / Kenneth John Lovatt, W. M. Russell and T. McMurray. Belfast: W. M. Russell, 1951.
80p; illus   BL: 7920.l.37

185 Danie Craven on rugby / Daniel H. Craven. Cape Town, SA: R. Beerman, 1952.
211p; illus   BL: 7923.bb.24
    Of interest to players, club coaches, and spectators.

186 How to play rugger / Basil H. Travers. London: Eyre & Spottiswoode, 1952.
xvi, 248p; illus   BL: 7921.e.41
☞ Previous ed. F178; subsequent ed. F195

187 Let's talk captaincy / B. H. Travers. Australia?: 1952?
35p; pbk
    Aimed at schoolboys, this covers both rugby union and cricket.

188 The manual of rugby union football for coaches and players / edited by H. F. Ellis. London: 1952.
280p   BL: 7920.aaa.74
☞ See also: F208, F209

189 Rugby digest / J. N. Pargeter. Newcastle: Newcastle Journal and North Mail, 1952-1960.
    Continues: Rugby: some do's and don'ts
☞ See also: F179

190 Rugby union football / Harold L. V. Day. London: Nicholson & Watson, 1952.
203p; illus
(Country books; no. 9)   BL: W.P.2622/9

191 Play better rugby / Harold L. V. Day. London: Frederick Muller, 1954.
104p; illus
(Play better books)   BL: W.P.C.566/2

192 Rugby football / Louis T. Stanley. London: Hutchinson, 1954.
132p; illus
(Hutchinson's library of sports and pastimes)   BL: W.P.1156/35

193 Rugby wrinkles: a pocket manual of reflections, maxims and hints on 'the man's game' / Izak van Heerden; with illustrations by 'Louwtjie' and an introduction by Bill Payn. Durban, SA: c1954.
32p; illus; pbk

194 Bob Scott on rugby: in which is expressed the conviction that attack is the art of rugby football / R. W. H. Scott and T. P. McLean. London: Nicholas Kaye, 1955.
155p; illus   BL: 7922.b.45
    There are chapters on attacking play, captaincy, kicking goals, defensive measures, and training and preparation.

195 How to play rugger / Basil H. Travers. 3rd rev. ed. with the complete new rules. London: Eyre & Spottiswoode, 1955.
xvi, 272p; illus   BL: 7922.e.2
☞ Previous ed. F186

196 Rugby football: a guide book for teachers, coaches, and players / prepared by the New Zealand Physical Education Branch. Wellington, NZ: New Zealand Education Department, 1956.
☞ Subsequent ed. F260

197 Rugby, hockey and other games for boys / Stanley Wilson; illustrated by Donald Cammell. London: Allen & Unwin, 1957.
48p; illus   BL: Cup.1253.k.21
    With the aid of illustrations, the basic movement and rules of each game are described.

198 Tackle rugger this way / Gerwyn Williams. London: Stanley Paul, 1957.
82p; illus   BL: 7923.h.54
☞ Subsequent ed. F226

199 Rugby football for schools / John Trevor Hankinson. 2nd ed. London: Allen & Unwin, 1958.
171p; illus   BL: 7924.b.42
    The text is the same as the 1946 edition.
☞ Previous ed. F172

200 Rugby football tactics / John Gwilliam. London: Stanley Paul, 1958.
104p; illus   BL: 7923.o.5

201 All Blacks and Lions: an examination of rugby tactics and players / J. M. Wallace. Wellington, NZ: Reed, 1959.
208p; illus
    Subsequently published: London: Bailey & Swinfen, 1960
        BL: 7925.b.95

202 The ABC of rugby / C. K. Saxton with the assistance of D. J. Manning. Dunedin, NZ: Published at the request of NZRFU and printed by the Otago Daily Times, 1960.
40p; illus; pbk

203 The All Blacks' book for boys / Pat Booth. Christchurch, NZ: Whitcombe & Tombs, 1960.
111p   BL: 7925.de.24
    Includes a brief biography of Don Clarke, 'The story of an All Black' as well as coaching bits and pieces on New Zealand rugby.

204 All Blacks in chains / J. M. Mackenzie. Wellington, NZ: Truth, 1960.
152p; illus
    Mackenzie, sports editor of Truth, discusses the theme that New Zealand rugby is losing its magic touch through coaching too often directed into the

wrong channels. Instead of concentrating upon the fundamental techniques of the game, modern coaches too often drill their teams excessively in safety first tactics.

205   High speed rugby / E. S. Higham and W. J. Higham. London: Heinemann, 1960.
xxi, 334p; illus   BL: 7925.g.9

206   Instructions to young rugger players / Cedric Venables; foreword by C. H. Gadney. London: Museum Press, 1960.
112p; illus; index   BL: 7925.l.15

207   Rugger: do it this way / Mark Sugden and Gerald Hollis with photographs by John Barlee. 2nd ed. London: John Murray, 1960.
79p; illus   BL: 7925.l.41
☞   Previous ed. F173

208   The basic skills in rugby football: based on the 'Manual of rugby union football', part one. Twickenham: Rugby Football Union, 1961.
96p   BL: X.449/1558
☞   See also: F188

209   Coaching rugby footballers: some suggestions on the organization of coaching for young players. Twickenham: Rugby Football Union, 1961.
71p; index; pbk

Extracted from 'The manual of rugby union football', part two
                                                        BL: X.449/1004
☞   See also: F188

210   Rugby on attack / Ron Jarden. Christchurch : Whitcombe & Tombs, 1961.
xiv, 226p; illus

Also published: Cape Town, SA: Tafelberguitgewers, 1961
                                                        BL: X.449/640

211   Coaching for rugby football / Cedric Venables; foreword by Sir Wavell Wakefield. London: Museum Press, 1962.
79p   BL: X.449/346
For schoolmasters and part-time coaches. The book explains how to set about coaching junior rugby players.

212   Rugby: skills, training and tactics / Les Williams. London: Stanley Paul, 1962.
192p; illus   BL: X.449/402

213   Rugby / John Herbert. London: Weidenfeld & Nicolson, 1963.
77p; illus
(Sports for schools)   BL: 7926.r.1/2
Deals with coaching theory and training programmes, with some reference to the history of the game.

214   Rugger for schoolboys / Donald Ireland; photographs by J. C. Page. London: Pelham, 1963.
132p   BL: 7926.p.9
For the beginner in his first year, or a member of the school XV.

215   Teach yourself rugby football / Frederick N. S. Creek. 2nd ed. London: English Universities Press, 1963.
208p; illus
(Teach yourself books)
A teaching book which gives detailed lessons for every position on the field.
☞   Previous ed. F183; subsequent ed. F245

216   Modern rugby: a comprehensive guide for player and coach / Gerwyn Williams; foreword by Ian Beer. London: Stanley Paul, 1964.
109p; illus   BL: X.449/295

217   Better rugby for boys / D. Cyril Joynson. London: Nicholas Kaye, 1965.
95p; illus   BL: X.449/1634
☞   Subsequent ed. F231

218   The complete loose-forward / Izak van Heerden. Durban, SA: J. F. King, 1965.
36p; illus

219   Coaching, practising and training for tries / Izak van Heerden. Durban, SA: Drakensberg, 1966.
105p; illus

220   Schoolboy rugby / Gerwyn Williams. London: Stanley Paul, 1966.
144p; illus   BL: X.449/1684

221   Improve your rugby / J. T. Greenwood. Harmondsworth: Penguin, 1967.
188p; illus; pbk
(Penguin handbooks; no. P.H. 130)   BL: W.P.4003/130

222 Tactical and attacking rugby / Izak van Heerden; with a foreword by D. H. Craven. London: Herbert Jenkins, 1967.
293p; illus

223 This world of rugby / John Thornett. Sydney, Aust.: Murray, 1967.
160p; illus

> Approved by the Australian Rugby Football Union.

☞ See also: F237

224 A guide for coaches. Twickenham: Rugby Football Union, 1968.
408p; illus

> A ring-binder in three parts: basic coaching (attitude and fundamentals, individual skills, unit skills — forwards, backs — team skills); advanced coaching (advanced subjects); and special subjects (diagnosis of faults, selection of captaincy, organisation of practice sessions, the laws, aids to coaching).

225 Successful rugby / illustrated by J. C. Page; with plates by Donald Ireland. London: Pelham, 1968.
208p; illus   BL: X.449/3339

226 Tackle rugger this way / Gerwyn Williams. London: Stanley Paul, 1968.
98p; illus   SBN: 090397711
                                BL: X.449/3392

☞ Previous ed. F198; subsequent ed. F249

227 Your book of rugger / David C. N. Hudson and P. S. Dyer. London: Faber, 1968.
72p; illus
(The your book series)   SBN: 571082467
                                BL: X.449/3451

Elementary guide to tactics and seven-a-side rugby.

228 A guide for players. Twickenham: Rugby Football Union, 1969.
71p; illus; pbk   BL: X.619/10183

229 Rugby. Edmonton, Can.: Dept. of Education, 1969.
71p; pbk

> A curriculum guide.

230 Rugby success starts here / Derek Robinson; illustrated by John Gully. London: Pelham, 1969.
147p; illus   SBN: 720702860
                                BL: X.449/3850

☞ Subsequent ed. F247

231 Better rugby for boys / D. Cyril Joynson, with 91 photographs by the author. 2nd ed. London: Kaye & Ward, 1970.
95p; illus
(The better sports series)   ISBN: 0718201434

☞ Previous ed. F217; subsequent ed. F239

232 Fred Allen on rugby / Fred Allen and Terry McLean. London: Cassell, 1970.
viii, 242p; illus   SBN: 30493433X
                                BL: X.629/2679

233 Proceedings report of the Centenary Congress: the development and enjoyment of the game. Twickenham: Rugby Football Union, 1971.
70p; illus

> During the periods 23rd-25th September and 30th September-2nd October 1971, delegates from 44 countries who were the guests of the county constituent bodies of the RFU participated in the Congress at Corpus Christi College, Cambridge. In broad terms the topics covered were: the laws, coaching, referees, and 'what rugby football has meant to me'.

234 Rugby for coach and player / Don Rutherford. London: Arthur Barker, 1971.
186p; illus   SBN: 213002434
                                BL: X.629/3165

235 Rugby, the players' game / J. Gavin Reid. Dubuque, US: W. C. Brown, 1971.
vii, 52p; illus
(Physical education activities series)

> *Bibliography: p50*   ISBN: 0697070417

236 Soccer and rugby training schemes for schools / Harcourt Roy; illustrated by Roy L. Alexander. Kettering: Schoolmaster Publishing, 1971.
127p; illus; pbk

> *Includes bibliography*   ISBN: 090064222X

> Maps out a series of lessons for training in soccer and rugby. The suggestions are accompanied by coaching points and comments on organisation. In addition, sections are included on a variety of circuits, conditioning, equipment and nutrition.

237 How to play rugby union / John Thornett. Wollstonecraft, Aust.: Pollard, 1972.
157p; illus
(Jack Pollard Sportmaster)

> *Based on material published in 1967 as 'This world of rugby'*
                                ISBN: 0909950091

☞ See also: F223

238 Rugby under pressure / Brian Jones and Ian McJennett in collaboration with Brian Dobbs. London: Faber and Faber, 1972.
211p; illus   ISBN: 0571097375
                                BL: X.629/4113

239 Better rugby for boys / D. Cyril Joynson. 3rd ed. London: Kaye and Ward, 1973.
95p; illus   ISBN: 0718214609
                                BL: X.629/5473

☞ Previous ed. F231; subsequent ed. F263

240 Even better rugby / Martin Underwood and Ken
     Bartlett. Twickenham: Rugby Football Union, 1973.
     140p; ringbound
     ☞ Subsequent ed. F315

241 Rugby for beginners / Ray Williams. London: Souvenir,
     1973.
     112p; illus   ISBN: 0285620932
                                         BL: X.620/6984

242 Rugby union. London: Training Associates, 1973.
     91p; illus; pbk
     (Sport coaching series / National Westminster Bank)
                                         ISBN: 085961011X

243 Proceedings report of the international conference on
     the development of rugby football for the young, at
     Rugby School 13-21 December 1973. Twickenham:
     Rugby Football Union, 1974?
       *Eleven lecturers and 42 delegates from over a dozen
       countries attended the conference.*

244 Rugby handbook / D. H. Craven. Cape Town, SA:
     Tafelberg, 1974.
     9, 250p; illus

       *Subsequently published: Wellington, N.Z., London: Reed,
       1976. ISBN: 058900915X*   ISBN: 062400662X
                                         BL: X.620/16610

     ☞ Subsequent ed. F262

245 Rugby / F. N. S. Creek and Don Rutherford. London:
     Teach Yourself Books, 1975.
     ix, 162p; illus; pbk
     (Teach yourself books)   ISBN: 0340198184
                                         BL: WP.706/605

     ☞ Previous ed. F215

246 Rugby sevens / Mike Williams. London: Faber and
     Faber, 1975.
     164p; illus; index
           ISBN: 0571105238 (cased) • 057110679X (pbk)
                                         BL: X.629/6898

       Coaching for sevens.

247 Rugby success starts here / Derek Robinson; illustrated
     by John Gully. Revised ed. London: Pan Books, 1975.
     159p; illus; index; pbk   ISBN: 0330241680
                                         BL: X.619/15341

     ☞ Previous ed. F230

248 Rugby union / John Dawes. London: Pelham, 1975.
     64p; illus   ISBN: 0720707927
                                         BL: X.622/2216

249 Tackle rugger / Gerwyn Williams. Rev. ed. London:
     Stanley Paul, 1975.
     96p; illus   ISBN: 0091253705 (cased) • 0091253713 (pbk)
                                         BL: X.629/10432

     ☞ Previous ed. F226

250 This is rugby. Auckland, NZ: Auckland Rugby Football
     Union, 1975.
     32p; illus

251 All about rugby football / Wallace Reyburn. London: W.
     H. Allen, 1976.
     143p; illus; index   ISBN: 0491017170
                                         BL: X.629/10837

252 Focus on rugby / compiled by Gordon Slatter.
     Christchurch, N.Z., London: Whitcoulls, 1976.
     136p; illus; index; pbk   ISBN: 0723304572
                                         BL: X.615/1811

253 Inside rugby: the team game / John T. Powell. Chicago,
     US: Regnery, 1976.
     vii, 102p; illus; index
           ISBN: 0809280809 (cased) • 0809280795 (pbk)

254 Radlauers' kickoff! / created for Bowmar by Radlauer
     Productions. Los Angeles, US: Bowmar, 1976.
     48p; chiefly illus   ISBN: 0837223792
       *Photographs with brief text to introduce the
       positions and plays of football, rugby, and soccer.*

255 The rugby game: a manual for coaches and players / Jim
     Wallace. London: Kaye and Ward, 1976.
     ix, 176p; illus   ISBN: 0718211146
                                         BL: X.620/16383

256 Skilful rugby / Ray Williams. London: Souvenir, 1976.
     239p; illus
       Bibliography: p219   ISBN: 0285622331
                                         BL: X.620/16453

257 Teaching rugby to boys: a graduated programme for
     schools and clubs / Gordon Banks; illustrations by Reg
     W. Hepple. London: Bell, 1976.
     111p; illus; pbk   ISBN: 0713519444
                                         BL: X.619/17063

258 Guide book for rugby coaches / compiled by D. J.
     (Don) Griffin. Petone, NZ: Petone RFC, 1977.
     78p; illus; pbk

259 Rugby coaching manual / R. J. P. Marks. Australia:
     Rothmans National Sport Foundation, 1977.
     156p; illus; pbk
       *Marks was the first National Director of Rugby
       Coaching appointed in Australia.*

260 Rugby football: a guide book for teachers, coaches, and
     players / text by R. R. Heale; edited by M. Campbell;
     photography by F. Mahoney. New Zealand: Curriculum
     Development Unit, Dept. of Education, 1977.
     79p; illus
     (Sports instruction series; no. 4)
     ☞ Previous ed. F196; subsequent ed. F326

261 Rugby for teachers, coaches, and players / Alan Morton and Rob Lynch. Adelaide, Aust.: Rigby, 1977.
137p; illus; pbk
(Seal books; Australian sports series)　ISBN: 0727003461
BL: X.629/22902

262 Rugby handbook / D. H. Craven. New ed. Wakefield: EP Publishing, 1977.
9, 250p　　ISBN: 0715806165
BL: X.629/11463

☞　Previous ed. F244

263 Better rugby for boys / D. Cyril Joynson. 3rd ed. reprinted with corrections. London: Kaye and Ward, 1978.
95p; illus　　ISBN: 0718214609
BL: X.629/12302

☞　Previous ed. F239

264 It's rugby: an introduction, or, C'est le rugby: une introduction / D. W. Roberts. Ottawa, Can.: Canadian Rugby Union, 1978.
12p; pbk
Bilingual English and French text.

265 Murray's guide to rugby union: a how-to-play book of the game / compiled by Bob Ryan. Ultimo, Aust.: Murray, 1978.
136p; illus; pbk　　SBN: 855664053
Covers the history of the game, the equipment needed, positional play, and teaching yourself the game.

266 Rygbi. Llanelli: Gwerin, 1978.
2, 85p; illus; pbk　　BL: P.611/806

267 Total rugby: 15-man rugby for coach and player / Jim Greenwood. London: Lepus, 1978.
xii, 282p; illus; index　　ISBN: 086019034X
BL: X.629/11764

☞　Subsequent ed. F320

268 Creative rugby: how to improve your game / J. J. Stewart. Petone, NZ: John Paul, 1979.
119p; illus　　ISBN: 0908585020

269 Rugby / John Hopkins. London: Cassell, 1979.
192p; illus; index
(The Schweppes leisure library sport)　ISBN: 0304302996
BL: X.622/12175

270 Rugby: a guide for players, coaches, and spectators / A. Jon Prusmack. New York, US: Hawthorn Books, 1979.
ix, 182p; illus; index　　ISBN: 0801564905

271 Rugby skills / Gareth Edwards with Ian Robertson. London: Stanley Paul, 1979.
64p; illus　　ISBN: 0091400104 (cased) • 0091400112 (pbk)
BL: X.620/19004

272 Thinking rugby: the London Welsh way / Geoff Evans, Denis Horgan and Gareth James; edited by John Dawes. London: Allen and Unwin, 1979.
xvii, 172p; illus; index　　ISBN: 0047960515
BL: X.629/14428

273 Back play: an introduction. Ottawa, Can.: Canadian Rugby Union, 1980.
23p; illus; pbk
Aimed at secondary school level.

274 Centre / edited by Neil A. Pidduck; foreword by Jim Renwick. London: Published for the Rugby Football Union by Rugby Publications, 1980.
16p; pbk
(Positional skills)

275 The evolution of the teaching of rugby football and its relationship to education and physical education / D. Rutherford. University of Leicester, 1980. *Master's thesis.*

276 Flanker / edited by Neil A. Pidduck; foreword by Tony Neary. London: Published for the Rugby Football Union by Rugby Publications, 1980.
16p; pbk
(Positional skills)

277 Forward skills / Gareth Edwards with Ian Robertson. London: Stanley Paul, 1980.
64p; illus　　ISBN: 0091426103 (cased) • 0091426111 (pbk)
BL: X.622/9663

278 Full back / edited by Neil A. Pidduck; foreword by Andy Irvine. London: Published for the Rugby Football Union by Rugby Publications, 1980.
16p; pbk
(Positional skills)

279 Hooker / edited by Neil A. Pidduck; foreword by Peter Wheeler. London: Published for the Rugby Football Union by Rugby Publications, 1980.
15p; pbk
(Positional skills)

280 Lock / edited by Neil A. Pidduck; foreword by Bill Beaumont. London: Published for the Rugby Football Union by Rugby Publications, 1980.
16p; pbk
(Positional skills)

281 Mini rugby: it's the real thing / Don Rutherford. London: Rugby Football Union, 1980.
150p; illus; pbk　　ISBN: 0901123315
The book complements a 16mm film launched in the 1979-80 season by the RFU. It is aimed at coaches, teachers and young players to make full use of mini rugby as a means of developing and raising the standard of rugby.

282 No 8 / edited by Neil A. Pidduck; foreword by Derek
     Quinnell. London: Published for the Rugby Football
     Union by Rugby Publications, 1980.
     16p; pbk
     (Positional skills)

283 Outside half / edited by Neil A. Pidduck. London:
     Published for the Rugby Football Union by Rugby
     Publications, 1980.
     16p; pbk
     (Positional skills)

284 Prop / edited by Neil A. Pidduck; foreword by Fran
     Cotton. London: Published for the Rugby Football
     Union by Rugby Publications, 1980.
     16p; pbk
     (Positional skills)

285 Running rugby / Ray French; foreword by Des
     Seabrook; preface by Mike Davis; line drawings by Ken
     Tranter. London: Faber, 1980.
     80p; illus   ISBN: 0571115977 (cased) • 0571116000 (pbk)
                                              BL: X.629/14615
       Aimed at middle schools.

286 Scrum half / edited by Neil A. Pidduck; foreword by
     Terry Holmes. London: Published for the Rugby
     Football Union by Rugby Publications, 1980.
     16p; pbk
     (Positional skills)

287 Small side game. Ottawa, Can.: Canadian Rugby Union,
     1980.
     15p; illus; pbk
       Aimed at secondary school level.

288 Success in rugby / Ian Robertson. London: John
     Murray, 1980.
     96p; illus
     (Success sportsbooks)   ISBN: 0719537231
                                              BL: X.629/12860

289 Successful rugby / Malcolm Lewis. London: Letts, 1980.
     95p; illus; index; pbk
     (World of sport)   ISBN: 0850974623
                                              BL: X.629/19038
       Aimed in particular at the under-19 player,
       emphasising the principles of team play.

290 Wing / edited by Neil A. Pidduck; foreword by Mike
     Slemen. London: Published for the Rugby Football
     Union by Rugby Publications, 1980.
     16p; pbk
     (Positional skills)

291 Developing skills for rugby using grid and channel
     systems / Alan R. Morton, David Docherty, E. Gwyn
     Evans. Perth, Aust.: ACHPER, 1981.
     84p; illus

292 How to play rugby / David Norrie. London: Hamlyn, 1981.
     61p; illus, 1 plan   ISBN: 0600346595
                                              BL: X.622/11135

293 Learn rugby, play rugby: a coaching manual / edited by
     Maurice Graham and others. Sydney, Aust.: Management
     Development Publishers for Gordon Rugby Club, 1981.
     68p; illus; pbk   ISBN: 0959333703
       Produced for the Australian Rugby Football Schools
       Union by Gordon Rugby Club.

294 Rugby union back play / David Duckham with the
     assistance of Michael Blair. London: Pelham, 1981.
     110p; illus
     (Sporting skills series)   ISBN: 0720713161
                                              BL: X.629/16574

295 Rugby union captaincy / David Frost with Roger Uttley.
     London: Pelham, 1981.
     111p; illus
     (Sporting skills series)   ISBN: 0720713013
                                              BL: X.629/15582

296 Rugby union forward play / Ian McLauchlan and Bill
     Dickinson. London: Pelham, 1981.
     120p; illus
     (Sporting skills series)   ISBN: 0720712815
                                              BL: X.629/16567

297 Seven-a-side rugby including tactics suitable for
     mini-rugby / J. C. S. Bass. London: Pelham, 1981.
     143p; illus; index   ISBN: 0720713390
                                              BL: X.629/16573

298 Helping youngsters to discover rugby: national rugby
     coaching plan level 1 / R. J. P. Marks. Sydney, Aust.:
     Rothmans National Sport Foundation in co-operation
     with the Australian Rugby Football Union, 1982.
     106p; illus
     ☞ See also: F323

299 The maroon magic in simple terms / R. J. P. Marks.
     Sydney, Aust.: Rothmans National Sport Foundation in
     association with Queensland Rugby Union, 1982.
     88p; illus; pbk
       Youth coaching.

300 New Zealand rugby skills & tactics / Ivan Vodanovich,
     technical editor; Peter Coates, graphic editor. Auckland,
     NZ: Lansdowne Press, 1982.
     255p; illus
       Includes bibliography   ISBN: 0868660647

301 Rugby football: the All Black way / Ivan Vodanovich,
     technical editor; Peter Coates, graphics editor. London:
     Orbis, 1982.
     256p; illus
       Bibliography: p256   ISBN: 085613466X
                                              BL: X.622/15044

302 Rugby union / Geoff Cooke. Wakefield: EP Publishing, 1982.
144p; illus, plans
Bibliography: p144
ISBN: 0715805835 (cased) • 0715807242 (pbk)
BL: X.629/21031

303 Cais!: llyfr ar rygbi i blant ysgolion Cymru / Alun Wyn Bevan. Caernarfon: Ty ar y Graig, 1983.
71p; illus; pbk
ISBN: 0946502188
BL: X.622/20908

Welsh text for schools.

304 The effects of in-season rugby training and non-training on the physical work capacity / Hans-Oldag Daehne. University of Pretoria, SA, 1983. *Master's thesis.*

305 Focus on rugby: an international coaching book based on the television series 'Focus on rugby' / Carwyn James. London: Stanley Paul, 1983.
189p; illus; pbk
ISBN: 0091502713
BL: X.622/18279

306 International rugby for players, coaches and spectators / Don Rutherford; foreword by Bill McLaren. London: Heinemann, 1983.
143p; illus, plans; index; pbk
ISBN: 0434659150
BL: X.622/15863

307 The principles of rugby football: a manual for coaches and referees based on papers delivered at the Welsh Rugby Union centenary international conference for coaches and referees. London: Allen & Unwin, 1983.
x, 189p; illus, maps, plans
ISBN: 0047960671
BL: X.629/20603

☞ Also listed at: F70

308 Tackle rugby / Bill Beaumont with Ian Robertson. London: Stanley Paul, 1983.
93p; illus
ISBN: 0091536006 (cased) • 0091536014 (pbk)
BL: X.622/20162

309 My kind of rugby: a coaching manual / Norman McFarland. Johannesburg, SA: J. Ball, 1984.
175p; illus; pbk
ISBN: 0868500674

310 Rugby coaching the New Zealand way / Bruce Robertson and Bill Osborne; foreword by Bill Freeman. London: Hutchinson of New Zealand, 1984.
94p; illus; pbk
ISBN: 0091590116
BL: X.622/22873

311 Rugby football / Ron Tennick. London: Batsford Academic and Educational, 1984.
64p; illus, plans; index
(Competitive sports series)
Bibliography: p64
ISBN: 0713411937
BL: X.622/21637

312 Rugby union / Howard Gilfillan. Cambridge: Cambridge University Press, 1984.
56p; illus; pbk
(Sport masters)
ISBN: 0521275342
BL: X.622/20573

313 Winning rugby: a handbook for players and coaches / compiled by Pat Walsh. Auckland, NZ: Novalit Books, 1984.
218p; illus; pbk
Subsequently published: London: Macdonald, 1985. ISBN: 0356105970
ISBN: 0959770208
BL: X.629/27155

314 Doc Craven's rugby: playing and training / Danie Craven; line drawings by M. Field; translated by Paul Dobson. Cape Town, SA: HAUM, 1985.
142p
ISBN: 0798615796

315 Even better rugby / Martin Underwood, Ken Bartlett with the assistance of Ken Morley. Rev. ed. Twickenham: Rugby Football Union, 1985.
140p; illus
☞ Previous ed. F240

316 Mini-rugby: the cartoon coaching book! Book 1 / written & drawn by Rod Jordan. Beaconsfield: Ruck & Maul, 1985.
28p; chiefly illus; pbk
ISBN: 0951101706
BL: YV.1986.b.1025

317 Rugby and me / Paul du Plessis. Cape Town, SA: Tafelberg, 1985.
50p; illus; pbk
ISBN: 0624021637
Children's book. Photographs and brief text promote the game. 'Paul du Plessis' is Servan Zatarain.

318 Rugby union: the skills of the game / Barrie Corless. Marlborough: Crowood, 1985.
128p; illus; index
ISBN: 0946284067
BL: YK.1987.b.3837

319 The science of rugby football / Mike Davis and Donald Ireland. London: Pelham, 1985.
296p; illus; index
ISBN: 0720715970
BL: X.622/25512
Training exercises and drills to cover all aspects of the game.

320 Total rugby: fifteen-man rugby for coach and player / Jim Greenwood. 2nd ed. London: Black, 1985.
xii, 288p; illus; index; pbk
ISBN: 0713655607
BL: X.629/26512
☞ Previous ed. F267; subsequent ed. F353

321 My way: improve your rugby kicking skills / Naas Botha in collaboration with Nelie Smith and Wally Rautenbach. Pretoria, SA: De-Jager-HAUM, 1986.
60p; illus; pbk
ISBN: 0798609966

322 Rygbi / Alun Wyn Bevan a Mel Morgans. Talybont, Ceredigion: Y Lolfa, 1986.
84p; illus; pbk
(Dewch i chwarae)   ISBN: 0862431115
                              BL: YK.1987.a.4121

323 The second decade: national rugby coaching plan level 1 / R. J. P. Marks. Sydney, Aust.: Rothmans National Sport Foundation in co-operation with the Australian Rugby Football Union, 1986.
300p; illus
☞ See also: F298

324 Think rugby: a guide to purposeful team play / Jim Greenwood. London: Black, 1986.
240p; illus; index; pbk   ISBN: 071365631X
                              BL: YC.1986.a.5564

    ☞ Subsequent ed. F364

325 An approach to teaching rugby football for the 9-13 age group / J. M. Bates. London: University of Newcastle for the Northumberland Rugby Union, 1987.
1 looseleaf portfolio

    This emanated from a workshop organised by the University of Newcastle's Centre for Physical Education and Sport.

326 Rugby: a guide for teachers, coaches and players / New Zealand Rugby Football Union. New ed. Wellington, NZ: Government Printing Office, 1987.
95p; illus; pbk
(Sports instruction series)   ISBN: 0477013783
    ☞ Previous ed. F260

327 Rugby: a tactical appreciation / J. J. Stewart. Marlborough: Crowood, 1987.
176p; illus; pbk   ISBN: 1852230428
                              BL: YK.1988.a.5059

    ☞ Subsequent ed. F345

328 Sports instruction series. Wellington, NZ: Government Printer, 1987-
    Prepared in conjunction with the New Zealand Rugby Football Union.

329 Youth rugby guide: creating the spirit of the game / Tony Spinella. Goleta, US: The author, 1987.
57p; illus

330 Improving back play. Twickenham: Rugby Football Union, 1988.
7p; illus; pbk

331 Rugby / Donald Ireland. Hove: Wayland 1988.
64p; illus
(World of sport)   ISBN: 1852101598
                              BL: YK.1989.b.3505

    For children.

332 Rugby: the battle of the boot / G. N. Walker. Pietermaritzburg, SA: The author, 1988.
9p; pbk

    Examines the influence in rugby of the specialist kicker and questions the validity of awarding penalties. The author suggests that changing the laws will lessen the need for 'the boot' and will encourage adventurous play.

333 Get ready for rugby union: a complete training programme / Stuart Biddle and others. Marlborough: Crowood, 1989.
128p; illus; index; pbk   ISBN: 1852231904
                              BL: YK.1990.b.6239

    Divided into: rugby practices, physical fitness, nutrition, injury prevention, mental training.

    ☞ Subsequent ed. F383

334 Rugby union / Ian Morrison. London: Ward Lock, 1989.
80p; illus; index; pbk
(Play the game)   ISBN: 0706367677
                              BL: YK.1990.a.3034

    ☞ Subsequent ed. F361

335 Take up rugby union / principal contributor, John Shepherd. Huddersfield: Springfield Books, 1989.
64p; illus; pbk   ISBN: 0947655670

336 How to coach rugby football / Alan Black. London: Willow, 1990.
128p; illus

    At head of title: National Coaching Foundation
    Bibliography: p108-9
         ISBN: 0002183749 (cased) • 0002183250 (pbk)
                              BL: YK.1991.a.1742

337 Rugby / Bernie Blackall. Melbourne, Aust.: Macmillan Education, 1990.
30p; illus; index
(Young players)
         ISBN: 0333500210 (cased) • 0732901529 (pbk)
    Primary school level.

338 Rugby training / Peter Winder. London: A & C Black, 1990.
128p; illus; pbk   ISBN: 0713632674
                              BL: YK.1990.a.7497

    Designed for use by teachers and club coaches 'wishing to improve performance of players'.

339 Skills practices for all. Twickenham: Rugby Football Union, 1990?
98 looseleaf pages

340 Start coaching rugby union / compiled by H. V. White and F. A. Biscombe. Twickenham: Rugby Football Union, 1990.
40 looseleaf pages

341 Coaching accreditation manual, level 2 / edited by R. A. Guy and others. Wellington, NZ: New Zealand Rugby Football Union, 1991.
183p; illus; pbk

342 Improving attendance at rugby practice: a behavioural approach / David Scott. University of Victoria, Can:, 1991. *Master's thesis.*
87p

As might be expected, the conclusion of this study is that attendance at training sessions is affected by seasonal and personal factors.

343 Let's get into Walla rugby / Rob Bradley; illustrated by Liisa Kuisma. Surry Hills, Aust.: Aussie Sports Books, 1991.
31p; illus

For children.

344 The name of the game is – rugby union / Rob Bradley; illustrated by Liisa Kuisma. Surry Hills, Aust.: Aussie Sports Books, 1991.
63p; illus

Bibliography: p61
Aimed at secondary school students.

345 Rugby: the All Blacks' way / J. J. Stewart. Marlborough: Crowood, 1991.
162p; illus; pbk   ISBN: 1852236299
                           BL: YK.1991.b.7144

☞ Previous ed. F327

346 Rugby tactics / Peter Winder. London: Black, 1991.
128p; illus; pbk   ISBN: 0713634499
Includes a chapter on rugby sevens.

347 Skilful rugby union / Geoff Cooke. London: A & C Black, 1991.
96p; illus; index; pbk   ISBN: 0713634448

348 What times [i.e. time] does the bus leave?: concepts in rugby team management / David Lewis. Canberra, Aust.: Australian Sports Commission, 1991.
2 vols.

☞ Subsequent ed. F375

349 An investigation into player management and development of top class Welsh rugby / Victoria Constantine. Cardiff Institute of Higher Education, 1992. *Master's thesis.*

350 Rugby / Chris Jones; foreword by Roger Uttley. London: Ward Lock, 1992.
80p; illus; index; pbk
(Tactics of success)   ISBN: 0706371003
                           BL: YK.1993.a.8526

351 Rugby Football Union: cross curricular project for primary schools. Twickenham: The Union, 1992.
81 leaves

352 Staged development of rugby union football for players in the 8-18 age group, June 1992. Edinburgh: Scottish Rugby Union, 1992.
12p

353 Total rugby: fifteen-man rugby for coach and player / Jim Greenwood. 3rd ed. London: Black, 1992.
viii, 312p; illus; index; pbk   ISBN: 071363443X
                                   BL: YK.1992.a.1803

Examines the new laws and gives advice on individual and team skills and fitness tips.

☞ Previous ed. F320; subsequent ed. F395

354 Winning rugby / Roger Uttley. London: Stanley Paul, 1992.
126p; illus; pbk   ISBN: 0091740525
                           BL: YK.1993.b.1213

355 The complete book of mini rugby / Don Rutherford; foreword by Will Carling. London: Partridge, 1993.
253p; pbk   ISBN: 1852251964
                           BL: YK.1994.a.12189

Aims to simplify the game of mini rugby for teachers, coaches, parents and players who are involved with coaching youngsters.

356 Play England rugby: a cross-curricular project for secondary schools. Sunderland: University of Sunderland, 1993?

357 Rugby / David Jennings. Dunstable: Folens, 1993.
48p; illus; spiral   ISBN: 1852764058
                           BL: YK.1995.b.3434

358 Rugby / Terence O'Rorke. Hove: Wayland, 1993.
48p; illus
(Go for sport)   ISBN: 0750208686
                           BL: YK.1993.b.14181

For children.

RUGBY *FOR*
THREE-QUARTERS
with Richard Hill

Peter Johnson

359 Rugby for three-quarters with Richard Hill / Peter Johnson. London: A & C Black, 1993.
xi, 114p; illus; index; pbk   ISBN: 071363782X
                                 BL: YK.1994.a.11040

360   Rugby union / Gill Lloyd and David Jefferis. Hove:
Wayland, 1993.
32p; illus   ISBN: 0750207000
                                  BL: YK.1994.b.2603

      For children.

361   Rugby union / Ian Morrison. Rev. ed. London:
Blandford, 1993.
80p; illus; index; pbk
(Play the game)   ISBN: 0713724188
                                  BL: YK.1993.a.14787

      ☞   Previous ed. F334

362   Rugby union: the skills of the game / Barrie Corless.
Marlborough: Crowood, 1993.
121p; illus; index   ISBN: 1852237686

363   Talent identification: a guide to selection. Abertillery:
Published on behalf of the England Rugby Football
Schools' Union by Old Bakehouse, 1993.
                                  ISBN: 187453800X

364   Think rugby: a guide to purposeful team play / Jim
Greenwood. 2nd ed. London: Black, 1993.
viii, 240p; pbk   ISBN: 0713637811
                                  BL: YK.1994.a.762

      ☞   Previous ed. F324

365   Working for rugby on and off the field: conference
report, Taunton School, July 1993. London: Sports
Council, 1993.

366   Blackheath FC mini rugby coaches' handbook.
Blackheath: The Club, 1994.

367   Coaching and medical manual 1994-95. Edinburgh:
Scottish Rugby Union, 1994.
40p; pbk

368   Hard-core rugby: tough men in a tough game / Bryan
Williams and others. London: Blandford, 1994.
155p   ISBN: 0713725001
                                  BL: YK.1995.b.6757

      Instructional; covers all playing positions, explaining
      the technique and tactics of the modern game.

369   Pick me up and run: a simple guide to rugby / David
O'Neil; illustrations by Scott Rigney; introduction by
David Campese. St Leonards, Aust.: Winky Press, 1994.
93p; illus; pbk   ISBN: 0646173332

      This lighthearted guide to rugby for newcomers to the
      game is endorsed by the Australian Rugby Football
      Union.

370   Planning for rugby union: a workbook for rugby coaches
and also for candidates on the RFU coaching award
scheme / edited by Penny Crisfield. Leeds: National
Coaching Foundation, 1994.
90 looseleaf pages   ISBN: 0947850988

371   Rugby / David Marshall. Oxford: Heinemann Library, 1994.
30p
(Successful sports)   ISBN: 043107433X
                                  BL: YK.1995.b.5891

372   Rugby lesson plans for three-quarters / Peter Johnson
with Jonathan Webb. London: Black, 1994.
110p; illus; index; pbk   ISBN: 0713640413
                                  BL: YK.1995.a.7885

373   Rugby skills / Will Carling with Ian Robertson.
Harpenden: Queen Anne Press, 1994.
128p; illus; pbk   ISBN: 1852915552
                                  BL: YK.1996.b.5850

374   Rugby union national coaching scheme level 1 / R. J. P.
Marks. Sydney, Aust.: Rothmans of Pall Mall, 1994.

375   What time does the bus leave?: concepts in rugby team
management / David Lewis. 2nd ed. Canberra, Aust.:
Australian Sports Commission, 1994.
77p; illus   ISBN: 0642222142

      Published under the auspices of the Australian
      Institute of Sport, Rugby Union. Includes excerpts
      from the Australian Rugby Football Union player's
      manual on banned and permitted drugs; and
      information on the legal liabilities of coaches.

      ☞   Previous ed. F348

376   Youth rugby: seal of approval. Winchester: Hampshire
Rugby Football Union, 1994.

377   101 rugby training drills / Ray Unsworth & Damian
McGrath. Cambridge?: White Horse, 1995.
53p; illus

378   Ben Clarke's rugby skills: a complete step-by-step guide
/ specially commissioned photography by Action Plus.
London: Hamlyn, 1995.
64p; illus; index; pbk   ISBN: 0600585115
                                  BL: YK.1996.b.645

379   The handbook of rugby / edited by Keith Miles;
contributors, Dusty Hare and others. London: Pelham, 1995.
207p; illus; index
      Bibliography: p202   ISBN: 0720719240
                                  BL: YK.1995.b.11443

380   The RFU journal: a technical insight into the game /
features editor Keith Bouser. Twickenham: Rugby
Football Union, September 1995.
32p; illus

      Eleven authors, including, Lisa Piearce, contribute
      articles on the management view, refereeing the 1995
      World Cup Final, nutrition — food for thought,
      motivation and team building, team play and
      performance, skills tests in rugby football, refereeing
      — an art or science?

      ☞   Also listed at: I198

381 Rugby Football Union preliminary coaching awards: tutor's pack. Twickenham: Rugby Football Union, 1995. 3 vols in folder

> *Contents: course handbook; tutor's notes; preliminary coaching award*

382 Rugby, the game: understanding developments in the field of play / J. J. Stewart. Palmerston North, NZ: Dept. of Management Systems, Massey University, 1995. xi, 84p; illus; pbk
(Occasional papers / Massey University, Dept. of Management Systems; 1995, no. 1)   ISBN: 0958341648

383 Rugby training: includes 100 practice drills / Stuart Biddle and others. Marlborough: Crowood, 1995. 128p; illus; index; pbk

> *Bibliography: 124-125*   ISBN: 1852238976
> BL: YK.1996.b.4012

> ☞ Previous ed. F333

384 Running rugby / Mark Ella and Philip Derriman. London: ABC Books for the Australian Broadcasting Corporation, 1995. 192p; illus   ISBN: 0733303595

385 Teaching students to play games 11-16: a resource for secondary teachers: rugby union football / project leader, Brenda Read. London: Sports Council, 1995? 40p; illus; pbk   ISBN: 1860780881
BL: YK.1996.b.8557

A manual which advises secondary school teachers on organising and teaching rugby as part of the national curriculum. Includes lesson plans and skills cards.

386 Try running!: a strategy for success in school rugby / Neil Emslie; illustrations by Tony Grogan. Port Elizabeth, SA: SA Bottling Company, 1995. 51p; illus; pbk   ISBN: 0620188952

387 Working with children. Twickenham: National Coaching Foundation, 1995.
> ☞ Subsequent ed. F389

388 Sport team leadership: coaching and captaincy in elite rugby union football / Robin C. McConnell. University of Waikato, NZ, 1996. *Doctoral thesis.* xvii, 671 leaves

389 Working with children in rugby union / edited by D. Houlston and A. Simpkin. Rev. ed. Leeds: National Coaching Foundation, 1996.   ISBN: 0947850589
> ☞ Previous ed. F387

390 Heading for the top: rugby for ambitious young players / Kerry Wedd; foreword by Jack Rowell; coaching advice and contributions from Brian Ashton and Richard Greenwood; international photographs by Russell Cheyne (courtesy of The Daily Telegraph). London: Quiller, 1997. viii, 87p; illus
ISBN: 1899163352 (coaching ed) • 1899163328 (pbk)

391 Modern rugby: the essential concepts and skills / Gerrit Pool. Cape Town, SA: Tafelberg, 1997. 119p; illus; pbk   ISBN: 0624032744

392 Off-season & pre-season training guide: injury free to be your best. Wellington, NZ: ACC Injury Prevention Services, New Zealand Rugby Union, 1997? 10p; illus; pbk   ISBN: 0478102437

393 Rugby for heroes: skills and techniques / Norman Harris; edited by Emrys Bowen; illustrated by Paul Trevillion. Godmanchester: Buckley-Bennion, 1997. 96p; illus; pbk   ISBN: 1901575004

394 Rugby union: technique, tactics, training / Peter Johnson. Malborough: Crowood, 1997. 121p; illus; index; pbk
(Crowood sports guides)

> *Includes bibliography*   ISBN: 1861260288
> BL: YK.1998.b.5532

395 Total rugby / Jim Greenwood. 4th ed. London: A & C Black, 1997. ix, 342p; illus; index; pbk   ISBN: 0713645458
BL: YK.1998.a.3973

> ☞ Previous ed. F353

396 Two-handed take / Martin McQuibban. London: Minerva, 1997. 344p; pbk   ISBN: 1858638801

397 Zinzan Brooke's competitive edge: a guide to training, toughness and sports nutrition / Lee Parore. Auckland, NZ: Celebrity Books, 1997. 102p; illus; pbk   ISBN: 0958364435

Fitness

398 Body size, strength, muscular endurance and power of top-flight English rugby and soccer players / C. R. Tattersfield. University of Oregon, US, 1963. *Master's thesis.*

399 Comparison of physical fitness of senior high school American football and English rugby athletes / G. J. Haensgen. University of Oregon, US, 1969. *Master's thesis.*

400 Power rugby: strength and fitness training / Tom Hudson. Swansea: Sports Forum, 1969.
68p; illus; pbk
(Power books; no. 1)   BL: X.619/9973

401 Fitness training for rugby. Twickenham: Rugby Football Union, 1978.
51p; illus; pbk   BL: DSC84/21330

402 Rugby. Ontario, Can.: Ontario Ministry of Culture and Recreation, Sports and Fitness Division, 1979.
9p; pbk

403 Fitness for training / edited by Don Rutherford. Twickenham: Rugby Football Union, 1983.
59p; illus; spiral   ISBN: 0901123285

404 Fit for rugby / Bev Risman; general editor Peter Verney; medical adviser Alan Maryon-Davis. London: Batsford, 1984.
96p; illus; index   ISBN: 0713442433

405 Fitness training for rugby / Michael Ardagh. New Zealand: Caxton, 1988.
32p   ISBN: 0908563264

406 Jim Blair's rugby fitness / Jim Blair. Auckland, NZ: SETO, 1990.
64p; illus   ISBN: 0908697554

407 Strength training for rugby league and rugby union / Bruce Walsh. Kenthurst, Aust.: Kangaroo Press, 1990.
135p; illus; pbk   ISBN: 0864172931

408 Fit for rugby / Rex Hazeldine and Tom McNab. London: Kingswood, 1991.
128p; illus; index; pbk   ISBN: 0413660109
                                         BL: YK.1991.b.8274

   Foreword by Don Rutherford.

409 Rugby / Jim Golby. London: Ward Lock, 1991.
80p; pbk
(Fit for the game)   ISBN: 0706369343
                                         BL: YK.1991.a.10463

410 The repeated high intensity jump test: a test developed for rugby union / Neil Harray. University of Otago, NZ, 1993. *Thesis.*
vii, 66 leaves; illus

411 Reebok fit for rugby / Jason Dance. Lancaster: Reebok UK, 1994.
28p; illus; pbk
(Fit for series)   BL: YK.1996.a.7868

412 Fitness manual for developing players / prepared by David McLean. Edinburgh: Scottish Rugby Union, 1995?
28p; illus

413 Rugby: fitness, testing & training: a scientific approach for coaches, fitness trainers and players / Richard Turnbull, Derik Coetzee and Theo McDonald. Scottsville, SA: R. Turnbull, 1995.
xii, 116p; illus; pbk   ISBN: 0620189428

   Endorsed by the South African Rugby Football Union.

Injury & Sports Medicine

414 The kinetics of rugby scrumming and the neck's force: capabilities as a cause of cervical spinal injuries / Davis-Etienne Du Toit. University of Port Elizabeth, SA. *Doctoral thesis.*

415 Rugby & sports medicine / Peter G. Stokes. Wellington, NZ: Alister Taylor, 1973.
94p; illus

   Bibliography: p94

416 International congress on injuries in rugby football and other team sports, Dublin, April 15th-18th 1975: collected papers and discussions with chapters on first aid etc. / compiled and arranged by Thos. C. J. 'Bob' O'Connell. Dublin: Irish Rugby Football Union, 1976.
333p; illus; pbk

   Spine title: Injuries in rugby football and other team sports
   At head of title: IRFU, 1874-1974   ISBN: 0950495506
                                         BL: X.319/16944

   A collection of papers on: physical preparation; analysis of risk; injuries and their treatment; first aid; statistical review of injuries; prevention of injuries; insurance; rehabilitation. Also covers topics like the danger of boot studs and touch flags, and the role of the referee.

417 The investigation into pain threshold, pain tolerance and augmentation reduction levels among rugby players / Hector Tahu. Brigham Young University, 1980. *Thesis.*
97 leaves

418 Rugby injuries / Tony Dunnill and Muir Gray. School ed. London: Edward Arnold, 1982.
xviii, 203p; illus; index; pbk   ISBN: 0713108479
BL: X.329/16068

419 Schoolboy rugby union injuries: a survey conducted by the Australian Schools' Rugby Union: report, conclusions and recommendations. Canberra, Aust.: The Union, 1983.
60p; illus

420 Bibliography on rugby injuries / compiled by Patricia Coleman, Jonathon Nicholl. Sheffield: Medical Care Research Unit, University of Sheffield Medical School, 1988.
☞ Also listed at: I17

421 Prematch anxiety levels and rates of injury in rugby / David Scott. University of Victoria, Can., 1988.

422 A study of the etiology, nature and incidence of injury in the 1988 Auckland Division 1 Senior Club Rugby Competition / Nicholas Ewart. University of Alberta, Can., 1989. *Master's thesis.*

423 The epidemiology of schoolboy rugby injuries / Charles Edward Roux. University of Cape Town, SA, 1992. *Master's thesis.*

424 Injuries in Edmonton rugby union: an epidemiological study / Leigh Garvie. University of Alberta, Can., 1992. *Master's thesis.*
129p

The study establishes the rate of injury at different levels of the game, the most common cause and location of injury and the effects of injury on the players' game. It also considers whether playing conditions, player positions and training impact in any way.

425 Medico-legal hazards of rugby union / edited by Simon D. W. Payne. Oxford: Blackwell Special Projects, 1992.
xv, 188p

Produced with the support of the Welsh Rugby Union
ISBN: 0632031832
BL: (B) HH 17(H)

Two of the 13 contributors are also consultant editors. Edward Grayson, a barrister, contributes a chapter on sports medicine and the law, and John Davies who is the medical director of Harley Street Sports Clinic, is also Honorary Physician to the Welsh Rugby Union and a member of the International Board Advisory Committee. Topics include the role of team doctors and physiotherapists, drug abuse, AIDS and HIV, and injuries in rugby.

426 The prevention of injuries: rugby / Helen Millson. Port Elizabeth, SA: The author, 1993.
50p; illus

427 Epidemiology of schoolboy rugby injuries at Craven Week 1993 / Ismail Jakoet. University of Pretoria, SA, 1994. *Master's thesis.*

Surveys the level and nature of injuries received by 600 schoolboys taking part in a youth rugby tournament.

428 Football injuries of the head and neck / National Health and Medical Research Council. Canberra, Aust.: Australian Government Publishing Service, 1994.
xvi, 134p; illus; pbk

Bibliography: p128-34   ISBN: 0644427116

429 Head and facial lacerations in rugby players / Gustav Johan Joyce. University of Pretoria, SA, 1994. *Master's thesis.*

A study to determine the incidence of this type of injury and how long injured players are out of the game.

430 Football injuries in Australia: a survey and comparison of the Australian Football League, New South Wales Rugby League, New South Wales Rugby Union and Victorian State Football League / Hugh Seward and others. Belconnen, Aust.: National Sports Research Centre, 1995.
29p; pbk
(Scientific report)

Bibliography: p22-3   ISBN: 0642227101

431 Head and neck injuries in football: guidelines for prevention and management: Australian football, rugby union, rugby league, soccer. Canberra, Aust.: Australian Government Publishing Service, 1995.
iii, 253p; illus; pbk

Accompanied by: Concussion: notes for referees, umpires and coaches, in back pocket   ISBN: 0644429321

432 Rugby without risk: a practical guide to the prevention and treatment of rugby injuries / Tim Noakes and Morné du Plessis. Pretoria, SA: van Schaik, 1996.
xvi, 351p; illus   ISBN 0627019471

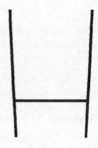

✽   *Additional References*

433   Medicine, sport and the law / edited by Simon D. W.
      Payne. London: Blackwell Scientific, 1990.
      352p; pbk   ISBN: 0632024399
                                                     BL: YK.1990.b.8096

      Rugby union is among the specific topics addressed.

434   ABC of sports medicine / edited by Greg McLatchie,
      Mark Harries, Clyde Williams, J. B. King with
      contributions from Richard Budgett and others.
      London: BMJ, 1995.
      vii, 109p; illus; index; pbk   ISBN: 0727908448
                                                     BL: YK.1996.b.1342

The Science of Rugby

435   A norm study in respect of neck strength in under-19
      schoolboy rugby forwards in the East Cape region / Lisa
      Paula Buckley. University of Port Elizabeth, SA. *Master's
      thesis.*

436   Analysis of rugby in Vancouver, British Columbia by
      statistical itemization of fundamentals / D. B. Howie.
      University of Oregon, US, 1970. *Master's thesis.*

437   Construction of a written knowledge test on rugby union
      football for secondary schoolboys / George T. Berwick.
      University College of Wales, 1971.
      223p

        Five chapters: the problem; review of related literature;
        procedure; results; summary and conclusions.

438   A kinematic and electromyographic analysis of the rugby
      punt using the preferred and non-preferred foot /
      Anthony Bauer. University of Alberta, Can., 1981.
      Doctoral thesis.

439   Attentional styles in rugby players / Ian W. Maynard.
      University of Victoria, Can., 1986.

440   A biomechanical analysis of the efficiency and safety of
      various rugby union scrummaging techniques: coaches
      report: a report presented to the Australian Sports
      Commission's Applied Sports Research Program / Peter
      D. Milburn. Australia: National Sports Research
      Program, 1986.
      26p; illus; spiral

        Bibliography: p25-6   BL: DSCq96/24608

441   The effect of imagery on tackling performance in rugby
      / Alex D. McKenzie. University of Victoria, Can., 1989.

442   The biomechanics of rugby scrummaging: a report to the
      Australian Rugby Football Union and the New Zealand
      Rugby Football Union, September 1990 / Peter D.
      Milburn. Wollongong?: Department of Human
      Movement Science, University of Wollongong, 1990.
      115p; illus; pbk

        Bibliography: p85-9   BL: DSCq96/24609

443   The effects of imagery on rugby goal kicking
      performance / Scott D. Pickford. University of Otago,
      NZ, 1994. *Thesis.*
      vii, 69 leaves; illus

444   Relationship of sprint running times with optimized and
      non-optimized power output protocols in rugby union
      players / Non Eleri Evans. Cardiff Institute of Higher
      Education, 1994. *Master's thesis.*
      207 leaves

445   The applied physiology of the elite rugby union player /
      Adrian J. J. Lombard. University of the Witwatersrand,
      SA, 1995. *Master's thesis.*

446   The relationship between communication and cohesion
      in inter-collegiate rugby players / Philip Joseph Sullivan.
      University of Windsor, Can., 1995. *Master's thesis.*

447   Variable-interval schedule of conditioned reinforcement
      and practising behavior of two rugby kicking skills /
      Brendan James Hoko. University of Victoria, 1995.
      Master's thesis.

✽   *Additional References*

448   The physics of ball games / C. B. Daish. London:
      English Universities Press, 1972.
      180p; illus; index   ISBN: 0340053992

        Divided into two parts, the book is aimed at 'players,
        commentators, students and scientists [who] will
        find the book to be a most instructive and
        entertaining account of the scientific principles
        governing ball games'. The first part analyses events
        which occur in games and the second part deals with
        the mathematical treatment of these topics.
        Outlined is the behaviour of the rugby ball when kicked
        – range, swerve and movement in the air.

449 Playing on their nerves: the sport experiment / Angela
Patmore. London: Stanley Paul, 1979.
272p; illus; index   ISBN: 0091395100
                                                      BL: X.629/12755

An examination of the pressure of top level sports
and its effect on the sportsman. Among the rugby
interviewees are Gareth Edwards and J. P. R.
Williams.

450 First World Congress of Science and Football,
Liverpool, 13-17 April 1987 organized from Liverpool
Polytechnic and held at the Albert Dock, Liverpool.
London: Spon, 1988.
xx, 651p; illus; index   ISBN: 0419143602
                                                      BL: DSC8134.005

Although the papers given at this important first
conference concentrated mostly on association
football, there was also some notable rugby content
on fitness test profiling.

451 Intermittent high intensity exercise: preparation, stresses
and damage limitation / edited by D.A.D. Macleod, R. J.
Maughan, C. Williams, C. R. Madeley, J. C. M. Sharp, R.
W. Nutton. London: Spon, 1993.
xiii, 605p; illus; index   ISBN: 0419178600
                                                      BL: YK.1993.b.9187

Contains selected papers from two scientific and
medical conferences which took place in Edinburgh
during the 1991 Rugby World Cup. The presentations
cover all sports but with particular emphasis on
rugby, football, and hockey.

452 Science and football II: proceedings of the second World
Congress of Science and Football, Eindhoven,
Netherlands 22nd-25th May 1991 / edited by T. Reilly, J.
Clarys and A. Stibbe. London: Spon, 1993.
xx, 480p; illus; index   ISBN: 0419178503
                                                      BL: YK.1993.b.6232

Papers include: D. J. Holmyard and R. J. Hazeldine on
'Seasonal variations in the anthropometric and
physiological characteristics of international rugby
union players'; W. Bell, D. Cobner, S-M. Cooper and
S. J. Phillips on 'Anaerobic performance and body
composition of international rugby union players';
W. J. Kirby and T. Reilly on 'Anthropometric and
fitness profiles of elite female rugby union players';
Werner Kuhn on 'A comparative analysis of selected
motor performance variables in American football,
rugby union and soccer players'.

453 Serum creatine phosphikinase changes in running,
football and rugby: an intergroup comparison / Mary
Kelly. Dublin: Cospoir, 1993.
23p; illus

Includes bibliography
At head of cover title: COSPOIR Sports Research Committee,
Department of Education

454 Science and football III: proceedings of the Third World
Congress of Science and Football Cardiff, Wales 9-13
April 1995 / edited by T. Reilly, J. Bangsbo and M.
Hughes. London: E & F N Spon, 1997.
xiv, 339p; illus; index   ISBN: 0419221603
                                                      BL: DSC8134.005

Includes several papers on the rugby union game
covering fitness test profiles of players, metabolism and
nutrition, training, medical aspects, and management
and organisation of the game.

Rugby &
Society

Contents

Racism

1 No Maoris, no tour: New Zealand protests, 1959-60: the case for CABTA (Citizens All Black Tour Association). Wellington, NZ: The Association, 1960.
15p; pbk

The story of the protest movement against the exclusion of Maori players from the 1960 New Zealand rugby team to tour South Africa.

2 The 1965 South African rugby tour of New Zealand: an appeal to conscience / Citizens' Association for Racial Equality. Auckland, NZ: Dobbie, 1965.
4p

3 The whole world watches: a record of Wellington protests against the All Black tour Thursday, Friday, Saturday June 11,12,13, 1970 / edited by Lyn Brooke-White, Alister Taylor and Chris Taylor. Wellington, NZ: Cockerell, 1970.

4 Don't play with apartheid: the background to the Stop the Seventy Tour campaign / Peter Hain. London: Allen & Unwin, 1971.
231p; index

Bibliography: p228　　ISBN: 0043010318
　　　　　　　　　　　BL: X.809/9013

5 The whole world watched: anti-apartheid, Queensland, Australia 1971 / Mark Steer. Torwood, Aust.: K. Howard, 1971.
84p; illus; pbk

Focuses on the demonstrations which accompanied the South African Springbok tour of 1971.

6 Political football: the Springbok tour of Australia, 1971 / Stewart Harris. Melbourne, Aust.: Gold Star, 1972.
256p; illus; pbk　　ISBN: 0726000175

'A football series in June and July of 1971 split the country. Young against old, black against white, students and trade unions against the government...'. Harris, Australian correspondent for The Times, toured the country with the South Africans, and was arrested during the demonstrations. This is a personal account of the events.

7 Attitudes towards the 1973 Springbok tour of New Zealand: an exploratory survey of attitudes to issues associated with the proposed tour, and the relationship between these attitudes and other variables / Alastair D. Pain. University of Canterbury, NZ, 1973. *Master's thesis*.
142p; illus

8 Springbok rugby tour: correspondence between the Prime Minister and the New Zealand Rugby Football Union, January-February 1973. Wellington, NZ: A. R. Shearer, Government Printer, 1973.
15p

Includes the statement by the General Assembly on Apartheid in Sports, signed 1997th plenary meeting, 29 November 1971.

Don't Play with Apartheid

The Background to the
Stop The Seventy Tour Campaign

by PETER HAIN

London · George Allen & Unwin Ltd
RUSKIN HOUSE MUSEUM STREET

9 Sinners at the stadium / Robert Fenton. Hastings, NZ: Ethos, 1974.
206p; illus

A critique of the anti-apartheid protests during New Zealand's sporting (mainly rugby) contacts with South Africa and Rhodesia.

10 Stop the 1976 tour. Wellington, NZ: P. Tyler for Halt All Racist Tours Movement, 1976.
6p; pbk

11 A whole new ball game: Norman Kirk's decision to stop the 1973 Springbok tour / John Alan Lipscombe. University of Auckland, NZ, 1979. *Master's thesis*
iv, 122 leaves

12 1981 Springbok tour of New Zealand: demonstrators handbook. Northern ed. Gisborne-Whangarei, Auckland, NZ: M.O.S.T., 1981.
25p; illus, maps; pbk

13   Barbed wire Boks / Don Cameron. Auckland, NZ: Rugby Press, 1981.
239p; illus   ISBN: 0908630050

The Springboks in New Zealand 1981. Cameron's book '...looks closely at all the aspects of the tour, and the problems it will leave behind. It looks at the Springboks themselves, and the demonstrators; the rugby officials, the police and the media...'.

14   By batons and barbed wire: a response to the 1981 Springbok tour of New Zealand / Tom Newnham. Auckland, NZ: Graphic Publications, 1981.
96p; illus; pbk

From the protestors' point of view.
☞ Subsequent ed. G23

15   The projected 1981 South African rugby tour of New Zealand: an eleventh-hour appeal for action on a major foreign policy issue of the day: addressed to the men and women of New Zealand's Foreign Service / H. J. Evans. Christchurch, NZ: 1981.
1 folded sheet

16   Proposed 1981 Springbok rugby tour of New Zealand. Wellington, NZ: Ministry of Foreign Affairs, 1981.
57p; pbk
(Special bulletin / New Zealand Ministry of Foreign Affairs; 1981/2)

17   Report and recommendation to the Prime Minister on representations regarding the proposed Springbok rugby tour of New Zealand. Wellington, NZ: Human Rights Commission, 1981.
12 leaves

18   Springbok tour: report to Prime Minister on representations on the proposed Springbok tour. Wellington, NZ: Human Rights Commission, 1981.
12 leaves

19   56 days: a history of the anti-tour movement in Wellington / editors, Geoff Walker, Peter Beach; contributors, Mark Stevens and others; photographers, Stephen A'Court and others. Wellington, NZ: Lindsay Wright on behalf of Citizens Opposed to the Springbok Tour (COST), 1982.
96p; illus; pbk   BL: YA.1989.b.1412

A record of the protestors' activities during the Springboks tour of New Zealand in 1981.

20   Operation Rugby, 19 July-13 September 1981 / New Zealand Police. Wellington, NZ: Police Headquarters, 1982.
130, 88 leaves; illus   BL: CSG700/818

21   The Red Squad story / Ross Meurant. Auckland, NZ: Harlen, 1982.
215p; illus, maps   ISBN: 0908630069

The police riot squad, the Red Escort Group, accompanied the South African side on their first rugby tour of New Zealand for 15 years. Meurant who was second in command of the police squad chronicles events throughout the tour: the public demonstrations and subsequent violence, the handling of these events by the accompanying police squad; the media's reportage of the events; the disbandment of the police group and criticism of its methods.

22   With all our strength: an account of the anti-tour movement in Christchurch 1981 / Juliet Morris. Christchurch, NZ: Black Cat, 1982.
133p; illus; pbk

23   By batons and barbed wire: a response to the 1981 Springbok tour of New Zealand / Tom Newnham; edited by Frank Stark; picture editor and captions, Tom Hutchins. 2nd ed. Auckland, NZ: Real Pictures, 1983.
96p; illus   ISBN: 0473002531 (cased) • 0473001128 (pbk)
BL: YA.1988.b.3313

From the protestors' point of view.
☞ Previous ed. G14

24   Report of the Chief Ombudsman on the investigation of complaints against the police arising from the South African rugby tour of New Zealand in 1981. Wellington, NZ: The Ombudsman, 1983.
130p

25   The scheduled 1985 New Zealand rugby tour of South Africa: HART, NZAAM's assessment of the position of the New Zealand government, the New Zealand Rugby Football Union, and the urgent need for a strong international response. Wellington, NZ: HART, 1983.
16 leaves; pbk

26   The dilemma of the All Black tour of South Africa 1985 / E. Te R. Tauroa. Auckland, NZ: Race Relations Conciliator, 1985.
11 leaves; unbound

27   The police and the 1981 tour: a survey of police attitudes: a report on Molesworth Street. Wellington, NZ: University of Wellington, 1985.
52p; pbk
(Occasional papers / Victoria University of Wellington, History Dept. ISSN: 0112-1774; no. 2)

Contents: 'The police and the tour' by Louise Greig; 'A report on the Molesworth Street incident' by Rachel Barrowman.

28   The possible dream in South Africa: an illustrated
      brochure showing the great All Black Springbok
      tradition, and why South Africa's participation in
      international rugby should be not only permitted, but
      positively encouraged. Newlands, SA: South African
      Rugby Board, 1985.
      20p; illus; pbk

      A presentation compiled by the South African Rugby
      Board highlighting the changes that have occurred in
      South African rugby. 'Significant [changes] are that
      non-whites can now sit anywhere in the grounds, and
      the Executive Committee of the South African Rugby
      Board and the Selection Committee now contains
      "non-whites"! We in the South African Rugby Board
      say: "Don't just take our word, come and see for
      yourself. We do not want visits from destructive
      critics or apologists, we want constructive dialogue." '

29   SPRI: New Zealand Organisation for Sporting Freedom.
      Christchurch, NZ: SPRI, 1985.
      12p; illus

30   Rugby, race and religion: the Catholic Church and
      controversy over sporting relations with South Africa,
      1959-1981 / S. G. Brosnahan. University of Canterbury,
      NZ, 1986. *Master's thesis.*
      292 leaves

31   Race and rugby in South Africa. Pretoria, SA: Australian
      Embassy, 1988.
      18p; pbk

32   Rugby integrasie, or, Rugby integration. Cape Town, SA:
      South African Rugby Board, 1988.
      32p; pbk

      In Afrikaans (16 pages) and English (16 pages). This
      was the year of full integration and this brochure
      summarises the decisions made by the South African
      Rugby Board.

33   You're black, you're quick, you're on the wing: a
      sociological analysis of the experience of England's elite,
      black rugby union players / Mike Wedderburn.
      Loughborough University, 1989. *Master's thesis.*

34   Rugby and politics / Kevin Boon; edited by Allan R.
      Kirk. Wellington, NZ: Kotuku, 1993.
      24p; illus; pbk
      (The story of the All Blacks; 11)   ISBN: 0908947046
        For children.

35   Trifling with their games: Australian reactions to the
      1971 South African rugby tour / David Ward. University
      of New South Wales, Aust., 1993. *Thesis*

36   'A colour line affair': race, imperialism and rugby
      football contacts between New Zealand and South
      Africa to 1950 / Mike Buckley. University of Canterbury,
      NZ, 1996. *Master's thesis.*
      iii, 129 leaves

✱   *Additional References*

37   Race and sport / Richard H. T. Thompson. London:
      Oxford University Press, 1964.
      73p   BL: 7926.s.51

      The writer lectured in psychology at the University of
      Canterbury in New Zealand. In the opening chapter he
      writes on sport and race relations. He then goes on
      to examine the exclusion of Maori players from the
      New Zealand All Blacks team which toured South
      Africa in 1960. The book was issued under the
      auspices of the Institute of Race Relations in London.

38   Race discrimination in New Zealand-South African
      sports tours: a bibliography / Richard Thompson.
      Christchurch, NZ: University of Canterbury, 1966.
      23p; pbk

      In the sporting tours to the respective countries,
      non-white participants have been excluded. In 1967 the
      New Zealand Rugby Union took a stance by advocating
      the inclusion of Maori players in the side to tour
      South Africa, otherwise the tour would be cancelled.

      ☞ Also listed at: I21; subsequent ed. G39

39   Race discrimination in New Zealand-South African sports
      tours: a revised bibliography / Richard Thompson.
      Christchurch, NZ: University of Canterbury, 1972.
      59p; pbk

      Revised and updated, the sixth and final chapter is
      on rugby and covers the period October 1958 to
      December 1972.

      ☞ Also listed at: I22; previous ed. G38

40   Retreat from apartheid: New Zealand's sporting contacts
      with South Africa / Richard Thompson. Wellington,
      NZ, London: Oxford University Press, 1975.
      vii, 102p; pbk   ISBN: 0195580133
                                             BL: X.519/25783

      Documents the story of apartheid, shedding light on
      the place of sport in New Zealand society. A great
      deal of the content is on the rugby contact between
      New Zealand and South Africa.

41   Black and white / Donald Woods; with a foreword by
      Conor Cruise O'Brien. Dublin: Ward River Press, 1981.
      142p; pbk   ISBN: 0907085121
                                             BL: X.529/41333

      The story of the controversy over sporting links with
      South Africa: what rugby means to the South
      Africans, how apartheid works in sport, and how
      'integration' was progressing.

42   The South African game: sport and racism / Robert
      Archer and Antoine Bouillon. London: Zed, 1982.
      viii, 352p; illus; index
      (Africa series)
        Bibliography: p337-45
          ISBN: 0862320666 (cased) • 0862320828 (pbk)
                                             BL: X.529/68791

Originally published as 'Sport et apartheid' (France, 1981). Rugby takes up a great deal of the book with three chapters devoted to the game: Rugby: the chosen sport of chosen people; Rugby: the force of conviction; and International responsibility: lessons of the 1981 New Zealand tour.

43   The politics of sport / edited by Lincoln Allison. Manchester: Manchester University Press, 1986. 240p; index

ISBN: 0719018714 (cased) • 0719023343 (pbk)
BL: YK.1988.a.90

44   Sport, racism and ethnicity / edited by Grant Jarvie. London: Falmer, 1991.
224p; index   ISBN: 1850009163 (cased) • 1850009171 (pbk)
BL: YC.1991.b.3106

Includes a chapter by Joe Maguire on 'Sport, racism and British society: a sociological study of England's elite male Afro/Caribbean soccer and rugby union players'.

45   The changing politics of sport / edited by Lincoln Allison. Manchester: Manchester University Press, 1993. viii, 238p; index   ISBN: 0719036704
BL: YC.1993.a.1267

46   'Welsh, gifted and black': a socio-cultural study of racism and sport in Cardiff / Mark Burley. Cardiff Institute of Higher Education, 1994. *Master's thesis.*

Violence

47   A study of violence in rugby union: 1973-1995 / Benny Peiser and David Glaves. Liverpool: Liverpool John Moores University, 1995.
94p

Offences in domestic and international matches, as well as world cups, are analysed in this unpublished study. Although fewer violent offences are committed, the nature of the offences are more serious. Where punching, butting, late tackles and obstruction are in decline, the incidence of stamping on a player on the ground is on the increase. The authors make a number of recommendations on how to reduce the number of stamping incidents, and these findings have found their way to rugby's governing bodies.

✱   *Additional References*

48   Blood & guts: violence in sports / Don Atyeo. New York, London: Paddington Press, 1979.
384p; illus; index

Bibliography: p378-9   ISBN: 0709200005
BL: X.620/18592

Atyeo, Australian born, London based journalist and author, spent three years observing and cataloguing violence in sport in the United States, Britain and elsewhere. Of relevance here is the realisation that rugby has become an amateur game played to professional standards. Commitment to winning has become ruthless. Violence is one tactic used by teams to ensure victory. It seems that an increase in

injuries in rugby has been caused by fiercer physical contact and a rise in 'extracurricular violence'. Anecdotal evidence is given by, among many, Barry John who recalls the British Isles tour to New Zealand in 1971 and the notorious Canterbury v Lions match – 'it was frightening, absolutely frightening, thuggery hatched in the dressing room as a tactic. At half-time the scene in the Lions' dressing room was terrible, with some players suffering appalling injuries'.

49   Play and culture: 1978 proceedings of the Association for the Anthropological Study of Play / edited by Helen B. Schwartzman. West Point, US: Leisure Press, 1980. 328p; pbk   ISBN: 0918438527
BL: DSC80/24222

A paper by John F. Sherry explores the verbal aggression of rugby folksongs, 'Verbal aggression in rugby ritual' (pp 139-50).

☞   Also listed at: A244

The Rugby Personality

50 Personality and rugby football / E. D. Sinclair.
University of Leeds, 1968. *Thesis.*
i, 149 leaves

> Investigates whether personality determines the level
> which athletes reach in rugby. 132 players (32
> internationals, 48 county and first class players, and
> 52 junior club players) were interviewed.

51 The rugby football subculture and deviance: a
sociological analysis / Rex W. Thomson. University of
Calgary, US, 1975. *Doctoral thesis.*
60p

> The purpose of the proposal is to determine if
> participation in a rugby subculture acts as a
> deterrent to deviant behaviour or acts to encourage
> such behaviour. Includes an overview of the sociology
> of sport.

52 Sport and deviance: a subcultural analysis of rugby
football / Rex W. Thomson. University of Alberta, Can.,
1977. *Doctoral thesis.*
241p

> Does participation in sport act as a deterrent or a
> catalyst to deviant behaviour of members of one club
> in the rugby subculture who were observed for one
> season? Evidence suggests that deviant behaviour is
> commonplace within the group.

53 Stereotyping of the cricketer, rugby footballer and
footballer: a case study of Edinburgh male middle-class
adolescents / B. Young and L. B. Young. University of
Salford, Centre for Leisure Studies, 1980.
40p; pbk
(Occasional papers in the psychology of leisure; no. 1)

> Surveys data from 53 male pupils of 17-18 years of
> age at a public school in Edinburgh to determine
> stereotypes of three sporting groups: cricketers are
> attributed with qualities of passivity and aristocratic
> qualities; rugby players are seen to possess
> aggressiveness and strength; association footballers
> have emotional characteristics.

54 Personality, perceptual conflict and anxiety in rugby
players / S. R. W. Rowley. Loughborough University of
Technology, 1984. *Master's thesis.*

55 Antidote to depression: rugby and New Zealand society
1919-1939 / Alan Manley. University of Otago, US,
1991. *Thesis.*
111 leaves; illus

56 An evaluation of Project Rugby Week 1990 for high
school boys relating to interpersonal relationships /
Andrew Charles Peterson. University of Stellenbosch,
SA, 1991. *Master's thesis.*

57 A ruffian's game for gentlemen: rugby football in
sociocultural contexts / James Alan Wright. University
of Delaware, US, 1993. *Doctoral thesis.*
308p

> Examines the history and social structure of rugby
> union football in the United States.

58 Making men: rugby and masculine identity / edited by
John Nauright and Timothy J. L. Chandler. London:
Frank Cass, 1996.
260p; illus, map; index
ISBN: 0714646377 (cased) • 0714641561 (pbk)
BL: YK.1996.a.17075

> Eleven essays by ten contributors plus an
> introduction and conclusion by the editors.
> Manliness/masculinity and male identity appear in all
> the chapter headings, apart from Murray Phillips'
> examination of the two rugby codes in New South
> Wales during the period 1907 to 1918. Albert
> Grundlingh of the University of South Africa argues
> that rugby is an arena where gender relations are
> influenced and reinforced. 'Rugby', he continues, 'has
> acquired a reputation of being pre-eminently "a man's
> game".' The editors feel that 'much more needs to be
> done on the development of rugby union in the British
> Isles and France in the period since the First World
> War, and particularly in the television age and that of
> the rugby World Cup'. Perhaps this omission can be
> rectified by academics teaching in British and French
> universities, rather than collating material for this
> book from British-born, American-based contributors
> such as Andrews and Chandler.

MAKING MEN

Rugby and Masculine Identity

Edited by

JOHN NAURIGHT
and
TIMOTHY J. L. CHANDLER

FRANK CASS
LONDON · PORTLAND, OR.

59   Playing the ball: constructing community and masculine
     identity in rugby: an analysis of the two codes of league
     and union and the people involved / Carl Spracklen.
     Leeds Metropolitan University, 1996. *Doctoral thesis.*

     ✱   *Additional References*

60   Sport, culture, and society: a reader on the sociology of
     sport / John W. Loy, Gerald S. Kenyon, Barry D.
     McPherson. 2nd rev. ed. Philadelphia, US: Lea &
     Febiger, 1981.
     ix, 376p; illus   ISBN: 0812107810
                                                        BL: 82/30410

     Includes a contribution by Kenneth Sheard and Eric
     Dunning entitled 'The rugby football club as a type of
     "male preserve": some sociological notes'.

61   A man's country?: the image of the pakeha male, a
     history / Jock Phillips. Auckland, NZ: Penguin, 1987.
     ix, 321p; illus; index; pbk   ISBN: 0140093346

     Chapter 3: 'The hard man – rugby and the formation
     of character'.

62   Meaningful play, playful meaning / Gary Alan Fine,
     editor. Champaign, US: Human Kinetics Publishers, 1987.
     x, 245p
     (The Association for the Anthropological Study of Play;
     v. 11)

     *Proceedings of the 11th Annual Meeting of The Association
     for the Anthropological Study of Play (TAASP) held March
     14-17, 1985 at Washington, DC*

                                                        ISBN: 0873220870
                                                        BL: YA.1989.b.6943

     A paper by Dan Craig Hilliard, 'The rugby tour:
     construction and enactment of social roles in a play
     setting' (pp 173-192) observes the behaviour of a
     Texas rugby club during a tour of England. It is the
     contention of the author that the rugby tourist
     undergoes a process of dissociation from his
     dominant role, and then takes on an 'ephemeral role
     set' consisting of several interrelated roles: the
     macho role; the rugby player role; the American
     tourist role; and, the personal role. Also comments
     on the declining rowdiness of rugby behaviour in
     general, comparing English club rugby and American
     club rugby.

63   The perceptions of the FAI, GAA, IRFU and their
     respective games among Dublin males / Donall
     O'Keeffe. University College Dublin, 1991. *Master's thesis.*

Professionalism

64   An examination as to whether rugby union can remain a
     truly amateur sport in an increasingly professional
     environment / David Henwood. West London Institute
     of Higher Education, 1986. *Thesis.*

65   An investigation into the role of strategic planning in
     rugby union and whether it can remain a truly amateur
     sport in an increasingly professional environment /
     Andrew Downes. University of Sheffield, 1994. *Master's
     thesis*

66   The professionalization of rugby union football in
     England: crossing the Rubicon? / Andy White.
     University of Leicester, 1994. *Master's thesis.*

67   Open rugby: the right to decide / RFU Commission.
     Twickenham: Rugby Football Union, 1995.
     52p

     Following the declaration by the International Rugby
     Football Board at its interim meeting in August 1995
     that the amateur principles upon which the game had
     been founded should be repealed, the Rugby Football
     Union Commission, consisting of seven members
     under the chairmanship of A. P. Hallett, was formed
     on 7 September 1995. The Commission held twelve

     plenary meetings to consider the implications of the
     'Open Game' decision. The report declares the
     findings of the Commission. Twenty brief chapters
     consider issues such as: players' contracts; referees
     and officials; discipline; compensation and transfer;
     agents; player qualification and registration; finance
     and marketing; club and divisional structure.
     Appendices I-IV include a 'Model club contract'.

68   An evaluation of the effects that professionalism of
     Rugby Football Union has had on players and clubs:
     with special reference to the work of Henry Mintzberg /
     D. B. Selkirk. Loughborough University, 1996. *Master's
     thesis.*

69   The rugby war / Peter FitzSimons. Sydney, Aust.:
     HarperSports, 1996.
     x, 321p; illus; index; pbk   ISBN: 0732256879

     Chronicles the setting up of a professional 'rugby
     circus' by the World Rugby Corporation (WRC) in order
     to attract the top players of Australia, New Zealand
     and South Africa. Approaches were also made to
     players in the northern hemisphere. The threat
     seemingly posed by WRC proved an irritation to the
     national unions in the southern hemisphere who had

put in place substantial monetary rewards and a new rugby structure. WRC's plan for the game failed as the organisers had no experience in rugby administration and no financial backing.

70 The amateur past and professional present of rugby union: de-differentiating culture and loss of identity / B. Edwards. Ruskin College, Oxford, 1997. *Master's thesis.*

71 Mud, blood and money: English rugby union goes professional / Ian Malin. Edinburgh: Mainstream, 1997.
176p; illus   ISBN: 1851589384

72 Rugby's new-age travellers / Stuart Barnes. Edinburgh: Mainstream, 1997.
192p; illus   ISBN: 1851589171

73 A whole new ball game / Phil de Glanville with Leonard Stall. Edinburgh: Mainstream, 1997.
192p; illus   ISBN: 1851589767
Examines the changing face of professional rugby union. The author also considers his role as England captain and his relationship with a number of people in the game, and casts an eye over his own club Bath.

Sociology

74 Rugby football – a study in developmental sociology / Kenneth Sheard. University of Leicester, 1972. *Master's thesis.*

75 The socialisation processes of Heineken League Welsh rugby players / Peter J. Sommers. Cardiff Institute of Higher Education, 1994. *Master's thesis.*

Rugby in the Community

76 The Malone experiment: rugby union as a cross-community sport / R. Snowling. University of Ulster, 1993. *Master's thesis.*

77 Welsh rugby union facilities venues for further community integration / I. C. Hughes. Swansea Institute of Higher Education, 1994. *Master's thesis.*

Economics, Marketing & Business Studies

78 The 3 ppp's of rugby: promotion, publicity, public relations. Wellington, NZ: Air New Zealand for the New Zealand Rugby Football Union, 1978.
47p; illus; pbk
☞ Subsequent ed. G79

79 Rugby promotion guide / Tom Johnson and Paul Gleeson. Wellington, NZ: Air New Zealand for the New Zealand Rugby Football Union, 1983.
47p; illus; pbk
☞ Previous ed. G78

80 An investigation into the administrative structure and financial management of the Preston Grasshoppers RFC / N. Smith. Loughborough University, 1984. *Master's thesis.*

81 Nottingham Rugby Football Club: a marketing case study / J. Hudson. Loughborough University, 1990. *Master's thesis.*

82 Rugby union: a strategy for sport and recreation in the northern region. Durham: Northern Council for Sport and Recreation, 1992.
20p; pbk   BL: DSCq93/07075
Identifies priorities to develop rugby union in the north east: coaching, competitions, administration and marketing.

83 The disengagement of elite international rugby union football players 1970-1990 / Allan J. Martin. Cardiff: Cardiff Institute of Higher Education, 1993. *Master's thesis.*
Focuses on prominent players and the financial and other difficulties they face upon retirement from the game.

84   Economic impact analysis 1994 Springbok tour /
     prepared for New Zealand Rugby Football Union by
     Cecilia Burgess and Tony Molloy. Auckland, NZ: Price
     Waterhouse, 1994.
     34p; illus; pbk

85   Assessment of the level, economic value and
     composition of individual volunteer activity within rugby
     union in Nottinghamshire / Bennet Riley. University of
     Sheffield, 1995. *Master's thesis.*

86   English First Division clubs: a report to the Rugby
     Football Union Commission, October 1995.

     The English First Division Clubs Limited (EFDR Ltd.),
     consisting of the top ten Courage clubs plus
     Northampton, wrote this report after failing to get
     the RFU to agree to a representation from their
     body. The proposals are: one contract for the player
     between player and club; EFDR to become the
     collective voice and joint marketing company for First
     Division clubs; avoid midweek competitions; abolish
     divisional competition; introduce European or Anglo-
     Welsh competition.

87   English rugby union in the era of commercialism: a
     contemporary and critical account of the modern game /
     Andrew M. Adams. University of Warwick, 1995.
     Master's thesis.

88   An investigation into the relationship between on-pitch
     success and financial success of rugby union clubs in the
     national divisions of the Courage Leagues: evaluating if there
     is a direct relationship or if other factors are involved /
     Jonathon Puzey. University of Sheffield, 1995. *Master's thesis.*

89   England Rugby Football Union: a RFU guide to producing your
     club programme. Twickenham: Rugby Football Union, 1996.
     16p; pbk

90   Moving the goal posts / Meadowbank College of
     Technical and Further Education. Meadowbank, Aust.:
     KickStart Communications, 1996.
     82p; illus; pbk   ISBN: 0646301616
     Prepared for the North Sydney Rugby Union Football
     Club by final year marketing students at Meadowbank
     College of Technical and Further Education.

91   The acquisition of human capital in various currencies:
     the dual career dynamics of professional rugby / Lopeti
     Essendon Tuitupou. University of Auckland, NZ, 1997.
     Master's thesis
     136 leaves

92   Introduction of management budgets and valuation of
     Leicester RUFC / Scott Beattie. London Business
     School, 1997. *Master's thesis.*

93   Introduction of management budgets and valuation of
     Leicester RUFC / Thomas Brown. London Business
     School, 1997. *Master's thesis.*

94   Rugby football in the 1990s: some economic issues /
     Dennis Thomas. Aberystwyth: University of Wales,
     Aberystwyth, 1997.
     29p; pbk
     (Aberystwyth economic research papers; no. 97-05)
                                              BL: DSC0539.127(97-05)

✱   *Additional References*

95   The way to win: strategies for success in business and
     sport / Will Carling and Robert Heller. London: Little,
     Brown, 1995.
     xii, 340p; illus; index
          Bibliography: p317-8   ISBN: 0316914479
                                              BL: YK.1995.b.10581

Rugby in Art

96   Rugby mania / photographs by Fotopacific; artwork by
     Paul Rogers, Andrew Tristram and Gary Chaloner; text
     by John Lockyer. Auckland, NZ: Reed, 1991.
     109p; chiefly illus; pbk
                              ISBN: 0790002353

97   Rugby moods: a photographic essay of the moods of
     rugby / compiled by Michael Ingram. Port Erin: Moods
     of Mann, 1997.
     208p; illus   ISBN: 0952430479

✱   *Additional References*

98   Sport and the artist, volume 1: ball games / Mary Ann
     Wingfield. Woodbridge: Antique Collectors' Club, 1988.
     359p; illus, plans   ISBN: 185149071X
                                              BL: YV.1989.b.399
     Illustrated and historical survey of ball games. Rugby
     is covered on pages 318-28. Examples are given, in
     black and white and colour, of illustrations depicting
     the game, with brief biographies of the artists, and
     details on the locations of their work.

99   A dictionary of sporting artists 1650-1990 / edited by Mary
      Ann Wingfield. Woodbridge: Antique Collectors' Club, 1992.
      550p; illus
                                               ISBN: 1851491406
                                               BL: YK.1993.b.415

      48 artists have contributed work on rugby football.
      Biographies, and a brief description and location of
      the works, are given.

Collecting Rugby Ephemera

100   Rugby: a history of the game / text by Harry Langton.
      London: Sports Design, 1991.
      50p; illus; pbk

      'An illustrated catalogue for the 1991 London
      Exhibition of the Langton Collection of pictures,
      antiques and souvenirs illustrating the development
      of one branch of football games over a period of at
      least 1,000 years.' Langton has sold a number of
      items from his collection which have been acquired by
      the RFU Museum, Twickenham.

      ☞   Also listed at: A65

101   Rugby and philately: rugby football thematic catalogue /
      Giuliano G. Rossi. Milan, Italy: The Author, 1995.
      158p; illus; pbk

      Lists philatelic items and their current value. Also
      records examples of postcards and phonecards.

Guides to Special Collections

102   The New Zealand National Rugby Museum, Palmerston
      North, NZ. Palmerston, NZ: The Museum, 1976.
      47p; illus; pbk

103   Choet Visser Rugby Museum: the world's biggest private
      rugby museum / edited by Nico du Plessis.
      Bloemfontein, SA: The editor, 1994.
      132p; illus; pbk   ISBN: 062018518X

      Biography of Choet Visser and his rugby museum
      housed in his home in the Orange Free State.

104   History in the making: the Museum of Rugby.
      Twickenham: Rugby Football Union, 1995.
      12p; illus; pbk

      Describes what is available in the Museum with a
      'behind-the-scenes' tour of Twickenham stadium.

105   The Museum of Rugby Twickenham: a souvenir.
      Twickenham: The Rugby Football Union, 1996?
      30p; illus; pbk

The Media

106   The influence of sport on social values: an examination
      of persisting and changing themes in the depiction of
      New Zealand rugby union football c.1940s-1990s with
      particular reference to the publications of T. P. McLean
      / Richard Kay. University of Waikato, NZ, 1992. *Master's
      thesis.*
      vi, 125 leaves

107   The language of televised sport: World Cup rugby, a case
      study / Lynne Star. University of Auckland, NZ, 1993.
      Doctoral thesis.
      xvi, 364 leaves

108   Working with the media. Twickenham: Rugby Football
      Union, 1996.
      20p; pbk

      A guide for rugby club press officers on developing
      successful relationships with the media.

✴ *Additional References*

109 Games and sets: the changing face of sport on television / Steven Barnett. London: BFI Publishing, 1990.
214p; illus; index

Bibliography: p207-8

ISBN: 0851702678 (cased) • 0851702686 (pbk)
BL: YK.1990.a.6525

Examines the role of television and how it has changed people's attitude to sport. Also analyses the growth of satellite television and the influence of sponsorship.

110 Fields in vision: television sport and cultural transformation / Garry Whannel. London: Routledge, 1992.
xii, 243p; illus; index
(Communication and society)

Bibliography: p222-32

ISBN: 041505382X (cased) • 0415053838 (pbk)
BL: YK.1992.b.7447

Fashion

111 Rugby ties / Pierluigi Fadda and Renato Tullio Ferrari. Milano: Idealibri Sp. A., 1986.

Bilingual Italian and English history of ties in rugby.

✴ *Additional References*

112 English costume for sports and outdoor recreation from the sixteenth to the nineteenth centuries / Phillis Cunnington & Alan Mansfield. London: Adam & Charles Black, 1969.
388p; illus; index

SBN: 713610174
BL: X.421/2855

Rugby is well covered in the football chapter.

113 Tracksuits and casualwear with your overlocker / Linette Maritz. London: New Holland, 1995.
96p; illus

ISBN: 1853685402

Among the projects is a step-by-step guide to making a rugby shirt.

Games

114 Rugby guide, 1909 / Joseph Younglove Underwood. Brooklyn, US: 1909.
18p; pbk

Rugby (dice game). 'The game is supposedly played with a standard football ... a throw of five dice ... determining the extent of the movement.'

115 Five-a-side: rugby football in miniature (played on a squared board). Belfast: 1922.
1 sheet

BL: 1865.c.2(74)

116 Rules for playing the Morris table rugby and table association / P. J. O. Morris. Brighton: 1932.
9p; pbk

BL: D

117 BBC QS: a Question of Sport self-contained game based on a specialist subject: rugby. Huntingdon: 1992.

118 I-spy rugby union. Watford: Michelin, 1995.
48p; illus; index; pbk

ISBN: 1856711501
BL: YK.1995.a.9359

Points are scored for each sighting of a player, team, emblem, action sequence and so on as listed in the book. Once 1,000 points have been scored you can send off for a badge.

119 The rugby game manoeuvre. South Africa: Towny Toys, 1995.

Designed to teach players the laws of rugby union.

The Game For People With Different Abilities

120 Back to the basics of quad rugby. Winnipeg, Can.: Manitoba Wheelchair Sports & Recreation Association, 1984?
26 leaves; illus; pbk

121 Motivational participation incentives of elite quadriplegic rugby athletes / Thomas F. Ferr. San Jose State University, US, 1992. *Master's thesis.*
82p

The study was based on evidence collected during the USQRA Quad Rugby Nationals in April 1992.

122 New image rugby: introducing the game to people with different abilities. Leeds: Rugby Football Union North Leeds Development, 1993.
12p; pbk

The guide explains how new image rugby, a minimal contact version, can be adapted for people with disabilities.

Women's Rugby

123 Born again amateurs: a rugby subculture / K. Hodge. University of Montana, 1984. *Master's thesis.*

124 Rugby players' perceptions of women's participation in the game / Catherine Evans. University of Birmingham, 1987. *Thesis.*

125 A women's rugby subculture: contesting on the 'wild' side of the pitch / Elizabeth Ellen Wheatley. University of Illinois, US, 1988. *Master's thesis.*
198p

Based on observation in two university based women's rugby clubs over a period from February 1986 to June 1988. The study 'highlights the intersection of the women's rugby subcultures and gay and lesbian subcultures . . . examines gender and sexual relations within the subculture, and how members of the subculture construct, and reconstruct their femininities and sexualities through living out, negotiating, and struggling over the women's subculture style'.

✱ *Additional References*

126 Women, sport, and culture / Susan Birrell, Cheryl L. Cole, editors. Champaign, US, Leeds: Human Kinetics, 1994.
viii, 408p; index

ISBN: 087322650X
BL: YC.1995.b.6129

Contains 2 chapters relevant to rugby: 'Challenging the hegemony: New Zealand women's opposition to rugby and the reproduction of a capitalist patriarchy' by Shona M. Thompson; and, 'Subcultural subversions: comparing discourses on sexuality in men's and women's rugby songs' by Elizabeth E. Wheatley.

127 A girl's guide to ball games: what men need to know / Sue Mott. Edinburgh: Mainstream, 1996.
224p; illus; index

Bibliography: p219

ISBN: 185158868X
BL: YK.1997.b.4164

Considers the role of women in football, rugby, cricket, golf, and tennis.

128 Girls' guide to footy / Tracey Holmes. Sydney, Aust.: Bantam, 1996.
204p; illus

Bibliography: p204

Covers soccer, rugby union, rugby league, and Australian football.

Rugby in Literature

Contents

In the short story and poetry sections, individual short stories and poems have been listed alphabetically by short story or poem title, followed by the name of the author. The title in italics which follows the author's name is the title of the book in which the poem or short story first appeared. These works are then listed with full bibliographic information in alphabetical order by title.

Novels

❋ *Adult Novels*

Arnold, W. D.

1 Football: the first day of the sixth match. Rugby: Crossley and Billington, 1851.
24p; pbk   BL: Mic.A.7125(8) (microfilm copy)

William Delafield Arnold, the Doctor's son, gives an imaginary account of the first football match of the year. Arnold was one of three Rugbeians who drew up the first rules of rugby football in 1845. A facsimile of the novel was published in 1987.

Benson, E. F.

2 David of King's. London: Hodder and Stoughton, 1924.
318p   BL: NN.9715

Rugby at Cambridge University.

Bickers, Richard Townshend

3 The Hellions. London: Hale, 1965.
191p   BL: Nov.6432

Mark Stratton, intelligence officer, boxer, rugger player, and Olympic athlete opposes the five evil men that are the Hellions.

Bird, Richard (pseudonym of Walter Barradell-Smith)

4 The forward in love: an improbable comedy. London: Herbert & Daniel, 1911.
274p   BL: 012618.b.7

The College Dean's struggle to achieve a rugby blue.

Buchan, John

5 Castle Gay. London: Hodder and Stoughton, 1930.
320p   BL: NN.16813

Chapter 1 tells of a rugby three-quarter.

Calder, Jason

6 A wreath for the Springboks. Palmerston North, NZ: Dunmore Press, 1977.
179p

Subsequently published: London: Hale, 1978
ISBN: 090856404X (cased) • 0908564066 (pbk)
BL: YA.1989.a.1668

'In spite of world protests, the South African rugby team is about to tour New Zealand…'.

Curtin, Michael

7 The league against Christmas. London: Deutsch, 1989.
264p   ISBN: 0233983821
BL: Nov.1989/575

A tale of four characters. One, an Irishman, is haunted by a boyhood failure on the rugby field.

Davies, Tom

8 One winter of the holy spirit. London: Macdonald, 1985.
363p   ISBN: 0356106217
BL: Nov.53815

The rugby excerpt has been reprinted in anthologies as 'The big game'.

Evans, Bethan

9 Amdani! Talybont, Ceredigion: Y Lolfa, 1997.
206p; pbk   ISBN: 086243419X

The story in Welsh of a women's rugby team.

Gee, Maurice Gough

10 The big season. London: Hutchinson, 1962.
198p   BL: Nov.4422

Gee's first novel, set in a small town in New Zealand, concludes with the season's big rugby match.

Gill, Bartholomew (pseudonym of Mark McGarrity)

11 McGarr and the method of Descartes. New York, US: Viking, 1984.
289p

Subsequently published in paperback: Harmondsworth: Penguin, 1985
ISBN: 0670464325 (cased) • 0140084053 (pbk)
BL: H.86/1275

McGarr, a police officer in Dublin, investigates the murder of an Irish rugby player.

Hill, Reginald

12 A clubbable woman. London: Collins, 1970.
256p
(The crime club)   SBN: 002311208
BL: Nov.15870

A rugby player's wife is murdered and Dalziel and Pascoe are brought in to investigate. The finale is played out at an international match at Twickenham.

Hughes, Thomas

13   Tom Brown's schooldays / 'An Old Boy'. London: Macmillan, 1857.
viii, 420p

> Published pseudonymously on 24 April 1857. In a fifth edition by November of the same year, Macmillan published 47 further editions before other firms began to publish this classic title in 1892.

Hutchins, Graham

14   Tall half-backs: a ticket to ride to yesterday. Dunedin, NZ: John McIndoe, 1987.
116p; pbk   ISBN: 0868680966

> 'About the complexities of growing up in small town New Zealand during the 50s and 60s where rugby was the unifying force.'

Jones, Gwyn

15   Times like these. London: Gollancz, 1936.
319p   BL: NN.25463

> The rugby extract has been reprinted in A Cardiff anthology as 'Come on, Wales!'

Kidd, Heather

16   Operation intercept. Auckland, NZ: Harlen, 1984.
219p   ISBN: 0908630190 (cased) • 0908630204 (pbk)

> The kidnapping of the Ranfurly Shield holders thwarts the planned tour of South Africa by the All Blacks.

Llewellyn, Richard

17   How green was my valley. London: Michael Joseph, 1939.
651p   BL: NN.30681

MacDonell, A. G.

18   England their England. London: Macmillan, 1933.
299p   BL: NN.19417

> Chapter 11 contains an account of the Varsity match at Twickenham.

Middleton, Stanley

19   Live and learn. London: Hutchinson, 1996.
248p   ISBN: 0091792207
                 BL: Nov.1996/598

Mulgan, Alan

20   Spur of morning. London: Dent, 1934.
viii, 364p
         BL: NN.22793

> Rugby as played at Eden's Grammar School and later the University College.

Reed, Talbot Baines

21   The Cock-house at Fellsgarth. London: The Office of 'The Boys' Own paper', 1893.
320p   BL: 4419.o.30/12

> A public school story featuring a rugby match between Fellsgarth and Rendlesham.

Romanos, Joseph

22   Black. Auckland, NZ: Hodder Moa Beckett, 1997.
285p

Sinclair, Janette

23   In touch. Auckland, NZ: Secker & Warburg, 1995.
186p; pbk   ISBN: 0790004011

> Women rugby union football players.

Walpole, Hugh

24   Jeremy at Crale: his friends, his ambitions and his one great enemy. London: Cassell, 1927.
311p   BL: NN.13309

> Considerable rugby passages including 'The game against Raddan' and 'The match against Callendar' both won by Crale.

25   The prelude to adventure. London: Mills & Boon, 1912.
308p   BL: 12642.ee.12

Waugh, Alec

26   Guy Renton: a London story. London: Cassell, 1953.
v, 314p   BL: NNN.3682

27   The loom of youth / with a preface by Thomas Seccombe. London: Grant Richards, 1917.
335p   BL: NN.4494

> Public school story written when the author was just seventeen years old.

Wodehouse, P.G.

28   The gold bat / containing eight full-page illustrations by T. M. R. Whitwell. London: Adam & Charles Black, 1904.
277p; illus   BL: 012803.cc.10

> The Ripton match.

29   The white feather / containing twelve full-page illustrations by W. Townend. London: Adam & Charles Black, 1907.
284p; illus   BL: 12803.s.16

> Recounts a rugby 'rout at Ripton'.

✳ *Teenage Novels*

Bird, Richard (pseudonym of Walter Barradell-Smith)

30 The boys of Dyall's House / illustrated by H. M. Brock. London: Blackie, 1922.
256p; illus   BL: 12800.de.6
     Cheriton versus Wanderers.

31 Captain of Keynes / illustrated by John Walker. London: Blackie, 1930.
256p; illus   BL: 12818.bb.20
     Adderley v. City.

32 The deputy captain: a public school story / with illustrations by Savile Lumley. London: Humphrey Milford, 1922.
288p; illus   BL: 012802.cc.34
     Melton v. Bessborough and the return match.

33 The Moreleigh mascot / illustrated by T. M. R. Whitwell. London: Blackie, 1927.
256p; illus   BL: 12801.pp.9

34 Play the game, Torbury! / illustrated by H. M. Brock. London: Blackie, 1926.
255p; illus   BL: 012809.e.54
     Sportsmanship and adventures at Torbury School including the disappearance of the cup.

35 Queer doings at Aldborough / illustrated by Alfred Leete. London: Oxford University Press, 1927.
288p; illus   BL: 12801.t.3
     Aldborough v. Hammerton and the invisible scorer!

36 The rival captains: a public school story / illustrated in colour by C. E. Brock. London: Henry Frowde, 1916.
288p; illus   BL: 12800.aaa.3
     House matches and Dipcote v. Old Dipcotians.

37 A school feud / illustrated by Reginald Mills. London: Oxford University Press, 1930.
272p; illus   BL: 12818.bb.19

38 School House v. the rest: a public school story / illustrated by Frank Insall. London: Oxford University Press, 1928.
vii, 280p; illus   BL: 12816.d.9

39 A school libel / illustrated by Savile Lumley. London: Thomas Nelson, 1934.
285p; illus   BL: 12848.aa.1
     School v. City.

40 The sporting house: a school story / with illustrations by T. M. R. Whitwell. London: Humphrey Milford, Oxford University Press, 1921.
282p; illus   BL: 012802.cc.11

41 The Wharton medal / illustrated by Frank Insall. London: Oxford University Press, 1929.
259p; illus   BL: 12812.g.20
     House matches and Gaythorpe v. Royston.

Carr, Kent

42 Playing the game!: a public-school story. London: Partridge, 1908.
415p; illus   BL: 012804.i.11

Clark, M. R.

43 Hatherly's first fifteen / illustrated by F. E. Hiley. London: Humphrey Milford, Oxford University Press, 1930.
254p; illus   BL: 12818.c.20
     The main thrust of the story is rugby at Hatherly, an Australian public school, and the holiday home of the principal character.

Cleaver, Hylton

44 Captains of Harley: a school story / with illustrations by H. M. Brock. London: Humphrey Milford, 1921.
277p   BL: 012802.cc.15

45 The Harley First XV. London: Oxford University Press, 1922.
288p   BL: 12800.c.47

Elrington, Helen

46 The red house of Boville. London: Nelson, 1925.
335p; illus

Hadath, Gunby

47 Playing the game: a public school story. London: Latimer House, 1950.
150p BL: 12826.l.8

Hayens, Herbert

48 'Play up, Buffs!' / illustrated by Archibald Webb. London: Collins' Clear-Type Press, 1926.
314p; illus BL: 12813.dd

A school story in which several rugby matches feature.

Lockyer, John

49 Tough tackle. Auckland, NZ: Mammoth, 1993.
95p; pbk
(A Bungee book) ISBN: 1869480929

Maree, Kobus

50 Trial match. Cape Town, SA: Human & Rousseau, 1997.
87p; pbk

Rhoades, Walter

51 In the scrum: a school story. London: Humphrey Milford, 1922.
288p BL: 012802.bb.37

52 The last lap: a school story. London: Humphrey Milford, 1923.
288p BL: 12802.bbb.46

53 'Quills': a tale of schooldays at Bedinghurst. London: Blackie, 1919.
288p BL: 12801.c.27

Slatter, Gordon Cyril

54 The pagan game. London: Robert Hale, 1969.
239p ISBN: 070910524X

Describes how the tension for a big game at school level in New Zealand can build up. Ends with an account of the match between the rival schools.

Smith, Topsy

55 Leon the Rugger Captain. Cape Town, SA: Nasionale Boekhandel, 1963.
83p BL: 012845.c.2/1

Set in Clan College, this is the second book in the Leon series.

✻ *Children's Stories*

56 Freddy's football. c1890.

Shaped as a ball, this children's book tells the story of Freddy and his football.

Bond, Michael

57 Paddington in touch. London: Carnival, 1989.
32p; illus ISBN: 000194536X
BL: YK.1990.a.822

Paddington Bear goes to watch a rugby match at his old school and ends up playing for the Peruvian Reserves.

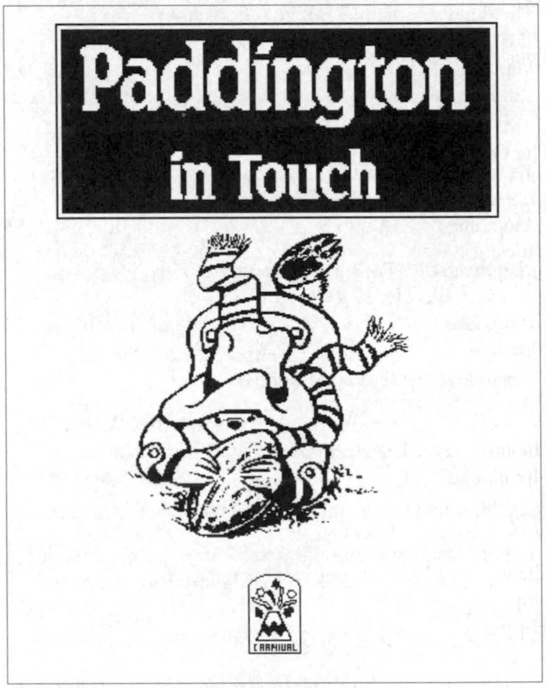

Byrne, John

58 Granny Sangoma. London: Macmillan, 1997.
59p; illus; pbk
(Mactracks. Sprinters) ISBN: 0333660021
BL: YK.1997.a.2319

For children and teenagers learning English as a second language. This is the new South Africa. Thabo attends an exclusive school in Johannesburg. Brought up playing soccer, he is the only black face in the school rugby team. With the help of his grandmother who dabbles in magic, he overcomes the prejudice of the team captain and scores the try that wins the prestigious Kingsman Cup for the school.

Gowar, Mick

59 Sir Gawain and the rugby sevens / illustrated by Clinton Banbury. London: Collins Educational, 1995.
60p; chiefly illus; pbk
(Comets)
ISBN: 0003230481
BL: YK.1995.a.7298

King Arthur introduces a rugby tournament to prevent his knights fighting amongst themselves, with disastrous results.

Grace, Kim

60 Bushy Park. South Freemantle, Aust.: Sandcastle Books, 1995.
30p; illus
ISBN: 1863681159

In a chain of catastrophes, Dad is run over by some burly rugby players.

Harold, Peter

61 The Greenbank rugby game. Auckland, NZ: Puffin, 1995.
32p; illus; pbk
ISBN: 0140555684

62 Little All Blacks. Auckland, NZ: Puffin, 1995.
24p; illus; pbk
ISBN: 0140556966

63 Little Jonah. Auckland, NZ: Puffin, 1996.
20p; illus
ISBN: 0140559507

A children's story based on the career of New Zealand player Jonah Lomu.

64 The little Silver Ferns. Auckland, NZ: Puffin, 1995.
24p; illus; pbk
ISBN: 0140558256X

Hill, David

65 The winning touch. London: Hippo, 1997.
146p; pbk
(Hippo sport)
ISBN: 0590136437

Hilton, Nette

66 Tough Lester / illustrated by Craig Smith. Norwood, Aust.: Omnibus, 1997.
32p; illus; pbk
ISBN: 1862913390

For 5-8 year olds.

McAra, Lynne

67 Claire's dream, or, The girl who wanted to play rugby / illustrations by Sally McAra. Auckland, NZ: Black Cat, 1989.
24p; illus
ISBN: 1869545001 (cased) • 1869545028 (pbk)

Morgan, Gwyn & Dai Owen

68 Zac yn y pac. Caerdydd: Dref Wen, 1994.
61p; illus; pbk
ISBN: 1855961180
BL: YK.1995.a.5851

It is the final of 'Cwpan y Swigod'. Zac Evans, the captain of Brynchwim, leads his team to victory over the unscrupulous side from Casgarw who have bribed the referee.

Owen, Dai *See* **Morgan, Gwyn & Dai Owen**

Wright, Geoff

69 Charlie-Not-So-Good plays rugby. Bedford: F. Coleman, 1985.
28p; illus; pbk
ISBN: 094810340X

Wyndham, Charles

70 The Lions abroad / illustrated by Hookway Cowles. Exeter: Haldon Books, 1967.
38p; illus
(They reached the top)
BL: X.0449/47

'In 1955 a British rugby union team toured South Africa. While they played there they were known as the Lions, and everywhere they went people flocked to see them...'. The story of the tour related for children.

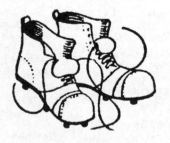

Short Stories

Accounts squared / Richard Bird. *Carton's cap*

The adventure of the missing three-quarter / A. Conan Doyle. *The return of Sherlock Holmes*

The big game / A. P. Gaskell. *The big game and other stories*

Cap Wil Tomos / Islwyn Williams. *Cap Wil Tomos*

Carton's cap / Richard Bird. *Carton's cap*

Dawson's score / Richard Bird. *Dawson's score*

The dream / Uys Krige. *The dream and the desert*

The drop-out / Alun Richards. *Dai country*

The eleventh hour / Richard Bird. *Dawson's score*

The fifteenth man: the story of a rugby match / Richard Marsh. *The seen and the unseen*

Fly half / Alun Richards. *Dai country*

Funk-shy, full-back / Sydney Horler. *Song of the scrum*

General post / Hylton Cleaver. *Captains of Greyminster*

The hero / Emyr Humphreys. *Natives*

Hon. Sec. RFC / Alun Richards. *The former Miss Merthyr Tydfil*

How Payne bucked up / P. G. Wodehouse. *Tales of St Austin's*

A little prep / Rudyard Kipling. *Stalky & Co.*

The man in the clean jersey / Sydney Horler. *Song of the scrum*

The man who took a chance / Sydney Horler. *Song of the scrum*

The mascot monkey / Richard Bird. *The third jump*

The match of the season / Richard Marsh. *Both sides of the veil*

The necessary action / Hylton Cleaver. *Captains of Greyminster*

The Oxton match / Richard Bird. *Touch and go*

Partners / Richard Bird. *Carton's cap*

Partners / Sydney Horler. *Song of the scrum*

Song of the scrum / Sydney Horler. *Song of the scrum*

Thanks to rugger / Richard Bird. *Thanks to rugger*

The third jump / Richard Bird. *The third jump*

Touch and go / Richard Bird. *Touch and go*

The way out / Hylton Cleaver. *The Harley First XI*

Why I play rugby / Daniel Curley. *Love in the winter*

The wing three-quarter / Liam O'Flaherty. *The tent*

With you, old man …! / Sydney Horler. *Song of the scrum*

---

71   The big game and other stories / A. P. Gaskell. Christchurch, NZ: Caxton, 1947.
142p

Author's real name is Alexander Gaskell Pickard
            BL: X.950/23453

'The big game' tells of a club final in Dunedin.

72   Both sides of the veil / Richard Marsh. London: Methuen, 1901.
306p   BL: 012639.a.7

Richard Marsh was the pseudonym of Richard Heldmann (1857-1915), a very prolific writer who wrote in a variety of genres including humour, horror and fantasy. The rugby story in this collection is 'The match of the season'.

73   Cap Wil Tomos / Islwyn Williams. Llandebie: Llyfrau'r Dryw, 1946.
56p; pbk   BL: W.P.5815/32

The story, 'Cap Wil Tomos' ('Wil Tomos's cap') appears in this collection. Tomos played rugby for both his University and Wales.

74   Captains of Greyminster / Hylton Cleaver. London: Collins, 1929.
288p; illus   BL: 12813.m.18

'General post' and 'The necessary action'.

75   Carton's cap and other school stories / Richard Bird; illustrated by Frank Gillett. London: Blackie, 1927.
255p; illus   BL: 12810.ff.25

Three rugby stories – 'Carton's cap', 'Partners', and 'Accounts squared'.

76   Dai country: short stories / Alun Richards. London: Joseph, 1973.
254p   ISBN: 0718111338
             BL: Nov.20550

Two rugby tales, 'Fly half' and 'The drop-out'.

77   Dawson's score and other school stories / Richard Bird; illustrated by Frank Gillett. London: Blackie, 1924.
255p; illus   BL: 012803.bb.52

Two rugby stories – 'Dawson's score' and 'The eleventh hour'.

78   The dream and the desert / Uys Krige. London: Collins, 1953.

       223p   BL: 12652.b.16

       A collection of nine stories including 'The dream' on pages 7-94. Jannie Kotze, son of Japie the great Springbok centre, dreams about his newly-born brother. Jannie's experiences are totally centred on rugby with descriptions of rugby in the Cape.

79   The former Miss Merthyr Tydfil: stories / Alun Richards. London: Michael Joseph, 1976.

       221p   ISBN: 0718114132

       Includes 'Hon. Sec. RFC'.

80   The Harley First XI / Hylton Cleaver; illustrated in colour by C. E. Brock. London: Humphrey Milford, 1920.

       272p; illus   BL: 12801.cc.25.

       Rugger was Harley's great game and is represented in this collection by 'The way out'.

81   Love in the winter: stories / Daniel Curley. Urbana, US, London: University of Illinois Press, 1976.

       118p   ISBN: 0252005511

                            BL: Nov.33256

       Includes 'Why I play rugby'.

82   Natives / Emyr Humphreys. London: Secker & Warburg, 1968.

       255p   SBN: 436209802

                            BL: Nov.12135

       Includes 'The hero'.

83   The return of Sherlock Holmes / A. Conan Doyle; illustrated by Sidney Paget. London: George Newnes, 1905.

       403p; illus   BL: 012631.aa.26

       Includes 'The adventure of the missing three-quarter'.

84   The seen and the unseen / Richard Marsh. London: Methuen, 1900.

       320p   BL: 012641.c.23

       'The fifteenth man: the story of a rugby match' included in this collection concerns one Frank Joyce who has had his skull broken in a match and is in hospital. A week later the team he played for turns up for a match with only 14 players, as the player who had been chosen to take Joyce's place fails to show. Throughout the game the team opposing Joyce's side fail to take advantage of a number of situations as they are thwarted by someone who to all appearances is Joyce. The game ends in a win to the side fielding 14 men, and a telegram announcing that Joyce died in hospital an hour before . . .

85   Song of the scrum / Sydney Horler. London: Hutchinson, 1934.

       287p   BL: NN.22413

       Six rugby stories in this sporting collection: 'Funk-shy, full-back', 'The man in the clean jersey', 'The man who took a chance', 'Partners', 'Song of the scrum', and 'With you, old man . . .!'.

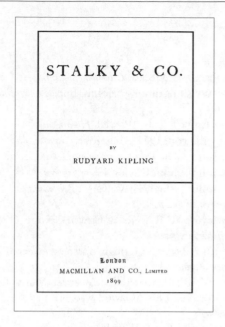

86   Stalky & Co. / Rudyard Kipling. London: Macmillan, 1899.

       ix, 272p   BL: 012643.h.42

       'A little prep'.

87   Tales of St Austin's / P. G. Wodehouse; containing twelve full-page illustrations by T. M. R Whitwell, R. Noel Pocck, and E. F. Skinner. London: Adam & Charles Black, 1903.

       281p; illus   BL: 012803.aaa.11

       Payne wins his colours in 'How Payne bucked up'.

88   The tent / Liam O'Flahertt. London: Jonathan Cape, 1926.

       288p   BL: NN.11828

       Includes 'The wing three-quarter'.

89   Thanks to rugger: and other school stories / Richard Bird. London: Blackie, 1928.

       256p

          Pseudonym of Walter Barradell-Smith

                            BL: 12810.eee.16

90   The third jump and other stories / Richard Bird; illustrated by Frank Gillett. London: Blackie, 1923.

       256p; illus   BL: 12800.ee.21

       Includes two rugger stories, 'The third jump' and 'The mascot monkey'.

91   Touch and go, and other school stories / Richard Bird; illustrated by Thomas Henry. London: Blackie, 1925.

       255p; illus

          Pseudonym of Walter Barradell-Smith

                            BL: 012807.bbb.29

       A collection of boys' school stories.

Poetry

Alun Pask / Dic Jones. *Caneuon cynhaeaf*

Anglo-Welsh testimony / John Tripp. *The province of belief*

Arthur Emyr / Robat Powell. *Haearn iaith*

Baled y Llewod, 1971 / Dic Jones. *Storom Awst*

Barry John / Dic Jones. *Caneuon cynhaeaf*

Barry John / John Davies. *Flight patterns*

Barry John / Rhydwen Williams. *Barddoniaeth Rhydwen Williams*

Barry John / T. R. Jones & Eirwyn George. *O'r Moelwyn i'r Preselau*

Big Arth / Roger McGough. *Sporting relations; We are the champions*

A bit of a ballad: Scotland v. Australia, Murrayfield, 18 December 1981 / Gavin Ewart. *We are the champions*

Cae'r Gnoll / Robat Powell. *Haearn iaith*

Cais i Gymru / W. Rhys Nicholas. *Y mannau mwyn*

Cardiff / Raymond Garlick. *Collected poems*

Cardiff Arms Park / Alun Rees. *A Cardiff anthology*

Carwyn / J. Eirian Davies. *Awen yr hwyr*

Carwyn / R. Gerallt Jones. *Cerddi 1955-1989*

Carwyn / Robat Powell. *Haearn iaith*

Carwyn / W. R. Evans. *Awen y moelydd*

Carwyn James / Robat Powell. *Haearn iaith*

Cliff Morgan / Dic Jones. *Caneuon cynhaeaf*

Clive Rowlands / Dic Jones. *Caneuon cynhaeaf*

The confusion of tongues / Alfred Jingle. *Rugby rhymes, rough and ready*

Cusan / Rhydwen Williams. *Barddoniaeth Rhydwen Williams*

Cyfarch y capten / Ifor ap Glyn. *Cywyddau cyhoeddus*

Cywydd Graf / Robat Powell. *Haearn iaith*

Dewi Bebb / Dic Goodman. *I'r rhai sy'n gweld rhosyn gwyllt*

Dewi Bebb / Dic Jones. *Caneuon cynhaeaf*

Dewi Bebb / Idris Reynolds. *Cywyddau cyhoeddus 2*

Dewin y bêl (Molawd I Barry John) / Gwilym R. Jones. *Y syrcas a cherddi eraill*

Y dyrfa / Cynan. *Cofnodion a chyfansoddiadau Eisteddfod Genedlaethol 1931 (Bangor)*

Er cof (am Carwyn James) / Bryan Martin Davies. *Lleoedd*

Er cof am Carwyn James / Dic Jones. *Sgubo'r storws*

The fence / Mike Jenkins. *Graffiti narratives*

Football in the mud / Alfred Jingle. *Rugby rhymes, rough and ready*

Football 'journalese' / Alfred Jingle. *Rugby rhymes, rough and ready*

For John Ormond / Gwyn Williams. *Collected poems 1936-1986*

Forwards of the North (after Kipling) / Alfred Jingle. *Rugby rhymes, rough and ready*

From the Triads / Nigel Jenkins. *Acts of union*

The game / Bob Reeves. *Club rugby*

Y gêm / T. James Jones. *Eiliadau o berthyn*

The Georgiad / Roy Campbell. *The Georgiad*

Gerald Davies / T. R. Jones & Eirwyn George. *O'r Moelwyn i'r Preselau*

Give it a welly / Mike Jenkins. *Graffiti narratives*

The great day / P. G. Wodehouse. *Rugby football*

Gwaed / Bob Reeves. *Club rugby*

In praise of the drop-kick / Alfred Jingle. *Rugby rhymes, rough and ready*

Inquisition / John Tripp. *Collected poems, 1958-1978*

Keith Jarrett / Dic Jones. *Caneuon cynhaeaf*

Kitchen conversation / Pat Cutts. *The poetry of motion*

Land of song / Nigel Jenkins. *Song and dance*

'The last of the Mohicans' / Alfred Jingle. *Rugby rhymes, rough and ready*

Lincoln, 1301 / John Tripp. *The province of belief*

Lines for Hamlyn Davies / Tony Curtis. *Letting go*

The loss of ancestry / John Tripp. *The loss of ancestry*

Max Boyce / John Davies. *At the edge of town*

Miracle at Arms Park / Harri Webb. *Harri Webb*

Morgannwg: gwlad y glo / Crwys. *Cerddi Crwys (detholiad)*

New Zealand Rugby Union / Hone Towhare. *Deep river talk*

Not up to date / Alfred Jingle. *Rugby rhymes, rough and ready*

Notes for an autobiography / Raymond Garlick. *Collected poems*

'Oh, oh, hear the whistle blow!' / Alfred Jingle. *Rugby rhymes, rough and ready*

One day / Harri Webb. *A crown for Branwen*

Parc y Strade / W. R. Evans. *Fi yw hwn*

Parc yr Arfau / Dic Jones. *Cyfansoddiadau a beirniadaethau; Sgubo'r storws*

Penarth / John Tripp. *Collected poems, 1958-1978*

Pictures in a school hall / Tony Curtis. *War voices*

Pitch / Chris Bendon. *Cork memory*

Prynhawn Sadwrn yn yr ysbyty / Prys Morgan. *Trugareddau*

Rugby / Owen Rhys-Roberts. *Kiwis and dragons*

Rugby club sex scandal romp! / Mike Jenkins. *A dissident voice*

The rugby match / Bruce Davies. *The poetry of motion*

The rugger match / John Collings Squire. *The rugger match*; *The poetry of motion*

Rygbi / D. Gwenallt Jones. *Eples*

Rygbi a socer / Brinley Richards. *Cerddi'r dyffryn*

Sgrym / J. Eirian Davies. *Darnau difyr, barddoniaeth i blant*

'The shock of Crew' / Alfred Jingle. *Rugby rhymes, rough and ready*

To Arthur / Tony Curtis. *The last candles*

To the whistle / Alfred Jingle. *Rugby rhymes, rough and ready*

The true spirit / Harri Webb. *Poems and points*

Vive le sport / Harri Webb. *The green desert*

Wales has never lost a rugby match? / Owen Rhys-Roberts. *Kiwis and dragons*

A weather trilogy / Alfred Jingle. *Rugby rhymes, rough and ready*

'Won by two tries' / Alfred Jingle. *Rugby rhymes, rough and ready*

The Yorkshire Challenge Cup / Henry Saville. *Picturesque history of Yorkshire*

---

92 Acts of union: selected poems, 1974-1989 / Nigel Jenkins. Llandysul: Gomer, 1990.
143p

ISBN: 0863835295
BL: YC.1991.a.3012

Pages 108-113 are taken up with 'From the Triads', stanzas X and XII.

93 At the edge of town / John Davies. Llandysul: Gomer, 1981.
75p; illus

ISBN: 0850889235
BL: X.950/3772

'Max Boyce' on page 61.

94 Awen y moelydd / W. R. Evans. Llandysul: Gwasg Gomer, 1983.
106p; pbk

ISBN: 0850889693
BL: X.950/29979

Includes two poems to 'Carwyn' on pages 15 and 48.

95 Awen yr hwyr / J. Eirian Davies. Dinbych: Gwasg Gee, 1991.
48p

ISBN: 0707402085
BL: YK.1992.a.1282

Includes 'Carwyn' on page 47.

96 Barddoniaeth Rhydwen Williams: y casgliad cyflawn, 1941-1991 / Rhydwen Williams. Felindre, Abertawe: Cyhoeddiadau Barddas, 1991.
360p

BL: YK.1992.a.4701

This collection includes 'Barry John' and 'Cusan (ar ôl darllen llythyrau Nelson Mandela y diwrnod y dychwelodd tîm rygbi o Gymry o Dde Affrig)' which translates as 'The kiss (after reading the letters of Nelson Mandela the day a Welsh rugby team returned from South Africa)'.

97 Caneuon cynhaeaf / Dic Jones. Abertawe: Gwasg John Penry, 1969.
104p

BL: YA.1994.a.18022

Page 21: 'Barry John'; 'Clive Rowlands'; 'Dewi Bebb'. Page 22: 'Cliff Morgan', 'Alun Pask', 'Keith Jarrett'.

98 A Cardiff anthology / edited by Meic Stephens. Bridgend: Seren, 1987.
197p; pbk

Includes 'Cardiff Arms Park' by Alun Rees.

☞ Also listed at: H156

99 Cerddi 1955-1989 / R. Gerallt Jones. Aberystwyth: Cyhoeddiadau Barddas, 1989.
186p

BL: YC.1990.a.6787

Includes the poem 'Carwyn (wrth ddychwelyd o gae rygbi'r Strade, Rhagfyr 1987)'.

100 Cerddi Crwys (detholiad), cyfrol II. Aberystwyth: Gwasg Aberystwyth, 1956.

'Morgannwg: gwlad y glo' (Glamorgan: land of coal) by William Crwys Williams describes in five short stanzas an international match at Cardiff Arms Park. The Welsh players are all from Glamorgan.

101 Cerddi'r dyffryn / Brinley Richards. Abertawe: Gwasg John Penry, 1967.
107p

BL: YA.1990.a.15067

The rugby poem is entitled 'Rygbi a socer'.

102 Club rugby: a visual celebration of the first-class club game in Wales / compiled by Paul Rees; introduction by Barry John. Cardiff: Oriel, 1985.
68p; illus; pbk

ISBN: 0946329176

'The game' and 'Gwaed' ('Blood') by Bob Reeves.

☞ Also listed at: B636

103   Cofnodion a chyfansoddiadau Eisteddfod Genedlaethol
      1931 (Bangor): barddoniaeth a beirniadaethau /
      golygwyd gan E. Vincent Evans. Wales?: Cymdeithas yr
      Eisteddfod Genedlaethol, 1931.
      viii, 132p; pbk

      'Y dyrfa' (The crowd), won the crown and the sum of
      £20 for Cynan at the 1931 National Eisteddfod. The
      adjudication of the entries is on pages 54-105 with
      the winning poem published on pages 106-14. The
      poem tells of the scoring of the winning try for Wales
      against England at Twickenham by future Christian
      missionary John Roberts. In the words of Cynan's
      biographer, Dafydd Owen, 'this dramatic ballad is a
      fervent expression of a profound Christian experience,
      and at the same time of a distinct facet of the Welsh
      tradition'. The crown was presented by the Cunard
      Company of Liverpool.

104   Collected poems 1936-1986 / Gwyn Williams.
      Llandysul: Gomer Press, 1987.
      xviii, 184p   ISBN: 0863833241
                                           BL: YH.1988.a.654

      'For John Ormond':
                      'April 27…
                  …My diary says Llanelli
            beat Cardiff in the final (I remember
            Albert Jenkins dropping a prodigious
                  goal from half-way)…'

105   Collected poems, 1958-1978 / John Tripp. Swansea:
      Christopher Davies, 1978.
      128p   ISBN: 0715404512
                                           BL: X.989/52806

      'Inquisition':
            '"Wales is more than a language", he sobbed,
               "It's landscape and rugby football
               and some people down in the south"…

      and, 'Penarth':
                  '…the Esplanade Hotel was full
              of touring rugby packs, their names
                hallowed in Playfair, boozing
              like galleons awash in the long bar…'

106   Collected poems: collected poems 1946-1986 /
      Raymond Garlick. Llandysul: Gwasg Gomer, 1987.
      165p; pbk   ISBN: 0863833187
                                           BL: YH.1988.a.155

      Includes 'Cardiff':
                  'Passing the Arms Park, hearing
                  The sixty-odd thousand fling
                  Their battle chants, bay uproar
                  For their game of ritual war …'

      and, 'Notes for an autobiography':
                  'And rugby's a more recent name
                  For turning life into a game;
                  Strolling off from reality
                  To players' bar or chapel tea…'.

107   Cork memory / Chris Bendon. Crewe: Stride, 1987.
      56p; pbk   ISBN: 0946699380
                                           BL: YC.1989.a.11329

      'Pitch':
                  'I seem so tall as against when
                  I was nose and knees to mud…
                      …rising leather
            - theat sewn up egg, its dark chocolate
               we had to chuck like hot goods…
            a runner who stole a Faberge from the elite
               up north - cheers egging us on…
               as across to the famous dropped h…
                      I plunge…'

108   A crown for Branwen / Harri Webb. Llandysul: Gwasg
      Gomer, 1974.
      76p   ISBN 0850882508
                                           BL: X.989/27415

      'One day':
                  'Bryn is still there after the others
               Have packed up training, gone for a pint.
                  Light fails, … no-one is watching,
                      Only the posts…
               As he practises placekick after placekick.
                      One day
                  In a red shirt he may run,
                  Out into the great roar…'

109   Cyfansoddiadau a beirniadaethau: Eisteddfod
      Genedlaethol Frenhinol Cymru, Caerdydd 1978 /
      golygydd W. Rhys Nicholas. Llandysul: Gwasg Gomer
      dros Lys yr Eisteddfod Genedlaethol, 1978.
      xvi, 207p; pbk   ISBN: 0850887704

      'Parc yr Arfau' (Cardiff Arms Park) is the winning
      poem written in a special metre at the 1978 National
      Eisteddfod.

110   Cywyddau cyhoeddus / golygwyd gan Iwan Llwyd,
      Myrddin ap Dafydd. Llanrwst: Gwasg Carreg Gwalch, 1994.
      140p; illus; pbk   ISBN: 0863813011
                                           BL: YK.1995.a.5884

      Includes Ifor ap Glyn's 'Cyfarch y capten (ar ôl tymor
      cynta' hynod aflwyddiannus Clwb Rygbi Ifor Bach)'
      which translates as 'Greeting the captain (following a
      notably unsuccessful season of the Ifor Bach Rugby
      Football Club)'.

111   Cywyddau cyhoeddus 2 / golygwyd gan Myrddin ap
      Dafydd. Llanrwst: Gwasg Carreg Gwalch, 1996.
      143p; illus; pbk   ISBN: 0863813720
                                           BL: YK.1997.a.277

      'Dewi Bebb' appears on page 74.

112   Darnau difyr, barddoniaeth i blant / J. Eirian Davies.
      Dinbych: Gwasg Gee, 1989.
      47p; pbk   ISBN: 0707401682
                                           BL: YC.1990.a.29

      Includes 'Sgrym' ('Scrum').

113 Deep river talk: collected poems / Hone Towhare;
    introduction by Frank Stewart. Honolulu: University of
    Hawaii Press, 1994.
    vii, 200p; index
    (Talanoa: contemporary Pacific literature)
                                        ISBN: 0824815882
    Includes a poem entitled 'New Zealand Rugby Union'.

114 A dissident voice / Mike Jenkins. Bridgend: Seren, 1990.
    86p; pbk   ISBN: 185411025X
                                        BL: YC.1990.a.5448
    'Rugby club sex scandal romp!' on page 38.

115 Eiliadau o berthyn / T. James Jones. Caernarfon:
    Cyhoeddiadau Barddas, 1991.
    55p   BL: YK.1996.a.11441
    Contains one rugby poem, 'Y gêm' (The game).

116 Eples: cyfrol o farddoniaeth / D. Gwenallt Jones.
    Llandysul: Gwasg Gomer, 1951.
    74p   BL: 11595.c.68
    'Rygbi'.

117 Fi yw hwn: hunangofiant / W. R. Evans. Abertawe:
    Christopher Davies, 1980.
    280p   ISBN: 0715405691
    'This is me: an autobiography' with a poem on pages
    276-78 entitled 'Parc y Strade' ('Stradey Park'), the
    home of Llanelli RFC.

118 Flight patterns / John Davies. Bridgend: Seren, 1991.
    77p; pbk   ISBN: 1854110446
                                        BL: YK.1991.a.10630
    'Barry John' appears on page 71.

119 The Georgiad: a satirical fantasy in verse / Roy
    Campbell. London: Boriswood, 1931.
    64p   BL: Cup.510.caf.2
    A section of this poem on pages 22-23 mocks J. C.
    Squire's poem 'The rugger match'.
    ☞ See also: H139

120 Graffiti narratives: poems 'n' stories / Mike Jenkins.
    Aberystwyth: Planet, 1994.
    70p; pbk   ISBN: 0950518816
                                        BL: YK.1996.a.4145
    Includes 'The fence' and 'Give it a welly'.

121 The green desert: collected poems, 1950-1969 / Harri
    Webb. Llandysul: Gwasg Gower, 1969.
    74p   BL: X.989/6081
    'Vive le sport':
             'Sing a song of rugby,
           Buttocks, booze and blood...
             When the match is over....
           If you think the game is filthy,
           Then you should hear the songs'.

122 Haearn iaith / Robat Powell. Llandysul: Gomer, 1996.
    109p; pbk   ISBN: 1859023991
                                        BL: YK.1996.a.23076
    A collection of Welsh language poems including poems
    on Welsh international players Arthur Emyr, Ray
    Gravell and Carwyn James, and the Gnoll rugby
    ground, Neath.

123 Harri Webb: collected poems / compiled and edited by
    Meic Stephens. Llandysul: Gomer, 1995.
    xxviii, 503p   ISBN: 1859022995
                                        BL: YC.1996.a.1354
    'Miracle at Arms Park'.

124 I'r rhai sy'n gweld rhosyn gwyllt / Dic Goodman.
    Caernarfon: Gwasg Ty ar y Graig, 1979.
    87p; pbk   BL: X.908/43490
    Includes 'Dewi Bebb'.

125 Kiwis and dragons: paintings in poetry, volume 1 /
    Owen Rhys-Roberts. Wellington, NZ: Owen, Owen and
    Owen Associates, 1988.
    xix, 86p; pbk   ISBN: 0473007169
    Welsh and New Zealand themes in the main. The rugby
    poems are 'Rugby' and 'Wales has never lost a rugby
    match?'.

126 The last candles / Tony Curtis. Bridgend: Seren, 1989.
    85p   ISBN: 1854110055
                                        BL: YC.1989.a.6773
    'To Arthur':
      'He was always the manic, serious sportsman,
    ex-international centre, buffeting through our flailing
    arms to ghost towards the memory of Stradey tries,
             lofting again and again
       that sweet dropped goal at Lansdowne Road...'

127 Letting go / Tony Curtis. Bridgend: Poetry Wales, 1983.
    57p; pbk   ISBN: 0907476252
                                        BL: X.958/21359
    'Lines for Hamlyn Davies':
         '...we're singing for another Triple Crown.
       The language and the rugby are romance...'

128 Lleoedd / Bryan Martin Davies. Caernarfon:
    Cyhoeddiadau Barddas, 1984.
    46p   BL: X.950/35849
    'Er cof (am Carwyn James)' which translates as 'In
    memory (of Carwyn James)'.

129 The loss of ancestry / John Tripp. Llandybie:
    Christopher Davies, 1969.
    57p   SBN: 853390096
                                        BL: X.989/5143
    'The loss of ancestry':
                   'The capital ...
              heave with sportsmen;
               the only cultural arena
            is the sacred turf in Arms Park...'

130 Y mannau mwyn: a cherddi eraill i'r ifanc / W. Rhys Nicholas. Abertawe: Penry, 1985.
70p; pbk
ISBN: 0903701766
BL: YC.1986.a.4020

'Cais i Cymru' (A try for Wales) is on page 16.

131 O'r Moelwyn i'r Preselau / T. R. Jones & Eirwyn George. Llandysul: Gwasg Gomer, 1975.
xii, 60p; pbk
ISBN: 0850882958
BL: X.909/40128

Includes 'Barry John' and 'Gerald Davies'.

132 Picturesque history of Yorkshire: being an account of the history, topography, antiquities, industries and modern life of the cities, towns and villages of the county of York, founded on personal observations made during many journeys through the three Ridings / J. S. Fletcher. Volume 5. London: Caxton, 1904?
BL: 2067.e-f

'The Yorkshire Challenge Cup' by Saville, a well-known Halifax writer, first appeared in 'The Yorkshireman'.

133 Poems and points / Harri Webb. Llandysul: Gomer, 1983.
43p; pbk
ISBN: 0850885264
BL: X.958/21490

'The true spirit':
'The game was fast and furious,
The final of the West Wales Cup…
There they were all at it,
Forwards, threequarters, halves,
Bruises all over their bodies
And teeth marks deep in their calves…'

134 The poetry of motion: an anthology of sporting verse / edited by Alan Bold. Edinburgh: Mainstream, 1986?
201p; index
ISBN: 0906391709
BL: YC.1987.a.2801

Includes 'Kitchen conversation' by Pat Cutts; 'The rugby match' by Bruce Davies; and, 'The rugger match' by Sir John Collings Squire.

135 The province of belief: selected poems, 1965-1970 / John Tripp. Ammanford: Christopher Davies, 1971.
65p
SBN: 853390835
BL: X.989/11922

'Anglo-Welsh testimony':
'At Twickenham a red-shirted jinking genius
still races the pulse; the huge choirs
induce a shiver of the spine…'
and, 'Lincoln, 1301':
'Seven centuries distant from Lincoln
in the swarming capital of the Welsh,
the latest incumbent is cheered
on a rugby field!'

136 Racist rugby: front-line poets respond / James Edwards and others. Auckland, NZ: Graphic Publications, 1981.
32p; illus

Foreword by Tom Newnham; contributions by Bob Orr, Chris Parr, Barry Metcalfe, Linda Collins, Rosemary Hollins, Gloria Stanford, Gary McCormick, James Edwards, Harry Goodwin, Tom Frewen, Don McRae. The individual titles of these poems were not available, so it has not been possible to list them.

137 Rugby football: an anthology / compiled by Kenneth Pelmear in collaboration with J. E. Morpurgo; with an introduction by O. L. Owen. London: Allen & Unwin, 1958.
357p; illus
BL: 7924.b.23

Contains 'The great day', a poem by P. G. Wodehouse, which 'sarcastically celebrates the great day when [Cyril] Lowe finally got the ball'.

☞ Also listed at: H152

138 Rugby rhymes, rough and ready: with Mr Jingle at the '92 International / Alfred Jingle. Cupar: Fifeshire Journal, 1893.
32p; pbk
BL: 11601.aaa.45(5)

An unusual little collection of twelve poems and a short prose piece on the 1892 England v. Scotland International. There are no clues to 'Mr Alfred Jingle's' true identity.

The Last of the 'Mohicans'

The forwards blamed the quarters, while in turn the halves they blamed,
In self-defence the halves declared the back should be ashamed —
That's how we got the licking; yes, that must have been the cause,
A proper dressing, though, we had, whosever fault it was.
we went to play some school-boys — thought we'd got a soft thing on,
Our halves were Tom, Dick, Harry, and our full-back's name was John;
Our quarters, Bob and Billy — forwards, Thomson, Robinson,
Smith, Jones, Brown, Higgins, Saunders, little Briggs, and Tomlinson.

The school-boys quickly showed us that they knew a thing or two,
Their forwards carried every maul and rushed the ball right through;
Their dribbling was the dickens — kind of thing you couldn't stop,
Not anyhow, I tell you — my, they had us on the hop!

And sometimes they'd pick up and chuck, and then we had a squint
At half-backs waltzing round us — 'gad, they showed us how to sprint!
And as for their drop-kicking, well, one goal was from half-way —
The kind of thing you don't see every other Saturday.

Besides, their tactics in defence weren't very far behind.
Poor Billy thought he'd got off once and tried to 'go it blind.'
Then one chap got him by the feet, another by the head —
Between them he had not much chance, a body would have said.
Indeed he hadn't, nor, by Jove, had either Tom or Dick
When once they tried some passing — one half dashed in mighty quick
Between them, got the ball, and had a run, upon my soul,
That only finished up when he was right behind our goal!

We 'took it fighting' to the last, but that did not prevent
Humiliation on our part as off the field we went.
For (tell it not in Gath nor in the papers, I implore)
Some eighty points to nothing was the total of their score!

We haven't quite decided yet who really was in fault.
Meantime the Club's defunct, and this is written o'er the vault —
'The forwards blame the quarters while in turn the halves they blame,
In self-defence the halves declare the back's not worth a d—mn!'

> Alfred Jingle
> Rugby rhymes, rough and ready, 1893

139   The rugger match / John Collings Squire. London: The
author, 1922.
14p

> *Limited edition of fifty copies, signed by the author*
>   BL: Cup.501.e.12

Commemorating a varsity match at Queen's Club.

☞ See also: H119

140   Sgubo'r storws: pedwaredd cyfrol a gerddi / Dic Jones.
Llandysul: Gomer, 1986.
80p; pbk   ISBN: 0863832539
                                            BL: YC.1987.a.3668

Includes the poems 'Er cof am Carwyn James' (In
memory of Carwyn James) and 'Parc yr Arfau' (The
Arms Park).

141   Song and dance / Nigel Jenkins. Bridgend: Seren, 1981.
Includes 'Land of song'.

142   Sporting relations / Roger McGough; with illustrations
by the author. London: Eyre Methuen, 1974.
64p; illus   ISBN: 0413327507
                                            BL: X.989/27740

> 'Big Arth from Penarth
> was a forward and a half
> Though built like a peninsula
> with muscles like pink slagheaps…
> A giraffe in the lineout
> a rhino in the pack
> he never passed forward
> when he should've passed back…'

143   Storom Awst: trydedd cyfrol o gerddi Dic Jones.
Llandysul: Gwasg Gomer, 1978.
101p; pbk   ISBN: 0850886708
                                            BL: X.908/41862

'Baled y Llewod, 1971' is a ballad to the Welsh players
in the British Isles (the Lions) side to Australasia,
1971.

144   Y syrcas a cherddi eraill / Gwilym R. Jones. Bala:
Llyfrau'r Faner, 1975.
74p   ISBN: 0901695262
                                            BL: X.989/40137

'Dewin y bêl (Molawd I Barry John)' on pages 50 to 54
translates as 'The wizard with the ball (In praise of
Barry John)'.

145   Trugareddau / Prys Morgan. Llandybie: Christopher
Davies, 1973.
75p   SBN: 715400584

Page 73: 'Prynhawn Sadwrn yn yr ysbyty' which
translates as 'Saturday afternoon in the hospital'.

146   War voices / Tony Curtis. Bridgend: Seren, 1995.
80p; pbk   ISBN: 1854111418
                                            BL: YK.1996.a.7979

'Pictures in a school hall':
> 'Rows of old school photographs…
> 1st XV 1939 – arms folded over their chests,
> Puffed like robins, hair cropped and oiled,
> These boys look like our father…'

147   We are the champions: a collection of sporting verse /
compiled by Caroline Sheldon and Richard Heller;
illustrated by Virginia Salter. London: Hutchinson, 1986.
124p; illus   ISBN: 0091634709
                                            BL: YC.1986.a.2541

Includes: 'A bit of a ballad: Scotland v. Australia,
Murrayfield, 18 December 1981' by Gavin Ewart which
relates in verse Scotland's victory against Australia
on that day; and, 'Big Arth' by Roger McGough.

Plays

Lewis, Geraint

148   Y cinio. Caerdydd: Dalier Sylw mewn cydweithrediad a'r
Ganolfan Astudiaethau Addysg, 1995.
86p; pbk

> *Perfformiwyd y ddrama am y tro cyntaf gan gwmni Dalier
> Sylw yn neuadd Ysgol Rhydfelen, Rhydyfelin ar Fawrth 16eg
> 1995 = The drama was first performed by the Dalier Sylw
> Theatre Company in the Rhydfelen school hall, Rhydyfelin, on
> March 16th 1995;*

Cast: 1 woman & 4 men   ISBN: 1856449475

'The dinner' – the setting for this comedy is the
annual dinner of Cwmbrain RFC.

McGee, Greg

149   Foreskin's lament. Wellington, NZ: Victoria University
Press, 1981.
96p; pbk
(New Zealand playscripts)

Cast: 2 women & 7 men   ISBN: 0864730314
                                            BL: YA.1988.a.18255

McGee was a former All Black trialist. The stage play,
set in 1976, analyses New Zealand society and its
values and explores why the game of rugby has
become a secular religion. Act 1 takes place in a rugby
changing room, act 2 at the after-match party.

Williams, Islwyn

150 Cap Wil Tomos: drama un act. Aberystwyth: Gwasg
Aberystwyth, 1951.
24p; pbk   BL: 11790.a.11
A play based on the short story of the same title.

Miscellanies

151 Rugger stories / edited with an introduction by H.
Marshall. London: Putnam, 1932.
xv, 303p   BL: 12602.s.10
Twenty six stories, some factual, some fiction by such
authors as John Buchan (from 'Castle Gay'); Alec
Waugh (from 'On doing what one likes'); J. B. Priestley
(from 'Apes and angels'); P. G. Wodehouse (from 'The
gold bat'); a poem from J. C. Squire; Thomas Hughes
(from 'Tom Brown's schooldays'); and Arthur Budd's
'Past development in rugby football'. Also includes a
biographical piece on Ronnie Poulton.

152 Rugby football: an anthology / compiled by Kenneth
Pelmear in collaboration with J. E. Morpurgo; with an
introduction by O. L. Owen. London: Allen & Unwin,
1958.
357p; illus   BL: 7924.b.23
☞ Also listed at: H137

153 Arms linked: women against the tour: poetry and prose
by New Zealand women opposed to the 1981 Springbok
tour / edited by Margaret Freeman and Rosemary
Hollins. Auckland, NZ: The editors, 1982.
46p   ISBN: 0473001357

154 Rugby digest / written and compiled by J. N. Pargeter.
The author, 1995.
140p; illus; pbk
*Illustrated by the late Dudley Hallwood, cartoonist for The
Journal*
The cover declares: 'a collection of rugby stories from
the author's highly successful series of "Rugby
digests". Though published between 1950 and 1961, all
the original articles still apply; others are very
relevant to the modern game'.

✱ *Additional References*

155 Modern sports writers: a collection of prose / edited by
John Byrne. London: Batsford Academic and
Educational, 1982.
173p   ISBN: 0713443030
                                                BL: X.629/18079
Rugby throws up five factual and two fictional pieces.
In the former David Irvine, Carwyn James, David Frost,
J. B. G. Thomas and Alun Richards have reproduced
their thoughts on: the joy of rugby; Irish great Mike
Gibson; Barry John; Keith Jarrett's contribution to
the Wales-England match at Cardiff in 1967; and
half-back play in the Welsh game. Extracts from
humorist Michael Green and Richard Llewellyn's 'How
green was my valley' complete the story.

156 A Cardiff anthology / edited by Meic Stephens.
Bridgend: Seren, 1987.
197p; pbk   ISBN: 0907476848
                                                BL: YC.1988.a.3357
Includes Tom Davies, 'The big game', Emyr Humphreys,
'After the match', Gwyn Jones, 'Come on, Wales!', and
some poetry.
☞ Also listed at: H98

157 Sporting literature: an anthology / chosen by Vernon
Scannell. Oxford: Oxford University Press, 1987.
320p; index   ISBN: 0192122509
                                                BL: YC.1987.a.3483

158 Sport the way I speak it / Peter Fenton. Sydney, Aust.:
Little Hills Press, 1992.
172p; illus   ISBN: 1863150382
Sporting anecdotes, prose and poetry on rugby,
cricket, boxing, and horse racing.

Essays & Reminiscences

✳ Single Author Works

Allan, Gordon

159   Not all mud and scrums: rugby union before
      professionalism. Brighton: Alpha, 1996.
      58p; illus; pbk   ISBN: 1898595194
                                         BL: YK.1997.a.2725

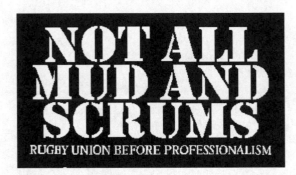

Alston, Rex

160   Taking the air / foreword by Lionel Gamlin. London:
      Stanley Paul, 1951.
      264p; illus; index   BL: 10857.bb.38

      Test matches, rugby internationals, Wimbledon ... all
      through the eyes of the well-known BBC sports
      commentator.

Barnes, Stuart

161   The year of living dangerously: rugby and the World Cup
      1995. London: Richard Cohen, 1995.
      viii, 247p; illus; index   ISBN: 1860660274
                                         BL: YK.1996.b.11289

      Reviews the 1994-95 season; the World Cup and the
      revision of the amateur regulations.

Batchelor, Denzil

162   Days without sunset. London: Eyre & Spottiswoode,
      1949.
      283p   BL: 7917. bbb.14

      '...a book of recollections of great sporting events.'
      Includes two chapters on rugby: Australia at
      Twickenham, and The unfading fern.

Beanland, Vincent A. S.

163   Great games and great players: some thoughts and
      recollections of a sports journalist. London: W. H. Allen,
      1945.
      151p; index   BL: 7916.e.44

      Includes chapters: 'Cradled in rugby football';
      'Somnolent rugby chiefs'; 'Bob' (R. F. Oakes); 'An
      historic episode' (Wales v New Zealand, 1905) and
      more.

Beaumont, Bill

164   Bill Beaumont's rugby year 1997 / edited by Matthew
      Petipher. London: Highbury House Communications,
      1996.
      98p; illus; pbk

Beaumont, Bill with Neil Hanson

165   Bill Beaumont's rugby masterpieces. London: Sidgwick
      & Jackson, 1992.
      xiv, 317p; illus   ISBN: 0283061316
                                         BL: YK.1992.b.8456

      An anthology in 16 headings, each subdivided.
      Contains fact and fiction.

Bray, Gordon

166   From the ruck: a commentator tells all / foreword by
      Nick Farr-Jones. Milsons Point, Aust.: Random House
      Australia, 1997.
      xviii, 210p; illus; pbk   ISBN: 0091830559

Brooke, Zinzan

167   The big black rugby book. Auckland, NZ: Rugby Press,
      1990.
      135p; illus; pbk   ISBN: 0908630336

Butler, Muriel

168   Tackling club rugby. Blackrock, Co Dublin: DBA
      Publications, 1997.
      64p; illus; pbk   ISBN: 0951969242

Cartwright, Justin

169   Not yet home. London: Fourth Estate, 1996.
      xi, 192p   ISBN: 1857024036
                                         BL: YC.1996.a.4482

Catt, Mike & Leonard Stall

170   The quest for the ultimate Grand Slam: Mike Catt's year.
Edinburgh: Mainstream, 1995.
192p; illus   ISBN: 1851587888
                                          BL: YK.1996.b.12142

Catt runs through the season – winning the Pilkington
Cup with Bath, the Five-Nations Championship with
England and reaching the semi-final of the World Cup
with England in South Africa, 1995. He also
discusses Will Carling's dismissal and reinstatement
as captain of England and the inevitability of
professionalism in the game.

Channer, J. 'Dad'

171   My fifty years of sporting and public life, notes on rugby
methods, hints and advice to players - young and old.
Uitenhage, SA: Uitenhage Chronicle, 1935?
63p; pbk

Chilcott, Gareth

172   Gareth Chilcott: my favourite rugby stories / Gareth
Chilcott with Les Scott; illustrations by David Farris.
London: Simon & Schuster, 1995.
xi, 287p; illus   ISBN: 0671714252
                                          BL: YK.1996.a.19270

Chilcott, the former England forward, recounts
humorous events in matches and on tour.

Gareth Chilcott

My Favourite Rugby Stories

GARETH CHILCOTT
with
LES SCOTT

Illustrations by David Farris

SIMON & SCHUSTER
LONDON · SYDNEY · NEW YORK · TOKYO · SINGAPORE · TORONTO

Collins, William John Townsend

173   Rugby recollections. Newport: R.H. Johns, 1948.
xix, 182p; illus   BL: 7917.bb.35

Craven, Nico

174   Try and run in search of rugby. Seascale: The author, 1975.
20p; pbk   ISBN: 0905467027
                                          BL: X.619/16768

Bit of a mixture, including The Mallaby Report and
rugby in Gloucestershire.

Edwards, Gareth

175   Gareth Edwards' most memorable matches with Terry
Godwin; cartoons by Roy Ullyett. London: Stanley Paul,
1984.
109p; illus   ISBN: 0091535905
                                          BL: X.629/25222

Fisher, Norman

176   Great days in sport. London: Mitre, 1943.
95p; pbk   BL: 7917.de.15
Includes: 'Wales beat All-Blacks at rugby, December
16, 1905', pages 36-38.

FitzSimons, Peter

177   Basking in Beirut: and other adventures with Peter
FitzSimons. North Sydney, Aust.: Allen & Unwin, 1991.
168p; illus; pbk   ISBN: 1863730524
                                          BL: YA.1993.a.18717

French, Ray

178   More kinds of rugby. London: Kingswood, 1989.
192p; illus; pbk   ISBN: 0413624803
                                          BL: YK.1990.a.360

Giles, Ben

179   'On the ball': tales of rugby in New Zealand.
Wellington, NZ: Organ, 1934.
63p
A very scarce book, only known from a copy held by
the New Zealand Rugby Museum.

Green, Michael

180   The boy who shot down an airship: the first part of an
autobiography. London: Heinemann, 1988.
vii, 232p; illus   ISBN: 0434304123
                                          BL: YC.1988.a.14842

181   Nobody hurt in small earthquake: the sequel to, The boy
who shot down an airship. London: Heinemann, 1990.
x, 245p; illus   ISBN: 0434304107
                                          BL: YC.1990.a.3552

Two part autobiography, both hilarious and moving,
from the author of the popular 'Art of coarse' books.

Grierson, Henry

182   The ramblings of a rabbit / foreword by Mark F. Waters. London: Chapman & Hall, 1924.
xi, 238p; illus; index   BL: 07911.eee.47

Reminiscences, mostly of rugby football, including a chapter on Leicester rugger.

Guiney, David

183   The days of the little green apples. Dublin: Gaelic Press, 1975.
118p; pbk

Sports columnist relates many tales, including rugby.

Hanson, Neil See Beaumont, Bill & Neil Hanson

Harding, Rowe

184   Rugby: reminiscences and opinions. London: Pilot Press, 1929.
154p; illus   BL: 07911.gg.55

Concentrates on the game in Wales.

Irvine, David

185   The joy of rugby. London: Luscombe, 1978.
144p; illus; index   ISBN: 0860021246
BL: X.620/18098

☞   Subsequent ed. H186

186   The joy of rugby. Rev. ed. London: Luscombe, 1979.
143p; illus; index; pbk   ISBN: 0860021254
BL: X.622/11569

☞   Previous ed. H185

John, Barry

187   Barry John's rugby world. London: Frederick Muller, 1982.
160p; illus   ISBN: 0584110367
BL: X.622/14840

188   O gwmpas y byd gyda Barry John. Llandybie: Christopher Davies, 1974.
82p; illus; pbk   ISBN: 0715401181
BL: X.619/8328

'Around the world with Barry John'.

Jones, Elias

189   The palmy days of Welsh rugby. Llanelly: The author, 1935.
30p; illus; pbk

Reminiscences of a veteran Welsh rugby forward.

Jones, G. V. Wynne

190   Sports commentary. London: Hutchinson, 1951.
191p; illus   BL: W.P.1156/17

Of the 15 chapters, 6 deal with rugby.

Jones, Stephen

191   Endless winter: the inside story of the rugby revolution. Edinburgh: Mainstream, 1993.
287p; illus; index   ISBN: 1851585613
BL: YK.1994.b.4457

☞   Subsequent ed. H192

192   Endless winter: the inside story of the rugby revolution. Edinburgh: Mainstream, 1994.
295p; illus; index; pbk

Updated to include England's South Africa tour
ISBN: 1851586849

☞   Previous ed. H191

Keating, Frank

193   Frank Keating's sporting century: the best, the worst, the weirdest. London: Robson, 1997.
260p   ISBN: 1861051123

The rugby chapter is divided into: Try scorer of the century; Tackle of the century; Prophet of the century.

194   Long days, late nights / illustrated by John Jensen. London: Robson, 1984.
224p; illus   ISBN: 0860512932
BL: X.629/24813

Pages 85-88 and 92-96 are concerned with rugby.

195   Up and under: a rugby diary. London: Hodder and Stoughton, 1983.
190p; illus; index   ISBN: 034034508X
BL: X.622/18677

Not so much a diary, more a journalistic examination by the Guardian correspondent of rugby played in all corners of the globe. Even finds space to reproduce, briefly, a treatise by a sports geographer on the number of rugby clubs per capita in Britain.

Kilburn, J. M.

196   In search of rugby football. London: Arthur Barker, 1938.
ix, 174p; illus   BL: 7911.eee.10

Comprising brief articles, most of which have been reprinted from the Yorkshire Post, this serves as a companion volume to 'In search of cricket'. There are pieces on the four national grounds, Twickenham, Cardiff Arms Park, Murrayfield, and Lansdowne Road. Potted biographies are also given for L. A. Booth, Wilfred Wooller, A. L. Gracie, Edward Myers, H. G. Owen-Smith, and W. J. A. Davies.

Labuschagne, Fred

197 Eye witness on sport. Wellington, NZ: Reed, 1970.
168p; illus

> *Also published in Cape Town, SA: Howard Timmins, 1970.*
>
> Labuschagne, a South African, looks at golf, swimming, tennis, cricket, the Olympics and six chapters on rugby in the International Board countries.

Lynd, Robert

198 Both sides of the road. London: Methuen, 1934.
viii, 183p   BL: 012352.bbb.71

> The author enthuses about Oxford University full-back, Tuppy Owen-Smith, in 'Storm troops at Twickenham'.

199 The cockleshell. London: Methuen, 1933.
viii, 183p   BL: 12355.ppp.46

> Chapter 21, 'Twickenham' is mostly about England v. Ireland.

MacCarthy, Winston

200 Rugby in my time: on New Zealand rugby football and personalities. Wellington, NZ: Reed, 1959.
200p; illus   BL: 7925.b.6

McKenzie, Norman

201 On with the game: the rugby reminiscences of Norman McKenzie. Wellington, NZ: Reed, 1961.
x, 166p; illus

> McKenzie was a player, selector, delegate and administrator.

McLean, Terry

202 The best of McLean. London: Hodder & Stoughton, 1985.
255p; illus   ISBN: 0340363959

> Mainly rugby, and a number of sports and wartime reports.

Mallalieu, J. P. W.

203 Sporting days: in which a travelling partisan views test matches, FA Cup finals, rugger and cricket matches, Irish hurling, billiards, boxing, racing & tennis & any other sport which fills in gaps between Huddersfield Town's home matches. London: Phoenix Sports Books, 1955.
190p; illus   BL: 7919.bb.52

204 Very ordinary sportsman. London: Routledge & Kegan Paul, 1957.
viii, 167p; illus; index   BL: 7923.r.10

> J. P. W. Mallalieu, MP, describes the annual Oxford v. Cambridge encounter at Twickenham on pages 126-144.

Mellish, Frank

205 My dear Danie: an open letter to Danie Craven / drawings by T. O. Honiball. Cape Town, SA: Maskew Miller, 1960.
92p; illus

> *English text bound tête-bêche with Afrikaans text*
>   BL: X.629/7531
>
> Frank Mellish gives his thoughts on aspects of the game in South Africa, including refereeing and coaching.

Morgan, John

206 John Morgan's Wales: a personal anthology. Swansea: Christopher Davies, 1993.
303p; pbk   ISBN: 0715406868
                           BL: YK.1993.a.16970

> Four sections including one on sport. Includes six well-crafted and analytical articles on rugby by this eminent author reproduced from the *New Statesman* and *The Observer*.

Mulgan, Alan

207 First with the sun / illustrated by Olivia Spencer Bower. London: Dent, 1939.
x, 243p; illus   BL: 2350.c.20

> Includes 'He's over' in which the author muses about sports writing.

O'Connor, Ulick

208 Sport is my lifeline: essays from the Sunday Times / foreword by Norris McWhirter. London: Pelham, 1984.
xviii, 141p; illus; index   ISBN: 0720715229
                           BL: X.629/24180

> Biographer of Oliver St. John Gogarty and Brendan Behan, Ulick O'Connor has divided this book into 5 chapters. The topics covered in the chapter on rugby range from: the Abbé Pistre lover of French rugby; injuries; Irish greats Jackie Kyle, Jammie Clinch, Mark Sugden, and Kevin O'Flanagan; to, Joyce's references to Irish rugby in *Finnegans Wake*.

Reyburn, Wallace MacDonald

209 The rugby companion. London: Stanley Paul, 1969.
122p; illus   SBN: 090979206
                           BL: X.441/1285

Sewell, E. H. D.

210 Rugger: the man's game / with a preface by C. B. Fry. London: Hollis & Carter, 1944.
xi, 276p; illus; index   BL: 7917.bb.16
☞   Subsequent ed. H211

211   Rugger: the man's game / with a preface by C. B. Fry.
      2nd ed. London: Hollis & Carter, 1947.
      xi, 276p; illus; index
      ☞   Previous ed. H210; subsequent ed. H212

212   Rugger: the man's game / with a preface by C. B. Fry.
      3rd ed. revised by O. L. Owen. London: Hollis & Carter,
      1950.
      xi, 276p; illus; index   BL: 7920.ee.3
      ☞   Previous ed. H211

Sharp, Richard

213   Winning rugby. London: Pelham, 1968.
      144p; illus   BL: X.449/3297

Stall, Leonard See Catt, Mike & Leonard Stall

Stewart, J. J.

214   Gumboots and goalposts: a collection of yarns from the
      country. Auckland, NZ: Rugby Press, 1985.
      160p; illus   ISBN: 0908630212

Swanton, E. W.

215   Sort of a cricket person. London: Collins, 1972.
      318p; illus   ISBN: 0002117487
                                              BL: X.520/6426

      Includes three chapters on rugby.

Thomas, J. B. G.

216   Fifty-two famous tries. London: Pelham Books, 1966.
      176p; illus   BL: X.449/2241

217   Great moments in sport: rugby football: thirty
      memorable moments in the rugby union game of the last
      20 years. London: Pelham, 1974.
      176p; illus   ISBN: 0720706882
                                              BL: X.629/6759

218   Great rugger matches: forty-one historic matches from
      1871 to 1958. London: Stanley Paul, 1959.
      210p; illus   BL: 7925.b.21

Thomas, R. S.

219   ABC Neb / golygwyd gan Jason Walford Davies.
      Caernarfon: Gwasg Gwynedd, 1995.
      100p; pbk   ISBN: 0860741249
                                              BL: YK.1996.a.13653

      Twenty short chapters. Each of the headings in
      alphabetical order: Aber, Bangor, Caer, and so on. In
      the chapter 'Maswr', R. S. Thomas recounts playing
      rugby during his school and university days at
      Holyhead, Bangor and Llandaff. While a student at
      the Theological College in Llandaff, he witnessed
      Wales' win over the 1935 All Blacks. He contends
      that, though Wales continue to produce talented
      threequarters, there is a need to coach forwards to
      compete in the modern game. Otherwise players will
      continue disappearing to the north of England to play
      rugby league.

Thomson, A. A.

220   Rugger my pleasure. London: Museum Press, 1955.
      192p; illus; index
          Bibliography: p189   BL: 7921.e.119

Watkins, Alan

221   Sports writer's eye: an anthology. London: Queen Anne
      Press, 1989.
      viii, 216p; pbk
          Spine title: Sportswriter's eye   ISBN: 0356176517
                                              BL: YK.1990.a.802

      Articles on rugby mostly written for The Field and The
      Independent during the 1980s.

Watson, E. H. Lacon

222   Notes and memories of a sports supporter. London:
      Herbert Joseph, 1931.
      287p; illus; index   BL: 07912.h.35

      Twenty chapters on a number of sports. Includes:
      early football; football gets organised; football —
      methods of play.

*Sort of a
Cricket Person*

E. W. SWANTON

COLLINS
ST JAMES'S PLACE, LONDON
1972

✳ *Anthologies*

223 Rugby football up to date / E. H. D. Sewell with chapters by E. Gwyn Nicholls, E. T. Morgan, H. T. Gamlin, C. H. Pillman, T. H. Vile, W. J. Martin, W. S. D. Craven, L. Q. Bulger, J. C. Jenkins, P. J. Ebdon, The Bishop of Bloemfontein, C. D. Stuart, E. B. Turner, Emile de Lissa, E. W. Ballantine, C. F. Rutherford, C. J. Wray. London: Hodder and Stoughton, 1921.

368p; illus   BL: 07911.g.14

In addition to general essays, there are individual chapters on the game in Scotland, Ireland, Wales, South Africa, New Zealand and France; also a look at the Barbarians, the London Hospitals and the Varsity games of 1894-97.

224 The game goes on / edited by H. B. T. Wakelam; with contributions by O. L. Owen, E. B. Osborn, Leo Munro, G. V. Stephenson, A. L. Gracie, J. E. Manchester, W. Wooller, B. C. Gadney, A. D. Stoop, J. Daniell, Howard Marshall, H. J. Henley, R. W. Harland, W. J. Hoare, A. Wemyss, H. B. T. Wakelam, F. Dartnell, L. Murray, R. Cove-Smith, D. J. Macmyn, F. D. Prentice, K. C. Fyfe, E. N. Greatorex, E. W. Swanton, Peter Lawless, T. H. Vile, F. J. Sellicks, D. R. Gent, T. H. E. Baillie, J. P. Jordan, E. De Lissa, Kenneth Rankin. London: Arthur Barker, 1936.

340p; illus   BL: 7915.s.11

34 essays grouped under nine headings: The game and its players; Here was a game; Points of view; Famous years; Mirrors of the game; Touring abroad; Here and there; Year in, year out; 'Mecca'.

225 Wickets, tries and goals: reviews of play and players in modern cricket, rugby and soccer / John Arlott, Wilfred Wooller, Maurice Edelston. London: Sampson Low, Marston, 1949.

x, 236p; illus   BL: 7917.f.22

226 With the skin of their teeth: memories of great sporting finishes in golf, cricket, rugby and association football, lawn tennis, boxing, athletics, rowing and horse-racing / edited by G. O. Nickalls. London: Country Life, 1951.

168p; illus   BL: 7919.f.35

Pages 48 to 68: 'Rugby football' by C. H. Gadney. Gadney writes on four matches played in the 1933-4, and 1934-5 seasons – England v. Scotland; Oxford v. Cambridge; Wales v. New Zealand; and Wales v. Ireland.

227 Crysau cochion (Cymru ar y maes chwarae) / golygwyd gan Howard Lloyd. Llandybïe: Llyfrau'r Dryw, 1958.

188p; illus

'Red shirts (Wales on the playing field)'. Nine articles on rugby by Carwyn James, R. T. Gabe, Howard Lloyd (2), V. G. J. Jenkins, Jac Elwyn Watkins, J. B. G. Thomas, A. M. Rees, and Llew Rees.

228 Sport in Wales / edited by Wyn Williams. Denbigh: Gee, 1958.

80p; illus   BL: 7924.d.1

Includes: 'Rugby a successful expression of Welsh people's way of life' by J. B. G. Thomas (p3-9) and 'Bleddyn Williams's appraisal of rugger in Wales' (p10-18).

229 Bryn Thomas's book of rugger. London: Stanley Paul, 1961.

123p; illus   BL: P.P.6758.fr

Includes contributions on aspects of the game by Tony O'Reilly, Cliff Morgan, Dickie Jeeps, Sam Walker, Clem Thomas, and Wilfred Wooller amongst others.

230 Best rugby stories / edited with an introduction by Wallace Reyburn. London: Faber and Faber, 1968.

176p   BL: X.449/3301

Nineteen extracts from books and journals.

231 Touchdown and other moves in the game / edited by Geoffrey Nicholson with Cliff Morgan and David Frost. Twickenham: Rugby Football Union, 1971.

126p; illus   BL: X.619/6357

In his foreword the President of the RFU (1970-71) explains: 'To mark our centenary we invited the Rugby Union Writers' Club to produce for us a colourful paperback on the game... aiming to reach as large and as youthful an audience as possible... [concentrating] on growth areas – the schools, colts and universities; the new rugby nations of the world; coaching, training, tactical evolution, the influence of the Sevens game...'. Also contains profiles of players, great tries, milestones and a quiz.

232 Game for anything / Alan Gibson, Derek Robinson, David Foot. 1973?

42p

The rugby union championship; Western Counties v. Fiji; John Blake's Bristol; and more.

233 Barry John's world of rugby. London: W. H. Allen; Swansea: Christopher Davies, 1978.

152p; illus   ISBN: 0491020570
                             BL: P.441/899

Players, critics and fans reminisce on past seasons and consider the future of the game.
See also: H234

234 Barry John's world of rugby, no.2. London: W. H. Allen; Swansea: Christopher Davies, 1979.

151p; illus   ISBN: 0491024193
                             BL: P.441/899

☞ See also: H233

235 The love of rugby / edited by Peter Walker; foreword by Bill McLaren. London: Octopus, 1980.
96p; illus; index
ISBN: 070641229X
BL: L.45/1954

236 Tries! / Gerald Davies; edited by David Parry-Jones. London: Harrap, 1984.
xi, 111p; illus
ISBN: 0245542035
BL: X.622/24567

125 players choose their most memorable try scored/participated in and their most memorable try witnessed.

237 Out of the ruck: a selection of rugby writing / edited by David Parry-Jones. London: Pelham, 1986.
240p; illus; index
ISBN: 0720716985
BL: YK.1987.b.427

238 Between the posts: a New Zealand rugby anthology / edited by Ron Palenski. Auckland, London: Hodder & Stoughton, 1989.
167p; illus
ISBN: 0340508345
BL: YK.1990.b.4075

Between the Posts

A New Zealand Rugby Anthology

EDITED BY RON PALENSKI

Hodder & Stoughton
AUCKLAND LONDON SYDNEY TORONTO

239 Take the ball and run: a rugby anthology / edited by Godfrey Smith; foreword by Cliff Morgan. London: Pavilion, 1991.
218p; illus; index
ISBN: 1851456058
BL: YK.1991.b.7140

Includes biographies compiled by Ian Buchanan of the four rugby international players who have been awarded the Victoria Cross, and a list of the international players from England, Ireland, Scotland, Wales, Australia, New Zealand, and South Africa who have been awarded military honours in the theatres of conflict.

240 The big black rugby book / introduced by Mike Brewer; edited by Bob Howitt. Auckland, NZ: Sporting Press, 1992.
124p; illus
ISBN: 095978843X

241 My game, your game: David Campese and Mal Meninga talk football with Peter Jenkins and Peter Frilingos. Chippendale, Aust.: Ironbark, 1994.
288p; illus; pbk
ISBN: 033035616X

A comparison between the two codes of rugby by players and journalists.

242 Nice tries: a collection of new rugby writing / edited by Stuart Barnes and Mike Seabrook. London: Gollancz, 1995.
187p

Variant title: Nice tries: an anthology of new rugby writing
ISBN: 0575059877
BL: YK.1996.b.13310

NICE TRIES

A Collection of New Rugby Writing

Edited by

Stuart Barnes and Mike Seabrook

VICTOR GOLLANCZ
LONDON

243 BBC Radio 5 Live, 50 years of Sports Report / edited by Audrey Adams; introduced by Desmond Lynam. London: CollinsWillow, 1997.
224p; illus
ISBN: 0002188066

Includes the reminiscences of former rugby internationals Ian Robertson and Cliff Morgan. An additional contribution by Bill McLaren, the one-time voice of BBC rugby gives a unique insight into life as a commentator.

244 Rugby / selected and edited by Graham Hutchins; foreword by Wilson Whineray. Auckland, NZ: HarperCollins New Zealand, 1997.
153p; pbk
(Classic Kiwi sport)
ISBN: 186950254X

Educational Aids & Reading Books

245   Rugby / compiled by Jack Cross. London: Jackdaw
       Publications, 1971.
       1 portfolio; illus
       (Jackdaw; no.121)

       *Contents: Introductory folder (6p), 2 reproductions of
       contemporary documents, 2 sheets of illus and 7 explanatory
       broadsheets*

                                        ISBN: 0305620401

246   Football / Mary McKay and Julia Forbes. New Zealand:
       1975.
       12p; pbk
       School reader featuring mice playing rugby.

247   The rugby pack, or, Y pecyn rygbi / Uned Iaith
       Genedlaethol Cymru ac Awdurdod Addysg Morgannwg
       Ganol (National Language Unit of Wales and Mid
       Glamorgan Education Authority). Cardiff: Hughes a'i
       Fab, 1987.
       45p; pbk

       Includes 3 audio cassettes

       A series of units in the form of a booklet and three
       audio tapes to help non-Welsh speakers to follow
       Welsh rugby commentary. The pack is based on the
       commentary of the rugby highlights shown on S4C's
       'Y maes chwarae' (Welsh Channel 4's 'The sports
       field'). The commentary by Huw Llywelyn Davies is on
       the tapes. The aim is to enable the user to
       understand most of the key terms and phrases used
       in the commentary. Separate sections deal with a
       set of terms associated with a particular aspect of
       the game.

Religious Tracts

248   Goals and tries / V. Brooke-Hunt; with an introduction
       by the Headmaster of Rugby. London: SPCK, 1897.
       63p   BL: 4413.ee.25
       A tale with a moral. The preface is by H. A. James.

249   On the winning side / Nico Bougas. Howard Place, SA:
       Christian Living Today Magazine, 1995.
       32p; illus; pbk
       Witness bearing.

Goals and Tries:

BY
V. BROOKE-HUNT,
AUTHOR OF "FACING THE FOE," ETC.

WITH AN INTRODUCTION BY THE
HEADMASTER OF RUGBY.

PUBLISHED UNDER THE DIRECTION
OF THE TRACT COMMITTEE.

S.P.C.K.,
NORTHUMBERLAND AVENUE, W.C.
1897.

Songs & Music Scores

250   To Andrew D. Thomson an old opponent, and good
      friend: on the ball, a football song / written and
      composed by E. W. Secker. Dunedin, NZ: Chas Begg,
      1887.
      1 song sheet

251   Skipper Gould: song complimentary to Mr Arthur J.
      Gould, and published as a souvenir of his 25th
      international rugby football match played at Cardiff
      January 25, 1896 (Wales v. Scotland) / Paul Brenton.
      Cardiff: Thomson & Shackell, 1896.
      4p

         Music and words. Includes a biography of Gould
         'Prince of Centres' on the final page.

252   Football greetings / music by Dorothy Spinks; words by
      Walter R. Burns. Wellington, NZ: Harry H. Tombs, 19--?
      1 music score (3p)

         For voice and piano; Maori translation of chorus printed as
         text

253   The All Blacks: rugby football boys / H. Hiscocks. 1925.
      1 music score   BL: Voc/1925/Hiscocks

254   Rugby: mouvement symphonique / Arthur Honegger.
      Paris: Salabert, 1928.

         Receiving its première on 31 December 1928 at
         Stade Colombes during half-time of the France-
         Ireland match, the composer had these comments to
         make, 'I am very fond of the game of football. Yet
         rugby has more meaning for me. It seems more
         spontaneous and more directly approaches nature
         than football, which is a hot-house game.... I feel
         more exalted by the more ungoverned and sudden,
         desperate and less-regulated rhythms of rugby... I
         wanted, quite simply in my own terms as a musician
         to express the thrust and parry, the rhythm and the
         colour of a match in the Colombes Stadium, and in all
         honesty I feel bound to indicate my sources. That is
         why this little symphonic piece will be called Rugby.'

255   Our football girl: (all Australian girl) a snappy fox trot
      song with special lyrics for Australian rules, rugby league,
      rugby union / H. S. Bridgeman and Arthur Wendling;
      music by Al Lewis; arranged by Art McKay. Melbourne,
      Aust.: Allan, 1932.
      1 music score (4p)

256   Why was he born so beautiful and other rugby songs /
      selected by Harry Morgan; with a preface by Michael
      Green. London: Sphere, 1967.
      187p   ISBN: 0722162251
                                            BL: Cup.702.i.4

257   March – sospan fach: the little saucepan: a prelude to a
      Welsh football match for brass band / Gordon Jacob.
      Sevenoaks: Novello, 1972.
      1 score (18p + 25 parts)   pl.19924

258   Max Boyce, his songs and poems / Max Boyce;
      introduction by Barry John; cartoons by Gren.
      St Albans: Panther, 1976.
      63p; illus; pbk   ISBN: 0586046216
                                            BL: X.907/25209

         All the songs in this book, including two in Welsh, have
         been recorded.

259   More rugby songs / compiled by Harry Morgan.
      London: Sphere, 1976.
      158p; pbk   ISBN: 0722162391
                                            BL: X.439/8184

260   The balls of the beaver: tune – Caviare comes from the
      virgin sturgeon / Gavin Ewart. Leamington Spa: Sixth
      Chamber, 1984.
      4p; illus; pbk

         Cover title: Rugger song
         Published in a limited edition of 56 copies signed by
         the poet. The score is not included, just the lyrics.

261   Here's to the union / words and music by John Pollock
      Young; arranged by Glyn Lehmann. Tasmania?: North
      Western Football Union, 1985?
      1 score (4p)

         For voice and piano. The official song of the North
         Western Football Union.

262   Sosban fach: 30 o ganeuon clwb rygbi, or, 30 rugby club
      songs / edited by Stuart Brown. Talybont: Y Lolfa, 1987.
      71p   ISBN: 0862431344
                                            BL: B.8.dd(1)

         Words and melodies with chord symbols for
         unaccompanied unison men's voices.

263   The rugby poet: a musical drama / Charles Harter. New
      Zealand: 1988.
      1 score (72p) + 1 libretto

264   Rugger off: a collection of the most outrageous and
      offensive rugby songs ever to be published. Woodford
      Green: International Music Publications, 1991.
      1 music score (90p)   Publ. no.: 17311; 215-2-625
                                            ISBN: 0863598102
                                            BL: G.788.yy(1)

265 The World Cup 1991: rugby songs and ditties / joint
     editors, Scott Milway & Jamie Macleod-Johnstone.
     Richmond: Expandgood, 1991.
     150p; illus; pbk   ISBN: 1873491050
                BL: YK.1993.a.15656

266 Raunchy rugby songs by Ron and the Rude Boys / D.
     M. W. Gop. Colyton: VR Products, 1992.
     30p; pbk + cassette   ISBN: 0951207180
     ☞ Subsequent ed. H267

267 Rugby songs (uncensored) by Ron & the Rude Boys /
     D. M. W. Gop. New ed. Colyton: VR Products, 1994.
     pbk + cassette   ISBN: 1897624042
     ☞ Previous ed. H266

Reference Books

Contents

Encyclopædias

1   The encyclopaedia of rugby football / compiled by J. R. Jones. London: Hale, 1958.
186p; illus   BL: 7923.tt.9

☞ Subsequent ed. I2

2   The encyclopaedia of rugby football / compiled by J. R. Jones; revised and edited by Maurice Golesworthy. 2nd ed. London: Hale, 1966.
196p   BL: X.449/2370

☞ Previous ed. I1; subsequent ed. I4

3   The Dunlop book of rugby union / David Guiney; cartoons by George Houghton. Lavenham: Eastland Press, 1974.
464p; illus   ISBN: 0903214067
                                              BL: X.629/10166

4   Encyclopaedia of rugby union football / compiled by J. R. Jones. 3rd ed. revised and edited by Maurice Golesworthy. London: Hale, 1976.
185p; illus; index   ISBN: 0709153945
                                              BL: X.629/10759

☞ Previous ed. I2

Encyclopaedia of
RUGBY UNION FOOTBALL

Compiled by
J. R. JONES

Revised and Edited by
Maurice Golesworthy

THIRD EDITION

ROBERT HALE LONDON

5   The encyclopedia of world rugby / Keith Quinn. Moffat: Lochar, 1991.
442p; illus; index   ISBN: 0948403616
                                              BL: YK.1991.b.7771

6   The encyclopedia of rugby union / Donald Sommerville. London: Aurum, 1997.
192p; illus; index   ISBN: 1854104810

7   The ultimate encyclopedia of rugby: the definitive illustrated guide to world rugby union / general editor, Richard Bath. London: Carlton, 1997.
224p; illus; index   ISBN: 0340695285
                                              BL: LB.31.b.14443

Contributors include Howard Evans, Barry Glasspool, Ron Palenski, Mark Reason, Alasdair Reid, and Chris Thau.

✱   *Additional References*

8   The encyclopædia of sport & games in four volumes / edited by the Earl of Suffolk and Berkshire. New and enlarged ed. with illustrations in colour & black & white. London: Heinemann, 1911.
4 vols.; illus   BL: 7920.d.19

The section 'Football, rugby' by A. Budd and J. E. Raphael appears in volume 2 ('crocodile shooting – hound breeding') p238-56. Arthur Budd had written his article in 1897. It was divided into: history of the game; hints on the game; the selection of teams; method of play (passing, dribbling, judgement kicking); departments of play (forward play, scrummaging, wheeling, heeling out, open play); half-back play, co-operation of the two half-backs; three-quarter back play, the centre, the wings; four three-quarter back play; full back play; general play (tackling); and, some general hints. J. E. Raphael, the former England player, looks at the principal changes to the game – defence and attack – since the publication of Budd's article. Also on pages 272-75 'International football – the rugby game' with results of international matches from 1871-1909.

9   The Macmillan dictionary of sports and games / J. A. Cuddon. London: Macmillan, 1980.
xxviii, 870p; illus
          ISBN: 0333191633 (cased) • 0333323874 (pbk)
                                              BL: X.622/7574

Pages 676-99 offer an in-depth summation of the game. The clubs formed between Guy's Hospital in 1843 and Coventry in 1877 are named. There is also a brief history of the founding of the game in England, its development in Scotland and Ireland and its transfer via the public schools to Wales, France, South Africa, New Zealand and Australia. A brief mention is made of rugby in Argentina, Fiji and the US. There is coverage of the various tours, beginning with the British one to the Antipodes in 1888, the Maori (Native team) tour to the UK in 1888-89, the British team to South Africa in 1891, 1903 and 1910, and New Zealand's 1905 and South Africa's 1906 tours of the UK and France. Presented chronologically, the final section lists the key players who have represented England, Scotland, Ireland, Wales, New Zealand, South Africa, Australia and France. Also covers the laws, tactics and skills of the game.

10   Encyclopedia of world sport: from ancient times to the present / David Levinson and Karen Christenson, editors. Oxford: ABC-CLIO, 1996.
3 vols (xxii, 1317p); illus; index   ISBN: 0874368197
BL: HLR796.03

Volume 2 covers handball to rugby union.

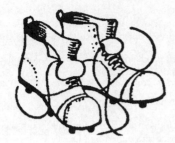

Dictionaries

11   Rugbyterme: Engels-Arikaans, Afrikaans-Engels / opgestel deur die FAK se Sporttermekomitee. Johannesburg, SA: FAK, 1959.
61p
(Handhaaf-en-bouveeks)

   ✳   *Additional References*

12   Sports dictionary in seven languages: English, Español, Français, Deutsch, Italiano, Magyar, Russkii: football / edited by Ferenc Hepp. Budapest: Terra, 1960.

13   The sportsman's glossary / F. C. Avis; diagrams by Pamela Mara. London: Souvenir Press, 1961.
301p; illus   BL: 7925.f.26

Defines sporting terms. 'Rugby' appears on pages 265-279.

Bibliographies

14   Bibliography on the history of South African rugby, 1862-1955 / D. L. Rance. Cape Town, SA: University of Cape Town Libraries, 1956.

This is unpublished, but available for consultation in the University of Cape Town library.

15   Danie Hartman Craven / Leon Redelinghuys. Stellenbosch: University of Stellenbosch School of Librarianship, 1974.

Craven was prominent in South African rugby as player, coach, and selector for his country, and president of the South African Board. He produced three doctoral dissertations and was a prolific writer on rugby. This bibliography is a result of the latter.

16   A handbook of rugby literature / David McLaren. Morrinsville, NZ: distributed by Crowsnest Books, 1985.
132p   BL: 2725.d.208
☞   Subsequent ed. I19

17   Bibliography on rugby injuries / compiled by Patricia Coleman, Jonathon Nicholl. Sheffield: Medical Care Research Unit, University of Sheffield Medical School, 1988.
☞   Also listed at: F420

18   South African rugby 1889-1989: a bibliography of monographs / compiled by the South African Sports Documentation and Information Centre in collaboration with H. P. Haubscher. Pretoria, SA: Human Sciences Research Council, 1989.
vi, 133p; pbk
(SASI publications; no. 2)

Bound in a ring binder, 673 items are recorded, taking in: annuals; biographies; coaching and training; clubs, universities, schools and regional rugby; research — theses and diverse projects; rules and refereeing; souvenirs; tours. An index of authors and titles completes the work.

19   A handbook of rugby literature / David McLaren. 2nd ed. Dunedin, NZ: The author, 1990.
188p   ISBN: 0473009900
☞   Previous ed. I16

20 Rugby catalogue of information sources / edited by the International Rugby Information Centre. Gloucester, Canada: Sport Information Resource Centre, 1994. 228p; index

    Annual supplements issued   ISBN: 0921817274

Produced in conjunction with the International Rugby Football Board, the bibliography is also useful for rugby coaches, referees, and players. The documents listed are arranged by subject. Also included is an international listing of national sport libraries and information centres.

✱ *Additional References*

21 Race discrimination in New Zealand-South African sports tours: a bibliography / Richard Thompson. Christchurch, NZ: University of Canterbury, 1966. 23p; pbk

Of the 196 books, pamphlets and articles recorded, items 48 to 196 cover rugby during the period October 1928 to May 1966.

☞ Also listed at: G38; subsequent ed. I22

22 Race discrimination in New Zealand-South African sports tours: a revised bibliography / Richard Thompson. Christchurch, NZ: University of Canterbury, 1972. 59p; pbk

Revised and updated, the sixth and final chapter is on rugby and covers the period October 1958 to December 1972.

☞ Also listed at: G39; previous ed. I21

23 A football compendium: a comprehensive guide to the literature of association football / compiled by Peter J. Seddon; introduction by Roy Hattersley; edited by C. McKinley and A. E. Cunningham. Boston Spa: The British Library, 1995. xix, 522p; illus; index   BL: 2725.g.1995

The first in a series of comprehensive subject bibliographies, A rugby compendium is the second.

Statistics & Records

24 The rugby union scoring book. London; Hayman, 1892. BL: D

25 Rugby union football: international, North v. South, and inter-university matches: teams, scorers, & results 1870 to 1912 / compiled by L. M. Holden. Birkenhead: E. A. Murray, 1912. 224p   BL: 7916.a.15

26 The Reed book of All Black records, 1884-1971 / R. F. Stokes. Wellington, NZ: Reed, 1972. vii, 201p   ISBN: 0589007246

27 The Guinness book of rugby facts & feats / Terry Godwin and Chris Rhys. Enfield: Guinness Superlatives, 1981. 258p; illus; index

    Bibliography: p258
    ISBN: 0851122140 (cased) • 0851122485 (pbk)
    BL: X.622/11913

☞ Subsequent ed. I28

28 The Guinness book of rugby facts and feats / Terry Godwin. 2nd ed. Enfield: Guinness, 1983. 256p; illus; index   ISBN: 0851122647
    BL: X.622/18865

☞ Previous ed. I27

29 Rugby football scorebook / Kenneth N. Carlson. Lynnwood, US: Rain Belt Publications, 1984. iv, 242p; illus; pbk   ISBN: 0938428047

All the known scores of 12 national teams (includes Brazil, Italy, Japan, but excludes Scotland and Wales) and 66 American and Canadian colleges and clubs.

30 Welsh club rugby guide results season 85/86: a comprehensive guide to the 190 affiliated Welsh rugby union clubs' playing records for the season 85/86. Cardiff: Western Mail, 1986. 90p; illus; pbk

31 The Phoenix book of international rugby records / John Griffiths. London: Phoenix House, 1987. 640p   ISBN: 0460070037
    BL: YK.1987.b.6331

32 Rugby: the records / Chris Rhys. Enfield: Guinness, 1987. 176p; illus, 1 genealogical table; index; pbk
    ISBN: 085112450X
    BL: YK.1987.b.7220

Includes coverage of the inaugural rugby World Cup; features on the major playing countries records, clubs, competitions and international grounds; profiles of a number of the game's most illustrious players.

33 A statistical history of Springbok rugby: players, tours and matches / Teddy Shnaps. Cape Town, SA: South African Rugby Board and Don Nelson, 1989.
383p; illus; index   ISBN: 1868060608

Pages 9-148: 'They played for South Africa: the complete record of South Africa's rugby football representatives, their matches played and points scored'.

34 The Guinness rugby union fact book / Chris Rhys. Enfield: Guinness, 1992.
223p; illus; index; pbk   ISBN: 0851125395
                                            BL: YK.1993.b.56

A compilation of records, results around the world, as well as information on players and grounds.

35 The rugby union stats book / John Wilby and Henry Sharp. 1997.
pbk

36 The who, when and where of English international rugby since 1947 / compiled by D.N. Stansfield. Welbourn: Stansfield, 1997.
648p; illus; pbk
    Includes bibliography   ISBN: 0953201007

✳ *Additional References*

37 The book of Blues: being a record of all matches between the Universities of Oxford and Cambridge in every department of sport / edited by Ogier Rysden. London: F. E. Robinson, 1900-1902.
3 vols.; illus; index   BL: D

38 South African sport, 1914: including a complete collection of records of all branches of the sport of this country / edited by H. P. Swaffer. Johannesburg, SA: Transvaal Leader, 1914.
viii, 174p; illus

Rugby is covered on pages 59-70.

39 Oxford versus Cambridge: a record of inter-University contests from 1827-1930 / compiled and arranged by H. M. Abrahams and J. Bruce-Kerr. London: Faber and Faber, 1931.
xx, 620p; index
    Supplement issued annually   BL: 07906.i.56

Details of the rugby matches played between the two universities between 1872 and 1930 are given: the date and venue; the score; and, a listing of the players.

40 The Lonsdale book of sporting records. London: Seeley, 1937.
xvi, 457p; illus
(Lonsdale library of sports, games & pastimes; vol. 25)
                                            BL: L.R.256.a.1/25

This is a modern version of the 'Badminton' series. In the rugby section Howard Marshall reviews the 1936 season, but the work is mainly statistical and there are 13 pages of records and results, including the playing records of some 200 English clubs for the 1935-36 season.

41 Complete handbook of sports scoring and record keeping / Jack Richards, Danny Hill. West Nyack, US: Parker, 1974.
266p; illus   ISBN: 0131612573

Details how to keep score for a variety of sports, including rugby. For children.

Annuals, Handbooks, Seasonal & Fixture Guides

✳ *British Isles*

42 John Lilywhite's football annual / C. W. Alcock. London: 1868.
    Only one issue published;
    Continued by: The football annual
    ☞ See also: I43

43 The football annual / edited by Charles W. Alcock. London: Sportsman Office, 1869-1908.
    Continues: John Lilywhite's football annual;
    Issues 1869-70 published by the Sportsman Office; issues 1871-75 published by Virtue; issue 1876 published by

Ward, Lock & Tyler; issue 1877 published by Ward, Lock; issues 1878-83 published by the Cricket Press; issues 1884-1894 published by Wright (Cricket Press); issues 1895-1908 published by Merritt & Hatcher
                                            BL: P.P.2489.wf

Concerned in the main with association football. Volume one has 'hints on the two styles of football play' with the rugby game covered on pages 7-14; and 'laws of the game ... the Rugby Football Union'. The final two editions, 1907/08 and 1908/09, bear the legend, 'founded by the late Charles W. Alcock'.

    ☞ See also: I42

44   Rugby union football annual: season 1874-75 / edited by
G. H. W. London: 1874.

Editor is George H. West   BL: P.P.2489.wg

45   Irish football annual / edited by Richard M. Peter.
Dublin: Dublin Steam Printing, 1880.

The author held two posts with the Irish Rugby
Football Union: honorary treasurer (1875-79) and
honorary secretary (1879-82). The annual provides
the histories and playing records of the clubs then
affiliated to the IRFU. In addition, there are
descriptions of the majority of the leading players in
Ireland at the time.

46   The Northern Counties rugby football guide: season ...
Hartlepool: 1886/7-1888/9?

BL: Mic.A.11007(14) (microfilm copy)

47   The Athletic News football annual. London: Athletic
News, 1887-1946/7.

*Subsequently incorporated into: Sunday Chronicle football
annual*   BL: P.P.2489.wfc

Primarily on association football, but included here as
it also contains some early notes on rugby.

48   The football handbook, 1888-9 / edited by N. L.
Jackson. London: 'Pastime', 1889?

Only one issue published

Includes: the rugby game; principal fixtures;
association and rugby union; unions and clubs – rugby
union rules.

49   The rugby union football handbook. London:
1890/1-1895/6?   BL: P.P.2489.wfb

50   Birmingham and Midland Counties football guide / G.
Roobottom. 1892.

Only one issue published

51   The 'Fred Pollard' football guide for Birmingham and
district: contains all the principal association and rugby
union fixtures for the season, laws of football association
and rugby union, records of all important past events,
etc. 1892-1897.

Also known as 'Fred Pollard's football guide'

52   Leighton's North-Western rugby football league card
1892-93 / J. A. Leighton. Kendal: The author, 1892.
1 sheet   BL: 1865.c.2(22)

53   Yorkshire Rugby Football Union: official guide, season
1893/4. Leeds: McCorquodale, 1893.

Only one issue published   BL: 7912.a.38

54   The handy football guide (Mortimer's) for South Wales
and Monmouthshire: containing the principal rugby and
association fixtures for the season and international
results, etc. 1895-96. Cardiff: G W & J J Lennox, 1895.

Only one issue published   BL: P.P.2489.wgf

55   The Hull and District Rugby Football Union official
guide 1895/6. Hull: The Union, 1895.

Only one issue published   BL: P.P.2489.wgs

56   Smirk's handbook of northern rugby-union matches,
season ... / Charles W. Alcock and E. H. Smirk. Wigan:
1895/6-   BL: P.P.2489.wge

57   Old Un's football handbook. Pontypridd: Glamorgan
Times Newspaper, 1896.
BL: 7912.a.69(6)

58   The rugby handbook: with special article by Arthur
Budd. London: All England Athletic Publishing,
1899-1900?

The 1900 edition, with a posthumously published
article by Budd, was published by Wright.

59   Leng's rugby handbook. 1906/07.

60   The Warrington football annual and sports record ... /
compiled by 'Ovalist'. Warrington: 1906-
BL: P.P.2489.wgw

61   Scottish athletic guide. Glasgow: Rowan, 1907-1921.

Covers hockey as well as rugby.

62   Football and athletic annual 1909/10. Belfast: Ireland
Saturday Night, 1909.

63   The 'Pall Mall Gazette' rugby football annual for
1910/11 / compiled and edited by W. Livingstone Irwin.
London: Pall Mall Gazette, 1910.

Only one issue published   BL: P.P.2489.wfg

64   Scottish football record. Edinburgh: R.W. Forsyth,
1910-1913.

Covers hockey as well as rugby.

65   Spalding's rugby union football annual: season ... /
edited by 'Old International'. London: The British
Sports Publishing Company, 1910/11-1911/12.

66   The rugby football annual. Twickenham: The Rugby
Football Union, 1913/14-1939/40.   BL: P.P.2489.wg(2)

67   Blackheath rugby football annual: season ... London:
Blackheath Football Club, 1919/20-1939/40.
BL: P.P.2489.wib

68   Scottish rugby record. Edinburgh: R.W. Forsyth,
1919-1986.

69   Commemoration book 1914-19 and, official handbook
season 1919-20. York: Yorkshire Rugby Football Union,
1920.
577p; illus   BL: YA.1993.a.19284

70   Rowan's rugby guide. Glasgow: Rowan, 1922-1963.

No issues published 1939-45

71   John Wisden's rugby football almanack for … London:
      Wisden, 1923/24-1924/25   BL: P.P.2489.wia

72   The Merseyside Rugby Union handbook for season ….
      Liverpool: 1926/27-1928/29.   BL: P.P.2489.wfw

73   Irish rugby football annual …. Dublin:
      1928/29-1939/40.

          Continued by: Irish rugby annual   BL: P.P.2513.ig

          Reviews seasons 1927/28 through to 1938/39,
          covering officials and clubs, international players,
          trials and inter-provincial matches.

          ☞ See also: I74

74   Irish rugby annual. Dublin: 1946-1950.

          Continues: Irish rugby football annual   BL: P.P.2513.ig

          ☞ See also: I73

75   Playfair rugby football annual. London: Playfair Books,
      1948/9-1972/3.   BL: P.P.2489.wic

76   Playfair Scottish rugby football annual 1949-50 / edited
      by O. L. Owen; foreword by J. Moir MacKenzie.
      London: Playfair Books, 1949.

          Only one issue published

77   Playfair Welsh rugby annual 1949-50 / edited by O. L.
      Owen & J. B. G. Thomas; foreword by Sir David Rocyn
      Jones; articles by Wilfred Wooller, D. R. Gent and C. B.
      Jones. London: Playfair Books, 1949.

          Only one issue published   BL: P.P.2489.wid

78   The Stratton rugby tables south-west region / Robert
      William Stratton and R. G. Stratton. Bath: 1949-
                                                   BL: W.P.14044

79   Rugby annual for Wales / edited by Arwyn Owen.
      Cardiff: Welsh Brewers, 1969/70-

80   Fred Cogley's yearbook of Irish rugby. Dublin: General
      Publication, 1970-1973.

          1973 ed. published by Maxwell Publicity;
          Continued by: Irish rugby annual and yearbook

          ☞ See also: I85

81   'Birmingham Evening Mail' Football Sports Argus
      annual. Birmingham: Birmingham Post and Mail, 1971?-
      Association football and rugby union coverage.

82   The Barry John book of rugby. Llandybie: C. Davies,
      1972-1973.

          Only two issues published

83   Rothmans rugby yearbook. London: Queen Anne Press,
      1972-1987.

          Continued by: Rothmans rugby union yearbook
                                                   BL: P.441/396

          ☞ See also: I96

84   Irish Rugby Football Union: yearbook of the centenary
      season 1974-1975. Dublin: Tara, 1975.

85   Irish rugby annual and yearbook. Dublin: Maxwell
      Publicity, 1976-

          Cover title: Fred Cogley's Irish rugby … annual and yearbook;
          Continues: Fred Cogley's yearbook of Irish rugby

          ☞ See also: I80

86   Bass, Mitchells & Butlers Midland counties rugby
      football handbook: official handbook for the Midland
      Group. Birmingham: The Midland Group Committee,
      1977-

          Published annually   ISSN: 0263-2551
                                                   BL: P.441/969

87   Rugby line-out / John O'Shea. Dublin: Tara, 1977-1984.

          A review of Ireland's previous season. John O'Shea
          edited the 1977 and 1978 editions; John Redmond
          edited the 1983 edition.

88   Rygbi, 1978/79 / golygydd John Jenkins. Llanelli:
      Gwerin, 1978.   BL: P.611/806

89   Nigel Starmer-Smith's rugby annual. Bristol: Purnell, 1984-

          Spine title: Rugby annual   BL: P.443/613

90   Playfair rugby union annual. London: Queen Anne
      Press, 1984.

          Only one issue published   BL: P.441/1082

91   ICL Irish rugby yearbook / edited by Karl Johnston.
      Dublin: Gill & Macmillan, 1986.

          Only one issue published   ISBN: 0717114732

          Review of Irish rugby at all levels for the 1985-86
          season.

92   The rugby annual. London: Pelham, 1986-
                                                   BL: ZC.9.a.777

93   Rugby union yearbook. London: W H Allen, 1986-
                                                   ISSN: 0959-1559

94   McEwan's rugby record. Edinburgh: 1987-

95   Courage clubs championship official rugby union club
      directory / edited by Bill Mitchell. London:
      Harmsworth, 1988-1996?

          Continued by: Official rugby union club directory
                                                   BL: ZK.9.a.4397

      A number of contributors cast their net over the
      Courage leagues; the three national divisions and
      area leagues north and south; the four divisions; and
      results for the previous season. All editions follow the
      same format but there have been a number of
      editors. From 1991-92, the directory was published in
      Taunton by Tony Williams.

          ☞ See also: I120

96 Rothmans rugby union yearbook. London: Rothmans Queen Anne Press, 1988-

　　Continues: Rothmans rugby yearbook　　BL: P.441/396

　☞　See also: I83

97 Rugby football union Courage clubs championship official guide. London: Courage, 1988.

　　Colour coded, the sections are divided from A to H and each section is numbered. Lacking a contents page, the sections note: media contacts; areas and divisions with addresses, contracts, telephone numbers, and fixture lists for the forthcoming season; the final section is an index to the clubs.

98 The Whitbread rugby world ... / edited by Nigel Starmer-Smith and Ian Robertson. Oxford: Lennard, 1988-1993.

　　Continued by: Flowers Whitbread rugby world

　　　　　　　　ISSN: 0959-342X
　　　　　　　　BL: ZK.9.a.1482

　☞　See also: I112

99 Rugby union yearbook / edited by Mick Cleary. London: Virgin Optomen, 1989.

　　Only one issue published　　BL: ZK.9.d.397

　　Gives a 'challenging review' of the season just past with an additional chapter by David Lawrenson on the history of the varsity match.

100 The Scotsman rugby year book: the Scottish season ... / Harry Pincott, John Davidson. Edinburgh: John Donald, 1989/90-　　BL: ZK.9.a.1763

　　Season's events include the fortunes of the national side; all seven divisions of the National League's scores and teams; and the National League tables from 1973 to the present.

101 Smithwick's Ireland's rugby annual / compiled by John Redmond. Dublin: 1989-

102 Women's Rugby Football Union handbook. London: Women's Rugby Union, 1990-

　　The 1992 handbook was published in Shipston on Stour.

103 Courage clubs championship official rugby union London & South East Division club directory 1992-93 / edited by Steve Lyon. Birmingham: Nicholas Publishing, 1992.

　　Only one issue published　　ISBN: 1897612036

104 Courage clubs championship official rugby union Midland Division club directory 1992-93 / edited by Steve Lyon. Birmingham: Nicholas Publishing, 1992.

　　Only one issue published　　ISBN: 1897612028

105 Courage clubs championship official rugby union North Division club directory 1992-93 / edited by Steve Lyon. Birmingham: Nicholas Publishing, 1992.

　　Only one issue published　　ISBN: 1897612001

106 Courage clubs championship official rugby union South West Division 1992-93 / edited by Steve Lyon. Birmingham: Nicholas Publishing, 1992.

　　Only one issue published　　ISBN: 189761201X

107 Dragons annual. Cardiff: Rugby Vision, 1992-

　　English and Welsh text　　ISSN: 0967-1331
　　　　　　　　BL: ZK.9.b.5557

108 The official Scottish rugby union annual 1992-93 / edited by Ian McLauchlan. Edinburgh: Mainstream, 1992.

　　Continued by: The Scottish rugby book
　　Only one issue published;　　ISBN: 1851584846

　　Includes chapters on the domestic and international seasons (the 1991 Cup and the 1992 Five Nations championship) and the season ahead.

　☞　See also: I111

109 Rugby club guide 92/93. London: AFCC, 1992.

　　Only one issue published

　　A directory of rugby union in England, Scotland, Ireland and Wales.

110 The international rugby almanack. London: Blandford, 1993-

　　Published annually　　BL: ZK.9.a.2918

111 The Scottish rugby book '94 / edited by Ian McLauchlan. Edinburgh: Mainstream, 1993.

　　Only one issue published;
　　Continues: The official Scottish rugby union annual
　　Continued by: The Scottish rugby year book

　　　　　　　　ISBN: 1851585788

　　Five authors review the previous season at club, league, inter-district and international level.

　☞　See also: I108, I113

112 Flowers Whitbread rugby world / edited by Nigel Starmer-Smith and Ian Robertson. Harpenden: Queen Anne Press, 1994-1995.

　　Published annually;
　　Continues: The Whitbread rugby world;
　　Continued by: Wooden Spoon Society rugby world

　☞　See also: I98, I119

113 The Scottish rugby year book 1995 / edited by Derek Douglas. Edinburgh: Mainstream, 1994.

　　Continues: The Scottish rugby book;
　　Only one issue published　　ISBN: 1851586296

　　A review of the previous season at club, district, league and international level. Also features a 'player of the year' profile of Gary Armstrong, with a statistics and fixtures section.

　☞　See also: I111

114   The year of rugby … / edited by Barrie Fairall. London: Harrington Kilbride, 1994-

Described as the official yearbook of the Rugby Football Union. Though concentrating on rugby in England, the first issue also included contributions on rugby in South Africa, Hong Kong sevens, and women's rugby. Coverage in later issues was confined to the game in England. From the second issue this was published by Sporting World Publications.

115   Rugby world annual … Princes Risborough: Annuals Publishing, 1995-   ISSN: 1363-2620
                                         BL: ZK.9.b.9377

116   Playfair rugby union annual / edited by Bill Day and Brendan Gallagher. London: Headline, 1996-
                                     ISSN: 1365-974X
                                     BL: ZK.9.a.4906

Information on the Courage Leagues, biographies of players appearing in the top two divisions, league and cup results in the four home countries, and results of international matches played during the previous year.

117   Rugby … / edited by Matthew Pettipher. London: Highbury House Communications, 1996-

Published annually

An official publication of the Rugby Football Union.

118   Rugby union …: the official RFU annual publication. London: Absolute Sports, 1996-   ISSN: 1365-3784
                                     BL: ZK.9.b.11066

119   Wooden Spoon Society rugby world, … / edited by Nigel Starmer-Smith and Ian Robertson. Harpenden: Queen Anne Press, 1996-

Continues: Flowers Whitbread rugby world;
Published annually   ISSN: 1366-2260
                                     BL: ZK.9.a.1482

☞   See also: I112

120   Official rugby union club directory / edited by Stephen McCormack. Taunton: Tony Williams, 1997-

Continues: Courage clubs championship official rugby union club directory

☞   See also: I95

✳   *South Africa*

121   Peirson's rugby union annual / compiled by A. R. Peirson. Natal, SA: 1890.

The only copy believed to be in existence was bequeathed to the Natal Rugby Union in 1947.

122   The South African rugby annual / edited by Ron Aldridge. Johannesburg, SA: Donaldsons, 1950-1957.
                                     BL: P.P.2579.egk

123   South African rugby yearbook, or, S.A. rugby jaarbock. 1962-

Publisher and sponsor varies;
Contributions in English and Afrikaans

124   South African rugby writers annual / edited by Quintus van Rooyen. Bloemfontein: 1971-

Publisher and sponsor varies   ISSN: 1011-4106

125   S.A. rugby year book. Cape Town, SA: Promco, 1979-1989.   ISSN: 1010-7983

126   South Africa rugby review / edited by Wynand Claassen. Durban, SA: Rugby 15 International, 1993-

Published annually   ISSN: 1022-2499

127   The international rugby yearbook / Johann Botha. Cape Town, SA: Struik, 1995-

✳   *New Zealand*

128   The New Zealand rugby football annual for 1885 / edited by S. E. Sleigh. Dunedin, NZ: 1885.   BL: P.P.2667.r

129   The Auckland rugby union annual. Auckland, NZ: Auckland Rugby Football Union, 1899.

130   The New Zealand rugby annual. Wellington, NZ: Geo. W. Slade under the auspices of the New Zealand Rugby Football Union, 1920-1945.

131   The rugby almanack of New Zealand. Wellington, NZ: Wright and Carman, 1935-

Publisher and sponsor varies; published annually

This publication has undergone a series of title changes brought upon by different sponsors – The DB Draught rugby almanack of New Zealand, and The National Mutual rugby almanack of New Zealand, are two examples. Since 1983 the almanack has been published in Auckland by Moa Beckett.

132   Radio New Zealand Sport rugby annual. Auckland, NZ: Moa Beckett, 1970.

Continued by: The New Zealand rugby annual 1971

☞   See also: I133

133   The New Zealand rugby annual 1971 / edited by R. J. Howitt. Auckland, NZ: Australasian Mail Order Associates, 1971.

Only one issue published;
Continues: Radio New Zealand sport rugby annual;
Continued by: The D.B. rugby annual   ISSN: 0113-1346
                                     BL: P.441/386

Pen portraits, match reports, club statistics, and interviews.

☞   See also: I132; I134

134   The D.B. rugby annual. Auckland, NZ: Moa Publications [and] Dominion Breweries, 1972-1985.

 Continues: The New Zealand rugby annual;
 Continued by: The New Zealand rugby annual
        ISSN: 0110-1560

 ☞   See also: I133, I136

135   The New Zealand Barbarian rugby book / Murray Reid. Auckland, NZ: McGregor, 1978-1981. ISSN: 0111-7491

136   The New Zealand rugby annual. Auckland, NZ: Moa Publications, 1986.

 Only one issue published;
 Continues: The D.B. rugby annual;
 Continued by: Radio New Zealand Sport rugby annual
        ISSN: 0113-1354

 ☞   See also: I134, I138

137   Rugby 86: television and radio's official rugby union guide. Auckland, NZ: TVNZ Publishing, 1986. ISBN: 0908690339

138   Radio New Zealand Sport rugby annual. Auckland, NZ: Moa, 1987-1993.

 Continues: New Zealand rugby annual
 ☞   See also: I136

139   Canterbury rugby review. Christchurch, NZ: Sports Communications, 1991-

 Alternative title: Trust Bank Canterbury rugby review;
 Published annually   ISSN: 1171-1906

140   Handbook. Wellington, NZ: New Zealand Rugby Football Union, 1995-

141   International rugby ... / edited by John Blondin; photographic editor Colin Whelan; statistics by Rod Chester. Auckland, NZ: Moa Beckett in association with Action Photographs and the International Rugby Football Board, 1994-1995.

 This title started off as a de-luxe production aimed at the collectors' market. A trade edition was also produced in 1995.
 ☞   See also: I154

✳ *Australia*

142   List of clubs belonging to the Southern Rugby Football Union: with the fixtures for the season 1889 and notes for guidance of umpires & referees. Sydney, Aust.: Southern Rugby Football Union, 1889.
35p

143   The New South Wales Rugby Football Union annual. Sydney, Aust.: H. T. Dunn, 1900-1901.

 Continued by: The New South Wales Rugby Union annual
 ☞   See also: I144

144   The New South Wales Rugby Union annual. Sydney, Aust.: H. T. Dunn, 1902-1907.

 Continues: The New South Wales Rugby Football Union annual;
 Continued by: New South Wales rugby annual
 ☞   See also: I143, I145

145   New South Wales rugby annual. Sydney, Aust.: New South Wales Rugby Union, 1908-

 Continues: The New South Wales Rugby Union annual
 ☞   See also: I144

146   The illustrated football annual. Sydney, Aust.: NSW Bookstall, 1909.

 Only one issue published

147   The rugby annual 1934 / edited by D. K. Rodgers. Sydney, Aust.: New South Wales Rugby Union, 1934.

 Only one issue published

148   The Australian rugby union almanac. Sydney, Aust.: New South Wales Rugby Union, 1959-1963.

 Continued by: The Australian rugby almanac
 ☞   See also: I149

149   The Australian rugby almanac. Sydney, Aust.: New South Wales Rugby Union, 1964-1970.

 Continues: The Australian rugby union almanac;
 Continued by: The Australian rugby yearbook
 ☞   See also: I148, I150

150   The Australian rugby yearbook. Sydney, Aust.: 1971.

 Only one issue published;
 Continues: The Australian rugby almanac;
 Continued by: Australian rugby
 ☞   See also: I149, I151

151   Australian rugby. Sydney, Aust.: 1972-1973.

 Continues: The Australian rugby yearbook
 ☞   See also: I150

152   Rothman's Australian rugby yearbook. Chatswood, Aust.: 1981-1984.

153   Rugby yearbook of Australia / edited by Donald Smillie. Brisbane, Aust.: The author, 1994.
iv, 124p; illus; pbk

 Only one issue published ISBN: 0646195514

154   International rugby yearbook / editorial director John Blondin; photographic editor Colin Whelan; statistics by John Griffiths. Rydalmere, Aust.: Hodder & Stoughton, 1995.
256p; illus   ISBN: 0733600824

 This was the Australian version of a yearbook first published in New Zealand.
 ☞   See also: I141

155   Rugby … / Greg Thomas & Col Whelan. Sydney, Aust.: Pan Macmillan, 1995-

> *Also known successively as: Mastercard rugby (1995); Ford rugby (1996); Schweppes rugby(1997)*

Official yearbook of the Australian Rugby Football Union. Coverage is mainly rugby in Australia, with additional coverage of the important events in world rugby. From 1996, published by Mandarin.

✳ United States

156   Illinois cricket and rugby annual for … / edited by K. A. Auty. Chicago, US: The author, 1935-

> Section 1 covers cricket; section 2 covers rugby.

Periodicals

✳ British Isles

157   Rugby monthly

158   Rugger sport.

159   Wales rugby international.

160   Huddersfield rugby news. 1908-1910?

161   Rugby football and cricket. Oct. 1911- Dec. 1911.

162   Rugby football (a weekly record of the game). Sept. 1923-Dec. 1924.

> *Continued by: Rugby news and notes*
> ☞ See also: I163

163   Rugby news and notes. Dec.1924-Feb. 1925.

> *Published weekly;*
> *Continues: Rugby football (a weekly record of the game)*
> ☞ See also: I162

164   Rugby football weekly. London: Campbell, Dec. 1928-Dec. 1929.

165   Rugger. London: Sept. 1931-Mar. 1932.

> *Published weekly*

166   Rugger. London: Eric Beaumont, Dec. 1946-

> *Published weekly until 15th January 1947, then monthly during the season*   BL: P.P.1832.mb

'Rugger sets out to reflect by fair and representative reports, articles and photographs the broadest possible aspects of rugby union football….' Coverage also extends to junior XVs and schools rugby.

167   Rugger: the national magazine of rugby union football. International series. London: Eric Beaumont, 1952-   BL: P.P.1832.mbb

168   Rugby world. Sutton: IPC Specialists & Professional, 1960-1985.

> *Published monthly; merged with Rugby post to become Rugby world & post*   ISSN: 0035-9777
>   BL: P.P.7613.it
> ☞ See also: I179

169   Welsh rugby. London: Geoffrey Lace Marketing, 1960-

> *Published monthly*   ISSN: 0260-7441

170   Welsh rugby / edited by Fred Croster. Feltham: Western Sporting Press, 1961-   ISSN: 0043-2466

171   Scottish rugby. 1975-1977

172   Irish rugby. Dublin: Sean Graham Publications, 1976-1981.

> *Later issues published by Olympic Press*   ISSN: 0790-2271

173   Rugby post. London: Burlington Publishing Company, 1979?-1985.

> *Eight issues per year; merged with Rugby world to become Rugby world & post*   ISSN: 0268-9804
> ☞ See also: I179

174   Intacta: news & views of rugby at Maidenhead. 1980s-   BL: ZC.9.b.188

175   Scottish rugby: the national rugby newspaper of Scotland. Dunfermline: G.T.G. Sports Publications, Oct. 1981-1989

> *Published monthly*   ISSN: 0260-9843
>   BL: P.2000/1139

176   Rugby Ireland: the national rugby magazine of Ireland. Manchester: Fitness Shop, 1982-1983.

177   Rugby Scotland: the national rugby magazine of Scotland. 1982-1983.

178 Irish rugby review: Ireland's only rugby magazine. Dalkey: Victory Irish Promotions, Dec. 1983-

Published by Irish Rugby Review from 1989 onwards
BL: P.443/563

179 Rugby world & post. Bray-on-Thames: Rugby Post Publishing, Aug. 1985-Apr. 1996.

Merger of: Rugby post, and Rugby world; published monthly; Continued by: Rugby world (1996) ISSN: 0268-9804
BL: P.443/595

☞ See also: I168, I173, I203

180 Rugby in Scotland. Edinburgh: Scotsman Communications, 1986-1989.

Newspaper format

181 Rugby international. 1986-
Published monthly

182 Rugby Wales. 1987-

183 Rugby news. Ashurst: Sporting Magazines and Publishers, Oct. 1988-

Published monthly ISSN: 0954-7428
BL: ZK.9.b.1864

184 Provincial rugby. Portadown: Provincial Rugby, 1989-1990.

185 Scottish rugby. Glasgow: Scotrun, Oct. 1990-

Published monthly ISSN: 0960-2917
BL: ZK.9.b.3461

186 Dragons. Cardiff: Rugby Vision, 1991-

In English with some Welsh text; six issues yearly
ISSN: 0967-3040
BL: ZK.9.b.5115

187 Munster rugby news: Munster's brightest rugby magazine. Limerick: PSC, 1991-

188 Rugby World Cup weekly. Windsor: Burlington, 1991-
ISSN: 0963-6870
BL ZK.9.d.684

☞ Also listed at: D39

189 County rugby: the magazine for Sussex rugby. Worthing: M Cobbs, 1992-

Published monthly ISSN: 0964-9115
BL: ZK.9.b.4400

190 SRU voice. Edinburgh: Scottish Rugby Union, 1992-

191 Kickoff!: rugby world cup ... review. Bristol: IRFB Services, 1993- BL: ZK.9.b.9203
☞ Also listed at: D25

192 Leinster rugby magazine / edited by Pat Fitzgerald. Dublin: Padema, Sept. 1993-

Published monthly ISSN: 0791-9549

193 The oval world. Bristol: International Rugby Football Board (IRFB) Service Ltd, 1993-

This is the official magazine of the International Rugby Football Board.

194 Rhondda rugby news. Treorchy RFC, 1993-

195 Rugby west: Connacht's rugby magazine. Galway: Rugby West, 1994-

Published monthly

196 Ulster rugby. Belfast: Greer, 1994-

Published monthly ISSN: 1363-2515
BL. ZK.9.b.9484

197 First XV: the rugby magazine / edited by Stuart Barnes. Bath: Future, Dec. 1995-1996.

Published monthly; Continued by: Rugby magazine
ISSN: 1360-7464

Edited by the former Bath and England fly half.
☞ See also: I201

198 The RFU journal: a technical insight into the game / features editor Keith Bouser. Twickenham: Rugby Football Union, September 1995.
32p; illus

Only one issue published.
☞ Also listed at: F380

199 Rugby journal. London: Lookturn, 1995-
ISSN: 1358-3220
BL: ZK.9.b.9340

200 Tennents scrumdown. Glasgow: Tennents, 1995?-
Published irregularly

201 Rugby magazine. Bath: Future, Oct. 1996-

Published monthly; Continues: First XV ISSN: 1364-7482
BL: ZK.9.b.9064

☞ See also: I197

202 Rugby the Five Nations Championship ... magazine. London: Stonehart Sports Magazines, 1996-

Published annually ISSN: 1361-5203
BL: ZK.9.b.9285

☞ Also listed at: D7

203 Rugby world / edited by Peter Bills. London: IPC Magazines, May 1996-

Published monthly; Continues: Rugby world & post
ISSN: 1363-9633
BL: P.443/595

☞ See also: I179

204   Inside rugby. London: Brackenbury, Mar. 1997-

       Published monthly   ISSN: 1365-8832
                                   BL: ZK.9.b.11026

205   Rugby Ireland international. Mar./Apr. 1997-

   ✱   *Fanzines & Club Newsletters*

206   Every time, ref, every time (ERE).
       Bath supporters' magazine.

207   In touch. Ilford?: Essex County Rugby Football Union.
       Eight issues of this newsletter are published annually.

208   In touch.
       Kirkcaldy Club newsletter.

209   From the blindside. 1963?-
       The official organ of Corstorphine

210   Loose maul. 1963?-
       Northampton Old Scouts' RFC's monthly newsletter.

211   The dead ball. July 1986-January 1988.
       A general magazine put together by enthusiasts of the game.

219   Tryline: official magazine of the Young England Rugby Club. London: Brass Tacks, Sept. 1992-

       Published quarterly   BL: ZK.9.b.7758

220   Jackattack: official magazine of Swansea Cricket and Football Club. Swansea: The Club, 1994-
       A statement from the Marketing Executive declares: 'Jackattack is aimed at increasing awareness and participation not only at the elite level of performance, but also at grassroots level by raising awareness in schools, local sports associations, etc. emphasising the benefits of sport and attracting individuals not only to rugby, but to sport in general'. In a subsequent issue, not dated, the magazine's presentation is more professional. Now edited by Mike Burrows, the founder of 'Scrumbag', the fanzine is produced at irregular intervals.

221   Squad: the magazine of the Scottish Life Young Scotland Rugby Squad. Edinburgh: Scottish Rugby Union, 1994-

       Published quarterly   ISSN: 1357-213X
                                     BL: ZK.9.b.8363

222   Tiger fan. Leicester: Gemini, Jan.-May 1994.
       Leicester RFC's fanzine consisted of five issues produced from January to May 1994.

212   Scrumbag: monthly rugby fans magazine. Swansea: Newrite Projects, October 1989-

       Published monthly   ISSN: 0963-7982
                                   BL: ZA.9.b.545

213   White Rose review / edited by Tony Simpson. Keighley: T. Simpson, 1989-
       Yorkshire RU newsletter. Produced irregularly.

214   The great fester: Scotland's top (and bottom) rugby fanzine. Edinburgh: The Great Fester, 1990-

215   The acorn / edited by Neil Levis. 1991-1994.
       A magazine about Woodford RFC.

216   Club blazer. Blackheath: Blackheath Rugby Football Club, 1991-
       The official Blackheath club newsletter, issued twice a year.

217   Programme. Old Wesley Rugby Football Club. 1991-

218   The Middlesex County RFU informer. 1992-

223   The unicorn: Bristol Rugby Club newsletter. Bristol: The Club, 1995-
       It is the intention of the club to publish the newsletter three times a year.

224   Dragon news: the magazine of the Dragons Rugby Trust. Sept. 1996-
       For children.

225   Shedhead. 1996?
       A magazine for Gloucester RFC. About eight issues were produced.

226   West edition / edited by Steve Smith. 1996-
       First five issues of a newsletter/fanzine of West Hartlepool RFC.

227   Newsletter of the International Guild of Rugby Theme Collectors. The Guild, 1997?-
       For philatelists

✳ South Africa

228 The South African referee. Western Province, SA: Van Reibeek Rugby Board, City & Suburban Rugby Football Union, Western Province Rugby Referees Union and the Motor Drivers Association of South Africa, Sept. 1912-Sept. 1913.

A newspaper which also covered cricket.

229 Ruggerite: SA's national rugby weekly. Johannesburg, SA: Times Advertising, Apr. 1947.

Only one issue published

230 Footballer: South Africa's rugby and soccer weekly. Johannesburg, SA: May 1947-Sept. 1947.

231 SA rugby. Cape Town, SA: SA Rugby Board, Mar. 1963.

This was possibly produced as a pilot or 'mock-up' for 'Rugby' which began publication later the same year.

☞ See also: I232

232 Rugby. Northlands, SA: Souvenir, July/Aug. 1963- July 1970.

Text in English & Afrikaans   ISSN: 0035-9726
BL: P.P.8003.lr

Published monthly it was the official organ of the South African Rugby Board.

☞ See also: I231

233 Rugby SA. Pretoria, SA: Northern Transvaal Rugby Union, Apr. 1974- Mar. 1976.

234 Rugby in Natal. Durban, SA: Natal Rugby Union, 1975-1976.

235 Rugby news, or, Rugbynuus. Johannesburg, SA: Rugby Supporters, Feb 1977-July 1977.

Weekly newspaper

236 SA & overseas rugby. Durban, SA: Cotswold, 1980-Mar. 1983.

Nine issues per annum;
Continued by: SA rugby

Publisher varies; contributions in English and Afrikaans.

☞ See also: I237

237 SA rugby. Cape Town, SA: SA Rugby, Apr. 1984- Apr. 1986.

Continues: SA & overseas rugby

From mid 1985 the magazine was published at Johannesburg by Independent Media Promotions.

☞ See also: I236

238 On the ball: the rugby magazine of the Western Province. Cape Town, SA: Royston Lamond International, 1990-

Published monthly

239 Rugby XV. Durban, SA: Rugby XV, May 1991- July 1991.

Continued by: Rugby 15   ISSN: 1018-0087

☞ See also: I240

240 Rugby 15. Natal, SA: Natal Rugby Union, 1991-

Continues: Rugby XV

The current issues are published in Durban by Sports Publications.

☞ See also: I239

241 South African rugby. Cape Town, SA: Sable Media, Apr. 1995-

Ten issues per year

✳ Fanzines & Newsletters

242 Fluit-fluit. Pretoria, SA: Northern Transvaal Referees Association, 1986-

Published monthly

This was only made available commercially in 1993.

243 Bokkie!: official newsletter of the South African Rugby Football Union. 1997-

✳ New Zealand

244 New Zealand rugby footballer. 1966-1967.

245 Rugby news. Auckland, NZ: Rugby Press, 1970-1981.

Published weekly   ISSN: 0110-3679

246 New Zealand rugby. June 1978-

247 New Zealand rugby referee. Auckland, NZ: J D Publications, 1980-1982.   ISSN: 0111-5693

248 Summer rugby news. Auckland, NZ: Rugby Press, 1980-1981.   ISSN: 0111-4662

Continued by: New Zealand rugby news

☞ See also: I249

249 New Zealand rugby news. Auckland, NZ: Rugby Press, 1981-1987.   ISSN: 0111-9672

Continues: Summer rugby news;
Continued by: Rugby news

☞ See also: I248, I253

250 Red & black: Canterbury's rugby weekly newspaper. Christchurch, NZ: South Island Sports Publications, 1983-1994.
12 vols; illus

Published biweekly between April and August/September;
Continued by: Canterbury rugby post

☞ See also: I258

251 Scrum down: rugby weekly. Auckland, NZ: Sports Media Enterprises, Mar. 1983-

　　Published weekly during the winter season

252 Rugby news preview. Auckland, NZ: Rugby Press, 1987?-

　　From 1995 published tête-bêche with The All Black
　　　　　　　　　　　　　　　　　　ISSN: 1171-5030

253 Rugby news. Auckland, NZ: Rugby Press, 1988-

　　Published weekly during the season with occasional issues off-season;
　　Continues: New Zealand rugby news　　ISSN: 0114-1406

　　Electronic access to this periodical is also available at: http://www.rugbynews.co.nz/
　　☞　See also: A202, I249

254 Touch football news. Auckland, NZ: Sponsors for Sport, 1988-

　　Seven issues each year　　　　　ISSN: 1171-4158

255 Referee: the official magazine of the New Zealand Rugby Referees' Association. Auckland: Percival Publishing, 1991-1992

　　Three issues a year　　　　　　ISSN: 1171-7289

256 Points unlimited. New Zealand: Association of Rugby Historians and Statisticians, 1992-

　　Published quarterly

257 The All Black: the official magazine of the All Blacks Club. Auckland, NZ: Rugby Press, 1995-

　　Published annually;
　　Issued tête-bêche with Rugby news preview
　　　　　　　　　　　　　　　　　　ISSN: 1173-5030

258 Canterbury rugby post. Christchurch, NZ: Canterbury Rugby Post, Mar. 1995-

　　Continues: Red & black
　　☞　See also: I250

259 NZ rugby. Auckland, NZ: Front Row, 1997-

　　Ten issues a year　　　　　　ISSN: 1174-2046

✱　*Fanzines & Newsletters*

260 North Harbour rugby union magazine. 1985-

✱　*Australia*

261 Waratah rugby news.

　　The official journal of the New South Wales Rugby Union.

262 The Queensland cricketer and footballer. Brisbane, Aust.: Sept. 1892-Apr. 1894.

　　Covers rugby union, athletics, and cricket.

263 Rugby news. Sydney, Aust.: Sydney Rugby Union, 1922?-1975.

　　Thirty-six issues per year;
　　Continued by: Rugby

　　For rugby supporters in Sydney. Contains statistics, team lists, club and general articles.
　　☞　See also: I268

264 The New South Wales Rugby Union news. Sydney, Aust.: The Union, 1923.

　　Continued by: The New South Wales rugby news
　　☞　See also: I265

265 The New South Wales rugby news. Sydney, Aust.: New South Wales Rugby Union, 1923.

　　Continues: The New South Wales Rugby Union news;
　　Continued by: Rugby news
　　☞　See also: I264, I266

266 Rugby news. Sydney, Aust.: New South Wales Rugby Union, 1924-

　　Continues: The New South Wales rugby news

　　'Published every match day.' Published by the NSW Rugby Union until 1969; thereafter by the Sydney Rugby Union.
　　☞　See also: I265

267 Victorian Rugby Union news. Melbourne, Aust.: The Union, 1974-

268 Rugby. Sydney, Aust.: Sydney Rugby Union, 1975-1986.

　　Continues: Rugby news
　　☞　See also: I263

269 Rugby country. Darlinghurst, Aust.: MJS News, 1980-

　　Published monthly
　　　　　　　　　　　　　　　　　　ISSN: 0725-5144

270 Rugby news. Melbourne, Aust.: Victoria Rugby Union, Aug. 1986-Sept. 1989.

　　Continued by: Victorian Rugby Union;
　　Title varies
　　☞　See also: I272

271 Rugby news. Canberra, Aust.: Australian Capital Territory Rugby Union, 1989-1990.

　　Continued by: ACT rugby news
　　☞　See also: I273

272 Victorian Rugby Union. Melbourne, Aust.: The Union, Mar. 1990-

　　Continues: Rugby news (Melbourne)
　　☞　See also: I270

273 ACT rugby news. Canberra, Aust.: Australian Capital Territory Rugby Union, 1991-1994.

> *Continues: Rugby news (Canberra);*
> *Continued by: ACT Rugby Union program*

☞ See also: I271, I276

274 International rugby review. Darlinghurst, Aust.: The National Publishing Group, Apr./May 1992-Sept./Oct. 1996.

> *Published monthly;*
> *Continued by: Australian rugby review*

Issue number six onwards published at PO Box 8, Strawberry Hills, NSW 2012. John Blondin was the editorial director.

☞ See also: I277

275 Australian rugby news. Jan. 1993-

> *Published weekly*

276 ACT Rugby Union program. Barton, Aust.: Australian Capital Territory Rugby Union, 1994-

> *Continues: ACT rugby news*

☞ See also: I273

277 Australian rugby review. Potts Point, Aust.: National Publishing Group, Apr. 1996-

> *Continues: International rugby review*   ISSN: 1326-4303

☞ See also: I274

✱ *Fanzines & Newsletters*

278 Journal: Western District Rugby Union Club. Macquarie, Aust.: The Club, Oct. 1982-Oct. 1991.

> *Continued by: Wests: the official journal of Western District Rugby Union Club Inc.*

☞ See also: I280

279 Dara eagle Daramalan Rugby and Social Club. Dickson, Aust.: The Club, Aug. 1987-Nov. 1987.

280 Wests: the official journal of Western District Rugby Union Club Inc. Macquarie, Aust.: The Club, Mar./Apr. 1992-

> *Continues: Journal: Western District Rugby Union Club*

☞ See also: I278

281 Newsletter. Jamison, Aust.: Western District Rugby Union Club, 1993-

282 Try time: the official Club Wallaby magazine. Potts Point, Aust.: National Publishing Group, 1997-

Club Wallaby is the official Junior Supporters Club of the Australian Rugby Union.

Periodicals ~ Rest of the World

✱ *Africa*

283 African rugby magazine. Nairobi: 1995-   ISSN: 1028-6799

✱ *Canada*

284 Cricket and rugger times. Canada, 19??-

285 National rugby post. Edmonton, Can.: 19??-

> *Published monthly*   ISSN: 1195-4248

286 Canadian rugger. Canada: 1954-

287 Scrum down. Vancouver, Can.: Buchanan-Sousa, Sept. 1978-June/July 1981.

> *Published irregularly;*
> *Continued by: Canada rugby news.*
> ISSN: 0706-7542

☞ See also: I288

288 Canada rugby news. Vancouver: Sports Marketing Consultants, Oct./Nov. 1981-

> *Only one issue published;*
> *Continues: Scrum down;*
> *Ten issues a year*   ISSN: 0712-3280

☞ See also: I287

289 Rugby communicator. Ottawa, Can.: Canadian Rugby Union, Aug./Sept. 1985-1989.

> *Published bimonthly*   ISSN: 0834-793X

The official publication of the Canadian Rugby Union.

✱ *Fanzines & Newsletters*

290 Newsletter / Canadian Rugby Union. Vanier, Ontario: The Rugby Union, 197?-1978?   ISSN: 0820-3121

✻ *Ceylon*

291 Ceylon rugby / edited by Austin Daniel. Apr. 1977-

✻ *The Netherlands*

292 Rugby nieuws: official organ of the Nederland Rugby
Board. Sept. 1977-

> *Published irregularly*

✻ *United States*

293 Rugby USA. May 1966-

294 Rugby / edited by Edward Hagerty. New York: Rugby
Press, 1975-

> *Eight issues per year*   ISSN: 0162-1297

295 Rugby union. Denver, US: North American Rugby
Publishing, Oct. 1993-

> *Published monthly*

296 US rugby news. Worcester, Massachusetts: Mad
Adventures Unlimited, 1994-

> *Published monthly, except January and August*

Wit &
Humour

Contents

Humour

1 The evolution of rugby football: nonsense verses / A. Podmore; drawings by Francis Brown; lettering by E. W. Brown. London: Ashley & Smith, 1911.
29p; illus; pbk

2 The book: test series 1949 New Zealand v. South Africa / edited by Pat Swanepoel with cartoons by John Jackson. Johannesburg, SA: Central News Agency, 1949.
32p; illus; pbk BL: 7919.ee.61

> As New Zealanders and South Africans fought side by side in World War II, 'somewhere between Cassino and the Alps, out of all the chaff and ragging about rugby, there came into being an imaginary volume containing the rules and general hints on the game, which each side began to recommend to the other for intensive study. This volume became known as "The Book".' This evocative and fragile item is 'The Book'.

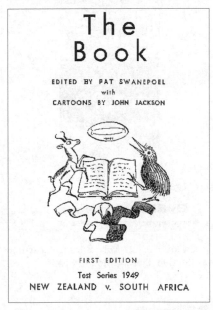

3 The art of coarse rugby, or, Any number can play / Michael Green; illustrated by John Jensen. London: Stanley Paul, 1960.
128p; illus BL: 7925.f.44
☞ Subsequent ed. J6

4 Even coarser rugby, or, What did you do to Ronald? / Michael Green; illustrated by Haro. London: Hutchinson, 1963.
119p; illus BL: 7926.t.18
☞ Subsequent ed. J9

5 Heard in the scrum——: a light-hearted look at the game of rugby / edited by Robert Anderson. London: Stanley Paul, 1964.
131p; illus BL: X.449/606

> Amusing anecdotes and reminiscences from Tony O'Reilly, Ray Chesterton, J. B. G. Thomas, Cecil Bear and others.

6 The art of coarse rugby / Michael Green; illustrated by John Jensen. Rev. ed. London: Arrow Books, 1967.
184p BL: X.449/2780
☞ Previous ed. J3; subsequent ed. J8

7 Fifteen men on a dead man's chest / written and illustrated by Murray H. Ball. Wellington, NZ: Reed, 1967.
143p; illus

8 The art of coarse rugby, or, Any number can play / Michael Green; illustrated by John Jensen. Rev. ed. London: Hutchinson, 1969.
126p; illus SBN: 090600320
BL: X.449/3881
☞ Previous ed. J6; subsequent ed. J49

9 Even coarser rugby, or, What did you do to Ronald? / Michael Green; illustrated by Haro. Rev. ed. London: Arrow, 1969.
192p; illus SBN: 90002270X
BL: X.449/3914
☞ Previous ed. J4; subsequent ed. J31

even COARSER RUGBY

or

What Did You Do to Ronald?

MICHAEL GREEN
ILLUSTRATED BY HARO

HUTCHINSON OF LONDON

10   Heard in the line-out: a humorous look at the game of rugby / edited by Robert G. G. Anderson; illustrated by Ray Chesterton. London: Stanley Paul, 1969.
120p; illus
                            SBN: 090997603
                            BL: X.449/3976

11   A funny thing happened on the way to Twickenham / edited by Robert G. G. Anderson; cartoons by Doug Smith. London: Arthur Barker, 1970.
121p; illus
                            SBN: 213002280
                            BL: X.629/2843

Eleven contributors depict the lighter side of rugby.

12   Michael Green's rugby alphabet / Michael Green; illustrated by Ray Chesterton. London: Pelham, 1971
176p; illus
                            SBN: 720704030
                            BL: X.629/3747

13   The wit of rugby / written and compiled by L. H. W. Paine. London: Frewin, 1972.
95p; illus
                            SBN: 856320110
                            BL: X.989/16833

Part of the 'wit series'. Contains 'stories, quips, bon mots, anecdotes, quotes: the barbed and the bawdy, the acid and the asinine'.

14   Loosehead Len's big brown book / 'Loosehead' Len Lacey; cartoons by Darryl Kirby. Auckland, NZ: Harlen, 1974.
64p; illus; pbk

Satirical articles on rugby football in New Zealand. Len Lacey is the pseudonym of Philip Douglas Gifford.

15   Loosehead Len's practical guide to troublemaking / 'Loosehead' Len Lacey; cartoons by Darryl Kirby. Auckland, NZ: Harlen, 1975.
64p; illus; pbk

16   Loosehead Len's bumper thump book / 'Loosehead' Len Lacey; cartoons by Darryl Kirby. Auckland, NZ: Harlen, 1976.
64p; illus; pbk

17   Loosehead Len's last tango in Te Kuiti / Loosehead Len; cartoons by Darryl Kirby. Auckland, NZ: Loosehead Enterprises, 1977.
64p; illus; pbk

18   Loosehead Len's Saturday night frosties / Loosehead Len; illustrated by Darryl Kirby. Auckland, NZ: Loosehead Enterprises, 1978.
64p; illus; pbk

19   'I was there!' / Max Boyce; with drawings by Gren. London: Weidenfeld and Nicolson, 1979.
94p; illus
                        ISBN: 0297776096
                        BL: X.435/674

Includes two songs in Welsh.

20   Loosehead Len's gluepot greats / 'Loosehead' Len Lacey; illustrated by Darryl Kirby. Auckland, NZ: Gifford/Kirby Productions, 1979.
64p; chiefly illus; pbk

Cartoons originally published in the 8 o'clock newspaper.

21   Never marry a rugger player! / Eileen Hollands; illustrated by Christine Townsend. Sidmouth: Quill, 1979.
146p; illus
                        ISBN: 090459601X
                        BL: X.950/11300

Humorous piece of fictional writing.

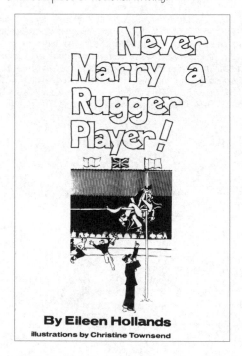

22   Tight heads, loose balls / Mike Burton; illustrations by Bill Tidy. London: Queen Anne, 1981.
88p; illus
                        ISBN: 0362005621
                        BL: X.950/7653

23   The world's best rugby book ever / Sherwood & Alderdice. Hong Kong: Lincoln Green, 1981.
97p; illus

    Authors are Peter Sherwood and Gary Alderdice
                        BL: X.622/18273

24   Have balls will travel: the story of a rugby tour / Mike Burton. London: Willow, 1982.
87p; illus
                        ISBN: 0002180057
                        BL: X.950/17970

25   Loosehead Len's Tokoroa mon amour / 'Loosehead' Len Lacey; illustrated by Darryl Kirby. Auckland, NZ: Gifford/Kirby Productions, 1983.
64p; illus; pbk

26 Rugby rabbits / Graham Hutchins. Auckland, NZ: Rugby Press, 1983.
96p; illus   ISBN: 0908630093

27 Tommy David: he velly big man / Tommy David. 1983.
91p; illus

28 Leo and Jilly Cooper on rugby / pictures by Ross. London: Bell & Hyman, 1984.
61p; illus; pbk   ISBN: 0713524111

29 The alternative coaching manual, or, Leg over-foot up / Mike Burton; illustrations by David Hughes. London: Pelham, 1985.
119p; illus   ISBN: 0720716039
                              BL: X.622/24586

30 Boots en bols / Weyni Deysel, Leon Schuster, Wessel Oosthuizen. Linden, SA: Deysel, Oosthuizen en Schuster, 1985.
104p; illus; pbk   ISBN: 0620091088
    Text in Afrikaans and English.

31 Even coarser rugby, or, What did you do to Ronald? / Michael Green; illustrated by Haro. New ed. London: Arrow, 1985.
158p; illus; pbk   ISBN: 0099434601
                              BL: H.86/163

    ☞ Previous ed. J9

32 Ripley's rugby rubbish: the essential ego and massage book / Andy Ripley. London: Allen & Unwin, 1985.
112p; illus   ISBN: 0047961058
                              BL: X.622/25800

33 Rugby: the dictionary / Jim Webster; illustrated by Bill Mitchell. Newton Abbot: David & Charles, 1985.
80p; illus; pbk   ISBN: 0715387642
                              BL: X.958/32446

    From Abuse through to Zzzzzz.

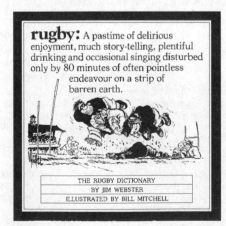

34 Bedside rugby / Bill Beaumont; illustrations by Edward McLachlan. London: Willow, 1986.
88p; illus   ISBN: 000218219X
                              BL: YC.1986.b.3061

35 Paid â blino dy fforwards! / Lynn Davies. Caernarfon: Gwasg Gwynedd, 1987.
95p; pbk
    'Don't tire your forwards!'. Caricatures of each position in the game; originally broadcast on Radio Cymru. In Welsh.

36 Rugby is a funny game: have you heard the one about the Scotsman, the Englishman, the Irishman and the Welshman? / Gordon Brown and others; illustrations by Jake Tebbit. London: Stanley Paul, 1987.
118p; illus   ISBN: 0091714702
                              BL: YK.1987.b.6698

37 The game of rugby football as played by elderly gentlemen / Shigeru Llewellyn. North Vancouver: Next Century Communications, 1989.
110p
    Based on the original Japanese manuscript: Boru! boru! boru! dozo   ISBN 0969395701

38 The lighter side of All Black rugby / edited by N. Park. Auckland, NZ: SeTo Publishing, 1989.
31p; chiefly illus; pbk
    Cover title: What the ref saw, Volume 2
                              ISBN: 0908697465

    A photograph per page with humorous comments in 'bubbles'.

39　The lighter side of rugby / T. W. Ickenham. 1989.
32p, illus

40　Ripley's very rough guide to rugby / Andy Ripley and
Geoff Atkinson; illustrations by Borin van Loon.
London: Stanley Paul, 1989.
112p; illus　　　　　　　　ISBN: 009174072X
　　　　　　　　　　　　　BL: YK.1990.b.6723

41　Nicks & cuts: Wallaby tales / Nick Farr-Jones & Steve
Cutler. Neutral Bay, Aust.: Elan, 1990.
189p; illus　　　　　　　　ISBN: 0646018884

42　Bluff your way in rugby / Alexander C. Rae. Horsham:
Ravette, 1992.
64p; pbk
(The bluffer's guides)　　　ISBN: 1853045527
　　　　　　　　　　　　　BL: YK.1993.a.6299

43　From the terraces / Dennis Scott; illustrated by J. Kay
Scott and Tania K. Scott. Morrinsville, NZ: Scottie, 1992.
143p; illus; pbk
　　Cover title: A look at New Zealand rugby from the terraces
　　　　　　　　　　　　　ISBN: 047301596X

44　A front-row guide to rugby union clubs: the First
Division / written and illustrated by Dick Tyson;
foreword by Gareth Chilcott. London: Stanley Paul in
association with Umbro International, 1992.
62p; illus, maps, plans; pbk　ISBN: 0091775388
　　　　　　　　　　　　　BL: YK.1993.b.7933
　　*Promises 'all the clubs, the nearest pubs and no long
　　words'.*

45　Ruck me: and other hilarious yarns / Stu Wilson and Phil
Kingsley-Jones. Auckland, NZ: Moa Beckett, 1993.
128p; pbk　　　　　　　　ISBN: 1869580125

46　Rugby stories: some rucking good yarns / Peter
FitzSimons. St Leonards, Aust.: Allen & Unwin, 1993.
xii, 192p; pbk

47　Well, I'll be ruggered / with Jeff Sayle, Chris Handy &
John Lambie. Randwick, Aust.: Ironbark, 1993.
xiv, 204p; illus　　　　　　ISBN: 187547126X
　　Humorous anecdotes.

48　More rucking fun / Stu Wilson & Phil Kingsley-Jones;
illustrated by Darryl Kirby. Auckland, NZ: Moa Beckett,
1994.
127p; illus　　　　　　　　ISBN: 186958063X

49　The art of coarse rugby / Michael Green; illustrated by
John Jensen. Rev ed. London: Robson, 1995.
159p; illus; pbk　　　　　　ISBN: 1861050011
　　　　　　　　　　　　　YK.1996.a.19947
　　☞　*Previous ed. J8*

50　Tight head, loose balls: South African rugby's funniest
stories / Paul Dobson and Rufus Papenfus. Cape Town,
SA: Sable Media, 1995.
96p; illus; pbk　　　　　　　ISBN: 0958406243
　　*Tales of eccentric characters; quirky on and off the
　　field events and jokes.*

51　The world's gone ruckin' mad / Stu Wilson & Phil
Kingsley-Jones; illustrated by Darryl Kirby. Auckland,
NZ: Hodder Moa Beckett, 1995.
111p; illus　　　　　　　　ISBN: 1869581652

52　The funny book of rugby / words selected by Bob Hale;
cartoons by Douglas Ingram. London: Brockhampton
Press, 1996.
61p　　　　　　　　　　　ISBN: 1860194613
　　*A collection of humorous anecdotes, quotations and
　　jokes.*

53　New Zealand rugby yarns / Graham Hutchins;
illustrated by Henry Nicholas; edited by Lorraine
Olphert. Wellington, NZ: Grantham House, 1996.
120p; illus; pbk　　　　　　ISBN: 186934054X

54　Ruckin' & maulin': stories and yarns from the pitches /
Dave Crowe. London: Chameleon, 1997.
112p; illus; pbk　　　　　　ISBN: 0233992006

55　There's no rucking business like rugby / Phil
Kingsley-Jones & Stu Wilson; illustrations by Darryl
Kirby. Auckland, NZ: Hodder Moa Beckett, 1997.
111p; illus　　　　　　　　ISBN: 1869585224

✳　*Additional References*

56　Play!: the best sporting stories / R. J. B. Sellar. London:
John Hamilton, 1927.
191p　　　　　　　　　　　BL: 012316.ee.39
　　*Sporting anecdotes, now somewhat dated, with a
　　chapter devoted to rugby and association football.*

57　New Zealand sporting disasters, disappointments &
curiosities / Keith Quinn; cartoons by George Martin.
London: Stanley Paul, 1986.
119p; illus　　　　　　　　ISBN: 0091660300
　　　　　　　　　　　　　BL: YK.1988.b.1459

　　*Commemorates prominence of the 'wrong kind' and
　　indignities suffered in New Zealand sport. Rugby,
　　union and league, is covered on pages 14 to 50 and
　　the tour of Britain, Ireland, Australia and New
　　Zealand in 1888-89 by the New Zealand Football
　　team on pages 110 to 119.*

58　Great sporting failures / Geoff Tibballs. London:
CollinsWillow, 1993.
192p; illus; pbk　　　　　　ISBN: 0002185261
　　　　　　　　　　　　　BL: YK.1994.a.788

　　*Rugby union is covered on page 91 through to page
　　101.*

Quotations

59 The book of world rugby quotations: wit, wisdom and wisecracks from the rugby union game / compiled by Derek Douglas. Edinburgh: Mainstream, 1991.
287p; illus; pbk   ISBN: 1851584358
                            BL: YK.1993.a.3650

✻ *Additional References*

60 The Guinness dictionary of sports quotations / compiled by Colin Jarman. Enfield: Guinness, 1990.
298p; pbk   ISBN: 0851129226
                            BL: YK.1991.a.551

The quotations are arranged by sport or by general theme.

61 'We knocked the bastard off': great New Zealand sports quotes / compiled by Joseph Romanos. Auckland, NZ: Moa Beckett, 1994.
130p; illus   ISBN: 1869580532

Records & Trivia

62 The book of rugby disasters and bizarre records / general editor Fran Cotton; introduced by Bill Beaumont; illustrations by Colin Whittock; compiled by Chris Rhys. London: Century, 1984.
119p; illus   ISBN: 0712609113
                      BL: X.622/21921

A light-hearted delve into true bizarre moments in rugby: lowest drop goal; most costly miss; played in international, but did not touch ball; capped in error; and so on.

63 The book of rugby lists / introduction by Gareth Edwards; edited by Norman Giller. London: Sidgwick & Jackson, 1984.
224p; illus   ISBN: 0283991259 (cased) • 0283001267 (pbk)
                        BL: X.622/23092

64 Rugby shorts / Chris Rhys; illustrations by David Arthur. London: Guinness, 1990.
128p; illus   ISBN: 0851123244
                      BL: YK.1990.a.5365

Records and trivia, such as the commonest surnames and the highest grounds.

Cartoons

65 Lodge laughs at the Springbok tour: cartoons and comments / Neville Lodge. Wellington, NZ: Reed, 1956.
36p; all illus; pbk

66 Lodge laughs at the Lions tour: cartoons and comments / Neville Lodge. Wellington, NZ: Reed, 1959.
40p; all illus; pbk

67 Lodge laughs at the 1960 All Black tour: cartoons and comments / Neville Lodge. Wellington, NZ: Reed, 1960.
40p; all illus; pbk

68 Lodge laughs at the 1961 French tour: cartoons and comment / Neville Lodge. Wellington, NZ: Reed, 1961.
40p; all illus; pbk

69 Rugby is ...: a muster of sidestepping cartoons perpetrated by Malc Evans, and dreadful doggerel fabricated by Geoff Whyman. Auckland, NZ: Hodder & Stoughton, 1972.
1 vol. (unpaged); illus   ISBN: 0340166045

70 Anyone for rugger?: a must for every rugby fanatic / Mike Richardson. Wellington, NZ: Sporting Aids, 1977.
115p; chiefly illus

71 A is for All Black / Paul Clarkson. Christchurch, NZ: Christchurch High School Old Boys' Rugby Club, 1978. 36p; chiefly illus

   Caricatures of past and present All Blacks.

72 'And the tanker spent a comfortable night': Welsh rugby in the 70s / Tom Bellion; illustrations by Gren. London: Boondoggle Limited, 1979. 64p; illus; pbk

   Spine title: Welsh rugby in the 70s   ISBN: 0861480015
   BL: X.909/44260

73 Boots, balls and banter: a collection of rugby stories / edited by David Parry-Jones, cartoons by Gren. London: Arthur Barker, 1980. vi, 88p; illus   ISBN: 0213167808
   BL: X.958/8307

74 The golden rules of rugby / Ian Heath. London: Corgi, 1984. 47p; illus; pbk   ISBN: 0552125911
   BL: X.629/25998

   Captioned cartoons.
   ☞ Also listed at: F72

75 The official duffer's guide to rugby / Gren; introduction by Max Boyce. London: Columbus, 1984. 80p; illus; pbk   ISBN: 0862871727

76 The duffer's guide to rugby: yet another try / Gren. London: Columbus, 1985. 80p; illus; pbk   ISBN: 0862872324

77 Men in the pink: a lighter shade of rugby / Grant Winter & Tom Hepburn. Auckland, NZ: SeTo; Halcyon, 1985. 56p; chiefly illus; pbk   ISBN: 0908697031
   Caricatures and cartoons.

78 Portrait of a rugbyholic / illustrations by Gren. London: Columbus, 1986. 96p; illus; pbk   ISBN: 0862872960
   BL: YV.1989.a.1355

Cartoons and text by Gren of the South Wales Echo.

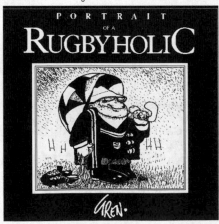

79 Up and under!: rugby cartoons / Malcolm Walker; foreword by Loosehead Len. Auckland, NZ: Reed Methuen, 1987. 29p; all illus; pbk   ISBN: 047400290X

80 Crazy world of rugby / cartoons by Bill Stott. Watford: Exley, 1988. 96p; illus   ISBN: 1850151105
   BL: YV.1989.a.867

81 The duffer's guide to rugby: keep on rucking / Gren. London: Columbus, 1989. 80p; illus; pbk   ISBN: 0862878969
   BL: YK.1991.a.12918

82 Rugby for Hugh / drawn by Gus Hunter; words by Barbara White. Nelson, NZ: The author, 1989. 16p; chiefly illus; pbk

83 Rugby and the Rams / Barbara White; illustrated by Gus Hunter. Auckland, NZ: Macmillan, 1991. 16p; illus; pbk   ISBN: 0333416422

84 The Rams on tour / Barbara White; illustrated by Gus Hunter. Auckland, NZ: Macmillan, 1992. 16p; illus   ISBN: 033341652X

85 Lofty '93 / Rob and Dr Jack. Groenkloof, SA: Hobotoons, 1993. 30p; chiefly illus; pbk

   Cover title: The Pretoria News' Lofty   ISBN: 1874969027

86 Boyo ballads / Kyffin Williams. London: Excellent, 1995. 96p; illus   ISBN: 1854878034
   BL: YK.1996.b.9650

87 Gren's guide to rugby. Cardiff: Western Mail & Echo, 1995. 100p; illus; pbk   ISBN: 0950404268

88 The world's greatest rugby cartoons / edited by Mark Bryant. London: Exley, 1996. 80p; illus; pbk   ISBN: 1850158002

Joke Books

89 Rugby jokes. London: Sphere, 1969.
176p; pbk   ISBN: 0722193866
☞ See also: J92

90 Son of rugby jokes. London: Sphere, 1970.
172p; pbk   ISBN: 0722193831
☞ See also: J92

91 What rugby jokes did next. London: Sphere, 1970.
138p   SBN: 722122551
                         BL: Cup.805.a.29
☞ See also: J92

92 Best rugby jokes / selected by John Thomas. London: Arnold Barker, 1979.
213p

Originally published: in 3 vols as: 'Rugby jokes', 'Son of rugby jokes', 'What rugby jokes did next'
                         ISBN: 0213167182
                         BL: X.989/54028
☞ See also: J89, J90, J91

93 More rugby jokes. London: Sphere, 1984.
187p; pbk   ISBN: 0722161840
                         BL: X.958/22759

94 Even more rugby jokes. London: Sphere, 1986.
147p; pbk   ISBN: 0722175671
                         BL: YC.1987.a.1114

95 Rugby jokes score again. London: Sphere, 1987.
146p; pbk   ISBN: 0722172443
                         BL: YK.1987.a.7314

96 Hands up for rugby jokes / illustrated by Raymond Turvey. London: Sphere, 1988.
164p; illus; pbk   ISBN: 0722172567
                         BL: YK.1993.a.837

97 Rugby jokes in the office / illustrated by Raymond Turvey. London: Sphere, 1989.
137p; illus; pbk   ISBN: 0747403090
                         BL: YK.1990.a.2504

98 Rugby jokes in the locker room / illustrated by Raymond Turvey. London: Sphere, 1991.
151p; illus; pbk   ISBN: 0747407290
                         BL: YK.1991.a.11130

99 The complete rugby jokes omnibus. London: Warner, 1995.
1 vol.; pbk   ISBN: 0751517038

100 The world's best rugby jokes / Edward Phillips; illustrated by Andy Hunt. London: HarperCollins, 1997.
96p; illus; pbk   ISBN: 0006388663
                         BL: YK.1997.a.6199

Quiz Books

101 The rugby quiz book / compiled by Denis Dwyer and Craig McFarlane. Christchurch, NZ: Whitcombe & Tombs, 1972.
24p; pbk   ISBN: 0723303479

102 Playfair rugby quiz book / Michael Nimmo. London: Queen Anne, 1976.
116p; illus; pbk   ISBN: 0362002797

103 Rugby posers / Huw S. Thomas. Llanelli: D. Thomas, 1979.
100p; pbk

104 More rugby posers / Huw S. Thomas. Llanelli: Gwerin, 1980.
63p; illus; pbk

105 Rugby News quiz book / Bob Howitt. Auckland, NZ: Rugby Press, 1984.
93p

106 John Taylor's rugby quiz book. Newton Abbot: David & Charles, 1987.
104p; illus
(A Graham Tarrant book) ISBN: 0715389467
                         BL: YK.1987.a.6530

107 Rugby trivia: 1001 questions and answers / Graham K. Jooste. Johannesburg, SA: Penguin, 1995.
v, 147p; pbk   ISBN: 0140250190

108 A South African rugby quiz book: from a green meadow through isolation to winners of the World Cup 1995 / prepared by A. J. van der Schyf. Doornfontein, SA: Goods Galore, 1996.
100p; illus; pbk   ISBN: 0620201789

Name Index

This index lists the names of all individuals and organisations (other than trade publishers) which appears in A Rugby Compendium as authors or as subjects, i.e. entries are given for items written, or issued, by individuals and organisations, as well as items written about them. Entries are given for all authors, editors, compilers, illustrators etc, and for corporate bodies such as the Rugby Football Union or the Association of Rugby Historians and Statisticians. There are no entries under club names – these may be found in the separate Club Index. Names beginning with Mc or Mac have been interfiled as if spelt Mac. A number of qualifying terms, such as photographer have been used where it is thought this might be helpful.

A

A'Court, Stephen *(photographer)* G19
Abbotsholme School F25
Abrahams, H M I39
ACC Injury Prevention Services F392
Action Plus *(photography)* F378
Adams, Andrew M G87
Adams, Audrey H243
Adams, David B57, F95
Adams, P C F143
Adamson, J A B307
Addicott, S A149
Ainsworth, Kenneth J B44
Air New Zealand G78-79
Aitken, Anna E190
Akers, Clive A B812-813, B815
Akon, Paul F64
Alcock, Charles W A3, A12, A28, C241-242, F109, F114, I42-43, I56
Alderdice, Gary J23
Alderson, F H R B127
Aldridge, Ron I122
Alexander, David B538
Alexander, Harry F113
Alexander, Roy L *(illustrator)* F236
Allaby, David B293
Allan, Gordon H159
Allan, Walter D23
Allen, 'Bull' C1
Allen, C P B317
Allen, Fred C290, F232
Alley, G T E26
Alleyniensis F126-127
Allison, Lincoln G43, G45
Almond, H H A9-10
Alston, Rex B245, H160
American Olympic Committee, Seventh Olympic Games D24
Anderson, Brian F82, F84
Anderson, G F B418
Anderson, Paul Gerard A242

Anderson, Robert J5, J10-11
Andersson, John B782
Andrew, Arthur R B742
Andrew, Rob C2-3, D19, D58
Andrews, Ann A215
Andrews, David L A148, G58
Anthony, V S B305
Ap Dafydd, Myrddin H110-111
Ap Ifor, Glyn H110
Appleton, Edward B376
Archer, Ian C152
Archer, Robert G42
Ardagh, Michael F405
Arlott, John C238
Armour, G E242
Armstrong, Gary C4, I113
Army Rugby Football Union A61
Arnold, Edward Carleton B309
Arnold, Peter B112
Arnold, W D B316, H1
Arthur, C S B526
Arthur, David *(illustrator)* J64
Ashburton County Rugby Union *See* Mid-Canterbury Rugby Football Union
Ashton, Brian F390
Ashworth, John C271, C310
Association for the Anthropological Study of Play A244, G62
Association of Referees, Leinster Branch B496
Association of Rugby Historians and Statisticians I256
Atchison, George B22
Atkinson, Geoff J40
Atkinson, Philip T B603
Atyeo, Don G48
Auckland Rugby Football Union B791-793, I129
Australian Bowling Club E293
Australian Capital Territory Rugby Union I271, I273, I276

Australian Rugby Football Schools Union E307-308, F293, F419
Australian Rugby Football Union E303, F50, F75, F223, F298, F323, F369, F375, I282
Australian Services Rugby Union A221
Australian Society of Rugby Referees F64
Australian Sports Commisssion F375
Auty, K A I156
Auty, Timothy C291
Averis, Ernest B294
Avis, F C I13
Awdurdod Addysg Morgannwg Ganol H247

B

Baber, Selwyn B621
Babrow, Louis B662-663
Bachop, Graeme C310
Bailey, John B289
Baillie, T H E H224
Baker, Martin B201
Balaam, Len B165
Bale, John A151
Bale, Steve D46
Ball, Ken B84
Ball, Murray H *(illustrator)* J7
Ball, Steve B151
Ball, Vic B43
Ballantine, E W H223
Ballantyne, G H B400
Banbury, Clinton *(illustrator)* H59
Bangsbo, J F454
Banks, Gordon F257
Bannerman, J M C324
Barak, Monty B252
Barker-Davis, J R B93
Barlee, John *(photographer)* F173, F207

F

Fabian, A H A69
Fadda, Pierluigi G111
Fairall, Barrie D20, I114
Fairbairn, John E173
Fairbrother, Roger *(illustrator)* F104
Fallon, Brian B52
Fallon, Ivan C175
Fallow, K M B775
Fanning, Bernard A180
Fanning, Leo A180
Farmer, David B611, C284
Farmer, Stuart B157
Farr-Jones, Nick C68, H166, J41
Farris, David *(illustrator)* H172
Fatialofa, Peter C69
Fawcett, M J P B194
Fazey, Ian Hamilton B284
Fegan, J H C F111
Fennelly, Mary C327
Fenton, Peter E305, H158
Fenton, Robert G9
Fergusson, Donald B383
Ferr, Thomas F G121
Ferrand, Tony C34
Ferrari, Renato Tullio G111
Ferreira, Jannie B678
Ferrie, Kevin C296
Field, M *(illustrator)* F314
Fiji Rugby Football Union A232, E314
Fine, Gary Alan G62
Finnane, Steve C70
Firth, Gary B39
Fisher, Norman H176
Fitzgerald, Ciarán C270, C328
Fitzgerald, John C327
Fitzgerald, Pat I192
Fitzpatrick, Sean C71-72, C310
FitzSimons, Peter C68, G69, H177, J46
Flannery, Michael B458
Fleming, Jim F82, F84
Fletcher, J S H132
'Fly Half' *See* Thomson, Walter
Foot Ball Association of Canada F5
Foot, David H231
Forbes, Bill B398
Forbes, Julia H246
Forshaw, Brian B122-123
Forster, J L M B385
Fotopacific *(photographer)* C286, G96
Fougasse *(illustrator)* F44
Fowler, Brian B511
Fox, Bob B835
Fox, Douglas N B651
Fox, Grant C73, C286, C310

Francis, Hywel B607
Franklin & Districts Football
  Association Incorporated F63
Fraser, Bernie C74
Fraser, Ian B666
Frater, J R B408
Freeman, Bill F310
Freeman, Margaret H153
French, Carl A147
French, Ray C75, F285, H178
Frew, Gary B818
Frewen, Tom H136
Friedlander, C K F176
Frilingos, Peter H241
Frith, David C207
Frost, David B71, E1, E51, E77,
  E252, F295, H155, H231
Fry, Beattie C81
Fry, C B A13, C76-81, H210-212
Fry, Pierre Paul B443, B470, B492
Fyfe, K C H224

G

G H W I44
Gabe, Rhys T C249, E197, H227
Gadney, B C H224
Gadney, C H F62, F206, H226
Gage, Jeff A97
Gainsford, John C82, C303
Gale, Frederick A25
Gallagher, Brendan D37, I116
Gallagher, John A97, C83-84, C310
Gallagher, Peter J B747, B748
Gallaher, D E220, F117
Gamlin, H T H223
Gamlin, Lionel H160
Gane, Denis B539
Gardner, Les B641
Garland, Steven J D74
Garlick, Raymond H106
Garrard, W G B796
Garvie, Leigh F424
Gaskell, A P H71
Gasson, John B283
Gate, Robert C272, C279
Gault, Ian B835, C105, E79, E191,
  E278, E302
Gaunt, Philip B362
Gee, Maurice Gough H10
Geeson, George B167
Gent, D R F130, F137, F157-158, H224,
  I77
George, Eirwyn H131

George, Howard B624
Gerber, Danie C85, C303
The Geriatrics C271
Gerrard, Major R A C86
Gibb, Alexander B317
Gibbon, W D *See* Alleyniensis
Gibson, Alan C87, H232
Gibson, Alfred A175
Gibson, Mike A146, C267, C328, H155
Gidley, Isobelle E193
Gifford, Phil C15, C69, C206, C240
Gifford, Philip Douglas *See*
  Loosehead Len
Gilbank, P G B236
Gilbert, James A41
Gilbert, John B409
Gilbody, Arthur B105
Gildroy, A B137
Giles, Ben H179
Gilfillan, Howard F312
Gill, Bartholomew H11
Giller, Norman J63
Gillett, Frank *(illustrator)* H75, H77, H90
Gilpin, D J B476
Glanville, Phil de *See* De Glanville, Phil
Glasspool, Barry E271, I7
Glaves, David G47
Gleeson, John C322
Gleeson, Paul G79
Gloag, Matthew C296
Gloucester Referees' Society F89
Goddard, Keith B342
Godwin, Terry C51, C186, C273, D5,
  E59, F74, H175, I27-28
Going, Sid C88
Golby, Jim F409
Golding, Neil B260
Goldingham, Francis Quinn E37
Golesworthy, Maurice I2, I4
Goodman, Dic H124
Goodman, Jim B136
Goodwin, Harry H136
Gop, D M W H266-267
Gordon, Anne Wolrige C109
Gormack, R S E219
Goslett, Johnathan E146
Goulburn, Edward M B316
Gould, Arthur C267, H251
Goulson, Gavin B179
Goulstone, John A76
Gowar, Mick H59
Grace, J S B747
Grace, Kim H60
Gracey, Tom B272
Gracie, A L H196, H224
Graham, Maurice F293
Granny Sangoma *(fictional)* H58

H

K

S

X,Y,Z

Club Index

This index enables the user to locate books in the main listing which are either about specific rugby clubs or have been issued by them. Most of the items listed are club histories and these, together with other items which contain enough club-specific information to warrant particular mention, are listed under that subheading. This index does not contain references to Rugby Unions, which are included in the general Name Index (page 255). National touring sides are listed in the Subject Index (page 321), as Tourists, e.g. French Tourists.

A

Aberaman
Club Histories B501

Aberavon
Club Histories B502-504,
B635-636, B639

Abercarn
Club Histories B505, B639

Abercrave
Club Histories B640

Aberdeen University
Club Histories B421

Aberdeenshire
Club Histories B364

Abergavenny
Club Histories B506

Abertillery
Club Histories B507, B635-636,
B639

Aberystwyth
Club Histories B508-509

Aberystwyth University See University
College of Wales Aberystwyth

Aboyne
Club Histories B365

Albert
Club Histories B641

Albion (New Zealand)
Club Histories B683, B836

Albion (England) See Bridgwater and
Albion

Alexandra
Club Histories B684

Alhambra
Club Histories B685
See also North Dunedin/Alhambra

Alltwen
Club Histories B640

Altrincham (Kersal)
Club Histories B13

Amman United
Club Histories B510, B640

Amman Valley Grammar School
Club Histories B640

Ammanford
Club Histories B511, B640

Ardrossan Academicals
Club Histories B366

Ards
Club Histories BB425

Armagh
Club Histories B426

Army
Key Personalities C316

Army Rugby Union C260

Ashbourne
Club Histories B14

Ashford
Club Histories B15

Ashton-under-Lyne
Club Histories B16

Askeans
Club Histories B17

Aspatria
Club Histories B18-19

Aston Old Edwardians
Club Histories B20-21
Key Personalities C115

Athletic E217

Athlone
Club Histories B427

Athy
Club Histories B428

Avonvale
Club Histories B22

Awahou
Club Histories B836

Awatere
Club Histories B686-687

Ayr
Club Histories B367

B

Baildon
Club Histories B23

Ballinasloe
Club Histories B429

Ballyclare
Club Histories B430

Ballymena
Club Histories B431

Ballymoney
Club Histories B432

Balmy Beach
Tours E313

Bandon
Club Histories B433

Bangor (Ireland)
Club Histories B434

Bangor (Wales)
Club Histories B512

Bank of England
Club Histories B24

Barbarians H223
Club Histories B298-300, B323
Key Personalities C312, C316,
F174

Barclays Bank
Club Histories B25

D

H

I, J

K

Y, Z

Title Index

This is a list of every title which appears in A Rugby Compendium, together with its item number(s). Titles are arranged alphabetically. Articles (A, An, and The), in whatever language they may appear, are ignored for filing purposes. The filing order also ignores punctuation. When there is more than one item with the same main title the items are distinguished by the addition of subtitles. If the subtitles are also identical, or the items do not have subtitles, then the author's or editor's name is included in italics. Titles beginning with a date are filed at the beginning of the index, in chronological order of the first date in the title. Titles which include numbers are filed as if the number was spelled out, e.g. 100 years of rugby files under 'Hundred'.

1875-1975 centenary magazine: Durham University B103
1877-1977 centenary season: Blackburn RUFC B44
1878 Morley RFC B172
1878-1978 centenary gala *(Bridgend)* B519
1878-1978: Crediton RFC centenary B94
1878-1978 '100 not out' B641
1879-1978 history of a hundred years of rugby football in Sri Lanka A238
1881-1981 Olympic Football Club B652
1883 centenary year 1983 Bynea RFC B525
1883-1933: fifty years' record of rugby in Auckland B791
1884-1959 rugby in the Duchy (rugby heritage) B329
1884-1984 Hawke's Bay Rugby Union centenary special feature B807
1885-1960: 75 years of rugby in Taranaki B826
1886-1986: one hundred years of Cinderford rugby B85
1891-1981 Swifts RFC 90 years B659
1891-1991: Swifts Rugby Voetbal Klub eenfeesuitgawe B660
1905 and all that A146
1920-1971, Bishop's Stortford Rugby Football Club B42
1926-1976 Staines Rugby Football Club B264
1928-1978: fifty years of Chingford Rugby Club B84
1928/9-1978/9: Heath Rugby Union Football Club (formerly Heath Old Boys) golden jubilee brochure B132
1930-1980 brochure to commemorate the golden jubilee of the Old Brodleians Rugby Football Union Football Club B192
The 1947/8 Wallaby tour E294
1949-1974, Biggleswade Rugby Union Football Club B38
1950, the year of the Lions E28
1950-1975: twenty five years of Market Rasen and Louth Rugby Union Football Club B167
The 1951-52 Springbok rugby tour of the British Isles and France E170
The 1956 Springboks in New Zealand E173
The 1959 Lions in New Zealand & Australia E31
1962-1987 the jubilee years: the history of the first 25 years of Winscombe Rugby Football Club B294
The 1965 South African rugby tour of New Zealand G2
The '66 Lions in New Zealand E37
The 1968 Lions E41
'76 All Blacks in South Africa E268
1980 All Blacks in Wales E278
1981 All Blacks in France and Romania E281

1981 Springbok tour of New Zealand G12
The 1981 Springboks in New Zealand, E191
1981: the tour E189
1983 British Lions rugby tour E75
1983 Lions in New Zealand E79
1991 rugby union World Cup special D32
1994 Wesley College rugby union tour of the UK E309
1995 rugby World Cup review D44

A

A is for All Black J71
ABC Neb H219
The ABC of rugby / *De Kock* F54
The ABC of rugby / *Saxton* F202
ABC of sports medicine F434
Aberaman Rugby Union Football Club B501
The Aberavon Rugby Football Club 1876-1951 B502
Abercarn Rugby Football Club B505
Aberdeenshire Rugby Football Club 1875-1975 B364
Abergavenny Rugby Football Club B506
Abertillery Rugby Football Club 1883-1983 B507
Aberystwyth economic research papers *(series)* G94
Aberystwyth RFC 1947-1997 B509
Aberystwyth Rugby Football Club B508
Accounts squared H75
The acorn I215
The acquisition of human capital in various currencies G91
ACT rugby news I273
ACT Rugby Union program I276
Action replay C179
Acts of union H92
Adroddiad ar arolwg rygbi yn yr ysgolion A149
The adventure of the missing three-quarter H83
Africa series *(series)* G42
African rugby magazine I283
After the final whistle E272
After the match H156
The Aldin book of outdoor games F158
Aldin series *(series)* F157
Alex the Bruce C20

C

E

G

H

I

J

K

L

M

'More than a game' B399
More than just rugby C36-37
The Moreleigh mascot H33
Morgannwg H100
Mortimer's handy football guide for South Wales and Monmouthshire I54
Moseley Football Club 1873-1973 B173
Motivational participation incentives of elite quadriplegic rugby athletes G121
The Mountain Ash Rugby Football Club story B572
Mourie's All Blacks E274
Mourie's men E277
Moving the goal posts G90
Mr C. B. Fry C76
Mud, blood and money G71
Mud in your eye C126
Munster rugby news I187
Murray's guide to rugby union F265
The Museum of Rugby Twickenham G105
Musselburgh Rugby Football Club: Canada tour, August 1952 E96
Musselburgh Rugby Football Club: Canada tour, August 1992 E126
My dear Danie H205
'My dear victorious Stod' C207
My fifty years of sporting and public life, notes on rugby methods, hints and advice to players H171
My game, your game H241
My kind of rugby: a coaching manual F309
My kind of rugby: union and league C75
My life in rugby C106
My pride of Lions E92
My recollections and reminiscences E22
My reminiscences C236
My Scottish youth C140
My way F321

N

'N eeu van OP rugby, 1888-1988 B671
Naas C13
Naas Botha: rugby's golden boy C14
The name of the game is – rugby union F344
Namibian rugby A235
The Napier Marist Brothers Old Boys Rugby Football Club Inc. B730
Natal 100 B676
The Natal rugby story B675
The National Mutual rugby almanack of New Zealand I131
National rugby post I285
Natives H82
The nature and meaning of sport in New Zealand A219
Navan Rugby Football Club B468
Neath Athletic B577
Neath RFC 1871-1971 B575

Neath Rugby Football Club E290
The necessary action H74
Nenagh Ormond's century 1884-1984 B469
Never marry a rugger player! J21
Never stay down C24
A new beginning A211
New Brighton Rugby Football Club souvenir booklet for opening new clubrooms B175
New Brighton Rugby Union Football Club 1875-1975 B176
New image rugby G122
New image rugby manual F76
New rugby laws explained / *De Kock* F51
The new rugby union laws explained / *Fleming & Anderson* F84
New South Wales rugby annual I145
The New South Wales Rugby Football Union annual I143
The New South Wales rugby news I265
The New South Wales Rugby Union annual I144
The New South Wales Rugby Union news I264
New York Rugby Football Club 1930-1979 B874
The New Zealand Barbarian rugby book I135
The New Zealand football team souvenir of the visit to Wales December 1905 E216
New Zealand international rugby 1884-1975 A193
The New Zealand Maori rugby tour, 1926-1927 E285
The New Zealand National Rugby Museum, Palmerston North, NZ G102
New Zealand playscripts *(series)* H149
New Zealand rugby *(1978)* I246
The New Zealand rugby annual *(1920-1945)* I130
The New Zealand rugby annual *(1971)* I133
The New Zealand rugby annual *(1986)* I136
The New Zealand rugby football annual for 1885 I128
New Zealand rugby football: some hints and criticisms F152
The New Zealand Rugby Football Union (Inc.), 1892-1967 A186
New Zealand rugby footballer *(1966-1967)* I244
New Zealand rugby greats C259, C266, C310, C311
New Zealand rugby legends C277
New Zealand rugby news I249
New Zealand rugby referee I247
New Zealand rugby skills & tactics F300
New Zealand Rugby Union H113
New Zealand rugby yarns J53
New Zealand sporting disasters, disappointments & curiosities J57
Newark Rugby Football Club 1919-1969 B177
Newbold-on-Avon RFC B178
Newlands 100 B11
Newlands, the story of the stadium B12
Newlyn, Penzance and the Pirates B231
Newport Athletic Club B582
Newport Athletic Club, 1875-1975 B583
Newport Rugby Football Club, 1875-1960 B579
Newport Rugby Football Club 1875-1975 B581
Newport rugby greats C300
News of the World rugby World Cup 1991 D37

O

P

Q

R

S

T

Tackle rugby F308
Tackle rugger F249
Tackle rugger this way F198, F226
Tackling club rugby H168
Tackling rugby C212
Tactical and attacking rugby F222
Tactics of success *(series)* F350
Taffs acre B5
Taibach Rugby Football Club 1884-1984 B613
Taieri Rugby Football Club, 1883-1983 B771
Takapau Rugby Club 1886-1986 centennial B772
Takapuna Rugby Football Club Incorporated B773
Take the ball and run H239
Take up rugby union F335
Taking the air H160
Talanoa: contemporary Pacific literature *(series)* H113
A tale of two roads B142
Talent identification F363
Tales of St Austin's H87
Tales of Twickenham B333
Talking of rugby C151
Tall half-backs H14
Taranaki rugby almanac E169
Taunton RFC centenary 1875-1975 B270
Teach yourself books *(series)* F183, F215, F245
Teach yourself rugby football F183, F215
Teaching rugby to boys F257
Teaching students to play games 11-16 F385
The 'team of three' touch judging F94
'Tell my wife I tried' B365
Ten out of fifty B473
Tennents scrumdown I200
The tent H88
Terenure College RFC, 1940-1990 B480
A text book on rugby football F145
Teyrnged mawreddog i Barc yr Arfau B6
Thanet Wanderers Rugby Union Football Club B271
Thanks to rugby C8
Thanks to rugger H89
The theory of modern rugby football F154
There was also some rugby E186
There's no rucking business like rugby J55
They gave us rugby A217
They led the All Blacks C290
They made headlines C257
They missed the bus E265
They played for New Zealand: a complete record of New Zealand rugby representatives 1884-1947 and their matches C246
They played for New Zealand: a complete record of New Zealand rugby representatives 1884-1981 and their matches C265
They played for New Zealand, volume 2: 1884-1963 C253
They played for New Zealand, volume 3 C258

They ran with the ball A224
They reached the top *(series)* H70
They're off! A37
Think rugby F324, F364
Thinking rugby F272
The third jump H90
The third jump and other stories H90
30 rugby club songs H262
30 super Springboks C303
The 31st man B838
This is rugby F250
This world of rugby F223
The thistle A116
Thistle AFC B775
Those magnificent men B845
The 3 ppp's of rugby G78
Three score and more, 1920-1980 B698
Tiger fan I222
Tigers B259
Tigers review B156
The Tigers tale B157
Tight heads, loose balls J22
Tight head, loose balls: South African rugby's funniest stories J50
Timaru Old Boys' Rugby Football Club B776
Times like these H15
Tiverton Rugby Football Club B273
To Andrew D. Thomson an old opponent, and good friend H250
To Arthur H126
To Ashbrooke and beyond B268
To be a pilgrim C41
To the whistle H138
Tom Brown's schooldays H13, H151
Tommy David C49
Tommy David: he velly big man J27
A ton of rugby B540
A ton of time B710
Tonmawr RFC 1897-1997 B614
Tonna Rugby Football Club centenary year B615
Tooheys official Bledisloe Cup book 1987 D66
Top people *(series)* C18, C83
Top South African rugby playing schools B669
Tot siens to test rugby C168
Total rugby F267, F320, F353, F395
Totnes Rugby Football Club 1889-1989 centenary B274
Touch and go, and other school stories H91
Touch football news I254
A touch of glory A135
Touchdown and other moves in the game H231
Tough Lester H66
Tough tackle H49
Tour guide: Italy, UK, Ireland 1996 E303
Tour le France E146
Tour of New Zealand by Lions rugby team E61
Tour of the century E280
The tour of the third All Blacks, 1935 E229

U

V

A view from the Garth B612
Viewless winds C165
The Villager rugby magazine 1995-Brookside experience B665
The visitors E2
Vive le sport H121

W

The Waihou one hundred B783
Waikato RFU jubilee B832
Waikato Rugby Football Union (Incorporated) B829
Wairarapa Bush centennial 1886-1986 B837
Wairarapa Rugby Football Union jubilee issue 1886-1946
  B833
Waitohi Rugby Football Club B784
Wakefield Rugby Football Club B278
Walcot Old Boys RFC centenary 1882-1982 B279
Wales has never lost a rugby match? H125
Wales in New Zealand E103
Wales rugby international I159
The Wales test 1905 E219
Wales v New Zealand E230
Walkerburn Rugby Football Club centenary 1884-1984
  official brochure B417
The Wallabies '72 E299
The Wallabies in South Africa 1969 E297
Wallabies' walkabout E300
Wallabies without armour E298
The Wallabies' World Cup! D40
Wallaby greats C306
Wanderers FC tour of USA, May 22-June 8, 1980 E110
Wanderers Football Club 1869/70-1969/70 B487
War letters of a public school-boy C120
War voices H146
Waratah rugby news I261
Warlingham Rugby Football Club 1922-1954 B280
Warnes recreation books *(series)* F150
The Warrington football annual and sports record I60
Wasps in the Courage League 1987-1994 B283
Wat elke rugbyspeler behoort te weet F71
Waterloo FC 1882-1982 B284
Watsonian Football Club centenary 1875-1975 B418
Wattie's '84 Ross Shield tournament, Hastings D83
Waunarlwydd Rugby Football Club 1900-1975 B624
The way out H80
The way to win G95
We are the champions H147
'We knocked the bastard off' J61
Weary C62
A weather trilogy H138
Well, I'll be ruggered J47
Wellington's rugby history, 1870-1950 B834
Wellington's rugby history, 1951-1979 B835
Welsh club rugby guide results season 85/86 I30
'Welsh, gifted and black' G46

Welsh rugby *(1960)* I169
Welsh rugby *(1961)* I170
Welsh rugby in the 70s J73
Welsh rugby scrapbook A140
Welsh rugby: the crowning years, 1968-80 A136
Welsh rugby union facilities venues for further community
  integration G77
Welsh Rugby Union tour of Namibia E123
Welsh Triple Crown souvenir 1893-1952 D4
Wesley College Zimbabwe tour 1992 E127
West edition I226
West Hartlepool Rugby Football Club B286
West Hartlepool Rugby Football Club 1881-1981 B285
West of Scotland Football Club 1865-1965 B419
West out West E288
West Park RFC B287
Western Province rugby football season 1904 B679
Weston-Super-Mare Rugby Football Club centenary 1875
  to 1975 B289
Westport Rugby Football Club, 1886-1986 centennial
  jubilee B786
Westport Rugby Football Club official opening of playing
  pitches & clubhouse B488
Wests I280
The Wharton medal H41
What did you do to Ronald? J4, J9, J31
What every rugby player should know F71
What rugby jokes did next J91
What the ref saw J38
What time does the bus leave? F348, F375
Whineray's All Blacks E248
Whineray's men E249
The Whitbread rugby world I98
The white feather H29
White Rose review I213
The who, when and where of English international rugby
  since 1947 I36
A whole new ball game G73
A whole new ball game: Norman Kirk's decision to stop
  the 1973 Springbok tour G11
The whole world watched G5
The whole world watches G3
Who's who in international rugby C269
Who's who in sport *(series)* C269
Who's who in the sporting world C317
Who's who of South African rugby C313
Who's who of Welsh international rugby players C291
Why I play rugby H81
Why the 'All Blacks' triumphed! E220
Why the whistle went F34, F35, F39, F43, F47, F52, F57
Why was he born so beautiful and other rugby songs
  H256
Wickets, tries and goals C238
Wigan Old Boys Rugby Union Football Club jubilee
  bazaar B291
Will Carling C29
Will Carling: the authorised biography C30-31

Y

Z

Subject Index

Note that books about clubs are listed in the separate Club Index.